Susan Hawthorne is a feminist activist, writer and performer. She is the author of a novel, two collections of poetry and the (co-)editor of eight anthologies. She grew up on a farm in the Riverina, New South Wales, in the 1950s and has lived an urban existence for the last thirty years. She is a founding member of the Performing Older Women's Circus and in her spare time indulges her passion for aerials.

OTHER BOOKS BY SUSAN HAWTHORNE

FICTION

The Falling Woman (1992)

POETRY

The Language in My Tongue (1993)
Bird and other writings on epilepsy (1999)

NON-FICTION

The Spinifex Quiz Book (1993)

NON-FICTION ANTHOLOGIES

Australia for Women: Travel and Culture
    (co-edited with Renate Klein, 1994)
CyberFeminism: Connectivity, Critique and Creativity
    (co-edited with Renate Klein, 1999)
September 11, 2001: Feminist Perspectives
    (co-edited with Bronwyn Winter, 2002)

OTHER ANTHOLOGIES

Difference: Writings by Women (1985)
Moments of Desire: Sex and Sensuality by Australian Feminist Writers
    (co-edited with Jenny Pausacker, 1989)
*The Exploding Frangipani: Lesbian Writing from Australia and New
    Zealand* (co-edited with Cathie Dunsford, 1990)
Angels of Power and other reproductive creations
    (co-edited with Renate Klein, 1991)
Car Maintenance, Explosives and Love and other lesbian writings
    (co-edited with Cathie Dunsford and Susan Sayer, 1997)

WILD POLITICS

FEMINISM
GLOBALISATION
BIO/DIVERSITY

Susan Hawthorne

SPINIFEX

Spinifex Press Pty Ltd
504 Queensberry Street
North Melbourne, Vic. 3051
Australia
women@spinifexpress.com.au
http://www.spinifexpress.com.au

First published by Spinifex Press, 2002

Edited by Janet Mackenzie
Cover designed by Deb Snibson
Typeset and designed by Claire Warren
Made and printed in Australia by McPherson's Printing Group

National Library of Australia
Cataloguing-in-Publication data:

Hawthorne, Susan, 1951– .
    Wild politics.
    ISBN 1-876756-24-1
    1. Globalisation. 2. Feminism. 3. Economics. 4. International economic
    relations. 5. Biological diversity I. Title.

For Renate who insisted this was a work
of non-fiction and not a novel

ACKNOWLEDGEMENTS

This book had its genesis at a conference organised by Farida Akhter in Comilla, Bangladesh, in December 1993. I would like to thank Farida Akhter for organising the conference, and allowing me to participate in it. And for publishing "Wild Politics: A Manifesto", from which this book has developed. Of the sixty-four women who participated in the conference, many influenced my initial thinking on issues such as development, structural adjustment programs, GATT and intellectual property rights. I would especially like to thank Gena Corea and Maria Mies who insisted that my three-page manifesto should be developed into a longer piece of work.

The thinking and reading for the work began in 1993 as I ploughed my way through textbooks on economics, critiques of globalisation and first-hand writings from women living in a wide range of cultures. In 1997 I met Jenae Theraldson – a student at Victoria University, St Albans Campus – in a sausage line. After an energetic discussion on economics, ecology and feminism, Jenae assisted me in locating research materials which plunged me into more reading.

This book has developed out of a PhD completed in early 2002. I am immensely grateful for the wide-ranging and thought-provoking discussions with my supervisors, Verity Burgmann and Wendy Weeks at the University of Melbourne. They have jointly and separately offered insightful comments, criticisms, challenges and some insistences that I extend the analysis in particular areas. They have also been incredibly supportive of the work throughout.

In July of 2001 I was invited to run a weekend workshop as part of the Townsville Feminist Winter Institute. I'd like to thank the organiser, Betty McLellan, and the other participants for the discussions over that weekend, and for allowing me to talk endlessly about my research. Debbie Emerson, in the Baillieu Library at the University of Melbourne, rescued me when I thought I had lost an entire master document. Her assistance at a critical time was invaluable.

A number of friends have given different kinds of support throughout the progress of this project. Margaret Young provided me with a continuous stream of access to a number of magazine subscriptions over the past two years. Coleen Clare, Kaye Moseley, Alix Dobkin, Zohl dé Ishtar, and Renate Klein read different versions of early drafts and gave me feedback. I am grateful for their insights, enthusiasms, and sustaining friendships. Their ideas and views have encouraged me to think through the challenges. The shortcomings, however, remain my own. Janet Mackenzie agreed to edit the book, and I thank her for asking some difficult questions, for her insights and wide knowledge, and for saving me from my inconsistencies. Thanks to Deb Doyle for her assiduous proofreading, and to Max McMaster for the index.. My sincere thanks to Claire Warren, typsesetter extraordinaire for her unstinting care with the text, and for the design of the book. Suzanne Bellamy provided me with some ideas for placement of photographs, and thanks to Deb Snibson for cover design and the photographic collage on page 29. I would also like to thank everyone at Spinifex Press – Maralann Damiano, Laurel Guymer, Jo O'Brien and Johanna de Wever – for their support and patience.

I am grateful for the existence of the Diverse Women for Diversity email list (divwomen@ndf.vsnl.net.in), whose co-ordinator until early 2000 was Beth Burrows of the Edmonds Institute, Canada; it has contributed greatly to my understanding and knowledge of many of the issues, particularly, on legal matters, patents and multilateral trade agreements. A wider expression of gratitude is due also to the many feminist theorists, activists and creative women on whose work I draw. Without the groundbreaking work of Diane Bell and Vandana Shiva this project could not have started; without the more recent contributions of Marimba Ani and Linda Tuhiwai Smith this book could not have achieved its current shape. I am grateful to many others whose words are referred to throughout this work. Particular thanks to Diane Bell and Prue Hyman for their commentaries on my work.

I would also like to thank my parents. My mother, Primrose Hawthorne, inspired me with an extraordinary example of a life to live up to, and instilled in me respect for trees, birds and the integrity of nature. My father, Hugh Hawthorne, in discussion after my mother's death, provided me with details about farming. We talked at length about his seventy years of farming experience, from driving a bullock cart as a boy in the 1920s through to exporting animal feed crops to Japan in the 1960s and 70s. My experience and memory of growing up amid farming activity carried out by both my parents has deeply affected my thinking on many of the issues covered in this work.

My dog, River, has insisted that regular exercise is as necessary for a desk-bound researcher as it is for her. Finally, I would like to thank my partner, Renate Klein, who has not only accompanied us on many walks, but also ecouraged me, fed me, discussed many of the issues over years with me, and provided me with the inspiration to keep going. Her ability to listen, to challenge, to discuss at length has not only enriched this book, but also my life. I thank her with all my heart, with the hope that there is life after publication.

Susan Hawthorne

Melbourne, April 2002

CONTENTS

If I had to name one quality as the genius of patriarchy,
it would be ... the capacity for institutionalizing disconnection.

– Robin Morgan, *The Demon Lover: The Roots of Terrorism* (2002: 51)

Disconnection is critical for a system based on profit.
By contrast, biodiversity relies on connection and relationship.

– Susan Hawthorne

PERMISSIONS

I am grateful to the following individuals and organisations for their generosity in allowing me to reproduce the following images and texts:

Renate Klein for the photograph of the author (see p. i).

Michael Leunig for his cartoon (see p. 1) on the dangers of the mainstream first published in the *Age*, 20 April, 1996: 16. Permission from the artist.

Associated Press for the photograph: The western world's image of Dhaka (see p. 3). Published in the *San Francisco Chronicle*, 2 September, 1994: 1. Permission from Associated Press.

Robin Morgan for the quote on p. xv. Cited from *The Demon Lover: The Roots of Terrorism*, published by Piatkus, London, 2002: 51. Permission from the author.

Tom Thompson for the extract from Judith Wright (see p. xvi). "Eroded Hills" cited from *A Human Pattern: Selected Poems*, ETT Imprint, Sydney 1996: 49. Permission from the publisher.

Suniti Namjoshi for the extract from *St Suniti and the Dragon* (see p. 6). Published by Spinifex Press, Melbourne, 1993: 52. Permission from the author.

Pearson Education for the extract from Ama Ata Aidoo's poem (see p. 52). Published in *Sister Killjoy, or the Reflections of a Black-eyed Squint*. Permission from the publisher.

Eva Johnson for the extract from "Letter to my Mother" (see p. 91). Published in *Difference: Writings by Women*, edited by Susan Hawthorne, Brooks Waterloo, Sydney, 1995: 35. Permission from the editor.

Carcanet for the extract from "Search for My Tongue" (see p. 103). Published in Sujata Bhatt, *Brunizem*, Carcanet, Manchester, 1988: 65–66. Permission from the publisher.

Jully Makini for the extract from her poem, "Solomon Blue" (see p. 235). Published in *Sustainable Development or Malignant Growth?*

Perspectives of Pacific Island Women (under the name Jully Sipolo), edited by 'Atu Emberson-Bain, Marama Publications, Suva, Fiji: 1994. Permission from the author.

In some instances it has proven to be impossible to contact copyright holders. Any copyright holders not acknowledged here or acknowledged incorrectly should contact the publishers.

Parts of this book have previously appeared in different forms in the following publications:

People's Perspectives (Dhaka, Bangladesh); *Broadsheet* (Auckland, Aotearoa/New Zealand); *Radically Speaking: Feminism Reclaimed*, edited by Diane Bell and Renate Klein; *Feminist Theory Knowledge and Power*, edited by Renate Klein; *There is an Alternative: Subsistence and Worldwide Resistance to Corporate Globalization*, edited by Veronika Bennholdt-Thomsen, Nicholas G. Faraclas and Claudia von Werlhof; *Rain and Thunder: A Radical Feminist Journal of Discussion and Activism* (USA); *Women's Studies Quarterly* (USA).

All photographs, other than the one acknowledged here, are by the author. Permission to reproduce should be directed to the publisher.

Ants are even more remarkable than scientists had thought: they regularly swap seed crops of fungus, and occasionally return to the wild for seed crops after floods or blights. According to Ulrich Mueller, a biologist at the University of Maryland, this behavior shows that biodiversity may constitute a more basic need than anyone imagined. What the ants have demonstrated is that it may not be possible to maintain an agricultural life for long periods without some connection to free-living close relatives, Mueller believes.

Age (1 October 1998: 29)

> I dream of hills bandaged in snow,
> Their eyelids clenched to keep out fear.
> When the last leaf and bird go
> Let my thoughts stand like trees here.
>
> – Judith Wright, "Eroded Hills" in
> *A Human Pattern: Selected Poems* (1996: 49).

Consider a deck of 52 playing cards as representing the Earth's current biodiversity, and let the human uses of, and services provided by, biodiversity be represented by all the card games that could be made up. During *Homo sapiens'* existence until recently, the number of cards has been virtually constant since the creation and loss of biodiversity normally occur at very slow rates. We are now randomly tossing out cards at an increasing rate, but essentially no new cards are being made. As we play our card games (i.e., use biodiversity, benefit by its services) with fewer and fewer cards, the games will become harder and more unpredictable to play (because we don't know which cards are missing) until it will become impossible to play some games because important cards, or too many cards, are missing. In the beginning a few missing cards are not noticed. Each additional loss, however, leads to an exponentially greater impoverishment of the possibilities.

> – John Gowdy and Carl N. McDaniel, "One World, One Experiment"
> in *Ecological Economics* (1995: 188).

Opposite
Michael Leunig's view of the dangers of the mainstream (*Age*. 20 April 1996: 16).

How do I get real?
YOU MUST GO WITH THE FLOW
ENQUIRIES
Where is the flow?
THE FLOW IS IN THE MAINSTREAM
ENQUIRIES
Where does the mainstream go?
IT GOES DOWNWARDS AND INTO THE BIG DRAIN.
Does the big drain have a grille or a grate on it?
NO. EVERYBODY GETS SWEPT STRAIGHT DOWN INTO THE BLACK PIT.
What is the black pit?
I AM REFERRING TO THE COLD, BLACK PIT OF PAIN, DISINGRGRATION AND OBLIVION.
ENQUIRIES
In that case I'd like to know where can I buy a nice colorful pair of trousers for my canary?
THIRD FLOOR; BIRDWEAR.
Leunig

A FEMINIST CRITIQUE OF
WESTERN GLOBAL CULTURE

We are living in a watershed time. If we had not been aware of this before 11 September 2001, we are now. The events of that day focused in many ways the central issues explored in this book. An attack on the heart of capitalism is how one or more commentators described what happened on the day following 11 September. Others talked about power, about reliance on technology, forgetting the human factor in intelligence. Outside the American sphere of influence, some commentators tried to point out how Palestinians empathised with the victims in New York City and Washington, DC because they know intimately what this experience feels like. Others compared the devastation to the bombing of Hiroshima. All agreed that the consequences of the event would be far-reaching.

I believe that the events of 11 September create a space for re-imagining a world that might operate differently. For if we do not attempt to do this soon, the current path leads to escalating violence and destruction, through the development of a fortress mentality. In *Wild Politics*, I bring together many ideas developed over thirty years of feminist theorising and activism; key among them is the contention that the inheritors of western culture need to think in much longer time frames than we do; that western culture needs to move away from the profit motive as the be-all and end-all; and that we need to base policies on the goodness of people wherever they come from. As I will argue, a world structured from the ground up, from grass roots, through a wild politics, founded on a culture inspired by biodiversity and the diversity principle could lead western global culture away from the vicious cycles of violence that are perpetrated in international politics, in communities and inside family homes.

In *Wild Politics*, I explore the nature of contemporary western and global culture; I examine some of its key features, core institutions and approaches; and propose an alternative.

The western world's image of Dhaka is summarised in this photo.

Photo: Associated Press.

Feminist theorists[1] have critiqued the processes of male domination, and have also shed light on other kinds of domination that prevail in this world, among them domination by race, culture, class, sexuality, mobility, ability, age. Just as there are many lenses through which to gaze, there are also many means to explore these issues and many disciplines as points of departure. This book is unashamedly interdisciplinary and transdisciplinary, and crosses the barriers between science and the arts, between politics and poetics, between ecology and economics, between subjective experience and so-called objective research.

The work is also informed by my own cultural placement. I have grown up in a culture dominated by the values of white middle-class men. But I have also lived for nearly thirty years within the new culture of women as it has been constructed in Australia and worldwide. This culture is simultaneously central and marginal. Although one can argue for the longevity of women's culture (Gimbutas 1989, 1991), the excavating of these traditions by women over the past thirty years has been fraught with all sorts of difficulty, among them acceptance by the "reasonable man". In my lifetime, however, numerous women – some known to me personally, some not – have developed challenging ways of thinking about culture. These women have created theoretical, poetic and fictional works; they have also created works of visual arts, music, theatre, circus, multimedia and a whole range of arts which defy classification. They have created changes in government policy, in community attitudes, and in some of the key areas of cultural creation, among them shifts in how we think about human beings, about life on this planet, about animals, plants, and the earth itself. They have challenged modes of scientific and mathematical thinking, and extended the range of logical thinking. These are no mean feats in a process which has been consciously undertaken by feminists for the last three decades.

The developments in feminist thinking continue, and this book is an attempt to carry feminist thought forward into the twenty-first century in an optimistic way. Being a feminist requires optimism because the basis of feminism is a belief that things can change, that we are not entirely caught in a deterministic trap which allows us simply to shrug our collective shoulders and avoid responsibility for the shape of the

---

1.   For an in-depth discussion of feminism, see Chapter One.

world. I remember taking part in an anti-nuclear demonstration in the late 1970s or early 80s. A group of us carried a banner which read: LESBIANS HAVE ALWAYS KNOWN THAT MEN ARE NOT RESPONSIBLE. It was intended ironically, and we enjoyed our joke, and could not really explain that we did not mean "irresponsible". We meant rather that there was intention on men's part to not be responsible, and that the challenge to this refusal of responsibility was an important aspect of coming to grips with the nuclear industry and its male-dominated associates in the military and big business. But, at the time, our theory had reached only an intuitive form where we understood but could not explain.

This book began in much the same way, when I attended an international conference in Bangladesh on population control.[2] Bangladesh? said every second person and then tried to tell me I would need various injections and drugs in order to stay alive and well. But going to Bangladesh changed my life, and certainly changed my thinking in many ways. I knew that as the former state of Bengal it was famous for its literature and culture. I also knew the work of Bengali feminist, Rokeya Sakhawat Hossain, and her utopian vision, *Sultana's Dream*, of an entire country turned into a garden.

> We are all very busy making nature yield as much as she can. We do not find time to quarrel with one another as we never sit idle. Our noble queen is exceedingly fond of botany; it is her ambition to convert the whole country into one grand garden (1905/1988: 15).

The author of *Sultana's Dream* envisions a society in which women are not shut up in zenanas, but rather where men have been convinced to retire to their own kind of seclusion. For, as the character Sister Sara says, "But dear Sultana, how unfair it is to shut in the harmless women and let loose the men" (Hossain 1988: 9). I also knew of the work of Farida Akhter, her research organisation, UBINIG; the bookshop, sari shop and publishing house, Narigrantha Prabartana. I knew that the name Bangladesh provoked in me thoughts of disaster – the mass rape of women (Brownmiller 1976: 78–86), and the devastating floods, caused by

---

2   The conference was the International Symposium on People's Perspectives on Population, held in Comilla, Bangladesh, 12–15 December 1993.

deforestation in Nepal and India. As poet, Suniti Namjoshi, writing about
the 1970 cyclone in Bangladesh, expressed it:

> 100,000 human beings
> were swallowed by sea
> in a single day
> and then thrown up,
> because
> 2000 miles of polluted oil
> have made the sea
> less than tolerant.
> "Think of the loss," they said,
> "visualize in numbers.
> Sea-sodden corpses
> are useful to no one.
> 200,000 eyeballs
> never to be grafted.
> 100,000 heads of hair
> spoilt by sea-water.
> Next time it happens
> we'll have a freezer handy.
> Next time a battery
> of poets will be ready" (1993: 52).

Or Farida Akhter herself, reflecting on the response to the devastation
of another cyclone, this one on 29 April 1991.

> During the first few days after the cyclone, we heard about dead people only.
> We saw pictures of dead and deformed human beings amid the debris and
> piles of carcasses in the newspapers and on television. It was hard to stand
> such pictures but the media kept on publishing them without any concern to
> journalistic ethics. They were eager to increase their circulation. Repeated
> assaults on the senses with these pictures had soon imparted a numbness, the
> thingish lifelessness of the bodies had soon created an image of the people of
> coastal areas as a pile of numbers, items to be counted in a dotted map of a
> geographical location.

Interestingly, no one was interested to talk about the people who had survived (1992: 79).

The misrepresentation of Bangladesh is pervasive; it is described as a "basket-case of poverty" (Yapa 1993: 255) and as the most densely populated nation on earth. Yet no mention is made of the agricultural richness of the land, of the genuine possibility of a garden nation – indeed, Bangladesh could be described as a cornucopia. The photographs of crowded cities do not indicate how it is that the west has contributed to this crowding through the dispossession of rural people. Crowding has been intensified by "development" programs such as the building of huge bridges funded by the World Bank. Prior to the bridges, ferries carried people and vehicles across the river at a slow pace and provided a site for trading of food and services. The new bridges take away the economic livelihood of the ferry traders and replace it with a road on which no one stops any longer; transnational corporations, however, are able to move their trucks more quickly through the country. The bridge does not benefit the local people, but it does benefit those for whom the fast movement of goods creates profit. During the building of the bridge there is a temporary increase in employment, making it appear as though there is economic development. Once the bridge is built the workers are laid off, and they join the ranks of the unemployed, or flock to the already crowded cities. The long-term result is that the, probably uncounted (Waring 1988),[3] economic benefit of trading on the ferries and the existence of riverside communities ceases altogether – and they have no option but to migrate to the cities. In Madhya Pradesh, India, a similar process is occurring. The Kevats and Kahars, peoples whose "land" is the river, are dispossessed by the construction of large dams. Depending for their livelihood on the river as "ferrymen, fisherfolk, sand quarriers and cultivators of the riverbank when the water recedes in the dry season" (Roy 1998: 69) they are not considered for compensation, since they don't "own" land. In these examples, at least two groups of people, previously self-sustaining, are dispossessed. This, in itself, is not a new idea. Fritz Schumacher pointed out in 1973 that the Buddhist economist would

---

3   The Australian and New Zealand edition of Waring's book is entitled *Counting for Nothing*, while the US edition was changed to *If Women Counted*.

regard import and export as a "deterioration in the pattern of consumption" (Schumacher 1973: 45). Just as small is beautiful, the local too, is critical.

The poverty of Bangladesh is usually attributed to population growth and density, but as Betsy Hartmann argues, colonisation, debt, political dictatorships and free market forces, have all been more important on a global level than the activities of the poor (1994: 15). In one of the main squares of Dhaka there is a constantly changing lighted sign on which the *estimated* birth rate of Bangladesh is displayed. This creates in the spectator a sense of impending doom, of being swept away on a tide of human over-population. On page one of the *San Francisco Chronicle* on 2 September 1994, the caption to the main photograph read: "Pedestrian and vehicular traffic clogs the streets of Dhaka, capital of Bangladesh, the most densely populated country in the world" (McLeod 1994: 1).

The photograph (reproduced opposite page 2) was a lead-in to the article on the UN International Conference on Population and Development in Cairo. The photograph and its caption were clearly an effort to produce in the newspaper's readers an emotional response to over-crowding, hence pushing the line that over-population, not over-consumption, was the critical issue on the agenda for the conference. As Suniti Namjoshi's poem suggests, and as Farida Akhter's experience confirms, number counting numbs us.

My view of Dhaka in December 1993.

So there I was, in Bangladesh with sixty-three other women from every continent. After two or three days of listening, I sat down under a tree and scribbled out in my notebook what I came to call "Wild Politics: A Manifesto" (Hawthorne 1993: 26–27). I managed to write, in a semi-poetic form, the ideas that form the core of this work. I "knew" I had intuited a way of looking at the world that satisfied my sense of intellectual rigour in its completeness. But what I could not do was explain my ideas to those who did not instantly "get it". And so I began reading. I did some writing on the topic (Hawthorne 1996), but only began to do that with any seriousness when, in 1999, I enrolled in a PhD. It was not until late 2000 that I began to really get a full sense of what I had intuited under a tree in Comilla, Bangladesh, on that day in 1993. This introduction serves to explain the sources of my thinking as the ideas began to gel.

Cultural Logic

What I found myself looking for was a logic of the culture which is currently dominating the world. The culture is both global and western, and it appears to be finding its way into the many nooks and crannies which have managed to remain distant from it. How has this happened? What are the forces at work? What impact is it having on women in different countries and different cultural settings? And finally, is there any alternative?

A number of feminist authors have critiqued dominant culture, for example, Linda Tuhiwai Smith (1999), Marimba Ani (2000), Vandana Shiva (1993a), and have identified what might be called the "logic of the culture" (Bell 1983/2002, 1987), its driving force, its vital spirit (Ani 2000), and its characteristic features (Shiva 1993a; Ani 2000).

I discuss the different elements encapsulated in the work of these writers who bring a decentred approach to cultural analysis, coming from viewpoints informed by African-centred experience (Ani 2000), from India (Shiva 1993a), and from working with indigenous knowledge systems of the Pacific basin (Bell 1983/2002, 1998; Tuhiwai Smith 1999; Trask 1986).

Diane Bell, referring to the logic of the host culture (1983/2002: 28), also finds it possible to explore her own culture as an anthropologist (1987). She puts Australian women's culture under the microscope and asks much the same questions as she does when doing fieldwork in a culture not her own (see Bell 1983/2002 for a discussion of these issues). In *Generations: Grandmothers, Mothers and Daughters* (1987), Bell looks at the ways in which women's knowledge and family heritage are passed from one generation to another. She traces the objects, the "heirlooms and hand-me-downs" (1987: 243) passed through the hands of the women in a family. In a later study with the Ngarrindjeri people of South Australia, what is passed down "from generation to generation" is knowledge, and this is done through "story, ceremony, song, dance and ritual design" (1998: 16). In both these arenas, the culture is passed on through meaningful objects or ideas. And it is this sense of meaning, in its deepest form, which is critical to the sustainability of culture.

Indigenous people in Australia use numerous concepts that are quite distinct from western concepts. Two concepts have influenced my thinking in this book. They are the concept of *jukurrpa* (Bell 1983/2002: 90–94) and of *miwi* (Bell 1998: 218–225). *Jukurrpa*, usually translated as "dreaming", is widely used, and in this instance is the word used by the Warlpiri of the Central Australian desert. The *jukurrpa* is not only time past, but also time present; the framework of knowledge provided by the ancestral beings is "a force in the lives of the living" and "a moral code". The *jukurrpa* is not a fixed law/lore, but rather a fulcrum from which change within the culture can occur. It provides "the structural potential for change" within a particular framework of social and cultural forms. *Jukurrpa* provides a mechanism for interacting with the world. It "binds people, flora, fauna and natural phenomena into one enormous inter-functioning world" (Bell 1983/2002: 90, 91).

The way in which the Law works is to allow classification within this system of things and concepts not previously encountered. A crowbar can be classified as a digging stick; and the *jukurrpa* can be renewed through new acts of dreaming, song and ritual. Money can also take on ritual significance, but when it does, it fundamentally changes the system of reciprocity in the indigenous system. This occurs because money is not tied to land and its exchange, and receiving money cannot therefore be located within the system of reciprocity that characterises kin relationship to food and tools.

The "interfunctioning" nature of this Central Australian epistemology marks the direct engagement between the people of a community and their environment. This is reflected in the nature of land tenure systems of both the Arrernte and Warlpiri peoples, each of which is adapted to the nature of the "country" for which a particular person or group is responsible. The relationship with the land is one of responsibility, which is characterised by ritual maintenance, and knowledge of resources and areas where food may or may not be harvested. Intimate and detailed knowledge is integral to the sustenance of the land, kin and country, and in turn, to the culture. Plants, animals, rocks, the nature of the landscape and soil, its water courses, and the people all play a part in the interfunctioning system of the *jukurrpa*.

In her work with the Ngarrindjeri people of South Australia, in an area which encountered the forces of colonisation much earlier than Central Australia, Diane Bell writes about the Ngarrindjeri concept of *miwi* and the related concept of *wurruwarrin*. *Miwi* is a knowledge feeling, located in the stomach. It is a feeling which indicates the truth of knowledge claims, and it is felt. Bell points out that *miwi* is not something referred to lightly, and sometimes represents a feeling of "heightened emotion" (1998: 219). It is often related to place, so that a place can create a feeling of peace or of feeling ill-at-ease. *Miwi* allows for a direct emotional engagement with the environment, and the wisdom gained from *miwi* "is not disconnected from the physical world". "*Miwi* fuses the emotional and intellectual into true knowledge and it is this which creates understanding generated by feeling and knowing, in turn creating knowing and believing or *wurruwarrin* (Bell 1998: 223, 225).

What is salient in this discussion of these two knowledge frameworks is the direct engagement that occurs between an individual or a group and the local environment. In the case of *jukurrpa*, the dreaming framework provides a means of dealing with change in the environment through a cultural form. In the case of *miwi* and *wurruwarrin*, the direct emotional experience and engagement initiate intergenerational discussion, story-telling and passing on of knowledge. Those involved engage in commu-nity-oriented activity, and those who have authority and knowledge confirm the experience of *miwi*, thereby developing and maintaining belief systems.

These are just two examples from the many hundreds of possible examples from indigenous Australia, and they give an insight into the ways in which complex cultural and epistemological systems are developed and extended. Indigenous knowledge systems show a remarkable aptitude for adaptation to both small and large shifts in cultural dynamics. They are localised, contextualised, and are played out in individual bodies. They are also integrative, and, as Ngarrindjeri elder Daisy Rankine says of *miwi*, it "is all wrapped up in weaving and each stitch in weaving meant the part of our lives through the *miwi* wisdom" (Bell 1998: 219). The interlocking metaphor of weaving used here is indicative of the ways in which the elements are interdependent.

Decolonising Scholarship

The literature in this field goes back to the period of decolonisation which accelerated its pace in many countries during the 1960s and 1970s. During this period writers such as Paolo Freire (1971, 1972) Frantz Fanon (1963) and later Edward Said (1977) began to map some of the relationships between imaginative constructs and stereotypes of "the other", as well as the institutional formations which systematically supported the ideology of colonialism. Nevertheless, in my view, the failing of these texts, in spite of their insights and overall importance for increasing our understanding of "the persistence and durability of saturating hegemonic systems like culture" (Said 1995: 15), is that by and large they neglected the impact of colonisation on women. It took until the 1980s and beyond to excavate the more complex relationship between women and colonisation (Etienne and Leacock 1980; Lorde 1984; Bell 1983/2002; Gunn Allen 1986; Anzaldúa 1989; Shiva 1989; Tuhiwai Smith 1999). I argue that the relationship is more complex because it creates a further layering of oppressions, and the institutional formations of these oppressions are specifically tailored to the role of women within the culture.

Linda Tuhiwai Smith's *Decolonizing Methodologies* (1999) is a fine example of work that engages with the layered complexities of feminist and indigenous scholarship. The rupturing of the interconnected webs of culture, language, history and their own sense of self, is not unusual among colonised peoples; it is also a common feature in the experience of other oppressions outside the colonisation, such as racism, sexism, homo-phobia, as well as discrimination based on class and ability/mobility. These additional refracting oppressions amplify one another according to their prominence within the individual's or group's identity.

For Tuhiwai Smith, it is not simply the process of research which is fraught with difficulty but also the terms under which research is done. She points to the overwhelming influence of western, so-called objective knowledge systems in framing precisely what research is possible; what questions can be asked. Simply thinking about which areas to research raises questions about "what counts as real" (Tuhiwai Smith 1999: 44), and therefore about what constitutes real research. Feminist research has faced similar difficulties since the 1970s, some of which I have personally experienced within academic discourses. My interdisciplinary approach which enabled me to put sometimes women, sometimes lesbians at the centre of my research, has resulted in discriminatory marking practices, or in simple incomprehension and an urge to push me in another direction. As anyone who has worked at the margins of intellectual respectability will acknowledge, there are sanctions for those who overstep the mark, who go beyond what is considered "legitimate knowledge" (Tuhiwai Smith 1999: 63). In a globalised world, legitimate knowledge is that which is acceptable to the arbiters of western knowledge (primarily universities, but also governments and major media corporations). So-called universal knowledge, knowledge not claimed by any one group of people, becomes the global knowledge currency. Everything else can be ignored. Legitimate knowledge is decontextualised and unmarked by its author's perspective (or at least this is the accepted fiction). Val Plumwood (1996: 157) contrasts the "universality and impartiality" of the "disinterested" dominating rationality of western philosophical discourse with the discourse that has been developed by ecofeminists. Ecofeminist discourse encompasses "caring and love", which are regarded as "unreliable, untrustworthy and morally irrelevant" by the apologists for masculine reason.

More recently, Tuhiwai Smith argues, "the other" has become a tradeable commodity, and a profitable one (1999: 90). The ability to trade is at least two-way, but is not necessarily reciprocal. On the one hand, the cultural objects, works of art, language and cultural institutions can be sold on the global market, or to the global tourist who passes through. On the other hand, the "interesting little backwaters, untapped potentials" are themselves markets for other global products (Tuhiwai Smith 1999: 98).

Tuhiwai Smith proposes a "'local' theoretical positioning" that enables the researcher to draw on her own very "specific historical, political and social context" to develop an embedded critical theory. It is only in this way, Tuhiwai Smith argues, that the "oppressed, marginalized and silenced groups" will gain something from research and from the knowledge created (1999: 186). The creation of knowledge is a matter of means and ends, and if the ends are not achieved in a way that is consistent with the cultural framework, then the knowledge is not worth having.

I consider the issue of means and ends critically important to any politics which aims for social justice. That is, to use the example of violence – whether it be political and public or domestic and private – overcoming violence, changing attitudes to it will not be achieved by using violence, but rather by using engagement and non-violent means. Creating connection is a means which, with persistence, can turn around violence. Nor is it overcome by using strategies of silence.

Biodiversity and Seeds

Vandana Shiva has been at the forefront of critiques which centre on the problems of globalisation, in particular its interaction with, and impact on, the lives of poor people and on the environments in which the poor live and work.

Shiva conceives of biodiversity as a central principle for evaluating whether a particular course of action should be embarked upon, or whether a particular technology is useful. She uses the perspective of the poorest people as the basis of her evaluations. For instance, Shiva looks at the productive value of rice in the context of India, where, she claims, some 30,000 species have been grown (1993a: 67). She points to the "multiple yields" of rice in the Indian context.

> The destruction of diversity and the creation of uniformity simultaneously involves the destruction of stability and the creation of vulnerability. Local knowledge, on the other hand, focuses on multiple-use of diversity. Rice is not just a grain, it provides straw for thatching and mat-making, fodder for livestock, bran for fish ponds, husks for fuel (1993a: 48).

Rice also becomes a subject for storytelling and cultural memory. This is the view from the perspective of farmers, indigenous peoples and small land holders. Shiva applies the same principles to her discussions of forestry and fishing, in which the forest is seen as more than just "dead wood" because it supplies fruits, fodder, shade and location for diverse species' habitats. Usefulness is not a matter of markets, but of livelihood and long-term sustainability. She uses the examples of miracle seeds, the high-yield varieties of the Green Revolution, and miracle trees (in India the eucalyptus is promoted in this way). The term "miracle" is enough to make one immediately suspicious. A miracle is something out of the ordinary, lifted out of context; it has been removed from the determining features of its environment. And this is precisely how miracle seeds and trees are characterised. Added to by commercial research and development, stripped of their environments, they are transferred to other places where they have never previously grown. Supported by expensive inputs such as fertilisers and pesticides, in the first year or two the results are impressive. But after persistent usage, pests can decimate large areas under monocultural cultivation (Shiva 1993a: 73–78).

What Shiva is arguing is that diversity in and of itself has ecological value and that it is a useful principle to apply to other areas. She notes, for example, that biodiversity contributes to cultural diversity, and that sacred status is among the successful strategies used by many cultures to preserve biodiversity: "Sacred groves, sacred seeds, sacred species have been cultural means for treating biodiversity as inviolable" (Shiva 1993a: 88, 89). Sacred places, if one takes a connected view of the world as central, are often rich in natural resources, whether plants, animals and birds, or striking natural features such as rocks and water courses. Such places are havens for wildlife, and for the continuing sustenance and safety of people and other life. The olive groves of Greece, the tree circles of Ireland, Britain and Brittany, the sacred caves in India, the sacred sites throughout Australia are important for these reasons, as well as additional culturally layered, spiritual meanings.

However, even Shiva, who shows great sensitivity to local conditions, sometimes fails to step outside her own view of the world. In *Monocultures of the Mind* (1993a) she includes a long discussion of the misuses of eucalyptus planting as an exotic species throughout Asia. The eucalyptus is promoted as a miracle tree with fast growth, but it has none of the advantages of biomass production which trees indigenous to India have. In the context of India, therefore, eucalyptus planting has destroyed soils and water tables. In Australia, its efficiency in obtaining water from dry soils makes it highly adapted to the local conditions. And, ironically, in Australia, the eucalyptus is not promoted as a miracle tree; instead, it is clear-felled to make way for plantations of exotics such as *Pinus radiata*. This decontextualisation of commercial forestry appears to be an intentional process of displacement and dispossession. My surprise was compounded when I looked at the illustration of a eucalyptus (1993a: 38); the tree depicted did not resemble any eucalyptus I have ever seen, although I grew up entirely surrounded by eucalyptus in Australia. What it did remind me of was *Pinus radiata*. Is this, perhaps, the image of the ideal tree in the minds of the monocultural commercial foresters?

The inviolability of the seed lies at the centre of Vandana Shiva's analysis. Shiva makes an analogy between the demise of the spinning wheel and the increasing standardisation of fabrics produced through industrialisation, and the threats to the seed and the potential for increasing uniformity. This will result in the demise of biodiversity, in particular indigenous varieties or landraces. These are the seeds which represent the "wild type". Human interference has been minimal (although some selection for adaptation to the environment might have occurred) and the vigour of the plants is important as a way of maintaining genetic health.

Shiva argues that the so-called "elite" or "advanced"[4] seed created by transnational seed companies fails in two significant ways:

1. It does not *reproduce* itself, while by definition, seed is a regenerative resource. Genetic resources are thus, through technology, transformed from a renewable into a non-renewable resource.

2. It does not *produce* by itself. It needs the help of inputs to produce. As the seed and chemical companies merge, the dependence on inputs will increase, not decrease. And ecologically, whether a chemical is added externally [through fertiliser or pesticide] or internally [through genetic manipulation], it remains an external input in the ecological cycle of the reproduction of seed (1993a: 144, emphasis in original).

The gradual decrease in variety of seeds used – whether within a species or through monoculture cropping rather than mixed cropping – creates

---

4   It is instructive to look at the language applied to seeds by agribusiness. It reflects dominant culture value systems where "elite" is considered a marketable category, and "advanced" implies the idea of scientific progress so central to western culture.

a new kind of poverty among farmers. Farmers become increasingly dependent on the external inputs of chemical companies, on the cash from export markets, and on external advisers who know nothing about the local conditions of food production. The increasing commercialisation means that people can be growing large acreages of crops for export and have nothing to eat. The balance of foodstuffs might be markedly disrupted, even when food crops are grown, since those suited to local needs may be rejected in favour of crops grown to satisfy the demands of global markets and the dictates of food fashions.

Shiva rejects the increasing uniformity which characterises industrial approaches to farming, forestry and fishing, and suggests that we need to move in the direction of a logic of production which is based upon the idea of diversity. The global push for sameness, for profit, for maintenance of entrenched structures of power, is, she argues, a threat to the survival of the planet.

The Seed of Culture

Marimba Ani (2000), in her thoroughgoing critique of western culture, identifies the problem quite precisely. She proposes three important ideas about cultural logic and the accompanying behavioural and perceptual structures which determine how a culture is shaped, as well as outlining the characteristics which shape the driving force of the culture. She traces how institutions and ideological approaches develop out of these structures.

The first concept, *asili*, is what she calls the logos of a culture. It is the seed at the centre of a culture, its driving force, or the "germinating matrix" (Ani 2000: xxv, 498). It is the ideological stance which makes sense of the behaviours of the people in the culture, and of its major institutions and creations, and the kind of cultural ethic supported by various rewards and sanctions. Law, religion and worldview emerge from the chrysalis of the *asili*.

In western culture, the *asili* is characterised by separation and universalism. Implicit in the notion of separation is dividing the world from the person. So there is "the European" and "the other", there is "man" and "nature", there is "truth" and "falsehood". Such division and dislocation lead to the systematic negation of the existence of "the other", which is redefined as having the sole purpose of serving the desires and needs of "man" (European man). Trask characterises this as "an elaboration of the logic of domination, the will to power over nature which informs western civilization" (1986: 4; see also Fanon 1973; Said 1977/1995).

Universalism extends this separation, and applies the same cultural logic to all people, everywhere, as if all contexts were the same. On this principle, "as people become more 'rational', they become more 'universal'" (Ani 2000: 512). Indeed, the entire idea of liberal democracy is based on an ethic of sameness and equality. And although this idea has led to some degree of "freedom", it has done so most effectively in those societies which are culturally part of the European world. Those who have lost out in the equality stakes are those who fall outside the European culture: Africans, indigenous peoples, gypsies, "orientals" and, to some extent, women, the poor, the disabled, gays and lesbians. Universalism implies that context is irrelevant, and that all people strive to become a part of, be assimilated into, western European culture. The normative status of European culture is what drives the strategies of the World Bank, the International Monetary Fund (IMF), the World Trade Organisation (WTO) and a host of other international "development" projects. It also drives the three major unethical and illegal trades: in arms, in people (slavery and prostitution), and in drugs. Val Plumwood expresses the desire for a feminist ethics which takes account of relationship, and a move away from abstraction and disconnection. She writes:

> We must move toward the sort of ethics feminist theory has suggested, which can allow for both continuity and difference and for ties to nature which are expressive of the rich, caring relationships of kinship and friendship rather than increasing abstraction and detachment from relationship (1996: 168).

Marimba Ani describes the construction of thought forms and practices within European culture. She uses the term *utamawazo* to describe "culturally structured thought" (2000: 14–15). *Utamawazo* "is structured by ideology and bio-cultural experience" (2000: xxv, 15). It creates cultural authority and explains the ways in which different cultural perspectives evolve.

Her third concept, *utamaroho*, is what she characterises as the inspiration of a culture, its ethos, its emotional responses (Ani 2000: 15–17). A good example of this from Australia was the way in which the opening ceremony of the Sydney 2000 Olympic Games presented the Australian *utamaroho* or ethos to the world. Most Australians recognised a part of themselves in the ceremony, and this tapping into the cultural ethos assisted in making the Olympic Games a successful event, even among those who had been cynical about the Games for a very long time. *Utamaroho* can be thought of as the spirit of the culture. Ani argues that the *utamaroho*, or inspiration, of European culture is domination. She suggests that domination is carved into all of the structures of European culture. It is present in every institution and every sanctioned behaviour, especially those which dispossess "the other" or which offer a means of control over nature, land and resources. Ani critiques the way in which western culture has been imposed on peoples all around the world and made out to be a higher and more evolved form of "civilisation", thereby justifying the wholesale destruction or appropriation of languages and other aspects of culture.

Weaving the Strands

The work of these four theorists combined to create a way of understanding how I might tease out the different strands of western culture, how they operate in a global setting, and how they might have an impact on diverse groups of people – those who fall outside the cultural forms (Africans, "orientals", gypsies and indigenous peoples), or fall short of them in some way (women, the poor, the disabled, gays and lesbians). For the purpose of creating an analysis, I call the members of these groups the diversity matrix.

I propose a way of thinking outside the *asili* of western culture. What I am suggesting is that if the *asili* of western culture could shift, it would involve "fundamental changes in conception of the 'other' and of behavior towards others" (Ani 2000: 517). If the *asili* were to shift to the idea of the "wild" as a central metaphor for thought and ideology, a whole raft of cultural forms would have to change. The "wild" is comparable to the seed (as described by Shiva), to *jukurrpa* (as described by Bell).

In this new world, biodiversity would become the inspiration for the culture, the defining spirit or Ani's *utamaroho* (2000: 15–17). This spirit would create very different behaviours and institutions, the expressions of a particular kind of thought or *utamawazo* (Ani 2000: 14–15). Diversity would become the organising principle of institutions and behaviours, and in this setting, each cultural practice could be tested against the diversity principle.

Of the four theorists mentioned here, there are times when they are almost interchangeable in their approaches to cultural critique. Ani, for example, writes "Knowledge of the universe comes through relationship with it and through perception of spirit in matter" (2000: 29). This is very like the conceptual apparatus which Bell (1983/2002; 1998) identifies as central to indigenous Australian culture, whether it be the *jukurrpa* of the Warlpiri and Arrernte peoples, or the *miwi* and *wurruwarrin* of the Ngarrindjeri of South Australia.

Tuhiwai Smith's "local theoretical positioning" (1999: 186) shares much with Shiva's argument that diversity is an integral part of local knowledge (1993a: 48). The centrality of the seed to Shiva's argument is given the kind of weight that Ani suggests through her notion of the seed of culture, the generating matrix, a complexity which generates diversity. In Vandana Shiva's most recent book, she summarises the importance of the seed as a necessary element of biological and cultural diversity.

> The seed is the first link in the food chain. It is the embodiment of life's continuity and renewability; of life's biological and cultural diversity. Seed, for the farmer, is not merely a source of future plants/food; it is the storage place of culture, of history. Seed is the ultimate symbol of food security (2001f: 69).

If the "wild" were a central conceptual force of western culture, the culture itself would change radically. In turn, if the inspiration for such a culture were biodiversity, a whole range of institutional and individual behaviours would have to change. Some examples are economic systems; land tenure systems; farming, fishing and forestry; production, consumption and work; as well as a number of recently implemented multilateral agreements, in particular the Trade Related Intellectual Property rights system (TRIPs).

The wild seed, the "wild type" – a metaphor for minimal interference from humanity – becomes epistemologically equivalent to Ani's *asili*. Its health is dependent upon a thorough knowledge of local conditions, the maintenance of biodiversity, and a self-sustainable approach to life which gives at least as much as, and often more than, it takes. A wild politics approach is regenerative, life-sustaining, and contains an element of unpredictability: a level of responsiveness in adapting to change as it might occur in an ecological system. Wild politics also draws heavily on feminist theory, including in its use of the word "politics". Kate Millett's definition of "politics" to "refer to power-structured relationships, arrangements whereby one group of persons is controlled by another" (1972: 23) remains a useful touchstone for a general conception of what constitutes the "political".

Defining the Wild

Throughout this book I use the term "wild" because it brings together a range of possibilities for developing a new kind of politics. The term "wild" is intimately connected with the biophysical world, and carries a range of specific resonances which I will investigate.

In genetics, the term "wild types" refers to unregulated genetic structures. The "wild type" is a characteristic shared by most members of a species under "natural conditions". This commonality is also the source of diversity. Diversity, unconstrained by human interference, is critical to the continuing biological existence of the planet.

Although I use the term "wild" in this conventional sense of lacking human interference, I also recognise some of the problems inherent in this definition. Humanity has had a longstanding relationship of interdependence with nature. By "unregulated" and "unconstrained by human interference", I mean a relationship that does not seek to control, but rather recognises interdependence.

"Unconstrained by human interference" should not be taken to mean that there is no influence of humans on plants. If humans share the ecosystem, there will be influence; sometimes, through activities that promote selection of a genetic wild type, these activities might even affect future generations. I take human interference to mean intentional selective breeding, genetic engineering, and the "creation" of novel genetic forms which would be considered "innovations" under existing WTO patenting rules.[5]

Indeed, I do not wish to suggest that human beings are outside the ecosystem. On the contrary, I highlight the intimate relationship between human beings and the planet, its living organisms, and its natural resources. Just as a wild animal or a wild plant is embedded in a series of

---

5   See Chapter Seven for an in-depth discussion of patents and multilateral agreements.

relationships with all the other species around it – as well as with the land, the water courses and other natural features – so too are humans.

The relationship aspect is centrally important to the concept of wildness. Removing a wild animal from its locale to, say, a zoo, in order to preserve it, moves it away from its status as "wild". Even when zoos attempt to reproduce "environments", they can never replicate the local ecology and its relationships for the wild animal. The process involved in domestication of animals and plants gradually moves the organism from an embeddedness in its own ecological niche to the human niche. A wild approach involves taking account of relationship, biodiversity and cultural diversity, ecological systems, context, and a respect for the ongoing dynamics of the system, taking account of what might be called the ecological matrix.

These issues come to the fore when discussing "wilderness". Tracts of land declared as wilderness areas by governments are frequently areas of traditional occupation of indigenous peoples, and it is a mistake to assume that there has been no imprint on the land of its traditional inhabitants (Wright 1991). Wild plants used for medicinal purposes which are harvested by biodiversity prospectors on behalf of pharmaceutical companies are another case in point. The knowledge of their medicinal uses has almost always come from local indigenous populations. When there are profits to be made, the wild is perceived as "part of the public domain" (Posey 1996: 8) and therefore freely exploitable; but after it has been "discovered" by the pharmaceutical industry, it becomes private property protected by US patent laws. The privatisation of blood cells from individual blood samples as part of the Human Genome Diversity Project is one of the most extreme examples of the appropriative process. These are some of the issues which I discuss in greater detail.

Catriona Sandilands, in her discussion of "wild democracy", defines wild as "aspects of undomesticated life both outside and inside humanity" (1997: n.1, 145). This goes some way toward identifying her range of discussion, but her definition lacks clarity. For example, resistance to the process of cultural domestication carried on under colonisation might be considered to fall under the category of wild politics, but if that resistance is effected in order to catapult a social system into a repressive regime (such as the regimes in Burma and the Republic of Congo at the end of the twentieth century), it will not, in my view, be an instance of wild politics. Such examples clarify why context is so important.

Wherever disengagement, dislocation and disconnection occur, there the wild is being tamed or co-opted. A utilitarian approach to politics, for example, allows for a moral disengagement, as the person justifies an action because of its end. In the area of development, a host of economic activities – structural adjustment programs, Population Council family planning programs, IMF-sponsored economic "reforms", or World Bank-funded projects – and their utilitarian approach are wreaking havoc in the lives of ordinary people. Utilitarianism strips context from any situation. This philosophy is one of the most pervasive of the tools of western liberal individualism. Through revering utilitarianism, liberal democracies continue to regard the diversity matrix, the "other", as their means to wealth, "freedom" and individual life satisfaction (Plumwood 1996: 170, 171). As Plumwood points out, "Others are a resource" (1996: 171). Disconnection is what makes this objectification possible.

I argue for a consideration of context, and of consistency between means and ends. The world's ecosystem will not survive if unjust economic means are used to justify short-term economic ends. Helena Norberg-Hodge comments on this from her experience in Ladakhi society in which people used to rely on one another. With increasing westernisation, "the distance between people has increased so that it now appears that you no longer need one another" (1991: 122).

In a cultural sense, wild types are the unexpected connections made by artists, or when encountering a new culture, a culture not part of the dominant mainstream.

"Wild" also refers to rage and anger. Those of us with a politics informed by activism have much to be angry about in the real world: violence against women and children, poverty, and the increasing control the state and transnational companies have over our bodies, our identities, our movements. Not to be wild would be tantamount to denial, apathy or resignation. Moreover, our anger can be turned to productive political ends. Wild politics activists can turn the situation around by constructing an ethic to live by; one that is nuanced enough to allow for the local conditions, but which gives some guidance on how to treat one another. Wild politics provides enough leeway for humour and anger, hence steering clear of the charge of "political correctness", and enables a broadly outlined political ethic grounded in the local, but which may be useful on the global level.

When I use the word "wild" I mean to capture the whole range of meanings, from wild as in angry or vicious; wild as in diverse, wide-ranging, rebellious; and wild in the way it is used idiomatically, comparable to cool, neat: wild, outside the barriers of control by the dominant party. I certainly do not mean to romanticise "wild nature" as a longed-for state of being. Rather, I want to draw out the political implications of "wild".

But the idea of "wild" has also been misused, and detractors of the idea of wild politics may well point to the reconnection with the "wild" part of oneself so strongly promoted by New Age philosophy. The "wild woman" and "wild man" images of Clarissa Pinkola Estes (1992) and Robert Bly (1992) are two cases in point. As Michael Kimmel and Michael Kaufman point out:

> Bly and others wander through anthropological literature like postmodern tourists [for example, Sylvester 1995], as if the world's cultures were an enormous shopping mall filled with ritual boutiques. After trying them on, they take several home to make an interesting outfit – part Asian, part African, part Native American ... But can these rituals be ripped from their larger cultural contexts, or are they not deeply embedded in the cultures of which they are a part (1993: 8–9)?

Such injunctions from the popular culture to get in touch with the wild part of oneself are, in fact, misleading, since this "getting in touch" succeeds only in distancing people even further from themselves. Getting in touch through the culture of another, also demeans others. Having contacted another culture through the sanitised and commodified version offered by New Age gurus, those in search of themselves find only "plastic passions" (Daly 1984: 197), fake cultures, and tamed selves. The result is what I have called elsewhere "cultural voyeurism" (Hawthorne 1989a), "spiritual voyeurism" (Hawthorne 1994a) and Diane Bell refers to as putting beliefs through a "cultural blender" (1997: 52), a commodified reality that bears little resemblance to the real world and real cultures (Hawthorne 1996b).[6] Bell points to the blending of different beliefs of Native Americans in the work of Lynne Andrews, who combines

---

6   In a move reminiscent of Robert Bly's "wild man", tours for men to Central Australia capitalise on a sense of disconnection experienced by some men. See Tiggelen (2002: 14–19).

Lakota, Cree and Hopi as if they were one. Bell points out that this is "an assault on the integrity of the extremely personal and specific ties to kin and country that underpin their beliefs and practices" (1997: 52). It is also a homogenising of diversity, and a denial of the importance of local conditions.

The search for meaning that so often ends, these days, in fake realities can be traced back to the sense of disconnection and rootlessness experienced by many contemporary people, in particular urban dwellers, but also those uprooted by war, natural disaster, political exile, or removed from families by governments, churches, or even, the seemingly innocuous purpose of education at a boarding school. Rootlessness arises because we grow up these days disconnected from the local. Global culture, from Disneyland to Coca-Cola, from baseball to the World Wide Web, influences us, distracts us from the world of our senses and from our local conditions. Overwhelmed by meaninglessness and powerlessness, we long for something more from our increasingly global culture (Du Plessis 1995: 27). But my argument is that the quick fix, the appropriation of other cultures through shopping for meaning, is a dead end. It will not make western people more vital, nor help us make sense of the world. Nor can anyone do it alone. It will take commitment to relationship and co-operation across the many barriers which separate people. If enough people can make the imaginative leap, and connect imagination to responsible and respectful social behaviour, then perhaps some will be operating on the basis of a wild politics.

In my definition, wild politics is both an analysis of structural forces and a strategy for resistance. It takes into consideration the local and the personal, measuring the impact of these on the global and the local environments (see also Shiva 1993a; Norberg-Hodge 1996a, 1996b; Rogers 1998).

The links between environmental pollution and the well-being of people has been pointed out many times, most notably by Rachel Carson in *Silent Spring* (1962). Likewise, feminists have pointed out the link between the personal and the political. If personal well-being is affected by behaviour and large-scale political structure is contributing to ill-health then this link needs to be drawn out. For example, after the Chernobyl disaster happened, it was clear that many people were suffering as a result, and the levels of thyroid cancer in children amount to many thousands of cases (UN Scientific Committee on the Effects of Atomic Radiation 2000: 491ff).[7] Laurie Garrett, in her mammoth work, *The Coming Plague*, proposes:

> a new paradigm in the way people think about disease ... [and suggests] a far more challenging perspective... allowing for a dynamic, nonlinear state of affairs between Homo sapiens and the microbial world, both inside and outside their bodies (1994: 11).

In *Wild Politics*, I am elaborating on a new paradigm for thinking about the macro world and the micro world. It affects every aspect of life, including human relationship to the natural world, the wild world; to one another; to culture; to the way we think; and to the economic structures which control everyone more and more.

My definition of "wild" shares something of the irreverence of Mary Daly's view of the wild, which she represents as: "The vast Realm of Reality ... characterized by diversity, wonder, joy, beauty, Metamorphic Movement and Spirit" (1987: 101). For Daly, the wild is a recognition that the world is neither entirely knowable, nor entirely controllable. This is in stark contrast to the purveyors of the knowledge economy, the information revolution, and the researchers into controlling life: biotechnologists, reproductive technology scientists, and those keen on bridging the carbon-silicon divide through the downloading of brains and creation of nanorobots (Klein 1999).

I do not claim to have concrete answers for the current crisis of globalisation. *Wild Politics* is not a blueprint, for that would imply a depth and breadth of knowledge none of us has; it is a call to challenge ingrained ways of thinking, providing a tentative first step. It is a springboard for a different kind of approach, one that respects the interactions between humans and our environments, and suggests some ways of limiting the levels of destructiveness that are often taken for granted; justified on economic grounds; and increasing in intensity on more and more fronts.

---

7   Valerie Kuletz states that "Nine years after the Chernobyl accident an estimated 125,000 people have died" (1998: 85). Doctors expect the cancers to peak in the second decade after the accident. See also UN Scientific Committee on the Effects of Atomic Radiation (2000: 491ff).

I argue that each of us, as well as the communities and societies, the political and business regimes we inhabit, must come to grips with new concepts and levels of responsibility (Kappeler 1995). For too long, the so-called Third World[8] has borne the brunt of criticism for its population, but my argument here is that population size is rendered insignificant when set against the level of consumption and production which occurs at the behest of the rich nations, and among the extraordinarily rich trans-nationals and national military installations. I do not analyse the global military infrastructure in detail, since it seems to me so clearly to be an instrument of oppression and would need an altogether new approach in a social system which took wild politics seriously.[9] *Wild Politics* involves re-examining every aspect of life and lifestyle, from ways of thinking and behaving, to the structures of politics and economics, to the ways in which humanity relates to the world, to other people, and to nature.

---

8   The term "Third World" is attributed to Alfred Sauvy. A French economist and demographer, he first used the term in 1952, as an analogy to the Third Estate of pre-revolutionary France (Roy 1999: 3).

9   For sustained feminist critiques of militarism, see Enloe (1983a, 1989); Caputi (1987); Hynes (1993: 16–22); Stiglmayer (1994); Lentin (1997); Bertell (2000); Hawthorne and Winter (2002).

CHAPTER ONE

THE PRINCIPLE OF DIVERSITY

> *Feminist theory has much to contribute to moving*
> *toward methodological diversity. Its contributions*
> *can be seen as a rejection of the superiority of*
> *abstraction and a rejection of contextlessness*
> – Sabine O'Hara (1997: 151).

Diversity is a continuing theme of this book, and I use it in part as an organising principle, but also as the conceptual check for my hypothesis that a world organised around wild politics, around the principle of diversity, and inspired by biodiversity, would be organised very differently from the profit-driven globalised world we now live in.

There are a number of other key concepts which recur. In contrast to diversity are a cluster of concepts which are readily approved of in the mainstream culture. Among them is universalism. If something is good, it is universal. If it is universal, it is good. God, globalisation, western culture and science all claim universal appeal. Universalism is generally accompanied by homogenisation and abstraction. Homogenisation assumes a sameness which arises from a dominant culture ideology. Sameness is regarded as positive and is underpinned by an ideology of "equality" of inputs (not outcomes). It assumes that a diversity of approaches to the world will be misguided in all but one case: its own approach. The worldwide domination of US culture moves in this direction. Homogenisation is a conceptual position which is rarely reflected by reality. The natural world is full of diversity; street life in any city reflects the parade of human diversity. Homogenisation is an abstraction. Abstractions involve stepping back from the real world in an attempt to organise life in the simplest way. By imposing sameness, however, oversimplification occurs. Abstraction has its uses, but when engaged and diverse approaches are disparaged as unscientific, subjective, personal and local, such thinking ignores the importance of context. Abstraction, or "abstractification" (Ani

2000: 107), has been authorised and institutionalised in such a way that it negates other approaches, other points of view, other frameworks through which the world can be examined. Chandra Mohanty points to this ideology of "sameness" which comes through in liberal feminist work. Mohanty identifies it as "the discursively consensual homogeneity of 'women' as a group [being] mistaken for the historically specific material reality of groups of women" (1997: 81). In this book I draw on the conceptual framework of "local conditions" and the particularities of context. I use the word "multiversalist" in contrast to the overriding liberal concept of "universalist". The multiversalist recognises that there is not just one view of the world, or one way of organising knowledge to reflect "truth". The multiversalist rejects the idea that as human beings "progress" to a state of "civilisation" they become more rational, and more universal (Ani 2000: 512). Conversely, universalism results in a lack of "appreciation of diversity and plurality" (Ani 2000: 502).

Beginnings

The origins of this book lie in the 1960s with the publication of Rachel Carson's *Silent Spring* (1962) and Betty Friedan's *The Feminine Mystique* (1962) in the USA, and in France with Frantz Fanon's *The Wretched of the Earth* (1963). In the 1970s a range of books and articles on feminist issues began to appear, as did works which looked at race and culture (Said 1978; Freire 1971, 1972), issues which were highlighted by the spread of decolonisation. The 1970s were also a time when challenges to economics appeared (Meadows *et al.* 1972; Schumacher 1973). By the mid-1980s the beginnings of ecofeminist perspectives, some international, some local, had been published,[1] as had some works on indigenous issues (Bell 1983; Watson 1984; Johnson 1985; Trask 1986), on women in the Third World, and by those writing from the margins (Etienne and Leacock 1980; Fuentes 1983; Nwapa 1986; Anzaldúa 1987; Minh-ha 1989). From the mid-1980s to the late 1990s a shift occurred in the writings of feminists,

---

1	Susan Griffin	1978	*Women and Nature*
	Mary Daly	1978	*Gyn/Ecology*
	Carolyn Merchant	1980	*The Death of Nature*
	Cynthia Enloe	1983a	*Does Khaki Become You?*
	Robin Morgan	1984	*Sisterhood is Global*
	Rita Arditti *et al.*	1984	*Test Tube Women*
	Rosalie Bertell	1985	*No Immediate Danger*

ecologists and economists.[2] This book draws primarily on feminist writing about decolonisation, books and articles which critique the power structures of class and race, as well as work by those in the disciplines of ecology and economics. Many of these fields have "converged" over the last decade, and individuals from diverse backgrounds are asking similar questions.

This convergence occurred in parallel with the shift toward globalisation. Feminists have been among the most vocal and critical, with concerns ranging from militarism, the effects of radiation, structural adjustment plans, population control, the value of women's work, agricultural practices, international trade policies, toxic waste, war and refugees, food security, pollution, development policies, poverty, international financial institutions, global economics, women's health and public health, citizenship, commodification, and the concentration of power in transnational hands.

Alongside these critiques have appeared a broadening range of works which challenge the existing paradigms of western knowledge and scientific practice, masculine traditions and classical economic theory. The challenges presented by feminist thinkers have literally turned the world upside down and have created new ways of looking at the crisis of western capitalism. Many of the critiques have come from outside the major dominant centres of knowledge production. There are challenges from indigenous thinkers, from writers and thinkers in Asia and Africa, from lesbian thinkers in Australia, North America, New Zealand, from thinkers whose focus is class or race or disability. A new kind of politics is growing out of this literature, and its parameters are diversity, context, interaction, locality, justice and change, namely, wild politics.

The importance of context cannot be understated. Context is a core feature of wild politics; just as a plant is sensitive to its ecological context. Context includes experience, standpoint, personal history, reflection, analysis, synthesis, consciousness, and the tension between dissociative and associative elements in the culture.

2	Maria Mies	1986	*Patriarchy and Accumulation on a World Scale*
	Jane Caputi	1987	*The Age of Sex Crime*
	Andrée Collard	1983	*Rape of the Wild*
	Maria Mies *et al.*	1988	*Women: The Last Colony*
	Marilyn Waring	1988	*Counting for Nothing*
	Vandana Shiva	1989	*Staying Alive*

Thesis, Antithesis, Synthesis

The dialectical relationship represented by these three words forms the core of my approach. Dialectics is a dynamic relationship which characterises speculative thought.[3] The thesis, in the case of wild politics, is the universal system of globalisation; the antithesis is the host of resistances and competing positions put forward by members of the diversity matrix; the synthesis is wild politics. The dialectical relationship is a dynamic connection, one which is not caught in an endless moment of theoretical stillness, nor one which is dependent on intellectual stability. It is a theoretical position outside the major forces of power, wealth and institutional knowledge. The next step in developing knowledge would be for the synthesis to become the new thesis, thereby creating an endlessly changing and dynamic system.

FIGURE 1

Thesis, antithesis, synthesis

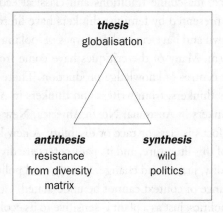

thesis
globalisation

antithesis
resistance
from diversity
matrix

synthesis
wild
politics

The dominant global forces at work are capitalist, masculine, white, western, middle-class, heterosexual, urban, and highly mobile.[4] In general a majority of these dominances is present in the institutions developed by

3   Dialectics emerges from the philosophies of Hegel and Marx. See, for example, Marx's *Economic and Philosophic Manuscripts of 1844* (Tucker 1972: 83–103). The classic feminist restatement of Marx's dialectic is Shulamith Firestone's *The Dialectic of Sex* (1971).

4   An analysis of *Wired* magazine shows a significant overlap of these demographies. See Millar (1998); Hawthorne (1999a); McGuire (2000).

this conglomerate, and most of the individuals are members of cultural elites. They are situated at the still point;[5] they are representatives of a cultural thesis which is buoyed up by the ideologies of western knowledge and science, by a masculinist view of history and the world, and by neoclassical economics.

For many years feminist thinkers have been developing critiques of these forces. The critiques are mostly argued from inside the thesis, the mainstream, that is, they challenge perhaps one strand at a time, or assume a certain kind of coherence among the subjects of their critiques. Critiques of the masculinist tradition are numerous, from Mary Wollstonecraft (1792/1970), Virginia Woolf (1929/1974), Simone de Beauvoir (1949/ 1972), Shulamith Firestone (1971), Kate Millett (1972), Juliet Mitchell (1973), Germaine Greer (1971) and a host of others responsible for the wave of activism which has characterised the women of the baby-boomer generation. Critiques of science (generally not specifically labelled as western in the early texts) began to appear in the 1970s.

Vandana Shiva, a physicist by training, has described the western, objective, scientific view as "reductionist" and as a local knowledge gone global (Shiva 1993a: 10); she has proposed an alternative contextualised reality in which *Prakriti* plays a part. *Prakriti*, in the tradition of India, is a primordial energy which encompasses both stillness and dynamism, and conceptually it is associated with women and the "female principle". Shiva has also challenged the economic assumptions of the masculinist approach to the calculation of value. She is not the only feminist theorist to put forward these arguments, but she was one of the earliest to bring all aspects together in a single critique of the forces of globalisation (Shiva 1989). Her view, and those of other feminists developing critiques in which all the strands are brought together, represent the synthesis. It is a rebellious, constantly changing, marginal position which has the

---

5   As an interesting aside, MacGregor, in his discussion of Hegel's "universal class", the class that makes up the majority of the civil service, notes that "Most members of Hegel's universal class are unaware of the distinct character of their place in the class structure" (1998: 197). I would attribute this to the mistaken view held by most members of the dominant/universal class that their experience is the only experience worth taking note of, thereby leaving them little room for critical reflection on their own experience. See my discussion of Dominant Culture Stupidities later in this chapter).

advantage of clarity because it lies outside the dominant culture. Synthesis is the theoretical style of *Wild Politics*.

Feminism

Feminist theorists have responded to changes in the world. This has resulted in ongoing developments and fine-tuning in feminist theory since the earliest writings appeared criticising different aspects of masculinist culture, whether it be Rokeya Sakhawat Hossain's (1905/1988) dream of another kind of culture, Mary Shelley's (1818/1987) critique of science, or Virginia Woolf's (1929/1974) interpretation of English history and literature. Likewise, feminism from the USA in the 1970s pushed many boundaries. But all of us are caught in our cultures and our times and our writings; dreams and theories are influenced by what we know and what we have experienced. Feminism, and the way it has changed, is no different. Feminists of the twenty-first century have access to much more knowledge about women – across all cultures, classes, sexualities, bodies, abilities – than any of us imagined would become available from the perspective of the 1970s. The theories of the 1970s were dreams of another world, imaginings sometimes way beyond our lived experience. There were many insights which still hold their own in the midst of our hard-won knowledge. Some theories and ideas turned out to be wrong, or limited in their approach, but they had to be thought in order to move on. An example is Shulamith Firestone's (1971) promotion of reproductive technologies as an escape for women from motherhood. Among the limited theories I would include those that promoted a reformist, liberal, white and heterosexual agenda such as Betty Friedan (1962/1973). Feminist theories of the past are often criticised as being out of date, of not taking account of differences now readily recognised (although this is not true of all), of not taking a critical stance on one's own position. Many feminists who have lived through the entire period would agree that there have been gaps; some of the insightful and far-reaching ideas, however, have been disappeared. They have not remained in print; they have not been cited by a generation of younger feminists impatient with the past; or they have been overlooked. The feminist of the twenty-first century has her own cultural traditions (for instance, as an indigenous woman, a lesbian, a rural feminist from South America) to draw on, and she cites from her own experience.

Chandra Mohanty (1997: 79) rightly criticises the homogenisation of the "other", particularly the "Third World woman" and, I would add, the "indigenous woman", both of which are evident in research "about" women, in contrast to research developed "with" women. In this book, I seek out work which has had significant input from the people being written about (Bell 1998; Norberg-Hodge 1991), or which is written by insiders to the culture (Tuhiwai Smith 1999; Gunn Allen 1998; Langton 1998).

The language I have at my disposal is limited, and I often have to resort to frustratingly inadequate terminology. I use, reluctantly, terms like "Third World", but I try where possible to be specific, including being specific about the location of those from dominant unmarked cultures. It is awkward, sometimes, to express oneself easily when experience and the categories used do not reflect my political intent. So "woman" remains a word that I use, for despite all its potential misunderstandings, it is still the most useful word we have. The word "gender" is often mistakenly used instead of either "woman" or "sex". For example, in most instances "gender discrimination" means discrimination against a woman on the basis of her sex; just as race discrimination usually means discrimination against someone who is not white. In some very specific instances, a man or a white may be discriminated against, but it remains unusual, and is marked because of its unusualness.

Likewise, the language of class, culture, and disability is fraught with difficulty. In different countries different terms are in use. For example, "the disabled" is accepted in Britain, while "people with disabilities" is the more acceptable term in Australia; "mixed abilities" is a term now being used in the USA (Guajardo 2001). Similarly, "women of color" (spelt this way) is used in the USA, "Black women" is used in Britain (even the word "Britain" is problematic). In Australia an array of words is used to describe Aboriginal people, and in general "Aboriginal" is used in preference to Aborigine. The word "Koori" is sometimes used in a general way, but it is more properly reserved for south and central New South Wales and Victoria (Butler 2001: 9). For more specific locaters of peoples' place of origin, the terms such as Wiradjuri (central south-west NSW), Warlpiri (parts of Northern Territory), Murri (parts of Queensland), Ngarrindjeri (coastal South Australia and western Victoria), Nyungar (Western Australia), Palawa (Tasmania) are used (and the spellings are often in dispute). The knowledge of "whereness" as well as "whoness" which is built into the naming conventions of Aboriginal people (and indigenous people elsewhere) says a great deal about the construction of knowledge in indigenous cultures, and their communications with the "other", be they indigenous neighbours or the colonising powers. Using the word "indigenous" can be problematic, in much the same way that "woman" has been problematised. In this book, I use "indigenous" as a word suggesting solidarity among the world's first nation peoples. It is important to have words which are inclusive of many people, but I do not mean them as homogenising or assuming sameness. I also use the term "diversity matrix" to describe the group of people who are most vulnerable to encroaching globalised systems. I use the word "western" to describe the culture which, although initially a local system of knowledge, has now become a global system.

It is precisely the importance of "whereness" that I want to highlight. Awareness of physical location is an important element in the construction of the knower's sense of self in colonised cultures. As an Australian, I was, from a very young age, aware of the disconnection of my experience of place from that of northern hemisphere inhabitants. I wondered how it was that that old European man, Santa Claus, was able to get to Australia in midsummer dressed in all that fur!

Locaters, of course, also occur in time. The emergence of feminism as a mass movement in the late 1960s determined the ways in which feminists described their project. My biggest quarrel with feminist theory of the 1970s is that it tends to be Eurocentric or US-centric. There were voices arguing for a Black perspective, a lesbian or class perspective. Disability and an awareness of age took longer. Lack of awareness of cultural domination is still rife in the USA as it moves toward greater and greater influence as *the* determinator of global culture. The social and political forces of every era spill over into the theoretical, just as in the 1990s the forces of globalisation and electronic communications have spilled over into the way in which feminism is described. Although many things remain the same (women's poverty, racism, dispossession of the marginalised), some conditions have changed (the relocation of large industrial and knowledge companies to countries where wages are low). These changes are reflected in the theoretical discussions arising out of local conditions.

Similarly, feminism in the 1990s retains continuity in its basic premisses, while adapting to the shifting ground of global and trans-national power. My own definition of feminism has arisen out of many years of activism, thinking, teaching and writing. A first step in becoming a feminist is acknowledging one's experience of oppression and the effects of systemic oppression on women as a group, but that alone is not sufficient, although it is a necessary condition. What makes the difference is the impetus to want to change the situation. Participating in creating change is an essential step to feminism, and when collectively recognised, feminism is not just an individual politics, but also a social movement. Acting on behalf of others, and for oneself, creates change not only in the conditions of our daily lives, but also in our knowledge and understanding of politics. This in turn creates a critical frame of reference and turn of mind, from which one can never retreat without violence to the self.

Some contemporary feminists go further. They ask the reader, the activist, to consider where she is coming from, her "whereness"; they ask her to consider where others are coming from; they ask everyone to respect difference, to be open-minded and sensitive to the context. These theorists do not ask her to be silent about the oppression of others – even others whose experience she does not share. But they ask her to begin the process of synthesising theory and practice. The personal is still political, but the range and depth of meaning has changed.[6]

Change

> In order to understand a thing, one must change it
> – Maria Mies (1991: 63).

Maria Mies' maxim on change is a good starting point for a work which focuses on the rapidly changing face of global economics, the effects of which can be felt in emerging ideas about globalisation, sustainability, development, and conceptual frameworks envisaging a different future. I write from a standpoint influenced by feminism and ecology, without

---

6   Robin Morgan, in her introduction to *Sisterhood is Powerful*, writes: "Women's Liberation is the first radical movement to base its politics – in fact, create its politics – out of *concrete personal experiences*" (1970: xvii, my emphasis). The slogan "the personal is political" is attributed to Robin Morgan, and has been used in feminist literature since the early 1970s. For a discussion of "the personal is political" as a methodological issue, see Stanley and Wise (1983).

limiting the boundaries of those two key cultural and political critiques of contemporary global culture.

Knowledge is dynamic, shifting as new insights are discovered, either through one's own experience or filtered through reading, writing, research, observation or conversation. These processes in themselves promote engagement and change through that engagement. In this respect, generation of feminist knowledge is no different from any other kind of knowledge. Some has been created through observation, participation and formal research. A great deal has been created through conversation via consciousness-raising groups, interviews, study groups, conferences, speak-outs and informal dialogue. Books and electronic media have spread a diverse range of information and knowledge about women. How was this vast array of research created? And what are the questions which have informed its progress?

Change is, of course, a process, and change is shaped by the context in which it occurs. Understanding the process of change means also understanding the contextual conditions for change. In the last quarter of the twentieth century, feminism, ecology, shifts in communications systems, and the processes of globalisation were some of the contexts of social and biological processes undergoing change.

Change is inherent in natural and biological systems. Indeed, central to the idea of biodiversity is continuous adaptation to change, dynamic relationship with the environment and changing influences or conditions. Biodiversity presupposes a dynamic relationship, one not caught in stasis, rather like the idea of the dialectical relationship in the movement of ideas and processes of political change (see Figure 1).

Creating Feminist Knowledge

How do we know what we know? What are the cultural constraints on our knowledge? How can we step outside the frameworks in which we come to know things? What experiences have shaped this shift in position and awareness? These are critical questions. Linda Archibald and Mary Crnkovich, among many others, call for feminist research to be "rooted in diversity" (1995: 124).

Feminist research is a style of knowing and knowledge making that is both critical and reflective. My knowledge is based on my existence in the actual world, a world created from my interactions in the social sphere, with the biophysical environment and with my own body. To this end, from time to time I include aspects of my experience, many of which reflect my childhood on a farm. I have included these reflections in order to ground the theory, and in some instances show how movements in international politics affect decision making in individual lives. It is, as Dorothy Smith points out, "important to avoid conceptualizations that lift phenomena out of time and place" (1999: 7). Sally L. Hacker pre-empted this call in her early critique of women's role in agribusiness, which she begins: "The most powerful social research, regardless of ideology, is embedded in social action. One informs the other and interaction often yields new ways of knowing and doing" (1990: 89).

Against those who suggest, solipsistically and post-modernly, that we can know and speak only those things that are like what we have experienced, I would argue that our imaginations have more strength and depth than this post-modern maxim suggests. Our ability to move outside our own knowledge frameworks and experience is part of our human capacity to recognise the past and the future, to understand history and applaud the visionary.[7] Attention to context and to relationship, as well as to consequences, can assist us in acquiring skill in these areas. These are precisely the knowledge styles of women, indigenous peoples and others marginalised by the mainstream.

The politics of knowledge is a recurring theme in feminist research, and it encompasses issues of judgement as well as of perception. The four writers whose work I discuss in the introduction – Marimba Ani, Diane Bell, Vandana Shiva and Linda Tuhiwai Smith – provide us with models for reconsidering our assumed frameworks and the amount of weight we give to research findings. How knowledge is framed has also come under scrutiny, and nowhere is this more clear than in the development and building of "marginal" knowledges – building upon women's diversity – by lesbian researchers, indigenous researchers, African-American researchers. When taken together, these knowledges increase the complexity of "marginal" knowledges, thereby decreasing the applicability of stereo-types. What kind of knowledge frames the work is a central issue for all researchers, although many mainstream researchers persist in not recog-nising their own heavily framed knowledge claims. Francis Fukuyama is

---

7   For a discussion of this, see Young (1997), Chapters I and II.

a good example of this with his claim that "liberal democracy may constitute the 'end point of mankind's ideological evolution'" (1992: xi). His
inattention to his framework pervades the work.

Indigenous knowledges are characterised by an incredible diversity of
knowledge systems and reflect the particularities which are "unique to
given cultures, localities and societies" (Dei *et al.* 2000: 19). Njoki
Nathani Wane took up this challenge in her research to recover the
missing parts of her own partial education which has "divorced" her from
her Kenyan roots. She carried out her research by placing "women in the
centre" which allowed her to take into account their broad social context.
She found that it also provided a "space for the 'other' who has been
excluded in the knowledge production process" (2000: 55). She found a
depth of knowledge among elder women about the way in which the
Embu environment has changed since the coming of white western ways.

The following quotation exemplifies the kind of knowledge held by
elder women in many parts of the world; in this case the speaker is Cucu,
an Embu elder from Kenya:

> By the time you are my age the world will be completely destroyed... Look
> around you, where are the thick forests we used to have? ... Kirimiri [name
> of a forest] was thick and the canopy created by the trees would not allow the
> rays of the sun through ... These days people have cultivated up to the top
> of the mountain ... Man's greed has chased the spirits of our ancestors that
> used to live there ... For us this was a sacred mountain ... But its sacredness
> has been destroyed ... Gaka ... your generation needs to halt or ... slow
> down the pace of destruction (Wane 2000: 66; ellipses and brackets in
> original).

Cucu's insight on the destruction wreaked by the imposition of foreign
knowledge systems without the benefit of, or interest in, understanding local
conditions has wide currency, and could be applied to many other settings.
What makes it so is a depth of knowledge obtained by her through living
in close connection with the land, the local environment, and by maintaining respect for long-standing cultural knowledge and traditions.

The sheer act of creating knowledge produces new realities, insights
and constructions. Research, when carried out with respect for context, is
creatively synthetic. When it emerges from hitherto hidden knowledge

(in the sense of not being visible to the dominant culture) it contributes toward greater creativity within academic disciplines. For this reason, much of the most original thinking is going on in areas which have been previously ignored, including Women's Studies, Black Studies, Indigenous Studies, Lesbian Studies, Disability Studies. This is not surprising, given the structure of western knowledge systems and the areas that receive priority, both formally[8] and informally. Both Marimba Ani (2000) and Vandana Shiva (1989) are critical of the exclusive nature of western knowledge systems. Shiva identifies three ways by which this exclusion occurs:

> (i) ontological, in that other properties are just not taken note of; (ii) epistemological, in that other ways of perceiving and knowing are not recognized; (iii) sociological, in that the non-specialist and non-expert is deprived of the right both to access knowledge and to judging claims made on its behalf (1989: 30).

Marimba Ani draws attention to the universalistic assumptions of European culture (2000: 512 ff). She writes about how this is put into practice through expansionist policies on the material level (warfare, colonisation, slavery, extraction of resources), and on the intellectual plane (religion, specifically Christianity, intellectual colonisation, the idea of progress, and the work ethic). Likewise, Linda Tuhiwai Smith discusses how research itself is "underpinned by a cultural system of classification and representation [which] ... help determine what counts as real" (1999: 44).

The experiential basis of my research is central to its structure. Reinharz has teased out the components of experiential analysis which is so often a feature of feminist research. Comparing it with more conventional research methods, she finds the following distinctive features (summarised from Reinharz 1983: 170–172):

---

8   The research styles, categories and methodologies within Australian and other Anglo universities are a case in point. The forms, the systems of referencing, and the categories are almost totally inappropriate for researchers working outside the scientific canon, or for researchers whose work draws on complexity or diversity as its core.

- research is context-sensitive
- the focus is broad and inclusive
- feelings, thoughts, insights and experience are a part of research
- the topic is socially significant
- the research role is open to the environment and shaped by it
- the research material is involved, participatory and committed
- the research affects the researcher who may change during the process
- method is determined by unique characteristics, that is, context and particularity
- the study cannot be replicated
- theory emerges from the research
- data creates gestalts and meaningful patterns
- the research objective is understanding
- presentation includes narrative and documentation of the discovery process.

Another perspective is provided by Barbara Du Bois who writes about engaged feminist scholarship as "passionate scholarship" (1983: 105–116). The term "passionate" in this context is used with all its ancient connotations. It comes from the Greek πασχω (pascho) which means "to experience", "to suffer or to be affected by anything" (Liddell and Scott 1986). Its English meaning has connotations of strong feeling including anger. Feminist scholarship which is passionate draws on all of these resonances. It includes feeling and experience, and is sometimes described as angry. Certainly feminism "affects" us. It turns our heads and makes us engage with the world around us in a different way.

Experience is the basis of consciousness raising, which Catharine A. MacKinnon suggests is the "major technique of analysis, structure of organization, method of practice, and theory of social change of the women's movement" (1982: 5). This is similar to the concept of "conscientization", borrowed from Paolo Freire (1972) and used by Maria Mies to describe the process by which women come to appropriate "their history as subjects" and "collectivize their own experiences" (1983: 127). This process steers feminist research away from individualism and career imperatives. It encourages responsible and respectful scholarship which is grounded in the real world rather than only being of relevance within the "ivory tower".[9] Risky scholarship becomes the hallmark of conscientised and radical feminist scholarship.

When I speak of experience, I am thinking of my own experience as well as the experience of women in other cultures and other times. I am thinking about experience in the way described by Mies (1991): not simply a vague feeling connected with an individual, but rather something concrete connected with social reality, from the ways we experience our bodies, to the ways in which social groups are constructed by national politics. Experience is that which gives us a perspective "upon which we can stand" (Mies 1991: 66) and a reality which is convincing. In my own case, my social reality is deeply influenced by my radical lesbian feminist politics and activism which span nearly thirty years,[10] as well as my white middle-class history of growing up in the 1950s, and into politics in the 1970s. My bodily experience is influenced by my experience of epilepsy, but also by my rural background and, in recent years, my involvement with circus, in particular aerials. Finally, although this is by no means a complete list of influences, growing up and living in Australia has influenced me deeply, from the experience of the land through to the cultural irreverence many Australians exhibit; in addition, there is an abiding sense of political complacency in Australia which is most evident to me when I return from overseas trips.

With the feminist slogan "the personal is political" reverberating throughout the text, I also acknowledge the many other researchers who refer to their starting point, their process and their conclusions and relate them to personal elements in their research.[11] The personal, however, is not intended to move this book into an individualised theoretical space. Rather, it allows for depth and intimate understanding of the material, as well as engagement with the "minutiae of everyday life" (Stanley and

---

9   This is one of the problems of post-modern theorising, which unfortunately ceased to be grounded in the real world or take account of the actual lives of women and men. For critiques of post-modernism, see Brodribb (1992); Bell and Klein (1996).

10 Perhaps one of the most influential experiences was that of feminist consciousness-raising groups in which I participated between 1973 and 1978. Dorothy Smith writes of the "political logic of consciousness raising extended into the realms of culture and intellectual life" (1992: 2).

11 Some examples of fine scholarship combined with perspectives drawn from the particularities of the author's life are: Rich (1979, 1976); Lorde (1984); Anzaldúa (1987); Shiva (1989); Bell (1998); Tuhiwai Smith (1999).

Wise 1983: 200). It is this aspect of engaged research, rather than the false objectivity of disengaged research, that is at the centre of my investigation. Maria Mies uses the word *Betroffenheit*, which "expresses not only a concern, a state of being affected, but also reflection and the appeal to do something, to act" (1999: xi). This strikes me as just the right balance between thoughtfulness and action. Wild politics contains the seeds of action, but leaves it open to readers just how this action should be taken, based on their background, experience and expertise.

The personal standpoint, as expressed by feminist researchers, is comparable to the local position and connection to community expressed by indigenous researchers. Both systems express their engagement with the real world and base their theories on grounded experience. These forms of theorising are in stark contrast to disengaged, abstract, universalising and objective knowledge which is the norm for "authoritative knowledge" (Smith 1992: 3). Sabine O'Hara argues that there is a plurality of feminist knowledges, and that this diversity reflects "the fact that theories and valuation concepts are formed and informed not by isolated individuals but by communities living in social and ecological contexts" (1995: 539). Feminist knowledge, indigenous knowledge, the knowledges of the poor and the marginalised are systematically excluded from what Smith calls the "main business" (1992: 9).[12]

Who Is the Knower?

> *Our work requires that we see things in context, that we*
> *understand and explain our eventful, complex reality*
> *within and as a part of its matrix. It is only within*
> *its matrix that experience, reality, can be known.*
> *And this matrix* includes the knower
> – Barbara Du Bois 1983: 111; (emphasis in original).

The particular relationship which exists between the knowledge and the knower is what makes creative research distinctive. A conscious knower,

---

12 As Smith goes on to point out, the "main business" excludes issues of family, especially as they relate to women and children. The economics of this field is perceived as "soft", as one which will not earn the researcher or corporate economist points in the public world of business and governments. For further discussion, see Hewlett (1986) and Chapter Three.

one who is aware of her position in relation to the material, one who perhaps moves around looking at the material from several angles, is going to produce different research results than those whose methods and material are not constantly up for (self-)questioning. Members of the diversity matrix face this most of the time because their experience of the world, or reality, falls outside the range accepted by the dominant culture. As Dorothy Smith puts it

> the situated knower is always also a participant in the social she is discovering. Her inquiry is developed as a form of that participation. Her experiencing is always active as a way of knowing, whether or not she makes it an explicit resource (1999: 6).

Janice Moulton argues that experience has been underrated as a basis for philosophical investigation (1989: 18). She particularly points to the dismissal of different life experiences in forming worldviews and belief systems. And yet it is women's experience transformed into writing, into philosophical investigation, into knowledge which allows, as Jeffner Allen says, "women [to] beget women" (1989: 45). Sandra Lee Bartky points out that the label "feminist" requires participation since "To be a feminist, one first has to become one" (1977: 22). Many women became feminists, and transformed their lives, through the process of consciousness raising (Acker *et al.* 1991). As Patricia Hill Collins states, those "who become outsiders within are forever changed by their new status" (1991: 53).

With the culture moving ever more toward globalisation, the experience of fractures – which allows for the perception of more than one worldview – needs to be heard and seen if we are not to fall into a featureless grey[13] world of homogenised culture, knowing only the realities of one sector of humanity: the dominant classes. This gap is experienced by anyone falling outside the dominant culture, but who, as a consequence, has access to kinds of knowledge closed off to those of the dominant classes. These knowers have been described as inhabiting the "world with a 'double consciousness'" (Du Bois 1983: 111), "two-sights

---

13 For two very different uses of the imagery of greyness, see Schama (1996: 26), and Le Guin (1980). Schama uses grey as the metaphor of the Holocaust; Le Guin, in *The Lathe of Heaven*, imagines a world peopled with a grey-skinned populace.

seeing" (Raymond 1986), "the outsider within" (Hill Collins 1991), "intimate outsiders" (Archibald and Crnkovich 1995: 105), and as those with a multiplicity of knowledge fractures who see the world through multiple lenses, that is "multiversalists".

It is precisely the work of theorists who come from the margins that is most important here. A major stumbling block for all social movements whose goal is change is getting those in power not only to understand the problems, but even to see and acknowledge them. The inability of the dominant group to see has been noticed by writers and theorists from the diversity matrix. What distinguishes them from the dominant group is that they continue to be marked by their identity.[14] This can also be seen in the way the address system on the internet functions. The unmarked category is reserved for US addresses or companies who want to look as though they are US-based; historically, Britain's stamps reflect a similar pattern by omitting the name of the country.

Understanding diversity involves imagining oneself differently. It means learning to unpack the assumptions we pick up through our life experiences. Taking a similar stance to Linda Tuhiwai Smith (1999), Fantu Cheru points to the process of decolonising "the imagination" (2000: 123). Cheru goes on to argue that global change relies on the recognition that "poor people's knowledge about their own reality … counts most, even when that local perspective appears on the surface to be inconsistent with (or less relevant than) the analysis and wishes coming from the North" (2000: 130). Vandana Shiva argues that because many Third World women, "tribals" and peasants have been left out of the colonising process of "development", they have escaped the mental colonisation and, as a result "are in a privileged position to make the invisible visible" (1989: 46). The poor also challenge the western notion of poverty; indigenous Australians and indigenous Mexicans (Coburn 2000: 13) argue for the significance of cultural and spiritual richness as an integral part of material wealth. This is not to suggest that material poverty is acceptable, but many indigenous groups are fighting for their

---

14 If I use the word "doctor", "politician", "soldier" almost all readers in the western world will imagine someone white and male. A number of women (note the marker) friends who have acquired titles such as Doctor, Professor are constantly battling with the person on the other end of the phone, or on the other side of the counter, who thinks they should be male.

immaterial welfare which they refuse to give up in exchange for material wealth. Ashis Nandy argues that the slave's standpoint is the one we must choose because the slave "represents a higher order cognition which perforce includes the master as human, whereas the master's cognition has to exclude the slave except as a 'thing'" (Shiva 1989: 53).

The difficulty the dominant group has in seeing the knowledge of the marginalised is what I call Dominant Culture Stupidities[15] (Hawthorne 1996a, 1997). This syndrome is widespread among people who belong to several dominant cultures: white, male, able-bodied, heterosexual, rich and mobile are some of the groups most prone to the syndrome. It comes about as a result of not having to think about the consequences of one's actions. Examples are easy to find: the many men who do not take account of or responsibility for the consequences of sexual activity with women; the rich who can ignore the cost of petrol or milk or rent in a way that the poor cannot; the able-bodied who do not notice steps which are entirely inaccessible to those using wheelchairs. Similarly, whiteness is a prevailing norm in western European-based societies, and lack of knowledge about the contribution to history of non-Europeans remains the norm; lesbians and gays often "pass" for straight, and heterosexuals who accept the dominant culture ideology create other relationships such as mother/daughter or sister/sister to account for close relationships between two women.

Membership of the dominant culture goes hand-in-hand with political ideology. There is nothing essential or necessary about the connection. Nor is membership of the diversity matrix any guarantee of increased awareness. It is an advantage which is available to those whose life experience gives them access to multiple views of the world.

All these sensitivities can result in two strategies for survival among members of the diversity matrix: either they recognise across cultures and communities the systematised oppressions they face and develop solidarity; or they become fragmented, alienated, and despise other dispossessed peoples. The first contributes to collective survival; the second will sometimes promote the survival of an individual or a small group at the expense of everyone else.

---

15 For similar analyses, see Raymond (1986/2001: 203–242); Janeway (1980); Trask (1986: 180–181); and Guinier (1997: 98–101).

In contrast to Dominant Culture Stupidities, Diversity Matrix Intelligences constitute an awareness advantage, a knowledge of local conditions, a knowledge of how the personal is political, and this translates into a greater understanding of how the power structures of the world work to uphold the status quo.

Very few of the powerful understand the ways in which everyday power operates to keep the powerful happy. This sentiment is well expressed in the following emailed quotation from an interview with Federal Minister Tony Abbott on 2JJJ, Sydney.

> Freedom is a good thing, and the market is based on freedom. The market has been the best guarantee of human happiness we've come up with ... if you're not happy, if you're going to a psychiatrist, it's your own damn fault (Abbott cited in jenjen@vampirehunter.com 2001: 26 March).

The oppressed know their own worlds as well as their oppressors' world. The powerful transnational elites know only their own world.

Such perspectives can be established around any structural power imbalance, any relationship between the diversity matrix and the mono-culture sector. The outcome will always be the same. This "knowledge advantage" which the oppressed have could be put to good use, given a sufficient critical mass of the politics of oppression among the oppressed.[16]

When it comes to the generation of knowledge in these areas, the immediate analysis is of the attributes and behaviours of the oppressed. Only later, do analyses emerge of the dominating behaviours of those with power. The concept of "whiteness" as central to the discussion of racism has been eloquently discussed by Toni Morrison (1993: 9–10). Likewise in the discussion of disability, the able body is the neutral body; it is almost always white.[17] The marked body is outside what is regarded as the norm: it is too thin, it is too fat, it is crippled (Mairs 1992: 9), it is mad (Jeffs 2000), it is unpredictable (Hawthorne 1996a). While Lennard J. Davis in his discussion of deafness has many insights to offer on the

---

16 The Chipko women protesters put this to good use when they fought against the limestone miners in India, see Shiva (1993b: 246–250). Patricia Grace (1983: 25–44) has written a marvellous short story which exploits the knowledge that the powerless (the Maori, in this instance) have about the movements of the powerful (the Pakeha).

17 For a discussion which looks at the black body, see Mohanram (1999: 23–55).

construction of normalcy in relation to disability, race and culture, he fails to notice the categories of class, sex and sexuality (1995: 11). These are the failings of "the normative status of heterosexuality" (Purple September Staff 1995) or what Monique Wittig has called "the straight mind" (1992: 25).[18] She argues that "discourses of heterosexuality oppress us in the sense that they prevent us from speaking unless we speak in their terms" (1992: 25).

To begin to speak, to write about the powerful and the culture of the powerful involves many risks. How can I speak about something, that like Lewis Carroll's cat, appears smiling (or is it growling?) and then dissolves at the moment of recognition? How will I be able to distinguish the cultural from the naturalised? If whiteness, ablebodiedness and hetero-sexuality are difficult to perceive, how difficult is it to challenge our basic concepts of knowledge and our perception of our lives and the lives of people outside our circle of experience (TV and the internet notwith-standing)? The challenge I take on in this book is to acknowledge diversity, and use the concept of diversity as an organising principle. The problem of the "ruling classes" (Smith 1992) determining what is real is not new. Nor is the extent of power available to the ruling class in contemporary society, but its spread to almost every corner of the earth *is* new.

Dorothy Smith points out that citizens in contemporary society "generally do not participate in the making of its [the society's] culture" (1978/1989: 5), but rather that culture is developed by specialists. What is even more evident at the beginning of the twenty-first century is that culture is produced as a commodity for sale back to the non-participants. This is in stark contrast to the relationship of culture to the members of communities with strong oral traditions. As Diane Bell points out, "If all important knowledge is transmitted orally, it is possible to know who has been told what" (1998: 402). The words of particular individuals are "owned" – in the sense of responsibility; they are also precisely situated, unalienated and unalienable. Even the non-participating members of such a community are affected, since speaking "out of turn" (Bell 1998: 402) and without the required responsibility and respect has consequences.

---

18   See also Myron (1975); Hawthorne (1976, 1990b); Rich (1980).

Dorothy Smith's early insight on participation was extended (Bowles and Klein 1983)[19] to show how women were excluded from any consideration that they have contributed to the development of culture. Others, such as Marilyn Waring (1988), have highlighted how women have been excluded from any consideration that they actively contribute to economic development. My research in *Wild Politics* analyses the ways in which power, culture, economics and legal structures work together in complex ways that marginalise members of the diversity matrix, not only making their contribution invisible, but also devaluing it in economic and theoretical terms.[20] I also discuss how exclusions allow those in the diversity matrix to see clearly the structures and to develop critiques and practices which challenge the universalist assumptions of the mainstream.

Standpoint Theory

The standpoints of theorists whose work I consult represent important approaches within feminism. Reflection on women's position in society was challenged early in its development as feminists discovered that if they took the "objective", dominant view, they could not speak about a host of features of women's lives. These features were impossible to speak about because they were particular, that is, heavily influenced by context and situation. The paradox was that when these theorists spoke from a women-centred position, they were not taken seriously because the categories with which they dealt were invisible in dominant culture research. Nevertheless, the recognition of knowledge that exists within social location – of women, of poor people, of indigenous people, of ethnic minorities, of the disabled and of lesbians, and of various combinations of any of the above and more – led to the development of standpoint theory. Dorothy Smith, among others, has developed standpoint theory as a sophisticated analytical tool which takes account of the experiences, the context and locality of women's lives, the "everyday/everynight worlds" (1992: 17). Similarly, the search for the particularities of the local, of the very specific cultural and biophysical conditions of particular groups, can

---

19 Numerous references could be cited here because women's contribution to development of culture, as well as to cultural production, have been two of the core topics of feminist research since the late 1960s.

20 See Dove's (1993) analysis of how forest peoples are excluded from earning income from those parts of the forest deemed most valuable.

be assumed under the umbrella of standpoint theory. Such an approach resists the universalising impulse if it is accompanied by a distrust of homogenisation. Local conditions can be understood as signifying a common experience in the particular, but that signification should not be confused with universalised assumptions about real-life experience and generalised conditions.

Feminist standpoint theory is connected to what Sandra Harding calls "strong reflexivity" (1991: 163) which, she argues

> would require that the objects of inquiry be conceptualized as gazing back in all their cultural particularity and that the researcher, through theory and methods, stand behind them, gazing back at his [sic] own socially situated research project in all its cultural particularity (1991: 163).

Such a call is echoed by Linda Tuhiwai Smith's project of decolonising methodologies (1999) or Cheru's decolonising of the imagination (2000), in which it is precisely the positioning of the researcher and the researched which are most relevant.

Analysis

Analysis is a core feature of rigorous research and it takes many forms. In this book, textual analysis, content analysis and context-sensitive analysis all have a part to play.

Textual analysis has compelled me to step outside the cultural norms of white Australian middle-class reality and focus instead on how the material might best be read from a marginal position. My reading strategy shares something with the experience of a reader of fiction, reading as "other". It includes analyses of women's writing about their own lives, as personal reflections or transformed into poetry or fiction. My reason for using these texts, as well as more conventional academic writing, is that they tend to include emotional truths and very specific information about local conditions. They describe those conditions in ways which reflect the experiences of ordinary women in the community.

Flora Nwapa (1986), for example, synthesises into poetry a wealth of information drawn from her own experience as an Ibo woman in Nigeria as well as a government official. Her reflections in poetic form convey succinctly all the major issues around agricultural development and reflect what Vandana Shiva calls the "violence of the green revolution".[21] And the clarity of Ama Ata Aidoo's reflections on colonisation and knowledge in the following poem concentrates many of the themes explored in the research.

> Post-graduate awards.
> Graduate awards.
> It doesn't matter
> What you call it.
>
> But did I hear you say
> Awards?
> Awards?
> Awards?
>
> What
> Dainty name to describe
> This
> Most merciless
> Most formalised
>
> Open,
> Thorough,
> Spy system of all time:
>
> For a few pennies now and a
> Doctoral degree later,
> Tell us about
> Your people
> Your history
> Your mind.
> Your mind.
> Your mind (1977: 86).

Content analysis takes place alongside a political framework which questions the dominant norms. For example, I give the content of personal

---

21 Shiva first uses this term in *Staying Alive* (1989), and later in her book, *The Violence of the Green Revolution* (1991).

writing (poetry, fiction, autobiographical non-fiction) the same weight as "evidence" from academic research. Likewise, I compare the content of academic writing across different cultures for similarities and differences. This approach assumes an understanding of the basic tenets of feminism which I take to mean, firstly, a recognition that women are oppressed and/or discriminated against in contemporary global culture, and secondly, that one recognises the need to do something to challenge and change the situation. To go a step further, oppression and discrimination are not just individual experiences, but rather the result of systematic inequalities operating in society at large. It is this conscientisation (Mies 1983) and a passionate engagement with the research questions which distinguishes feminist research from the "authoritative knowledge of the expert" (Smith 1992: 3). The latter exemplifies much of the knowledge respected and privileged within universities, governments, corporations and mainstream international organisations.

Conscientisation and engagement are critical parts of the research process, but so too is analysis of the ways in which research results have been used in the process of colonisation of various groups. Here, I use the term "colonisation", not just in its spatial sense, but also temporally. And there are the echoes of Cheru, Tuhiwai Smith and Aidoo providing me with an awareness of the impact of colonisation on people's minds. In this regard the cultures of women, of people with disabilities, of lesbians and others located more in time than space, have also been colonised. Giving certain ways of knowing more weight and authority is a strategy which limits both the kinds of questions, and the kinds of solutions, that can even be considered.

In previous works (Hawthorne 1976, 1990b, 1997) I have analysed power and looked at the way in which access to, and exercise of, power by women is constrained by significant limitations. An analysis of the workings of power is best done by examining particular situations in which power is used by one party over another and signifies a particular kind of relationship of power. Although on an individual level, it is always possible to find counter examples, contextual analysis allows the researcher to see the way in which systemic weighting in one direction – namely in the direction of the dominant groups – affects the use of power across social classes. When power is concentrated through economic weight, military force, and the authoritative power of legitimacy (in the western legal sense), it is difficult to challenge it from within the system. The anti-globalisation protests have recognised this and have organised themselves using decentralised leaderless forms (Couch in progress).

Cultural power – the power of global domination through culture – has intensified in the last decade (Hawthorne and Klein 1999), to the detriment of less visible cultures, cultures who have something to show us if only we had the time to listen. Such cultures are those rooted in their local environments, attuned to the shifting patterns of land, seas, seasons, plant and animal life around them, or, if urban, the patterns of traffic, people movement, heat and cold, holidays and working hours. They don't have to be rural communities, as the communal gardens of New York City show us so clearly (Hynes 1996); or the multilayered, multi-temporal world of the Yaqui which exists within the city limits of Tucson – although not originally Yaqui territory – but is not confined by it (Silko 1996: 85–91). These communities have a sense of the importance of the immediate environment, and a sense of relationship to and engagement with the people in the locale. Tuhiwai Smith also points to the importance of localising approaches to critical theory, taking account of the "specific historical, political and social context" (1999: 186).

Synthesis

Although scientific "objectivity" has been shown, even by scientists, to be something of an illusion, academia, governments and corporations continue to hold on to it in their practice and theorising. In this book, I visit both the public domain of "objective knowledge" and the situated domain of personal and subjective knowledge. To dispassionately examine the materials in the public domain and then to question them, enables the knower to experience the knowledge through the "whole seeing" part of the brain. Shulamit Reinharz refers to this as "feminist synthesis" and describes the method as an immersion "in a deep nonchronological, nontopical intuitive process" (1992: 231).

I turn now to the third part of the dialectical triad. Synthesis is an activity which is possible only when one has sufficient information – a breadth of knowledge and a depth of understanding – to take the next leap and create a new piece of knowledge out of the ingredients. Patricia Hill Collins points to the "relationship between oppression, consciousness and action ... as a dialectical one". The perspective developed from the dialectical process is one "where intellectuals learn to trust their own personal and cultural biographies as significant sources of knowledge" (1991: 47, 53).

Linda Tuhiwai Smith describes her own research "with a community of Maori mothers and children" (1999: 137–140). She was a member of this group, and of other locally based groups. From this point of view she was an "insider". As a researcher, she had to distance herself and become an "outsider" for the duration of the project. Like Tuhiwai Smith, Maria Mies, in her discussion of the dialectical process, writes also of the importance of distance, of avoiding total identification with the participants of the research. Mies suggests that "being able to observe oneself from the outside is ... identical to that which is indicated by the term double consciousness" (1991: 78–79). *Wild Politics* is a synthesis of a wide range of ideas which are central to a number of different disciplines. My hypothesis is that biodiversity, consisting of wild types, is a useful metaphor for understanding social, political and economic relations in the globalised world of the twenty-first century. I test it within a range of disciplines to see whether it is applicable or not. The burgeoning interest in genetics and biotechnology affects how we understand ourselves. The aptness of the biodiversity metaphor has become more and more apparent as the book progressed, in contrast to the continuing use of genetics and biotechnology to hijack the agenda of the future.

Taking a metaphor as a central concept is a useful technique for decolonising the imagination. It involves an intellectual leap of faith on the part of the reader, and a suspension of belief sufficient to accept the "as if" (Turbayne 1971: 18) nature of the metaphor. The features of "wild type" are extracted from its original meaning, extended to incorporate the concept of biodiversity and then applied to social, political and economic systems. The use of a metaphor is freeing, and it resembles the usual method by which we build up concepts used in politics, economics and science. An example used by Colin Turbayne is "muscle fatigue and metal fatigue". Clearly the metal is not experiencing fatigue in the same way as the person whose muscle is fatigued. But both will cease to do their job if overly stressed.

In a similar way, the "wild", the unpredictable, the genetic material in its ecological niche can be seen as a system of non-interference and respect for locality in dealing with human affairs. Likewise, biodiversity applied to social and political diversity allows for integrity of context, a recognition of differing roles of the component parts – the individuals, and their nourishment. The metaphor acts as a "screen through which we look at the world" (Turbayne 1971: 21). It also provides a useful way of bringing things together, of synthesising complex concepts.

The synthesis achieved through this method is akin to poetic method (Namjoshi 1996), which gathers disparate ideas and examines them for their richness. Synthesis, analysis, hypothesis do not always proceed in an orderly fashion; at times, they tumble over one another in a great rush which is simultaneously insight, understanding, a hunch, a batch of discrete elements which fit together (and sometimes they don't). In research, this dynamic dialectical movement is stopped and each part pursued in depth, pulled apart, and put back together again. Further, with the added ingredient of feminism, synthesis takes on an activist garb.

"Dialectical politics" (Miles 1996: xii) allows for an approach to political change and theorising based on transforming the social system, not simply reforming and fitting in with it. What appear to be paradoxical and oppositional elements "become dynamic contradictions that, far from being mutually exclusive, are mutually constitutive, each transformed by the other" (Miles 1996: xii).

In this way, an exploration of the gene-based metaphor of the "wild type", instead of leading toward a genetically engineered future, results in an examination of language and conceptual frameworks, of the local and the global, of homogenisation and diversity.

Dissociation

A central theme of *Wild Politics* is the problem of dissociation. Dissociation – that is, disengaging from feeling, from what we know about our immediate environment, from our own connection with knowledge production – is one of the problems of current global structures. An economy relying on import and export for its survival is not paying attention to sustainability. Nor is a science which fails to consider the contextual origins and outcomes of its research (see Tuhiwai Smith 1999; Shiva 1988).

The idea of dissociation is not new to feminist theory. Susan Griffin called one chapter of her groundbreaking book, *Woman and Nature*, "Separation" (1978: 93) and she discusses the divisions created by civilisations intent on separating from their locale; similarly, Charlene Spretnak (1991) wrote of disengagement; Robin Morgan (1982) compared the objectivity of physics – in which the calculation must take into account the observer's presence and position – with the accusation that feminist theory is too subjective. In a later book, she writes of patriarchy's "capacity for institutionalizing disconnection" (Morgan 1990: 51).

The concepts of disconnection, dissociation, separation, apply not only to the personal and natural spheres, but also to our global economic system. A kind of doublespeak usually prevails in descriptions of the process. An interesting example is the description of the progress of China's move toward globalisation as "integration with the global marketplace" (Wo-Lap Lam 1999: 17). Of course, this means disconnection from the local. The legacy of western liberalism infused with utilitarianism is also deeply affected by disconnection. The push to export-orientation instead of local or regional sustainability is the foundation of global economics. The pace at which globalisation has moved in the last decade is symptomatic of the world's increasing disconnection. Downsizing, the transfer of entire companies from the western world to the developing nations, and the constant attempt to keep up with mobile money are manifestations of those symptoms.

Vandana Shiva and Marimba Ani have a great deal to say about the ways in which knowledge and power interact. Shiva, for example, writes in a critique of the values of western science: "The basic ontological and epistemological assumptions of reductionism are based on homogeneity" (1989: 22). She goes on to argue that an assumption of uniformity results in separability, which in turn "allows context-free abstraction of knowledge and creates criteria of validity based on alienation and non-participation, then projected as 'objectivity'" (1989: 22). Marimba Ani, discussing power, writes: "It is ultimately the European obsession with unlimited 'power over other' that brings universalism into their conceptions" (2000: 514). "Disinterest" (Ani 2000: 515), "indifference" (Hawthorne 1996a: 486) and "objectification" (Ani 2000: 517) become the touchstones of European knowledge systems. They are the legitimate power behind many of western culture's institutions. As Ani points out:

> The implications of a radical change in the definition of knowledge or "what it means to know" are not only a change in epistemological methodology,

but a change in the European conception of self with corresponding changes in the conception of "other" and behavior towards others as well. If the traditional mode of European science – "objectification" – loses its position of primacy on the scale of values, the redefinition of culture itself theoretically becomes possible ... Change would have to occur at the most fundamental level: the level of the *asili* (2000: 517).

Linda Tuhiwai Smith takes a similar view:

> Objectified knowledge, as we engage with it, subdues, discounts, and disqualifies our various interests, perspectives, angles, and experience, and what we might have to say speaking from them (1990: 80).

These modes of thinking and approaches to knowledge lead to an imposition of sameness (homogeneity) which is applied to everyone (universalism), and ignores location and local conditions (decontextualisation). As I will go on to discuss in this book, these processes have been structured into western approaches to economics and ecology; to land and natural resources and the ways in which they are utilised through primary industries; to work and the way it is structured in secondary industries, as well as in western levels of consumption; and finally to the evolving network of trade rules and agreements which have become an integral part of globalisation.

A feature of globalisation is the dominance of the USA in all areas of economics. Much of the discussion of globalisation speaks only about the global nature of it,[22] when in fact in any chart of the largest corporations, in any treaty pushed by the WTO and its agencies, US dominance is a given.[23] Perhaps there is a connection between the sense of disengagement experienced by many American feminists and the excessive amount of power their government holds.

---

22 Peter Brain (1999) traces how countries around the world have fared and created strategies for dealing with US economic dominance.

23 Of the world's largest 100 economic entities, US corporations account for forty-seven (Sheehan 2001: 32).

The police and the military rely on homogeneity.
Police at WEF forum, 11 September 2000 (S11).

An example of dissociation in science (and there are many others) is the Human Genome Diversity Project (HGDP). This project removes cell lines from individuals who belong to communities which have had limited contact with other populations. Among them are indigenous peoples from the Amazon Basin, from the desert regions of Australia, from Papua New Guinea and Irian Jaya (Papua), the Kurds from Iraq. The intention of the researchers is to isolate cell lines (usually without permission from the donors) and to abstract from the DNA analyses information about the nature of human genetic diversity. The HGDP ignores the welfare of the person whose cell line has been pirated; it ignores the knowledge context and religious beliefs of the culture the person inhabits; it ignores the international legal rights of the individuals. Moreover, it trespasses on the dignity of the person whose bodily substances are stored and potentially commodified for the benefit of geneticists or the companies for which the scientists work.[24]

Associative Thinking

Poetry, fiction and other forms of creativity rely on associative thinking (Namjoshi 1996; Buzan 1990), or something akin to what the engineers call fuzzy logic (Kosko 1993). The ability to create a patterning of images, symbols or a surprising synthesis of ideas is an essential element of the associative process. I have found that important insights often emerge when a synthesis is applied associatively. Earlier feminist research, such as that by Susan Krieger (1983), used a similar approach. Her intention was to highlight the non-authoritative (according to dominant culture) voices and to show how embedded lesbian culture is in the standpoint of the particular speaker or writer.

I have therefore included the voices of women from the Pacific, from Bangladesh, from Nigeria, and from many other places as women reflect on their own specific experience and knowledge. I consider this material to have the same weight as research conducted by the World Bank or internationally renowned scholars. This is a deliberate decision because these are the people who know what is happening in their very specific part of the world. They know about the medical value of indigenous plants; they know how to plant a mix of crops together to get the best yield

---

24   A lucid critique of the HGDP is made by Laurie Ann Whitt (1998).

and to sustain the small plot they have. As Diane Bell points out, "content, without an understanding of cultural context and etiquette, does little to advance one's certainty regarding the 'authenticity' of the cultural knowledge" (1998: 362).

Context plays a critical role in my research as it gives clues as to how to read and how to interpret the materials at hand. Bell's quotation makes reference to knowledge and experience of Ngarrindjeri culture of South Australia. In the same way, my speaking and writing come out of a cultural context of late-twentieth-century feminism affected by activism, experience and reflection in fields such as lesbian theory and culture. My life experience includes living with epilepsy. In my working life I have worked among women from diverse cultural backgrounds, including indigenous women, Arabic women migrants in working-class Melbourne, and women from different parts of Asia. I have also had a long-standing engagement with international movements in feminism.

Jill Vickers (1982) showed how feminist research challenges our ways of thinking and creates a need for "new tools of thinking" (Vickers cited in Reinharz 1992: 214); while Audre Lorde, in her influential essay "The Master's Tools Will Never Dismantle the Master's House" (1984), challenged feminists to go beyond the safe havens, "to descend into the chaos of knowledge and return with true visions of our future" (1984: 111). Or as Patricia Hill Collins suggests, to trust that which we already know.

Dorothy Smith named important "underground sources of intellectual power and assertion" (1978/1989: 9), and it is these sources which form the core of my work in *Wild Politics*. Smith writes that, "The ideological practices of our society provide women with forms of thought and knowledge which constrain us to treat ourselves as objects" (1978/1989: 19). *Wild Politics* takes the work of women as subjects and extends it into global systems of economics, ecology, politics and culture. The context of these global systems is the way in which power is used.

Central to the idea of this book are the concepts of multiversity[25] and diversity, for which the particular and the local are rich sources of knowledge. Multiversity respects systems of knowledge born out of experience as well as through research and study. Interactions between

---

25 It is interesting to note the relationship of the word "university" to the word "universal". See Aidoo (1977: 86) cited above.

knowledges are important in the development of systems which value the collective whole, the self-sustaining organism, the consequences and the contexts. Paul Wangoola (2000) has also proposed a multiversity. For him, multiversity is a challenge to the ways in which knowledge is structured in western systems, in particular in universities, where abstraction and disconnection from place result in specialist discourses which cannot communicate with one another across disciplines. He proposes an Mpambo Multiversity which actively resists modernisation and its accompanying "Disconnects from culture" (2000: 270–272).

> The guiding principle behind *Mpambo* is that being rooted in their own knowledge bases people can engage in dialogue, synthesis, articulation, partnership, collaboration, the building of synergies and cross-fertilization: all of this across sectors, knowledges, cultures and civilizations (2000: 274).

"Marginal knowledges" have contributed significantly to feminist knowledge. The "multiversalist", in contrast to the "universalist", recognises that universals tend to work against the most dispossessed members of society since they deny the worth of the knowledge of the dispossessed. The multiversalist, by contrast, recognises that there are many ways of organising knowledge, and that those who live close to the biophysical world have the best knowledge of it and are well-versed in the local conditions; likewise, the multiversalist recognises that the knowledge of the poor, of women, of people marginalised for a multiplicity of reasons have a great deal to offer with their perceptions and knowledges of the world. Wangoola explains the name, Mpambo:

> After the harvest the mother selects the best seeds for careful and safe keeping for planting the next season. Thereafter permission is given to eat the rest. In the Lusoga language of Uganda mpambo means the best of the seeds that are kept away for propagation (2000: 277).

Multiversity recognises that the existence of alternative knowledges is important to human knowledge as a whole (Wangoola 2000: 273). The caution here is that respect for the way in which knowledges are structured is important, and appropriation or commercialisation of such knowledges results in their distortion. For, just as money in Warlpiri society transforms its meaning (Bell 1983/2002), so does commercialisation of ideas which are structurally anathema to a monied economy.

The dialectics of analysis and synthesis is pursued throughout the book, moving between foreground and background as required. In a similar vein, my experience informs the analysis of the "authoritative" knowledge, and my synthesis attempts to draw together some disparate themes. The metaphor of wild politics, along with biodiversity and diversity, moves in and out of focus, and is an important shaping feature of the book. I look at the mechanisms which marginalise women, and at particular resistances to this marginalisation. I conclude with an examination of the structural impact of major international shifts in legal and economic systems, and consider associatively how these super-structures will have an impact on the lives of those in the diversity matrix.

CHAPTER TWO

POWER AND KNOWLEDGE:
GLOBAL MONOTONY OR LOCAL DIVERSITY?

> *The struggle for diversity is a struggle that*
> *concerns us all. Cultural diversity is essential*
> *to the health, beauty and survival of humanity*
> – Justin Coburn (2000: 13).

Power

The way in which power is used resembles closely the mechanisms for the global spread of western knowledge. For example, the knowledge spread most widely is that which is recognised by the powerful, but because they have access to a relatively narrow range of knowledges (due to Dominant Culture Stupidities) these are the ones which are actively continued (through education, publication, global media). These knowledges tend toward homogenising and decontextualising. They operate on the basis of the masculine view of the world, dominating and eradicating by force or by inducement.

Power is a web of interacting forces which, if one imagines a piece of cloth, is closely woven at the powerful end and loosely woven at the powerless end. The powerless are relatively easily torn, but they have the advantage of flexibility. At the tightly woven end, there is little movement, and as one moves, so do the rest. The tightly woven end is strong, it can withstand attack, and it can even kill by strangling. This metaphor can be seen to represent the way in which systematic power (closely woven) is supported by the power of violence or potential violence. Systematic power, institutions of law, as well as the supporting social sanctions of individuals or organisations, work in cahoots with one another. Because it is tightly woven, each thread appears to be the same. Its movement is in the direction of homogeneity.

By contrast, the loosely woven end displays what could be called weakness (Janeway 1980). But within the weak bonds, each individual

Test the West advertising for West cigarettes, Berlin, 1992.

thread can be seen, and there is flexibility. Its movement is in the direction of diversity and multiversity.

My argument is that power, used globally, shares the same set of features as it does in its individual instances, and that the concentration of power currently being built up by the very wealthy, the transnationals, the highly mobile classes, is strangling those at the other end of the planetary cloth, the members of the diversity matrix. What unites these groups is their lack of access to strong forms of power (violence, reward, systems, backlash and obstacles). The wealthy, on the other hand, have ready access to a range of forms of power, power as control (Hoagland 1988: 118). I will briefly outline these forms of power,[1] giving examples of how they are used in the developing global systems. Next I discuss two forms of power (attraction and attitudes) to which members of the diversity matrix have more ready access, and how they are using these to create a groundswell of resistance to globalisation.

The relationship which stands out as significant in the global web of power is that of the deepening gap between the transnational sector and the diversity matrix.

The transnational sector is characterised by a cluster of features. The primary feature is its wealth. Because of its wealth (an attribute of power) it can force changes to occur in the way in which global trade and politics are structured. General Electric in March 2001 was the largest company in the world. It is an economically larger entity than most of the world's countries, and is the twelfth-largest economic entity in the world (Sheehan 2001: 32).[2]

---

1   I am indebted to an article by Anthony de Crespigny (1970) which I read many years ago, and which has influenced my thinking about power (see Hawthorne 1976, 1990b, 1997). I retain his concept of forms of power, recognising that they are not discrete in their actions, and several forms might be in use simultaneously. It is also clear that this mosaic of power varies in strength and its clearest examples occur when the difference in access to power and exercise of power is greatest. This is certainly the case between the diversity and transnational sectors. The different forms of power can manifest in individual, group, structural or institutional contexts. The intensity of power is also variable from soft individual persuasiveness through to military or economic violence.

2   There are numerous companies whose accumulated assets are worth more than those of nation states. Sheehan's list mentions seventy-one companies and only twenty-nine countries. Of those companies, forty-seven are US-owned, fifteen are European, three are Japanese, two are from Hong Kong and one is from Canada. For discussion of these issues, see also Martin and Schumann (1997); Chossudovsky (1998); Roy (1999).

General Electric is known for its household appliances, financial services, and nuclear reactors (among other things). In this regard, it appeals to a very large segment of the world's market – from women using kitchen appliances, to small businesses, to the largest governments in the world. The world's largest 200 companies control 28 per cent of the world's economic activity, but their employees represent, not 28 per cent of the workforce, but a mere 0.25 per cent of the global workforce (Roddick 2001: 199). If corporations were putting back even equal to what they gain from the workforce, this figure would need to go up by 11,200 per cent.

The transnational sector is also characterised by high mobility, and production moves to wherever it is most profitable. Sameness is promoted, and nothing should fall into the realm of the unpredictable; so in the walled shopping centre of Los Angeles, teenagers[3] are barred from entry (Beckett 1994: 37). It has a tendency to universalise even the most idiosyncratic of cultural norms: teenage boys wear their baseball caps backwards even if they have never seen a game of baseball.

At the other end of this dimension are women, the poor, and indigenous peoples, as well as large numbers of refugees, exiles and migrants (many of whom fit into the first three categories): those who belong to the diversity matrix. They tend to be poor, much less mobile, and are more likely to remain (unless they are refugees) in the area where they grew up. Their attachments, therefore, tend to be local. Poverty keeps many women immobile, but poverty can also create a status for women resembling the refugee as women move to follow seasonal work, or to accompany a male partner, even a corporate executive, willingly or unwillingly. Clearly, rich women fall into the transnational sector, but on a global scale this is statistically insignificant (see Wichterich 2000; Chossudovsky 1998).

The transnational sector is currently in the process of globalising the diversity matrix. It is taming it, removing the features of diversity from it, homogenising it, eliminating its uncontrollable "wild types".

Dorothy Smith points to the disjunction between women's experience of the world and the way in which ruling relations are maintained

---

3   It is not surprising that teenagers are frequently both the targets of consumption by global companies (the effect of peer-group pressure), and the targets of punishment by global companies (the effect of teenage rebelliousness and rule-breaking).

through objectified knowledge (1990: 11–18). A similar dynamic operates between the experience of the world from the point of view of the diversity matrix (it is marked, subjective and local) and the view put forward by the transnational sector (it is unmarked, objective and universal). This analysis reflects the elements identified earlier by Bell, Ani, Tuhiwai Smith and Shiva in their critiques of western modes of operating culturally. The primary gulf between the two groups – diversity and transnational – is that of power.

In the following pages I discuss systemic weightings of power in the hands of certain individuals or groups, and how this is translated into institutional power. I conclude that institutional power is the fulcrum from which systemic power depends.

I argue that systemic power tends toward the universal and toward the imposition of sameness, homogeneity, monopoly, monotony and mono-culturalism. The imposition comes from an inability to see beyond the dominant culture paradigm into the lives and circumstances of others. The "others", by contrast, have plenty of practice in knowing the world of the dominant culture and are therefore more sensitive to issues of culture and politics. This access to multiverses and to multiple knowledge systems is the one area in which people from the diversity group have an advantage of power over those in the transnational sector. The transnational sector suffers from having experiential and knowledge access to only a single knowledge system, namely the universalised dominant culture. This creates a tunnel vision, one-eyed seeing, a narrow worldview which allows for only the experience of those who hold power. Dominant culture knowledge diminishes the knowledge and understanding of the powerless, and because knowledges of the powerless are regarded with contempt, the powerful are cut off from greater understanding. The powerful suffer from the syndrome of Dominant Culture Stupidities (Hawthorne 1997: 53–55).

I suggest, therefore, that it is important to recognise that the universalists, the powerful, will use blunt methods to retain a hold on power. These blunt methods are most likely to be coercive and bludgeoning (violent suppression of demonstrations against globalisation are an example; as are disconnected[4] acts of violence against civilians who

---

4   By "disconnected", I mean that there is no knowledge of who the targeted individual is, no relationship to them, only an assumption that they can represent either American capitalism or Islamic support for Osama bin Laden. Both are incorrect.

represent the ills of a nation – victims of the Twin Tower bombings in New York *and* victims of carpet bombing in Iraq or Afghanistan equally fall into this category). But they might also be inducive: promises of catch-up development or of a consumer heaven are examples.

The Power of Violence

Violence is one of the major means of maintaining a position of power. I use the word "violence" when I am referring to "force", "coercion", "abuse", although other words such as "rape", "assault", "physical force" describe particular instances of violent power. Violent power implies strength. That strength may be institutionalised through the provision of arms to those in the dominant group (e.g. colonisers), or it may be individualised (e.g. rape of women, homosexual men or children). It takes non-physical forms,[5] such as the use of monetary and wealth resources to achieve ends which are against the interests of the subjected group; the World Bank debt schedules and structural adjustment programs are examples of this. Violent power also includes procedures of confinement. The high rates of imprisonment of Aboriginals in Australia, Maoris in New Zealand, people of colour in the USA are examples of this, as is the detention of refugees in Australia, and the more subtle confinements of women in the home that were prevalent prior to the women's movement in western countries.

Systematic individual use of violence tends to support socially sanctioned institutional forms of violence. To give two examples: slavery is clearly violent power. Writing of the antebellum southern states of the USA, George P. Rawick's comments on the nature of slavery reflect many of the practices found in the *maquiladoras* of Mexico under globalisation (see Biemann 1999; see Chapter Six):

> Whipping was not only a method of punishment. It was a *conscious device to impress upon the slaves that they were slaves*; it was a crucial form of social control particularly if we remember that *it was very difficult for slaves to run away successfully* (1972: 59, my emphasis).

---

5   In the event that readers think that money and wealth are primarily material or physical entities, economist Michael Rowbotham makes the following point: "People think of money as being note and coin, but in fact note and coin is only 3% of modern money. What is the other 97%? Well the other 97%, almost the dominant form of money, has no other existence than as numbers" (Garrett 2001: 6).

Likewise, the beating of women within marriage was, and in some places still is, socially sanctioned and legally permitted. And just as the use of violence against slaves was not considered a crime (Patterson 1982: 3), so too violence against married women has only slowly achieved recognition in the west as criminal. Violence against prostituted women and enslaved peoples in the contemporary globalised economy remains difficult to identify since it is informally encoded in these practices. The instruments of the International Labor Organisation (ILO) do not adequately protect the most dispossessed.

In the context of globalisation, similar kinds of social and legal systems are being enacted. Just as the human genome has been decoded, and bioprospectors are heading into the field to learn about the indigenous use of medicinal plants, the US patent system is universalised, and the WTO is attempting to multilaterally enforce systems which privilege the investments of transnationals (for further discussion, see Chapter Seven).

In an international setting, violence is generally described as either terrorism (an illegal form of violence) or war (in its international legalised form). The distinction between war and terrorism is a vexed one and depends a great deal on the political alignments between the speakers and the actions. To make an analogy at the individual level, it is like the distinction between a street rape (terrorism) and a legal rape in marriage (war).[6] In my view, none of these forms of violence, individual or international, is justifiable. Just as rape is backed by the generally greater economic power of individual men, so too war is backed by the economic power of the military industrial complex. Other feminist theorists have analysed the intimate connections between institutional international violence (war) and individual male violence against women and children (rape), as well as mass rape of women and children in war.[7]

The power wielded by the military is excessive, and is implicated in a raft of other violations, violences, and economic and ecological dispossession. I am thinking here of diamonds fuelling war in Angola; of unwilling

---

6   Enloe (1989: 195) makes this point and entitles her final chapter "The Personal is International".

7   See Brownmiller (1976); Caputi (1987); Enloe (1989); Morgan (1990); Copelan (1994); Stiglmayer (1994); Kappeler (1995); Mladjenovic and Matijasevic (1996); Boric and Desnica (1996).

conscripts to wars, as well as the tragic loss of life through landmines, unexploded bombs, and "collateral damage", all of which continue to be current problems in war zones around the world; of the impact of economic sanctions on Iraqi children; of the ecological impact of oil spills in Kuwait during the Gulf War. Those who bear the brunt of these violations are usually the poorest, and they have the least political and economic clout.

The systematic and generalised use of violence has been a critical tool to keep the powerless in their place, but it is not the only one. Among the other forms of power used against the powerless are systems of false reward, systematic obstacles and backlash spread by the media, as well as the more personalised forms such as attraction (discussed below) and critical mass attitudinal shifts.[8] Violence is a form readily available to those in power, and is endorsed by the culture of the powerful. It is also tempting for the powerless to resort to it as a form of resistance. However, an ethic of the means being consistent with the ends is important in achieving long-term stable peace. The most effective means of transforming violence are not the most violent forms. As Kappeler concludes:

> Resistance to *violence* however cannot consist of violence. Violence may change the direction of violence, invert the roles of violator and victim, but it necessarily affirms the principle of violence, whatever else it may achieve (1995: 258, emphasis in the original).

Resistance to violence is essential if justice is to occur; but violent resistance, like nuclear deterrence, simply risks more violence.

The transnational sector assumes that it will get easy compliance with its regime from those in the diversity matrix. And in most instances it makes practical sense for the diversity matrix to comply. For example, a poor Third World country, confronted by an IMF demand that it participate in a structural adjustment program, knows that the chance of successful resistance is low; the powerless nation may still attempt resistance, but it will run the risk of further economic violence.

If the powerless attempt to initiate violent power against the powerful, it is highly unlikely they will succeed without recourse to other forms of

---

8   This discussion draws on some elements from Hawthorne (1997).

power (which I will discuss in this chapter). For example, activists from the diversity matrix have stood up to large corporations and nations on environmental issues. In 1995 a wide range of individuals, organisations and groups sailed to Moruroa Atoll during the French nuclear tests. Zohl dé Ishtar, one of the few Australians among them, recollects that

> the most important element of the flotilla protest was the Maohi peoples of Te Ao Maohi/French (occupied) Polynesia who had been protesting French nuclear testing since the early 1960s. There was a Viking ship, sailed by a sword-waving Dane, dressed in a g-string and Viking horns who repeatedly challenged the French to a duel; the smallest boats had been sailed single-handedly from Chile; German boats with their sails signatured by hundreds of fellow-citizens; a Vaka from Cook Islands carried Polynesian warriors dressed in traditional garb. And much more. It was a celebration of life! (2001).

France, nevertheless, went ahead with the tests. Any back-down since is not due to the success of violent action, but rather to attitudinal pressure. The activists did not engage in violence, other than the act of resistance of sending ships into the exclusion zone, a territorial violation.[9]

With violent power, actual exercising of that power is not always needed. Threats of its use are usually sufficient for the powerful to achieve their ends. This is particularly successful if the powerful have previously used violence to achieve their ends. In contrast, if the powerless have previously resisted, they are less likely to succeed. Theresa Wolfwood makes the interesting observation that "violence is elitist" and the powerful perpetuate the belief that "there are good and bad kinds of violence and that we must choose between them" (2001: 2).

The successful exercise of power opens up further opportunities of access to power. The powerful, therefore, become more and more powerful, while the ability of the powerless to resist is reduced, and is rendered less and less effective. Such a vicious circle leads to wholesale disempowerment

---

9   That this is technically called a "violation" is an example of what Mary Daly has named as a reversal (1978: 364–365). The status of Moruroa is as an atoll which has been violently taken from the indigenous people by the colonisers, France, in order for it to be further violated through its continuous use as a site for nuclear explosions (a form of political gang rape). For more information on Pacific peoples' resistances to nuclear testing, see dé Ishtar (1994, 1998).

of large numbers of people. It is through these means that the few are able to control the many. Examples include the teacher in a classroom, a violent father, prison officers, invading colonists. In the international political arena it is interesting to observe this process in action among the protests against globalisation which have occurred globally since the 30 November 1999 protest in Seattle. By the time of the World Economic Forum in Melbourne, from 11 to 13 September 2000, the institutions of force – police, private security companies, military and intelligence personnel – believed they were well prepared with an escalating store of protective clothing for the police on the front line of the barricades. In spite of their preparations, on the first day of the forum, protesters managed to prevent around one-third of the delegates from getting in to the meeting. An escalation of violence occurred after the first day, and the police had more success after that. The preparations for security with these meetings moves in the direction of a one-size-fits-all approach (Guinier 1997). Homogenisation and standardisation are common strategies employed by the military, and obedience down lines of hierarchy is a symptom of the one-size-fits-all approach. The warlike defence systems put in place in Davos, Switzerland, in February 2001, the preparations for the Free Trade Area of the Americas (FTAA) meeting in Quebec on 2 April 2001,[10] and the near impossibility of access to the WTO meeting in Doha, Qatar,[11] from 9 to 14 November 2001, reflect the militarisation of global economics.

The use of violent power is not confined to relationships between people. It is frequently extended to the natural environment and its inhabitants, such as animals, or perceived threats such as disease, microbes, insects, drugs. But it is the use of violent power against other people which provides a model for institutional extensions of its use. Consider for example, the language of "the war against drugs" (McCoy 1991), "the war against malaria" (Garrett 1994), and even less convincingly, "the war

---

10 "A second wall is being built around the old walled city, and a prison is being cleared out to house troublemakers" (Walker 2001: 7). The violence of the Genoa meeting in August 2001 reflected a further escalation of the use of violent power by a government supporting the transnational sector against protesters, many of whom came from the diversity matrix. As Robin Morgan (1990) so cogently points out, violence can seem an attractive option for many men from both the right and the left who are caught in its cycle.

11 Qatar, alongside Brunei, Darussalam, Saudi Arabia and Oman, has never recognised women's right to vote (UNDP 2001: 229).

against poverty" (Mies 1994). "The war against terrorism" is the latest war imposed by the most powerful nations on earth. Interestingly, the "need" for all these "wars" can be traced back to excessive uses of power by the powerful in the past.

The Power of Reward

Violent power, for all its effectiveness, has bad press. In the liberal democracies which comprise the world's major powerful members and are home to all the transnational companies (see Appendix, Table 1) there is a desire to appeal to a system of power which pretends to be in the interests of the powerless. Such a system is one in which rewards are offered by the powerful to the powerless to participate. There are times when the powerless can even be fooled into thinking it was their own idea.[12] What needs to be stated clearly is that the power balance does not shift or change, only the mechanism of its use.

Under such a regime the powerless will comply with the wishes of the powerful because there is a perceived benefit in compliance. The benefits can include rewards such as money or career opportunities; access to knowledge, including educational scholarships and awards,[13] or information technologies; withdrawal of threats such as economic or physical sanctions; or withdrawal of instances of deprivation such as the status of social outcast.

The power of reward results in absence of social conflict between the powerful and the powerless. The powerless believe they will gain by complying, when in fact, this may not be the case. And although compliance by reward is inconsistent with the autonomy of the powerless, the powerless believe that the benefit of reward is greater than a resort to violent power.

A contractual agreement between the powerless and the powerful is a form taken by this kind of power. The marriage contract provides a useful example (Pateman 1988: 116–188). Benefits – physical protection against other men, financial benefits such as access to a higher wage or tax benefits, increased status – may all feature in a woman's decision to enter the marriage contract. Similarly, enterprise agreement contracts in

---

12 Andrea Dworkin analyses the mechanisms of this reward system in her book *Right-wing Women* (1983).

13 See Aidoo (1977); Bhatt (1988).

the workforce provide benefits to the employee in terms of security and dismissal procedures. *But nothing has changed in the balance of power. Men and employers still retain more power than women and employees.*

Not all the benefits are empty; there can be short- and long-term gains for some members of the powerless. But these benefits will never be evenly distributed. The few retain their power over the many.

In a global sense, a comparable situation is the promise of "development", whereby poor nations are offered the carrot of "catch-up development" (Mies and Shiva 1993; Mies 1994). The "development" inducement is often sufficient to draw poor nations into the global market economy with promises of rich rewards if only they will alter their farming practices to produce export crops, build bridges to enhance road transport, and allow their forests to be chopped down, their land mined, their seas fished. It is rare that the down-side of these "adjustments" is highlighted. Instead, cash-flow, television and consumer culture take the place of local and traditional self-sustaining economies (see Adams 1994; Mogina 1996; Shiva 1993a, 1996a; Mies 1994). But these are false promises. The widespread export of commodities causes prices to drop; bridges create unemployment once the construction is finished; deforestation and environmental damage from mining and overfishing cause poverty and dispossession of those depending on the land and the sea.

Interesting shifts have occurred in recent years around the discourses of prostitution and mining. It is instructive to look at these and see how the power game is being played out.

Libertarians argue that women, and some men, make rational choices about entering prostitution. They argue that, given the potential financial rewards offered in prostitution, it is a reasonable and free choice to make the most of those rewards. What is missing from this analysis is the question of who benefits most, and increased profits for the sex industry is where the main benefit lies. It does not lie with the few women and men who make more money (while the many are severely exploited on the streets, living lives dominated by violence), but rather with the easy and ready access of the powerful members to members of the powerless class.[14] The short- and long-term benefits accrue to members of the

---

14 For discussions of prostitution and trafficking, see Barry (1995); Raymond (1998); Jeffreys (1997); Hotaling (1996); Hughes (1999b).

powerful class, whereas very few of the powerless get rich and retire early. *The access to power, and the exercise of it, have not changed.*

A similar approach has been taken to mining the lands of indigenous peoples over the last decade or so. With the promise of large royalty payments, some groups have opted to allow mining on their lands. The proposed CRA mine in northern Queensland, Australia, has caused severe social conflict between those who thought the mine would bring more benefits than losses, and those who thought the loss was too great to provide any meaningful benefit. What is clear is that members of the powerless, the Aboriginal community, were in conflict among themselves, rather than in conflict with the powerful, in this instance the mining company. The mine was finally given approval in 1997 by Native Title claimants, and by then it had changed hands to be a Pasminco Century Mine (Aiken 2000). This distracts attention from the use of power of the powerful. The Aboriginal community, and in the earlier example, prostituted women and men, trade their autonomy for perceived benefits.

Resistance to the powerful's system of rewards is often difficult to sustain among the powerless, who may well be desperate for some relief from extremely difficult circumstances. Some groups have come up with original ideas for using the system of benefits, but all require some forfeiture of autonomy. The Native American communities who have provided gambling facilities[15] are an example of resistance by the powerless. The autonomy pay-off is that some members of the communities will suffer lung cancer and other health problems, or lose dignity through excessive gambling, or that violence will intensify (see Clark 1989). Power based on reward has little to offer to members of the powerless class, whereas members of the powerful have much to gain. But it is understandable that members of the powerless decide to trade a host of disadvantages for a few advantages.

The Power of Backlash

Both violent power and power of reward rest on the intentions of the active party, which can be either the powerless or, more likely, the powerful. There are other kinds of power which rely on the dynamic or

---

15   For example, the Mohawk on the border between the USA and Canada, Clark (1989); and the Seminoles of Florida, LaDuke (1999: 34); Slind-Flor (1996).

reactions of each party and come about because of what the powerless believe about the powerful, or vice versa. Through this belief, dynamic forces become the cause of the behaviour rather than any active interference through direct violence or reward giving. The situation is particularly applicable in an institutional context where the powerless refrain from certain activities because of what they believe about the powerful's position of power.

Norms of behaviour around class, sexuality and disability are pertinent here. In a class context, speech patterns, body language and accents carry enormous weight, and it is generally those without class privilege, the powerless, who are made to feel embarrassed or awkward about their speech (Mahony and Zmroczek 1996). Middle-class members will tend to uphold these norms, unless they are entering a community where they are in the minority and their accent marks their difference in the new context.

In the case of sexuality, heterosexuality is such a dominant norm that only members of lesbian and gay communities are likely even to notice it. Even relatively politicised heterosexuals are sometimes hard pushed to notice their homophobia. Disability tends to operate in similar ways (Hawthorne 2001b: 40–44). The results are normative and prescriptive modes of behaviour and perception. This form of dynamic power operates via strong social pressures to conform to whatever the acceptable behaviour is, to the point where many members of the dominant group, the powerful, are unaware of this kind of power.

Dynamic power is implicated in reactionary or backlash forces. The powerless (rightly) believe that if they do not conform then they will be deprived of some of their freedom. A working-class boy attending a private school on a scholarship soon finds out how he should speak; a disabled person who remains silent about his/her condition will be easily overlooked when provision of services is considered; a young lesbian will be asked why she is not dating boys when all her friends are. On a global level, being a signatory to the WTO[16] is a prerequisite for access to certain markets, even though becoming a signatory may eat into one's own natural and intellectual resources (see Shiva 1995: 272–275; and see

16   A Sony PlayStation game reportedly features a fictitious institution, the American Trade Organization. In many ways this is a more accurate definition of the WTO's main purpose (reported in Klein 2001: 4).

Chapter Seven). The reactions of the powerless to abuses of power by the powerful can be useful: an example is the series of demonstrations against globalisation which have occurred since 1999. The reactions of the powerless, however, decline over time, and the powerful members are more readily able to introduce ever more draconian policies and laws. Since the 11 September 2001 attack on the World Trade Center in New York, and the Pentagon in Washington DC, globalisation protestors in the USA have complained that it is impossible to protest against globalisation: in part because of increased security; in part because of the symbolic power (now negatively connoted) of gas masks and other paraphernalia used previously by protestors (Crouch 2001), or as Naomi Klein puts it, protestors "find themselves in an utterly transformed semiotic landscape" (2001: 4). Here one sees the powerless increasingly constrained, while the powerful are able to throw around their weight even more effectively.

The normalisation of abuse by the powerful is an essential part of this process. When that occurs, the powerful not only control the game, but constantly invent new and random rules which the powerless are obliged to obey. Dictatorships display inconsistent and randomly abusive behaviours such as these, and in some instances institutions become infected with them also.

The Power of Obstacles

Dynamic power also operates as a roadblock. All kinds of discrimination fall into this category. On a social level, the so-called glass ceiling is a useful example, while internationally, the myth of catch-up development provides a similar example (Mies 1994). Despite legislative changes, equal opportunity and access to better educational resources and training, the powerless rarely make it to the level of executive in large and powerful companies or in government. Internationally, in spite of the increased mobility of capital and resources through multilateral trade agreements, obstacles are placed on the mobility of people from poor nations to rich nations.

The manipulation of obstacles is in the hands of the powerful. Whereas the power of backlash is centred in the beliefs the powerless hold, obstacle power is centred on the powerful, and puts limits on the autonomy of the powerless. In its deliberateness it is similar to violent power, but it differs because the powerless may not realise they have been hindered in achieving their goals. International intelligence operates as a covert form of obstacle power, whereby certain events or blocks are deliberately set up to prevent the powerless from achieving a desired outcome. Legislative change can sometimes have an impact on the use of obstacle power, or it can simply drive underground those forces intent on setting up obstacles. In Australia, for instance, the ban on automatic and semi-automatic guns, introduced after the Port Arthur Massacre, in which thirty-five people were killed (28 April 1996), can be assumed to work only if there is significant compliance with the law. Only when all parties recognise the legitimacy of a law does the law become workable.

The escalation of overt obstacles can be seen in the treatment of asylum seekers as globalisation results in the increased mobilisation of peoples across borders. In Australia the construction of detention centres in isolated areas, the turning-away of the *Tampa* off-shore from Christmas Island in October 2001, and the increasing number of barriers put in the way of refugees seeking asylum are all examples of the power of obstacles.

The Power of Systems

Systemic power is what Max Weber (1947) refers to as authority with legitimacy and operates in legal, traditional and charismatic forms. When legitimacy is recognised, then the degree of conflict is very low, even if the commanded party disagrees with the decision. It is frequently backed up by threats of violence to ensure compliance; such threats may include economic or physical sanctions. Systemic[17] power is the power vested in the system, and upheld through the means of law or lore (the latter applies to oral-based cultures). These are the forms, the glue, which hold together the culture as an interconnecting system. The advent of international law as an expression of systemic power is not surprising in a era of increasing globalisation.

Systemic power, alongside violent power, is the no-nonsense, no-argument power. Systemic power, when combined with violent power, as it is in times of war and in the institution of the military, has enormous strength. Ultimately, this combination is the most powerful force available. It combines the strongest forms of power: violent power, the

---

17   For a clear analysis of systemic power as discrimination, see French (1992).

threat of death and injury, as well as environmental and civil damage); and systemic power: authority through legality, economic wealth, and cultural enforcement. I include the military in systemic power, because although it uses institutionalised violence, it is able to do this because of its authority as an institution. The greater part of its power comes from "underwriting" other government institutions through massive budgets which enable it to make or break large corporations or government departments; it provides a reserve force for dealing with insurrection, national emergencies, external threats, and for virtually any purpose a government sanctions.[18] The military also sponsors its own industries which spring up around military bases and installations, whether on domestic[19] or foreign soil. Among the most prevalent are the bars and brothels intended to "service" military personnel. The prostitution industry has an enormous impact on women's lives, with deleterious impacts on their health and well-being. I am not suggesting that women's only contact with the military is as prostitutes, since many other women, among them military and diplomatic wives, women working on bases as general staff or as soldiers, even the women protesters and activists outside the military base fence, are engaged in different ways with the military (Enloe 1989).

But legitimacy has its more subtle permutations also, ones which are not obviously institutionalised, but which are very strong forms because they are so pervasive. Racism and patriarchy on a global level are two powerful forms of systemic power (Williams 1991; Guillaumin 1995). They are structured into the system in so many subtle ways that it is virtually impossible to disentangle them. Marimba Ani analyses the ways in which domination is structured into European culture. She argues that "the culture constructs a universe of authorization" (2000: 15) which reinforces the values of the culture. Denise Thompson points to the connections between domination and the ways in which "ideological

---

18   A recent Australian example is the use of the Navy to patrol Australian shores in an attempt to prevent refugees and asylum seekers from entering the country. For background reading on this issue, see Mares (2001).

19   On domestic soil, military installations are likely to be found near indigenous communities. Valerie L. Kuletz notes that in New Mexico, near the Jackpile–Paguate uranium mine, located on the Navajo Reservation at Laguna Pueblo, a large number of transnational corporations have contracted with the US Department of Energy. The companies include "Kerr–McGee, Vanadium Corporation of America, Foote Mineral, AMEX, United Nuclear Corporation, Exxon, Mobil Oil and Gulf" (1998: 24).

meanings" are the things that make "domination palatable or acceptable, or natural, real and unchallengeable" (2001: 22). Authorisation often works in conjunction with normalisation, a process that resists analysis because it is camouflaged by social norms. Jeffner Allen (1996: 45–53) draws attention to the patriarchal food economy, which, she argues, involves women in extensive food production and in a prescriptive underconsumption of food. Centuries of such practices around the globe mean that in many places women are underfed, are physically weaker and more likely to be malnourished than are men. This systemic institution ensures that violent power is reasonably easy to enforce. Others extend domination into the natural world:

> Our society has been characterized by domination and control (of women, of classes, of ethnic or cultural groups, of other species and of natural resources) and the frames of reference we use to analyse and interpret the physical world reflect that character (Kloppenburg and Burrows 2001: 107).

Michel Chossudovsky (1998) details the ways in which the IMF and the World Bank through their processes of macro-economic "reform" have led to mass starvation and war in Somalia and Rwanda, while riots, the collapse of economic and civil institutions, have become standard for the powerless and poorest of nations.[20] Thompson's and Ani's analyses together point to the way in which institutional systems which do not necessarily benefit the poor nations, nevertheless are broadly accepted as legitimate in international political, economic and cultural fora.

Within the framework of systemic power, the issue of rights tends to be raised. Human rights are called for. But who establishes these rights? Calling for rights recognises the authority of the system, and of the institutions. As Colette Guillamin argues, the "right to be different" is not made by a member of the dominant group, the powerful:

> first of all because his practices and his ideal of existence are effectively the norm of society – what the dominator does goes without saying; then because he considers himself ... as exquisitely specific and distinguished; and because

---

20 See also Waring (1988) on women's contribution to work and food production; see Shiva (1993), and Wickramasinghe (1994) for a discussion of women's role in maintenance of biodiversity and feeding the family.

he exercises this distinction by right without having asked for, without ever having to ask for, anyone's authorization, individuality being a practical effect of the position of the dominator. On the contrary, the "right" to be different is a recourse to authorization (1995: 251).

As rights language is more and more frequently used in international agreements, such concerns are spread across not only the rights of individuals, but across the competing and always more powerful rights of corporations. The Bretton Woods institutions and the United Nations became such bodies for authorisation following World War II. Within the "new world order" of globalisation, this power of authorisation is vested in the WTO, with the United Nations steadily losing ground on issues such as human rights. Any nation wishing to uphold its individuality – to protect the livelihood of its indigenous peoples, to maintain environmental or labour laws, to break patent laws for the health of its people – must apply to the WTO for permission. The proposed Free Trade Area of the Americas agreement goes even further, including the worst aspects of the old Multilateral Agreement on Investment (MAI), such as open competition for services.[21]

Systemic power, as developed through the implementation of the WTO, is a more insidious form than at first is apparent. The WTO charter is written in terms of increasing the freedom of member countries, alleviating poverty and strengthening rights through provisions such as Intellectual Property Rights (IPR). However, because the rules are written from the perspective of the most powerful nations, in particular favouring US institutions and legal systems (e.g. patents law), the freedoms of poor countries are actually decreased.

The Power of Attraction

There are two forms of power (attraction and attitudes) to which the members of the diversity matrix have ready access, and these can be, and have been, effectively used by the powerless to effect personal and political change.

---

21 Clarke and Barlow's (1997) discussion of the implications of the MAI provisions for national health services, education and welfare applies to the proposed Free Trade Area of the Americas (FTAA) agreement.

A continuum from liking, or wanting to be liked, at the weak end, to love, lust, passion or devotion at the strong end, is the central feature of what might be called attractional power. If a member of the powerful or the powerless is the desired one, the other will comply with their wishes simply because the beloved wants it. In that respect it is similar to legitimate or systemic power as little conflict occurs. The power of attraction can be both productive and destructive, depending on the context and the other balances and imbalances of power between those involved. It is woven in a complex way with all the other forms of power. It can interact with violence, rewards, obstacles, backlashes, systems and prevailing attitudes. But its force should not be underrated. In children and adolescents it operates as peer-group pressure. In a global context, cultural imperialism affects the culturally colonised. Corporate advertising

Test the West advertising for West cigarettes, Berlin, 1992.

relies on this power to get people in, say, Nairobi or Manchester, to buy televisions, Coca-Cola and Big Macs. Cigarette advertising, for example, creates a fantasy high-flyer world. In 1992 on a visit to Berlin I saw an extraordinary example of this. A new cigarette brand called West had been launched, and advertisements lined the streets in both East and West Berlin. They advertised the cigarette alongside mixed images of wealth and decadence.

The more recent marketing exercises by IBM and Microsoft are descendants of the brand advertising which Coca-Cola and cigarette manufacturers pioneered.[22]

Love, especially its romantic manifestations in western culture, has been critically analysed by feminists, from Germaine Greer (1971: 139ff) to Shulamith Firestone (1971: 121ff), as a means of control when it is accompanied by misuses of power. And as Firestone points out, "the psychological dependence of women on men is created by continuing real economic and social oppression" (1971: 139). The power of attraction can be used (and misused) at both the individual and collective level. The "psychological dependence" of the powerless can be seen in global culture in instances of the allure of the western lifestyle presented to young people in countries where the west is still a fantasy world. The advertising for West cigarettes is intended to draw those who had lived under communist regimes for many years into the world of western consumerism. Love and attraction are complex forces and are often ignored in analyses of economics, where, in neoliberal discourse, decisions are assumed to be made by "rational economic man" (McMahon 1997).

The productive aspect of attraction power is when two or more people genuinely care about, like or love one another. Mutuality, support and acts of altruism occur frequently when this happens, and when the relationship is balanced, companionship and stability become determining features. The "companion lovers" of Monique Wittig and Sande Zeig (1979) are a fine example, as are many relationships between friends and family members (Raymond 1986/2001).

---

22 For a fine analysis of how branding operates in a globalised market, see Klein (2000); see also Chapter Six.

Given the importance of altruism to members of the powerless, it is interesting how unimportant it is within economic theory. Neoclassical economic theory is based on the view that all economic activity is selfish. Drawing women and indigenous peoples' concerns to a central position in economic theory challenges this assumption. I suggest it is not unusual for the dominant group not to recognise important social systems of the powerless.

The Power of Attitudes

The final major form of power is attitudinal power, which may be achieved through a process of rational or irrational persuasion. Rational persuasion is the power most frequently found between equals. It is grounded in respect for one another, and its centre moves among all the players. That is, it is not systematised or institutionalised. The individuals or groups involved are players without regular positions of dominance or oppression. Deception is not a feature, nor is withholding of information. This form is very stable. When applied to a global or mass context, persuasion has the power to shift attitudes and behaviours which remain stable over time. In some countries, such as Australia, the tobacco industry has come up against "Quit campaigns". These campaigns set about to alter people's perceptions about the attraction of cigarettes. Similar campaigns have been run about male violence and drunk driving, with considerable effect. Attitudinal shifts about global warming and other environmental concerns, including nuclear disarmament and racial vilification, could also be cited. The impact of the protests against globalisation have had a similar effect. The protests have put the critique of economic rationalism and the global economy on the front page of newspapers and on televisions around the world.[23]

Irrational persuasion, on the other hand, has much in common with marketing and advertising practices. In its worst form it takes on shades of Orwell's "Ministry of Truth" (1973) and sinks to propaganda and brainwashing. Individual instances may include emotional blackmail, intellectual trickery and misinformation parading as honesty. The ideology of

---

23 This is not to suggest that everybody everywhere will agree, but rather that once an attitudinal shift has occurred, it tends toward stability. As Jen Couch (2001) has pointed out, however, the events of 11 September 2001 have shifted this once again, especially in the US.

consumerist culture largely falls into this category, as does the claim that women benefit from globalisation through increased access to employment in export processing zones. Much political filibustering is readily captured in irrational persuasion. Duplicitous consent[24] in experimental medical procedures with adverse effects also falls into this category. However, unless the duped person becomes aware of the deception, it can be a very effective method of control. Many fundamentalist religious groups are founded on principles of irrational persuasion, to great effect.

One of the best examples of irrational persuasion in recent times has been the marketing of genetically modified organisms (GMOs). Transnational companies such as Monsanto,[25] Aventis and Novartis have been attempting to persuade the world's consumers that biotechnological farming will solve what is called the "world's food problem". They have also played down the dangers of GMO farming, and the pollution of wild types and unmanipulated domesticated crops. But contamination of ordinary unmanipulated corn by Starlink corn has already caused huge losses to farmers in the USA. The prospect that it is likely to take four years – or longer; no one really knows – to remove the contamination from the food supply is creating further havoc (see Anderson 2000; Kneen 1999; Shiva 2000; Tokar 2001; Bennholdt-Thomsen *et al.* 2001).

Irrational persuasion also has a positive face, and this is seen in the humour and jokes which make us laugh. Seeing an absurdity from another person's perspective can be an effective means of changing attitudes. Street theatre and political cartoons can shift people's attitudes in relation to political issues.

Knowledge

There is a place under the tongue, an enclosed space, a place of solitude and thoughtfulness. Coiled in that place is our original sense of place: the scents

---

24 For a critique of consent, see Hawthorne (1991a: 23); Raymond (nd: 6–9); and Thompson (2001: 22).

25 On 28 February 2001, Monsanto admitted it had not followed government guidelines in its growing and clean-up procedures in trial crops in Tasmania, Australia. It was also revealed that, instead of there being twelve trial sites, there were in fact fifty-eight. Contamination by GM canola of Tasmania's wild turnip plant is a possibility, and contamination of non-manipulated canola has been confirmed (*Lateline*, ABC TV, 28 February 2001).

of memory, the wild feelings of childhood, the forgotten dreams, the original words – our mother tongue. This is the place I write from …

My own place is a mix of wilderness and artifact. Stands of *callitris* (native cypress pine) remain virtually undisturbed in the midst of farmland: earth torn open to grow wheat, barley, oats; earth trodden by sheep whose hooves break up and destroy the native vegetation. And there is also a garden, a strange mix of native and exotic surrounded by a hedge that keeps the native world at bay. Inside the garden are caged budgerigars, native birds brought back to the land, but separated from it, just as we are separated from the place under the tongue, beneath the language we use. An aunt has a cockatoo, also caged, and featherless except for the unreachable tail feather. What does this say about our existence in this land? What does it say about our relationship to the place it was before it was seized by the colonisers? And they were colonisers of both place and language (Hawthorne 1991b).

I grew up in a multiple knowledge system. The accident of my birth in the southern hemisphere was the first knowledge dislocation I noticed. Later, with political activism around feminism, lesbian culture, Aboriginal culture and disability, I noticed other systems. But my first understanding of the dual system – northern hemisphere/mainstream, southern hemisphere/margins – occurred on a daily basis throughout my childhood. Christmas cards filled with snow and reindeer accompanied blistering hot days, withering grass and ice creams. My grandmother told us stories of innocuous rabbits such as Peter Rabbit, while my father went out on shooting expeditions to rid the land of the introduced pest: the European rabbit. At school the text books were filled with images of oaks and elms, God and the church; only in Nature Study classes did anyone mention the *eucalyptus* and *callitris*; no one mentioned the dreamings of the indigenous owners of the land. The history we learnt had more to do with the British Empire than the 70,000 years (and more) of continuous Aboriginal culture, or even the mere 200 years of white habitation. What was conveyed to us was that the knowledge of Britain or Europe was more important. It represented "Truth". What we learnt in Nature Study, or by living on the land, was incidental, only of interest to us, and not the sort of knowledge which would carry you through your life. This was the 1950s in rural New South Wales. We knew we were a long way from where the real and important events of the world occurred. Nevertheless, the first twelve years of my life gave me a rootedness in the local, in the land, and a real sense of my place. It is the background against which my thinking and imagining takes place.

Against this background which I carry with me, I am also aware that I had to leave. The narrowness of rural life before the advent of sophisticated communication systems[26] was significant. And unless I wanted to become a farmer, it was likely that my future lay elsewhere. Knowledge of the local has to be balanced against awareness of events outside the local sphere, and the outsider or a different perspective is not always respected in small communities (Hawthorne 1995: 114). Localism is, as John Wiseman points out "a two-edged sword" (1997: 75) and balancing the local and the global is not an easy task. However, many rural people are better informed about the city than the reverse, and knowledge of the local could become an important source, if respected, for governments, corporations and social institutions.

In the long term the knowledge which I had thought disadvantaged me, I have come to see as the most valuable heritage I have.

Assimilation and Appropriation

Assimilationist policies have affected colonised peoples deeply over the last 500 years. In Australia they have included introducing indigenous peoples to western mores and lifestyles (images of Aboriginal people in nineteenth-century clothing abound in the museums); pulling indigenous peoples into the market economy; removing children from their families in a policy which has spanned two centuries and affected every indigenous family in the country (Haebich 2000: 15) and has resulted in what Judy Atkinson calls "transgenerational trauma" (Atkinson 1997, 2002). Policies which forced colonised peoples to take on the culture of the coloniser, the powerful, stripped the colonised of their culture, their language, their sense of identity. Assimilation, integration, homogenisation, apply also in a range of other contexts. In the context of women, assimilation is usually glossed over. An example here is the way in which violence against women is renamed "family violence" (Smith 1990: 205); lesbian culture is assimilated into "queer"; women's studies is renamed "gender studies". In

---

26 Electricity came to our farm in 1951. Television was much later and was not introduced into my family's household until 1965. In 1993 a solar-powered telephone box was the talk of the town for months. My cousins now have internet access.

each case the active person at the centre is displaced and removed by tricks of language. The broader term is defended on the grounds that it is more useful, inclusive and unifying, when in fact it disguises the ruling relations of the most powerful by putting them at the centre. For example, in World Bank-funded "development" projects, the process of implementing new systems is determined by outsiders (organisations and individuals) who are not sensitive to the context and the local conditions (ecologically and socially). What is implemented in this context are systems developed outside the country, possibly in very different environments, which assume that within the country to be developed, the same inputs will result in the same outcomes. Assimilation covers diversity, pretends it does not exist, and makes it harder to find afterwards.

The so-called "Green Revolution" resulted in exactly the same problems: homogenisation of farming methods, imported and hybrid seed types, replacing mixed farming methods as well as traditional food staples (njahe beans in Kenya, taro in Hawai'i, maize in Mexico). The Green Revolution was a disguised colonisation of diversity. It was threefold, colonising the ground in changed cultivation practices; people's bodies in changed eating and nutritional practices; and culture, since both the above have a profound effect on cultural rituals, life styles and the symbolic content of people's lives. As Swanson points out:

> Biodiversity serves a distinct function within the R&D process. It acts as a source of new stocks of information which can then serve as the base from which to develop new innovations. Once brought within the process it is assimilated bit by bit into the commercial sector and investigated as such (1996: 6).

The assimilation of biodiversity is as destructive as the assimilation of cultural diversity. It results in the disappearance of the wild stock which originally gave rise to it. Vandana Shiva documents this process of disappearance of knowledge systems through fragmentation, erasure, and the homogenisation of agricultural and scientific practices (1993: 9–64). Mogina (1996: oral presentation) argues that formal education is the greatest threat to women's traditions and the maintenance of culture in Papua New Guinea, as it undermines not only traditional knowledge, but the sources of that knowledge, and the traditional processes of transmission:

In the past if a young woman wanted to find out about contraceptives and medicines she would have to follow the older women into the forest to collect food and medicinal plants. This is also where information about sex occurs – outside the village in the forest – because the village has many ears (Mogina 1996: oral presentation).

Environmental disasters, such as tropical deforestation, have resulted because external forces – the State, the capitalist market, the colonisers' systems of education – have appropriated the valuable resources while leaving those considered worthless in the hands of the forest peoples (Dove 1993: 17–24). Michael Dove makes the following observation of the way it works in Indonesia:

> forest people develop a resource for the market, and if and when this market attains sufficient importance, central economic and political interests assume control of it, based on self-interest rhetorically disguised as the common good (1993: 20).

It is interesting that in a metaphoric sense, diversity or the ability to distinguish one thing from another is equated with life. Simon Schama asks us to consider how we think about the Holocaust. He writes:

> In our mind's eye we are accustomed to think of the Holocaust as having no landscape – or at best one emptied of features and color, shrouded in night and fog, blanketed by perpetual winter, collapsed into shades of dun and gray; the gray of smoke, of ash, of pulverized bones, of quicklime (1996: 26).

The appropriation of indigenous and local knowledges is paralleled in academic discourse by the appropriation of "the all" in post-modern theories. "The all" is appropriated by allowing some (the forest peoples) to keep those things not valued by the market forces (read cultural difference, local knowledge and traditions). The post-modern theorist and knowledge keeper, meanwhile, appropriates anything the market values. Such things include products which can be commodified and sold; seeds or genetic information which can be value added through research and development, and owned through US patent laws; natural resources such as timber, metals, fisheries which can be exploited on a massive scale.

The post-modern equalises the value of everything else (read all positions) thereby devaluing it. Like Schama's view of the Holocaust, it has no features, no landscape.

Appropriation is the first step in the globalisation process, and relies on making invisible the knowledge of the diversity matrix, denying its existence and then remaking it in a form which suits the needs of the dominant group. Shiva has documented the way this is done with forestry and agriculture: trees are declared weeds, unmarketable, useless; when traditionally they, like the cassava of Nigeria, have been harvested by women and provided a range of sustenance for the local people (Shiva 1993: 22–27; 1997). In Australia, attempts at weeding out Aboriginal culture were made through the institutionalised stealing of Aboriginal children from their families. In spite of this policy rupturing generational links to culture, the persistence of a vibrant and lively indigenous culture in Australia is testimony to its strength.[27]

> I not see you long time now, I not see you long time now.
> White fella bin take me from you. I don't know why
> Give me to missionary to be God's child
> Give me new language, give me new name
> All time I cry, they say – "that shame" (Johnson 1985: 35).

Appropriation is not just an issue of material things: it has also entered the area of the cultural and the spiritual. Cultural voyeurism is the process by which the "exotic" person, literature, art or practice is romanticised,[28] incorporated and then commodified and marketed for the profit of the company (Hawthorne 1989). Spiritual voyeurism (Hawthorne 1994a), as exemplified by the New Age, disconnects the culture or spiritual by dislocating it from its geography, its locale. Cultural appropriation takes many forms. The more obvious examples – such as Marlo Morgan's *Mutant Message Down Under*, Lynn Andrews' Native American

---

27 For some first-hand stories relating to the stolen generation, see Wilson (1997); Bird (1998); Kartinyeri (2000); Haebich (2000).

28 In a note reminiscent of the analysis of romantic love mentioned earlier in this chapter, Maria Mies comments on the process by which the dominant culture engages in systematic exoticisation: "Capitalist patriarchy and science have first to destroy women or nature or other people as autarkic subjects. This is the basis of all romantic love, of romanticizing exotic peoples or 'natives'" (Mies 1986: 234n).

pseudofiction, Carlos Castaneda's and James Renfield's appropriations of Mexican and South American culture – have been identified as cultural appropriations.[29] Cultural appropriation also affects the poor within the western nations, where the markers of class are turned into new fashions or where linguistic appropriations give an impression of downward mobility.[30] For, as Rita Mae Brown wrote of middle-class existence: "We know that anytime you get tired of poverty you can go right back to them [material privileges]" (1974: 21).

Downward mobility has its equivalents in male-to-female transsexuals: men who through cosmetic surgery or hormone treatment join the ranks of women. They do so without acknowledging their role in appropriating women's culture. A significant number then become lesbians, further betraying the trust given to them as women.[31] For women, like men, like other colonised groups in the diversity matrix, have a culture. And women's culture is passed on to girls in ways which resemble the passing on of a forbidden language.[32]

Appropriation is a tool used against the members of the diversity matrix to gain access to their "private" culture[33] and then to use that access to gain market advantage.[34] The process of cultural homogenisation takes place through appropriation of the knowledge or practices of those in the

29 In the event that readers want to read these books, I suggest they be borrowed rather than purchased. It is interesting to consider the politics of publishing. Time–Warner, owner of Warner Books and publisher of Lynn Andrews, is number thirty-three in the world's largest 100 economic entities; see Appendix, Table 1.

30 Rita Mae Brown also wrote: "the irony of downward mobility ... is that they could afford to become downwardly mobile" (1974: 20).

31 For a lengthy discussion of transsexualism, see Raymond (1979/1994).

32 As a specific example of this occurring, see Silber (1995) and Morgan (1992) on Nüshi/Nüshu, a traditional form of women's writing. In Australia, Aboriginal women speak of women's business; similar traditions exist among women in many parts of the world. See also Mogina (1996).

33 The privacy is partly of the powerful's own making. His inability to see, recognise, acknowledge and respect the culture of the diversity matrix leads those in the diversity matrix toward silence, secrecy and non-public exposure, lest that lead to declarations of "weed" status, disrespect and another cycle of appropriation.

34 Examples are: Helen Darville (Demidenko), author of *The Hand That Signed the Paper*, who took on a false Ukrainian identity although she was of English parentage; Sandy (Rose Allequere) Stone, a male-to-female transsexual who publishes under a female name, which gives him an edge (at other women's expense) for being a "woman" in the field of computers, cyborgs, internet. Elizabeth Durack's paintings marketed under the name of Eddy Burak provide an example of appropriation in the visual arts. Elizabeth

diversity matrix. The process involves incorporation, commodification, export, dislocation, and finally homogenisation, a process of de-differentiation;[35] and as we will see in the next chapter, it is controlled by the economically and culturally dominant group.

The systematic appropriation of the knowledge, goods and culture of other peoples is a perverted form of the power of reward. Just as land was "traded" with indigenous peoples for beads and the goods of European culture – presented as valuable when in fact they held little value in a European context – so today, export and participation in the global market is presented as a lure. The value accorded to appropriated goods and knowledge in the field is nowhere near reflective of its value on the global market. Appropriation successfully transforms the resources of the powerless in the diversity matrix for the benefit of the powerful.[36]

A Clash of Knowledge Systems

The structure of knowledge systems is different across cultures. Western peoples tend to assume that all knowledge is accessible to all people. In spite of this rhetoric, there are many ways of protecting particular kinds of knowledge and the practice of it.[37]

Recent technological shifts, such as the internet, have extended the notion of public access to all "knowledge", or more correctly,

---

Durack's family owned large tracts of land in traditional Aboriginal lands. Magabala Books, an indigenous publishing house in Australia, has faced problems of authors who have masqueraded as Aboriginal in order to get work published, as in the case of Leon Carmen who pretended to be a descendant of the Pitjantjatjara people. Carmen took the name Wanda Koolmatrie, and his book, *In My Own Sweet Time*, was published in 1994.

35 For further elaboration of the process of corporate homogenisation, see Chapter Three.

36 Unlike Hardt and Negri, I do not believe that reversing the process of appropriation by engaging in reappropriation will result in any gain in power for the powerless. They write: "[Reappropriation] is how the multitude gains the power to affirm its autonomy, traveling and expressing itself through an apparatus of widespread, transversal territorial reappropriation" (2000: 398). Rather, it suggests an ignorance of the importance of the means remaining consistent with the ends.

37 Doctors and lawyers are the first to protect their ground when alternative systems are offered. An individual may know the knowledge as well as or better than many of its practitioners, but without a certificate, diploma or degree it is not possible for that person to make use of the knowledge. This system of accreditation has been used very effectively to keep out women practitioners. Various legal forms of protection have also been developed, including registered trademarks, copyright, patents, trade secrets and commercial-in-confidence regimes, see Chapter Seven.

"information". But this development too is fraught with problems of open access and transparency. It also encourages the individualisation of knowledge, which is exemplified in the production of individual websites.[38] Cybertechnologies are often referred to as the democratisation of knowledge, but democratisation on the internet will not be achieved while starvation, diarrhoea, and old-fashioned epidemics are still the norm for so many of the world's people.

Some cultures view access to knowledge as something which is earned, or secret with sanctions on spreading the knowledge publicly (see Bell 1998). Legal protection of secrecy is respected in draft legislation drawn up in Brazil (*Brazilian Indigenous Societies Act 1994*; the act has not yet been proclaimed; Posey 1996: 18). The draft legislation included the right "to maintain the secrecy to traditional knowledge ... to refuse access to traditional knowledge and to apply for protection under IPR [Intellectual Property Rights] law" (Posey 1996: 18). Access to knowledge also entails community responsibilities. For many indigenous peoples the creation of culture is a communal responsibility (Serote 1998: 5; Bell 1998), and the creative and intellectual products achieved cannot be sold or transferred by individuals because intergenerational protection is an important ingredient within the culture (COICA/UNDP 1994). This applies to natural resources as much as it does to intellectual and artistic creations.

Which returns the discussion to the core of the problem of exploitation of "wild" resources by western companies, even those who claim sensitivity to cultural difference. Katerina Teaiwa shows how the Body Shop has exploited indigenous Banaban resources. She suggests a community response, one which recognises the importance of "talk amongst themselves" and an awareness that "Self-determination must come before global participation or we will be swept away by the tide of 'boundarilessness'" (1997: 8). The absence of boundaries is not helpful to indigenous peoples whose lands have been colonised as it tends in the direction of assimilation and homogenisation. The lands were proclaimed as "wild" and uninhabited, and in recent years indigenous peoples have had to fight legal battles to re-claim their title over traditional land (see, for example, Melbourne 1995; Bell 1998).

---

38   For further discussion on this, see Hawthorne (1998).

The identification of differences in knowledge systems has important implications for the theory and practice of international law. Darrell Posey and Graham Dutfield refer to "integrationist language" of early conventions (the 1957 ILO convention, for example) as being culturally inappropriate (1996: 117). Integrationist language, like assimilationist social policies, attempts to impose western law *as if it were universal*. In reality, little has changed, and integrationist language can be found in very recent international agreements; the integration now is not cultural, it is economic. Economic integrationist language – free markets, free trade, the knowledge economy – is central to the framing of the multilateral agreements which form the backbone of global trade. Darrell Posey (1996) concludes that very few of the international laws[39] currently in place deal with appropriation and universalisation, and that those that do, such as intellectual property rights, tend to favour western industrialised countries with considerable access to, and holdings of, patents, copyright and other intellectual protections, rather than the biodiverse and culturally diverse nations.

Such developments are no surprise, given the unequal relations of power between these two groups. In some quarters, indigenous peoples have taken up the challenge of using new developments in global technologies, mapping their land and demarcating it using digital technology. This is a way of making their knowledge system visible to western eyes. In Australia, the Central and Northern Land Councils are using the latest digital mapping technology, Geographic Information Systems (GIS), combined with satellite data and remote sensing "to locate and identify every tree, every significant feature in their territory" (Turnbull 1997:

---

39 Posey's article (1996) outlines a number of strategies which might or have been used. A central problem of IPRs is that they cannot handle community ownership, nor do they respect intergenerational codes of protection, particularly where there is no written record. Other proposed systems include Traditional Resource Rights (TRR), a bundle of rights which have already been recognised; Material Transfer Agreements (MTAs), regulated transfers of biological resources with benefits returning to the supplier; and Information Transfer Agreements (ITAs), which are similar to MTAs but recognise knowledge about processes, formulas, conservation practices. India has led the way with lobbying for Community Intellectual Rights (CIRs), which recognise indigenous peoples as "innovators", and which come into existence simply by declaration, in a way that is similar to copyright law. Community registers, electronic databases, community-controlled research are some of the other methods used to maintain and protect indigenous knowledge. See Chapter Seven for a longer discussion.

560; see also Bartolo and Hill 2001). The Ye'kuana in Venezuela are doing the same (Posey 1996: 12). But as Ariel Salleh points out, the claim that the cultural knowledge embedded in the GIS data will remain in the hands of local people is "questionable". She writes:

> If LandCare requires open access to all GIS data gathered, and if the same information can be "presented" either in bush tucker or scientific terms, there is in fact no way of protecting local intellectual property (1997: 121).[40]

Despite the benefits of LandCare programs, the technologisation of indigenous knowledge – and hence its appropriation – is not neutral. And just as bioprospecting raises the need for intellectual property protections, so does the advent of GIS.

Europe, too, has its own history of a shift from multiple local knowledges to a centralised, standardised knowledge system. As Turnbull points out, the integration of local knowledges of map making in Europe finally emerged as a result of the "demands of a centralised economy which, in turn, brought with it a yet greater need for a more fully articulated knowledge space" (Turnbull 1997: 558). This gives us a clue to what is happening now. In Europe, it was national and regional economic forces. Today, these forces have become global, and we have to ask whether everyone on the planet wants to join the "market". Vandana Shiva, writing about the next phase in European expansionism, regards the western system of knowledge as "a local tradition which has been spread world wide through intellectual colonisation" (1993: 10).

The objective western system of knowledge attempts to create order in the world, but complexity and uncertainty require more open-ended approaches to knowledge. Without wishing to promote further appropriation, it is nevertheless instructive to look at systems and practices which have proven well suited to "handling uncertainty".

Turnbull describes two open-ended practices: the building of Chartres cathedral and Polynesian navigation of the Pacific (1997: 553–557). Both

---

40 Bartolo and Hill say that the Ramingining community would like to have control over GIS, as that would better allow them to protect "sensitive cultural information" (2001: 11). But like the system of patents, once such knowledge enters the public western system, it is nigh impossible to protect in ways that indigenous communities are used to being able to protect knowledge.

were built on local knowledge systems and traditions. Both involved discrete groups involved in a collective effort with guidance from a "master" [*sic*] mason or navigator. It is this approach to knowledge which may well assist us in dealing with the plethora of uncertainties we face in our contemporary world.

Not Seeing[41]

In the development of disciplines of knowledge, what is seen, what is given importance, is what is regarded as true, real, and of value. Nowhere is this clearer than in the economic systems developed under capitalism, and their extension to globalised economics in the late twentieth century. Neoclassical economics continues its objectified and universalising practices as if there had never been any critiques of objectivity, context stripping and universal knowledge.

Only members of the dominant culture, imbued with the belief systems of formal economics, could go on believing, in the face of so much evidence, that the economics of globalisation and its attendant institutions could be good for all the world's people (see Chossudovsky 1998). Only they could ignore the uncomfortable feeling, or "experience no dissonance with the default assumptions" (Hyman 1994: 53). Economics, like all other disciplines, is value laden, and in its latest globalised incarnation, creates a monoculture on a scale the planet has never before experienced. Marilyn Waring points out, "much of the economic discipline is a matter of perception, and what does or does not constitute production could depend on the way you see the world. And it does" (1988: 59).

"Not seeing" has been basic to colonisation. It creates a vacuum of invisibility where previously there had been a people, a culture, a language, a cluster of traditions around food, survival, shelter, as well as creativity in the arts, religion and social structures. The gap which precedes colonisation makes it possible to move into a land deemed *terra nullius*[42] and take it over without consultation or consideration of those who live there. It means that the coloniser does not see or consider of value the ecosystem of the place, and so brings in animals and foods unsuited to the environ-

---

41   See Frye (1983), in particular, her essay, "To See and To Be Seen: The Politics of Reality".

42   Salleh (1997: 121) makes the connection between *terra nullius* and the appropriative behaviour of transnational resource companies and the funding of educational posts.

ment except in the most gross sense, namely that the climate is sufficiently similar for exotics to grow and survive. "Not seeing" makes it possible to ignore the local traditions, disregard all but the most basic local conditions, and impose a monoculture of foods foreign to the land. This process has happened all around the world. In Kenya, njahe beans are supplanted by green beans and coffee beans; in Fiji, taro and yam are supplanted by cassava; in Australia, eucalyptus and native forests are supplanted by *Pinus radiata* as well as monoculture crops like wheat, oats and canola; in India, the native forest is supplanted by eucalyptus. By not seeing the world as it is, the coloniser can feel at home, but the colonised – people, animals and plants – are displaced, made homeless in their own homeland; like the abused woman who is "homeless in her own body" (Copelan 1994: 202).

The Perceptual Gap

"Not seeing" results in the opening up of a perceptual gap which is a feature of dominant knowledge systems, and the system currently dominating the globe is a pertinent example. The gap has a history going back to the separation of religion and science during the so-called "Enlightenment" (see Ani 2000; Asante 1999). The separation of science and religion was replicated by René Descartes (1596–1650) through the separation of mind and matter. Once the mind is dissociated from matter, all sorts of beliefs become possible. It is possible, for example, to begin to distrust the idea of other minds. This leads to a depersonalisation of humanity, for if one can doubt the existence of other minds, one can doubt their humanity. From this position, colonisation can be readily justified, and the imposition of the dominant worldview on "empty" minds and cultures can be regarded as a benefit.

Another result of the perceptual gap is that it is possible to imagine immortality. Again mind and matter are separated, only this time, mind becomes far superior to matter, particularly the matter of others. This allows for the possibility of using other people to practise the experimentation necessary for achieving immortality. In-vitro fertilisation (IVF), cloning, genetic engineering, robotics and the colonisation of outer space are some of its more recent applications (see Klein 1999).

The mind/body split also makes it possible to doubt the existence of divinity. It does not matter that doubting the existence of other minds, believing in immortality and doubting divinity contradict one another, for they are simply gaps which have opened in the dominant cultural ideology.[43] Doubting divinity means doubting the need to retain places which are sacrosanct. It means providing proofs which show that meaningful rituals – which are a source of joy to ordinary people, and the stuff of connectivity between people – have no scientific basis or purpose. Doubting divinity reduces social connectedness; recognising divinity creates respect for those things deemed sacred and creates a regard for the specialness of life.

The perceptual gap is utilised by those in control of capital: the military, the transnational corporations, and governments. It enables them to move or remove large numbers of people. Sometimes this occurs through mass extermination in war; the more subtle operators make it happen through mass migration to fill employment gaps, or mass movement of an industry to a jurisdiction where there are no rigorous labour laws, no trade unions and low pay.

The perceptual gap between mind and matter is the basis of consumerism. Filling the gap is what being a consumer is meant to do. "Thirty years of shopping, and I still have nothing to wear"[44] encapsulates the idea. We are urged to buy from a clothing company called "Gap". Fashion, whether it be global sports clothing or the latest technotoy, creates needs which did not exist prior to the advertisement or the product. Constantly updated and outdated technologies operate in exactly the same way. I am writing this book on a laptop computer with a colour screen. Five years ago, I did not know I'd ever "need" such a thing.

Science is constantly filling gaps in our knowledge, although as many writers have pointed out the knowledge often existed but scientists failed to ask. Or it existed, but in a different cultural or knowledge context which scientists refused to acknowledge, or simply had not "seen". Filling the gaps is not always a positive move. Florence Nightingale designed the sewerage systems for Delhi using standard knowledge available to anyone

---

43 A recent example which combines different aspects of the above is Omega Point Theory, described by Frank J. Tipler in his 1994 book entitled *The Physics of Immortality*. See Margaret Wertheim (1995) for a critique of modern physics and its Pythagorean origins.

44 The traveller arriving at Melbourne's Tullamarine Airport is greeted by a billboard which proclaims in similar fashion: "Melbourne, shopping capital of Australia".

in her era. This resulted in massive public health improvements. In contrast, providing ultrasounds to pregnant women a hundred years later in a culture which favours boys, fills the gap, but usually results in the elimination of girls.

The ultimate technologies in filling the gap include the new biological gap-fillers: gene technology, and multimillion-dollar enterprises such as the Human Genome Project. These come about in a way similar to consumerism. A phrase such as "solving world hunger" is repeated over and over in the media until a certain portion of the society begin to believe there is such a problem. The false "problem" is then solved with genetically modified foods. The military has created the outer space gap-filler of spacecraft colonising other worlds, exploring the moon, planets and soaring out beyond the solar system. Why is there so little interest in filling the inner gap, the emotions, the feelings, what all of us experience as "self"? Why is there so little interest in creativity and diversity?

Shiva supplies a partial answer to this when she connects the increasingly accepted view of knowledge "as capital, a commodity and as a means for exclusive market control" (2001f: 21). She argues that Trade Related Intellectual Property rights (TRIPs) represent a "privatization of the intellectual commons" with the final outcome "that the mind becomes a corporate monopoly" (2001f: 113).

How Knowledge Is Valued

Vandana Shiva introduces an important concept into her work, that of creation and production boundaries (1994: 140–141). The "production boundary" refers to the line between production for commercial use and production for domestic or non-commercial use. According to this regime, the free-range eggs which my family ate when I was a child, and the sheep which were killed for home consumption, were not produced. That is, they fell "outside the production boundary" (1994: 140). The outcome of this is that recycled products, home-produced goods for domestic consumption, and altruistic behaviour – all of which are regenerative, sustainable and responsible – are discouraged since it is accorded no value. The work women and children do – as farmers, fishers, weavers, recyclers – is not work. And self-sufficiency leads to low scores on GDP counts, and so is regarded as economic suicide in the global economy.

WEF protest, Melbourne 2000. Have a nice lunch.

The "creation boundary" refers to the knowledge input. Creation which takes place in the community, over long periods of time, gradually refined and passed on generation by generation, is turned into non-knowledge. In this schema, the knowledge of natural medicines used by traditional peoples all around the world does not count as knowledge. Jane Mogina's forest women in Papua New Guinea do not know anything (Mogina 1996); the women of Hindmarsh Island in South Australia are said to have no knowledge (see *Chapman v. Luminis Pty Ltd* (No. 5) 2001 FAC 1106; see also Bell 1998); the Cofan peoples of Ecuador do not know what is best for their environment (Tidwell 1996). Shiva writes:

> The creation boundary does to knowledge what the production boundary does to work: it excludes the creative contributions of women and Third World peasants and tribals and treats them as being engaged in unthinking, repetitive, biological processes (1994: 140–141).

The recognition of women's knowledge as valid and valuable is a long project that has been carried by numerous feminists inside and outside academia (for three quite different examples, see Bell 1983/2002, 1987, 1998). Likewise, the knowledge of indigenous peoples has only recently been recognised as valid and valuable, and has been accompanied by a rush to appropriate it as a profitable commodity. Similar forces have been operating in economics, in particular, in relation to the previously "uncounted" economic activities.

The trend in the western world has been away from recognising the use value of sustainable practices, away from biodiversity and ecological regeneration, and toward a system which highlights individualism at the expense of the community, homogeneity at the expense of diversity, efficiency at the expense of humanity, and the commodification of everything at the expense of creativity.

Cultural Homogeneity

Vandana Shiva, in her influential book *Monocultures of the Mind* (1993), points to the increasing homogeneity of knowledge and practice globally. Like Sabine O'Hara (1995), she is disturbed by the simultaneous decrease in biodiversity and cultural diversity. Monoculturalism, in the European languages imposed on the colonies, is an aspect of colonisation. In these technological times, the internet has become a major purveyor of this brand of monoculturalism, now structured around US-centred worlds.

Linguistic monoculturalism has another side. Shirley Geok-lin Lim is one of a generation exiled from her linguistic roots by an accident of history. She was raised to speak and write with ease in the colonist's language, English, but when independence came to Malaysia in 1957, she found herself barred from political participation because the only literature which counted was

> literature in the national language. This definition starkly underlies the movement to restrict national identity to a monocultural and monolinguistic position, a constitutional decision which cannot be debated under pain of imprisonment without *habeas corpus* (1994: 169).

Monoculturalism, imposition of the elite's belief system, is a feature of the culture of the powerful, even where it occurs – as in Malaysia – outside the global elite culture. The national elites used the same methods to suppress foreign culture as the former colonists had used in their suppression of the indigenous culture.

Indian poet Sujata Bhatt powerfully describes the process of loss of language, alongside culture and place:

> You ask me what I mean
> by saying I have lost my tongue.
> I ask you, what would you do
> if you had two tongues in your mouth,
> and lost the first one, the mother tongue,
> and could not really know the other,
> the foreign tongue.
> You could not use them both together
> even if you thought that way.
> And if you lived in a place you had to
> speak a foreign tongue,
> your mother tongue would rot,
> rot and die in your mouth
> until you had to spit it out (1988: 65–66).

These writers recognise "that a battle is being fought over their minds and their souls" (Coombs 1996: 41), a battle which ensures that the dominant worldview maintains its supremacy.

George Trevorrow in his testimony on the Hindmarsh Island case provides a fine example of the clash of knowledge systems between the Ngarrindjeri people of South Australia and the western legal system in South Australia (Bell 1998: 386–389). While Trevorrow persists in talking of spiritual and cultural matters, including *ngatji*,[45] the interrogating barrister hears him to be speaking of animals, wildlife and the environment. Because of the nature of Ngarrindjeri rules concerning who can speak about women's business and men's business – a distinction the western legal system[46] finds hard to acknowledge – George Trevorrow puts limits on what he can speak of. The Ngarrindjeri women's claims against the developers of the Hindmarsh Island bridge faced multiple knowledge clashes. Firstly, as Eileen McHughes states: "If it is printed by a white person, no offence, but if it is printed by a white person, then they believe it, but they won't believe us if it's oral" (cited in Bell 1998: 395). Secondly, this is an indigenous knowledge system with different rules, signifiers and conceptual structures, as well as a whole raft of words which don't translate readily into the English language. Thirdly, what counts as sacred to the Ngarrindjeri is interpreted in secular ways within the western legal system. And fourthly, the Ngarrindjeri claims were about women's business, women's knowledge, and the sacredness of women's bodies, all concepts foreign within a western, English-language, legal framework.

The Ngarrindjeri women's challenge is typical of the issues faced by indigenous peoples in different places. The specificities of each culture's battle with the dominant culture will vary: the broad outlines and the kinds of issues faced are similar. In the Chiapas region of Mexico, indigenous people are fighting for their lives against the Mexican military in an uprising that began on "1 January 1994, the day the North American Free

---

45 *Ngatji* can be defined as totem, friend, countryman, protector (Bell 1998: xiii).

46 In a study on women in the law conducted by Guinier *et al.* at an American Ivy League college, one of her co-authors concludes: "if law school is an attempt to engage and educate diverse students democratically and critically about the practices and possibilities of law for all people, then the failure of the institution is alarming. In the meantime, the price borne by women across all colors is far too high and their critique far too powerful to dismiss" (Fine cited in Guinier 1994: 76). Guinier *et al.* call the process of acculturation which women pass through "becoming gentlemen" (ibid).

Trade Agreement came into effect" (Coburn 2000: 13). Globalisation is a force which threatens not only the viability of local cultures, but their very existence. And because of the way in which the issues are framed within western discourse, a crucial part of that struggle is getting western eyes to move beyond not seeing.[47]

In addition to the dominant knowledge systems engendered by the west, the other ubiquitous and related global culture is men's culture. Men have developed a culture which is self-sustaining and which is carefully passed on vertically and horizontally – across generations and across cultures – to other men. As Anoja Wickramasinghe in her study of Sri Lanka points out:

> community forestry programmes in the developing world have become limited by traditions of male leadership and power. This has marginalized the women who actually practice forestry. Programmes have focussed on timber production alone; practicalities related to the multiple uses and sustainable management of the forests has been de-prioritised. Women's knowledge of the trees and plants that help to meet local needs has been ignored (1994: 25).

Although there have been men who have resisted this acculturation (Stoltenberg 1990), and some whites have resisted racism (Rich 1979), on the whole the dominant culture is successfully passed on. Monoculturalism pervades every aspect of the culture of the powerful. The law, even when couched in terms of equality, perpetuates one-dimensionality. Catharine MacKinnon makes the point that: "Equality has come to mean a right to be treated like the white man when you can show you are like him" (1987: 63). In order to become like him, members of the diversity matrix dress up in the accoutrements of the powerful: shoulder pads for corporate women, new accents for the working class,[48] cosmetic surgery

---

47 In a roundtable on intellectual property and indigenous knowledge, organised by the World Intellectual Property Organisation (WIPO), three speakers from South Africa, Panama and the Saami reflected on the importance of respecting indigenous knowledge systems as communal intellectual creations. See Serote (1998); López (1998); Baer (1998). The difficulty, as I have indicated elsewhere (Hawthorne 1998), is that opening up indigenous knowledge systems to organisations such as WIPO where indigenous communities are regarded "as the repository of hidden or lost knowledge" (Serote 1998: 4) may well open up those communities to further appropriation.

48 See Mahony (1996); Mahony and Zmroczek (1997, 1999).

for those with Asian eyes, and education for anyone who can't change the colour of their skin or the foibles of their marked body.

In Defence of Diversity

In the quotation that begins this chapter, diversity and the health of the communities and cultures are connected. But is diversity something we should cherish? Is it simply a great slogan which provides consumers with more and more options and choices in the marketplace? Biodiversity is a system of interconnecting relationships, and when an ecosystem is in balance, most of its elements remain dynamically stable. Its condition is not static but changes over time, and among the changes which take place are shifts in species composition. When disaster strikes an ecosystem either in the form of a naturally occurring event – drought, flood, volcanic eruption, tidal wave – or through human causation – an oil spill, nuclear contamination, poisoning by pesticides, excessive tourism or development – there might be sudden shifts in the composition of the species which inhabit that ecosystem. The ability of the ecosystem to return to its previous dynamically stable condition will mostly depend on how many times it has faced and recovered from this situation previously, that is, on its diversity, complexity, adaptability and overall resilience. Intermittent but regular drought or flood can, over time, be adapted to, and so its long-term impact will not be as severe as the rare cyclone, tidal wave or volcanic eruption. But what of the human-caused disaster? Is it an argument to increase the intensity of pollution, to sort out those species which will recover and those which will not? The difference, I believe, is that the human-caused disaster is avoidable. Allowing environmental destruction is comparable, in a moral sense, to choosing to violate another person (see Kappeler 1995: 253–258). It is comparable to misuses of power in the political and social arenas. It is a case of Dominant Culture Stupidity (DCS) in ignoring the consequences of one's actions on the world. In this case the DCS is the stupidity of the human species in relation to the other species of the world.

On a practical, rather than moral, basis it simply makes good sense to continue the state of dynamic stability. It is very costly to help disaster areas recover. Within the framework of wild politics it does not make sense to create new products which increase the waste quotient, and which then have to be cleaned up. As Veronika Bennholdt-Thomsen and

Maria Mies describe, "the export of organic waste from West German villages to a composting plant in Thuringia in East Germany was an ecological and economic absurdity" (1999: 155). They suggest that we should be considering how to reduce our waste and look after it ourselves.

And what of cultural diversity? Why should we value this? Like species, cultures come in and out of existence. The demise of racist, sexist and homophobic cultural values would be a real achievement, so why

S11 Melbourne. No jobs on a dead planet.

support the continuation of cultural diversity?

The issue, again, is not the survival *per se*, but who is responsible for the survival or demise of cultures. The problem of colonisation is that it is the coloniser who decides that children should no longer speak their native tongue; it is the coloniser who steps in to prohibit certain activities which the coloniser regards as reprehensible. Suttee, footbinding and female genital mutilation are three "cultural practices"[49] which have been variously defended and criticised; the last is the only one with any remaining serious defenders.[50] Since the advent of the second wave of the women's movement in the 1960s, women both outside and inside the cultures continuing these practices have begun to scrutinise why these practices were initially implemented, and whether there are any good reasons for continuing them. What made the difference, in terms of cultural shift, was when those within the cultures[51] began the process of changing attitudes toward the practices.

In the area of cultural diversity, my argument is that it matters where the force for change is coming from. When a powerful outsider steps in to make changes, change often becomes a hostile act. When change comes from within, it is more like the shift that occurs within the framework of dynamic stability in an ecosystem. Power, its effects, who is responsible, and the consequences of change are all important factors in maintaining cultural integrity. If the integrity of the culture is still in place – it has not been linguistically fragmented or culturally appropriated in massive ways – then the shifts which occur will not be a threat to diversity. The problem humanity faces, as a homogenised global culture, is that cultures are under pressure to change and conform to the more powerful norm. And, in some instances, such as in Chiapas, Mexico, people are

---

49   Mary Daly (1978) was one of the first to analyse these as violence against women.

50   I suspect that part of the reason for having defenders is that this is not a publicly visible violation. Suttee results in the death of the woman; footbinding results in visible impairment of mobility for the woman; female genital mutilation (FGM) remains hidden under garments and taboos on speaking about sexuality. See Rioja and Manresa (1999).

51   In the case of footbinding, when the communists outlawed the practice from within China, it achieved much more success than any earlier efforts by colonising powers. Likewise, the most successful campaigns against female genital mutilation have been those headed by women who are insiders, see Dirie (1998); Dorkenoo (1994).

52   Justin Coburn writes of the massacres of indigenous people in the community of Acteal in December 1997 by paramilitary forces (2000: 13). Twenty-two women, fourteen children and nine men were killed that day.

losing their lives as well as their cultures.[52] In Australia, at the time when the British boat people first came to these shores, there were many hundreds of living Aboriginal languages; the vast majority of these have now disappeared through the results of massacre, disease, cultural dispossession, the stealing of children, and the demands of government policy. The consequences of these activities should by now be obvious to members of the educated global community. The dominant cultures have the chance to change their/our approach. In much the same way that we should be renouncing environmentally hazardous policies, so too should we be renouncing culturally hazardous policies.

Power and knowledge intersect within and between cultures, affecting the overall shape of the society. When the strong forms of power (violence, especially when it is systemic) are evident, diversity retreats, and homogeneity in cultural practices and forms of knowledge becomes the norm. The treatment of women by the Taliban in Afghanistan is an example of this kind of cascading dispossession. Women were deemed invisible, could not engage in education and learning,[53] and were brutally beaten when they "violated" the Taliban's laws. Violence requires disengagement, and as women were further dehumanised and segregated under the burka or were banned from going outdoors, disengagement escalated, and violence became increasingly likely.

When power is decentralised and knowledge of others is respected, then diversity can thrive. Homogeneity is diminished, and violence is less likely to be institutionalised. In order to solve conflict non-violently, engagement needs to occur, and engagement requires respect for differences.

Dominant culture practices have been institutionalised widely, and with globalisation, such practices have been encoded in economic, legal, social and political institutions. The following chapters examine the framework of universalisation and the practice of disconnection which shape global institutions.

---

53 The Taliban excepted from this rule a limited number of female medical students in order to avoid women being examined by male doctors.

CHAPTER THREE

ONE GLOBAL ECONOMY OR DIVERSE DECOLONISED ECONOMIES?

Our current economic system is
incompatible with an ecological society
– Sonja A. Schmitz (2001: 49).

The Logic of Neoclassical Economics

The prevailing theory of neoclassical economics is based on an abstraction,[1] which is driving the profit margins of western powers through a competitive so-called "free market". Neoclassical economics focuses on efficiency, as opposed to sustainability, and does not concern itself with where goods come from or how they leave the economic system. One of its key flaws is that it takes no account of content or of context. "The human subject of neo-classical investigation is a timeless, classless, raceless and cultureless creature, although male, unless specified" (Amsden 1980: 13). For instance, if textiles coming from one country are cheaper than comparable fabric coming from another, that is an efficient source of textiles and to be preferred over others. No account is taken of how the workers in the textile industry are treated or paid, and no account is taken of pollution or any environmental costs, of what economists call "externalities". Even further away from consideration is whether cultural traditions around say, fabric dyeing, are sustained or destroyed (Mamidipudi 2000).

In neoclassical economic theory, individuals as consumers and producers are assumed to pursue their own self-interest. Such an assumption takes no account of altruism, or the sustenance of resources considered to be part of the community commons (water, forests, beaches, the air and public space). Nor does it take account of the growing number of women-headed households (see Report of the

---

1   For a detailed critique of abstraction, or "abstractification", as she calls it, see Ani (2000: 107); this is similar to Shiva's critique of scientific reductionism (1989: 22).

Secretary-General 1995: 55–61). Economic Darwinism tends to ignore the roles women play as carers, sustainers and altruistic givers within the economic system, which depends on their labour much as wealthy European colonisers depended on the free resources of the colonies (Mies, Bennholdt-Thomsen and von Werlof 1988). In neoclassical economics, the notion of collective good is concealed by the value of competition in the market. The assumption is that "everyone is equal" to compete for the scarce resources.

"Globalisation is our chance" proclaims this poster displayed at Frankfurt Airport, Germany. The poster promotes the idea that globalisation is simply another aspect of multiculturalism and presents a false picture of who benefits from globalisation.

Neoclassical economics constitutes a Global Politic: a single, universal, homogenising view of everything. It continues to take "man" as the norm in its view of "economic man" who is a self-interested, separated individual. This "economic man" believes in neoclassical economics, liberalism, privatisation and globalisation. The individualised economic man has also become corporatised, and is busily going around the world privatising knowledge, resources and a whole host of other things through the new range of multilateral agreements on intellectual property rights. The Global Politic is supported by the most powerful of groups in the world: those in the transnational sector.[2] It is on their behalf that globalisation operates.

Although neoclassical economics claims to be "value neutral" (Gowdy and O'Hara 1995: 6), by excluding altruism on the part of women, it automatically excludes the contribution of women to the survival of the next generation; by ignoring the sustainability of the commons, neoclassical economists fail to see indigenous and traditional subsistence economic regimes. Given the increasing exploitation of traditional knowledge by bioprospectors, such exclusions distort the calculation of inputs and outputs. Under neoclassical economics, the inputs of traditional knowledge are free (just as the land was free to the colonisers of Australia, the Americas, India, Africa, the island nations and elsewhere). The outputs – profit and the accumulation of capital – would indicate that this is a profitable industry in which to engage. By minimising costs and maximising profits, it is clear that exploitation of land, resources and knowledge can turn a tidy profit for shareholders. Critics such as Hazel Henderson, suggest that corporations should be accountable for the consequences[3] of their actions (1999: 46), and that there should be a shift from focusing on what is good for shareholders to what is good for stakeholders (2000: 75; see also Schumacher 1973: 29).

But making corporations accountable means making a shift away from neoclassical economic theory since it pays no attention to "how the

2   The transnational sector, in its private form, is represented by huge transnational companies; in its governmental form, it is represented by the military who tend to be trading with the transnational companies. For example, a company such as General Electric trades with numerous governments. General Electric is the largest company in the world (Sheehan 2000: 32).

3   For cogent discussions of consequences, see Diamond (1994); and on responsibility, see Kappeler (1995).

economic activity of producers and consumers affects the stocks of natural resources" (Gowdy and O'Hara 1995: 7). The place of the biophysical world is ignored. Given the impact of human activity on the planet – about 40 per cent of all biological resources are appropriated by humans – this has become a huge distortion of so-called growth figures. As Marilyn Waring (1988) argued, the UN System of National Accounts needs revising in order to take account of gross environmental destruction, which within neoclassical economic theory is calculated as national growth through the logging of forests, mining of land, prospecting of bio-materials, development of lands and fishing of the seas.

Economic activity can only take place within a biophysical setting, and it matters what kind of biophysical setting it is. It makes a difference whether it is desert or rainforest, whether it is rural or urban, whether it is geologically stable or unstable. The homogenising of significant differences in environments is typical of the homogenising impetus of neoclassical economics. It extends also into the value put on different kinds of work. As Prue Hyman points out:

> The neoclassical world is a tidy one, containing units of homogenous labour, perfect competition, clear distinctions between short/long term and what factors are fixed and variable in each, and with defined and measurable production functions and demand and supply curves. Equilibrium is stable (1999: 4).

Because it is fundamentally a system which models for order and control rather than for contextualised variation, in the real world it is systematically imperfect. Neoclassical economics has been characterised as based on the following assumptions:

- there is perfect information
- there is perfect competition
- prices are accurate and up-to-date
- there are no externalities[4]
- no monopoly (sole seller)

---

4   Joan Martinez-Alier argues that all attempts to calculate the money values of externalities have failed because their effects are uncertain and there might be irreversible effects which simply cannot be calculated, for example, the Human Genome Project, cloning, GMOs, and radioactive waste (2000: 149). The problem is one of sightlines. It is simply not possible to calculate value over tens of thousands of years, especially

- no monopsony (sole buyer)
- no individual transaction can move the market[5]
- all resources equally employed
- no transaction costs[6]
- no subsidies or distortions[7]
- no barriers to entering or exiting the market
- no regulation
- no taxation
- everything can be traded in uniform and standardised chunks
- unlimited capital is available to everyone[8]
- everyone is motivated by maximising personal utility (self-interest) (paraphrased from Hawken, Lovins and Lovins 2000: 263).

Add to this list the following assumptions:

- it is an objective science[9]
- consumption and greed are the primary motivations of people[10]
- the economy is self-regulating
- capitalism is the most efficient system of economic organisation (paraphrased from Sparr 1994: 13–15).

Most laypersons reading these lists will be startled by several of these items. Anyone with a basic understanding of economics will baulk at many

---

when government plans are for one term (of between three and seven years) not tens, hundreds or thousands of years. He goes on to say that: "Monetary indicators are believable only to captive audiences of professional economists" (2000: 150). Presumably this is so because economists have been trained to suspend belief.

5. With investments of ever-increasing size through superannuation fund managers, it is certainly possible that one transaction could affect price patterns globally.

6   One only has to have a bank account to know how ludicrous this is.

7   See Moore (1997: 50–63) for a humorous spin on subsidies paid to transnational corporations.

8   If the reader hasn't paused in shock at this list, this one will do it.

9   For an extensive discussion of feminism, economics and objectivity, see Nelson (1996a); see also O'Hara (1995: 538); McMahon (1997: 165). See also the critiques mentioned earlier by Ani (2000); Shiva (1989); Tuhiwai Smith (1999).

10 Julie Nelson (1996a: 134) posits an interesting straw "man" when she asks why it is that co-operative behaviour is so puzzling. She cites Joseph Harrington (1989): "the challenge to economists has been to explain cooperative behavior as consistent with individual rationality". The model, as she argues, does not notice that individuality and competition remain unquestioned. For a hint, see my discussion in Chapter One on Dominant Culture Stupidities.

of them. Hugh Stretton challenges these principles and assumptions from the outset: "Economic beliefs are working parts of economic systems. *The systems change as beliefs about them change,* and beliefs change as systems do" (2000: 10, my emphasis).

Economic systems, like other systems, contain feedback loops. Just as in quantum physics the observer and the observed influence one another, so economists' belief systems have heavily influenced economic theories. Western knowledge systems have largely developed from the seventeenth-century worldview of thinkers such as Descartes. Julie Nelson affirms that this is also the case with economics, the core of which "has remained firmly planted in the seventeenth century" (1996a: 131).

Neoclassical economics limits its feedback system to the mechanism of setting prices. The context in which the prices are set is not considered relevant. This would be fine if the world were more like a sterile laboratory, unaffected by atmosphere, poverty and oppression of all kinds. But the world is not such a place. Its atmosphere and temperature are dependent on levels of carbon dioxide, chloro-fluorocarbons, sulphides and ozone (among other things) in the atmosphere. The social atmosphere is dependent upon distinctions in wealth and poverty, access to power, histories of abuse or oppression, and a whole range of behaviours determined by the level of give and take in a society. Prices, in this setting, are only a part of the story. How they are arrived at, and at what cost to the biophysical and social atmosphere, is important to understand. Since biodiversity is the touchstone of the biophysical sphere, and local knowledge is the most important feature in its management, an economics which takes no notice of these elements can never adequately describe environmental systems or be accountable.

Universalising and homogenising in the economic sphere is as destructive as it is in the ecological sphere. In the ecological sphere it results in clear-felling, in monocultures, and in a mindset that can regard nuclear fallout with equanimity. In the economic sphere, it results in dehumanising people as "fodder" for production and profit. As stated earlier, slavery is one result; export processing zones are another, while the exploitation of "free" resources through bioprospecting is yet another.

This attitude to economics is exemplified by comments such as: Margaret Thatcher's claim "There is no alternative!" (cited in Wiseman

1997: 72) and the statement by George Bush senior prior to the 1992 Earth Summit in Rio de Janiero that "the American standard of living was not negotiable" (cited in Falk 1999: 178).

I argue that an alternative exists (Bennholdt-Thomsen, Faraclas *et al.* 2001) and that the American way of life is by no means sacred. Indeed there is plenty of evidence to suggest that it is wasteful and hugely inefficient (Martinez-Alier 2000: 158). There are problems with a system that devalues the welfare of people in exchange for increased profits (Pronk 2000: 49). Decontextualised globalisation based upon money exchange is producing victims (Pronk 2000: 47; Forrester 1999; Khor 1996). The universalising of markets, the creation of seemingly porous borders for money and goods, is creating what Chossudovsky (1998) calls a "globalisation of poverty" and what Martin and Schumann term "killer capitalism" (1997: 122).

Michel Chossudovsky's research shows a systematic misuse of coercive economic power by the transnational sector (this includes corporations and institutions such as the IMF and World Bank). Recent examples of the misuse of corporate economic power abound, from Enron and auditors Arthur Andersen in the USA to HIH and Ansett in Australia; in the governmental sphere, political and economic downward spiralling can be seen in 2002 in Argentina, in the 1990s in Russia, and over time in Japan. Chossudovsky comments:

> The restructuring of the world economy under the guidance of the Washington-based financial institutions increasingly denies individual developing countries the possibility of building a national economy: the inter-nationalisation of macro-economic policy transforms countries into open economic territories and national economies into "reserves" of cheap labour and natural resources (1998: 37).

"Open economic territories" are instances of homogenisation in practice in an economic setting. Context is ignored, and the culture is treated as if it were moving in the direction of acceptance of "universal" (western) values.

Many of the structural adjustment programs (SAPs) being foisted on the Third World and Eastern Europe[11] have also been implemented in

---

11 There are numerous critical discussions of the impact of SAPs and IMF-sponsored plans; among those that focus on women are Sparr (1994); Dalla Costa and Dalla Costa

Australia and New Zealand.[12] In Australia this policy has been accompanied by deregulation of the banks; former federal minister Peter Reith's attempts at deunionising the workforce;[13] implementation of a Goods and Services Tax;[14] reduction of tariffs; sell-off of family farms to the transnational sector, particularly to foreign investors; the increasingly widespread user-pays principle for education, health and social services of all kinds (crèches, nursing homes); privatisation of prisons and of aged-care, and unemployment services; deinstitution-alisation in the area of mental health; and an increasing orientation toward export.[15]

Macro-economic reforms in developing countries which face significant external debt have resulted in a blurring of sovereign boundaries. In a move reminiscent of post-modern blurring of bodily boundaries, the IMF forces poor nations to surrender economic sovereignty.

Globalisation and its attendant ideologies of homogenisation, increased shareholder profit, free flow of capital, increased inputs and export orientation are having an impact on women in vastly different settings. The effect on women farmers has been discussed by Vandana Shiva (1989; 1991, looking at India), Claire Robertson (1997, looking at Kenya), and Flora Nwapa who derides food grown for the "All Mighty foreign exchange" (1986), rather than for nutrition. As these and other

---

(1995); Kelsey (1995); Sassen (1998); Matsui (1999); Wichterich (2000); Mantilla (2000); see also Teeple (1995); Mander and Goldsmith (1996); Correa (2000).

12   Indeed, New Zealand began the process of deregulation earlier than many other countries and has embedded it more fully into its economic system than have other OECD countries of comparable size. Jane Kelsey (1995) argues that there have been significant economic, social, democratic and cultural deficits.

13   Peter Reith, the Liberal (conservative) government's Minister for Industrial Relations, in 1998 threatened the power of the Maritime Union of Australia by arresting strikers in the middle of the night and using guard dogs against them. The union and the government sued and counter sued in increasingly higher courts. The courts eventually upheld the rights of the unions. The passing of the *Workplace Relations Act* 1996 was the catalyst for the ensuing battle between the union and Patrick Stevedores. For a full discussion, see Trinca and Davies (2000).

14   The Goods and Services Tax (GST) of 10 per cent came into force in Australia on 1 July 2000.

15   The above reforms have bipartisan support, many of them having been first implemented (as in New Zealand) by Labor governments. For a discussion of the impact of economic rationalism on women in the state of Victoria under Liberal leader Jeff Kennett, see Ford (2001).

writers demonstrate, women's knowledge of the environment is either overlooked or appropriated by bioprospectors, once again ensuring that if the resources are sold back to the community from whence they came, it will be at a profit. Women workers in export processing zones have also been the subject of considerable research.[16] Just like the environment, women are used up, turned over at a high rate under conditions which threaten their future well-being.

Women's informal "cottage industries" are industrialised and passed into men's hands, thereby depriving women of income, as happened in Sri Lanka in 1977 when the economy was liberalised (Jayaweera 1994: 104–106; Mantilla 2000: 9–10). As Christa Wichterich points out in relation to women as export labour:

> The export of women is by now a well-calculated item of economic planning, an indispensable raw material plundered all the more ruthlessly, the heavier the external debt burden grows (2000: 59).

In the atopic zone of cyberspace women are commodified once again. In the trade in women through prostitution and trafficking it is women's bodies which are the raw material, to be picked up by mobile prospectors and discarded after the use-by date has passed (see Hughes 1999; Sassen 1998).

The commodification of women – as exported labour, as sexual product – has become a new way of participating within the dominant ideology of free markets, free-flowing capital, and global exploitation. Although it is clear that both women and men are affected by the movements of global capital, it is my contention that the impact on women is even greater. It links to the ways in which women have traditionally worked, as well as to the new ways in which women's work practices have been appropriated, dislocated and commodified. Flexibility is appropriated in the Mexican *maquiladoras*; women's knowledge is appropriated for pharmaceutical developments. Women's farming practices and bodily experiences are dislocated. And in each case the application of capital creates a new commodity.

---

16 See Manuh (1994); Çagatay and Berik (1994); Jayaweera (1994); Floro (1994); Elabor-Idemudia (1994).

Globalisation can be compared to a military approach to economic, social and cultural structures. The global voice is a single voice; it does not allow for responsiveness or disagreement; it is also loud. It has been described as a "monotonous American 'screech' all over the world" (Martin and Schumann 1997: 17). Like the scorched-earth policy of military commanders, it pays no attention to context and creates a disengagement from the self, from the community and the local environment, and from the culture. Everything everywhere is the same: identity and sovereignty – hard-won only recently by most of the powerless groups – are pushed aside in the interest of shareholder profit, productivity and efficiency. Like post-modernism, globalisation moves in the direction of something usually attached to the word "free" (free markets, free flow of information and capital) but which is really an individualised "free" only for the well-off, elite and powerful, and results in increased marginalisation and poverty for the poor and powerless. The global market represents a new level of what Schumacher called "the institutionalisation of individualism and non-responsibility" (1973: 29). Thatcher and Reagan presented it as the "freedom struggle on behalf of capital" (Martin and Schumann 1997: 109). Its goal is to turn the entire world into one huge free-trade area, an export processing zone in which the poor work for appalling wages in appalling conditions and the transnationals take all they can. As futurist Robert Theobald comments: "The worship of free markets is ... the most extraordinary triumph of theory over reality in human history" (1996: 37).

Nike has pursued a policy of absolute advantage in its production of footwear. Other companies have followed suit in order to increase profits, increase efficiency, and uncover "huge productivity reserves" (Martin and Schumann 1997: 117). The result for members of the diversity matrix and the governments of the poorest countries is joblessness, reduction in growth, and budget deficits. In the period from 1973 to 1991, Nike recorded an overall growth rate of nearly 150,000 per cent; in other words, they multiplied their initial turnover nearly 1500 times in the 18 years to 1991.[17] This profit came about through several successive shifts in

---

17 These figures have been calculated on the basis of material cited in Korzeniewicz (1993) reprinted in Lechner and Boli (2000). Beginning with a turnover of $US2 million in 1973, by 1991 Nike had a turnover of $US3 billion. When I checked these calculations with a mathematician friend, she commented that it was so obscene that it made one doubt one's figures.

company policy. In 1980, Nike relocated factories "to the periphery (particularly China, Indonesia and Thailand)", which resulted in large cuts in production costs, but was accompanied by some sacrifices in quality and production flexibility (Korzeniewicz 2000: 164, 165). By the late 1980s, Nike had shifted its focus from production to "design, distribution, marketing and advertising" (Korzeniewicz 2000: 158), and it was this shift which has created the global company with its well-recognised logo.

One of the great problems of a narrow view of economics is that it tells one nothing about the relationships between the different factors of the equation, of the impact of, say, Nike's move to China, or more recently to Vietnam and Cambodia, on the social institutions and conditions of the countries within which the company bases its operations.[18] Indeed, neo-classical economists would consider social institutions and conditions outside the equation altogether. Nor does it give us any sense of outcomes and consequences of decisions made simply on the basis of figures. There are some interesting theoretical crossovers here between different ways of making moral, ethical or legal judgements, and different ways of making economic judgements.

The former, when subjected to a homogenising influence, will come up with a one-size-fits-all arrangement. A relevant example is the debate which occurred in Australia around mandatory sentencing laws in two states, or the US three-strikes legislation. In these instances the law allows no leniency or consideration on the basis of outside context and circumstances. The consequences are all the same. The homogenising influence in mandatory sentencing, or mandatory detention, in the case of asylum seekers, is that everyone is treated the same. This may sound fair and equal, but when unequal outcomes and context are ignored in such situations, injustice prevails.

A feminist dimension of the debates about perception of the "other" is exemplified in the work of Carol Gilligan (1982) and her co-researchers, in what they call the difference between the "generalized" (universalised, homogenised) other and the "concrete" (specific, contextualised) other. I mention feminist research in this area because the discussion of "generalised" and "concrete" knowledge is a continuing theme of the book and

18   See Klein (2000: 328–329); see also the broadcast of *The Cutting Edge*, on 6 March 2001, in which SBS TV exposed the use of child labour in the June Textiles factory in Phnom Penn.

arises in my later discussion of Sabine O'Hara's characterisation of ecological economics and diversity debates (1995a; 1995b; 1996; 1997). Susanne Kappeler raises similar questions to Gilligan by asking "Is the political psychological?" (1995: 67), and goes on to discuss the "legitimation of irresponsibility" (1995: 83). Universalising and generalising the "other" leads to institutionalised irresponsibility. Indeed, irresponsibility becomes systemic. Relationships, whether they be social or intimate or economic, and whether they be personal or on a national scale, replicate themselves in a further cycle of relationships. The reproduction of relationships based on a generalised other means that both sides of the relationship are connecting on a monodimensional basis, one which tends toward flattening and diminishment. The contextualised, concrete other, by contrast, enables an expansion of knowledge and understanding, and takes account of local circumstances, conditions and expertise.

Global irresponsibility, writes Hazel Henderson, has become systematised into our global economy which

> functions like a global behavioural sink, rewarding corporate and government irresponsibility, levelling rainforests, and homogenizing the world's precious cultural diversity just as it plunders the planet's biodiversity (2000: 72).

Further, the continuing process of universalising of economic strategies for globalised markets threatens precisely the people, cultures and knowledge that are most vulnerable to exploitation on a global scale. When a country enters the global market, cultural diversity tends to be reduced along with biological diversity. Biological homogenisation occurs when people are no longer able to live in the local environment, as in the case of deforestation or agriculturalisation of indigenous living areas. Under these circumstances, systems of reciprocity between people, the land and the environment break down as traditional systems fragment. An example of this is the reduction in mosaic burning patterns in Australia, traditionally carried out by Aboriginal peoples, which has had a severe impact on the environment, particularly in the drier regions of the continent. Mosaic burning has been reintroduced in National Parks such as Kakadu that are now under the management of Aboriginal communities.[19] This

---

19 For an extensive discussion of Aboriginal fire regimes from an indigenous perspective, see Langton (1998: 40–55).

fracturing is intensified as members of the group become involved in the cash economy of the dominant culture (McNeely 1997: 184).

The Multilateral Agreement on Investment (MAI), although not ratified in October 1998 as was planned, continues to pose a threat to managing diversity. Mobile capital is premissed on disconnection, and the incoming investor believes he bears no responsibility for returning the fruits of his[20] investments to the community. Social cohesion collapses, and as soon as profits slump, the investor moves on to another place which offers greater absolute advantage. Nor does the investor worry about environmental damage.[21] He is likely to be living on the other side of the world in a security-patrolled walled community of his own. Social cohesiveness is not a priority: since when it fails, he is not there. When riots erupted in Indonesia, the wealthy flew out to Hong Kong, Singapore and Sydney.

Nations used to take pride in their manufactured goods, labelling them with their origin. Mercedes-Benz has symbolically shifted attention away from Germany by replacing the "Made in Germany" tag with "Made by Mercedes-Benz". Even this is misleading, since much of Mercedes-Benz's manufacturing is subcontracted to other automobile companies such as Volkswagen. Gap manufactures clothing in Saipan, an island near China that is wholly owned by the USA. Gap can label the products made in Saipan as "Made in the USA", although the employees, before they leave China to work in Saipan, sign "shadow contracts" in which they waive basic human rights that citizens of the USA take for granted.[22]

In language that evokes ecological crisis, Stephen Roach, a former economic rationalist, recanted: "The new US economy was based on something like 'slash-and-burn restructuring strategies', which destroy for short-term gain the soil on which people depended for a living" (quoted in Martin and Schumann 1997: 123). Just as land cannot be squeezed for more productivity forever, so workers too will simply collapse and cease to produce if they are pushed too far.[23]

---

20 I use the masculine pronoun here intentionally as the vast majority of mobile capital for these purposes comes from sources owned by men, or controlled by men. This does not exclude the possibility of elite and wealthy women's money being invested in such companies, but the decision-making power remains in men's hands.

21 For a thorough critique of the MAI, see Clarke and Barlow (1997); Clarke (1996). See also the extensive discussion in Chapter Seven.

22 Broadcast on *The Cutting Edge*, 6 March 2001, SBS TV.

23 Although, as Kevin Bales (2000) argues, in the global economy, people have become

Although the issues around global environmental degradation cannot be attributed to any one corporation, they are attributable to a particular approach or ideology. Growth economics as criticised by Meadows *et al.* (1972, 1992) combines with a philosophy which seeks to decontextualise the real world to contribute daily to environmental problems. Neoclassical economics enshrines irresponsibility and disconnection in its practices. A move away from neoclassical economics as the dominant system of economics would achieve extraordinary changes in the social fabric, and in the shape of international trade and politics. Such a shift would entail considerable changes to global structures and institutions, as well as in the ways in which power is used and misused; it would entail the abandonment of ideologies of universalism, domination, progress and objectification.

How Women Are (ac)Counted

One of the key tools of economists is figures. These figures are used to decide whether an economy is functioning in ways which would benefit investors. Numerous critics have identified shortcomings of the figures, including the over-reliance on GNP and GDP, and the use of words such as "uneconomic" (Schumacher 1973: 27) to justify cutting programs which contribute socially, environmentally or culturally, but do not turn a financial profit. Marilyn Waring (1988), Prue Hyman (1994) and Susan Donath (2000) identify ways in which "the other economy" operates around women's and children's lives, but their work is neither acknowledged nor accounted by number-crunching institutions. Ecological economists such as Sabine O'Hara (1995: 33b) have criticised the market-centred approach to analysing biodiversity and socio-diversity, and others such as Vandana Shiva have questioned the language: "'normalcy' is determined by the demands of the market; the non-marketable components of the natural ecosystem are seen as 'abnormal'" (1993a: 51).

In spite of these criticisms of the nature and usefulness (or otherwise) of figures, to ignore them altogether would be like trying to create social change without acknowledging the structures of power which not only influence, but often determine, social, political and economic institutions.

---

disposable and slavery is alive and well; see also Chang (2000). See Chapter Six for a further discussion of production and work.

Figures used in economics come from a range of sources, and although they vary according to what they are measuring and when it was measured, they are nevertheless instructive in providing a framework for what follows. Figures,[24] for all their shortcomings, provide a sense of how women are situated in the global economy and what issues are important when thinking about the ways in which economics has an impact on women's lives.

"Women constitute the single biggest group of the poor. They are among the poorest of the poor" (Seager 1997: 121). This is borne out by Michael Watts: "Of the 1.3 billion people in poverty, 70 per cent are women" (2000: 137; UNIFEM 2001).[25] And the Report of the UN Secretary-General indicates that poverty in developing countries consistently increased between 1985 and 1993 (Report of the Secretary-General 1995: 48). Meanwhile, in the developed countries of the Organisation for Economic Cooperation and Development (OECD), although women's labour force participation rate rose from about 48 per cent in 1973 to about 62 per cent in 1991, men's labour force participation rate in that period fell by only about 5 per cent, leaving women with a participation rate around 20 per cent lower than men's (Report of the Secretary-General 1995: 26). In Australia (Milburn 2001: 3), the USA, Japan, the UK and Sweden men are recorded as having higher rates of unemployment (Report of the Secretary-General 1995: 27). This may partly be due to women not registering as unemployed, as their time is taken up with unpaid domestic, community or caring work. A further factor noted by numerous commentators is "the feminization of poverty … in the context of developed market economies" (Report of the Secretary-General 1995: 53). In spite of these trends, globalisation enthusiasts can be heard to argue that women are the main group profiting from globalisation (Plant 1997: 41). After all, as Christa Wichterich writes: "Cheap, docile and flexible, they have a competitive advantage over men

24 Many national and international figures do not include women as a separate category, or women are sometimes subsumed into the category "family", so that measures of wealth or income cannot be ascertained.

25 These figures are very high and based on categories which are used by the counting institutions. It is likely that the categories themselves could contribute to the shocking gap between women's and men's poverty because women might not be included as having income (their income might be subsumed under the names of male heads of households, or be held in the names of fathers, uncles, brothers, husbands – even sons).

in meeting the new requirements of the labour market" (2000: ix).[26]

Women's major "advantage" is cheapness of labour (Cravey 1998; Mitter 1986; Matsui 1999), an advantage which they share with children and with poverty-stricken men in developing countries (Bales 2000; Chossudovsky 1998), with refugees or illegal migrants within the developed world (Bales 2000: 1–3; Wiseman 1998: 61), and with indigenous peoples throughout the world (LaDuke 1999; Wiseman 1998: 61).

What do the figures tell us about women's income in the global marketplace?

Between 1965 and 1988, the number of rural women living below the poverty line increased by 47 per cent; by November 2001, the figure was reported to be 50 per cent (UNIFEM 2001). The corresponding figure for men was less than 30 per cent (UNDP 1996 cited in Watts 2000: 137).

Between 1960 and 1991, the share of global income of the richest 20 per cent rose from 70 per cent to 85 per cent (UNDP 1996 cited in Watts 2000: 137).[27] Since the richest group is composed mainly of male elites, including individuals whose assets have become disguised as corporations, or institutions run mainly for and by men (such as the military, prostitution, drug and criminal rings), the richest 20 per cent have moved into a group which could be described as having excessive disposable income for luxury and mobility (Hynes 1999a: 46 ff).

The share of global income for the poorest quintile fell from 2.3 per cent of global income to a mere 1.4 per cent. Between states, the ratio "of the shares of the richest to the poorest increased from 30:1 to 61:1" (UNDP 1996 cited in Watts 2000: 137). The poorest of the poor are women, children, refugees (mostly women), landless (mostly women) and indigenous peoples (where again women are less likely to be a part of the cash economy). However, women do have a larger share of income than wealth, since women do manage to earn income for themselves and their

---

26 In an interesting, though contestable, variation on this argument, Barbara Ehrenreich (2001: 15) speculates that the rise of the fundamentalist Taliban in Afghanistan may be due to the negative impact (displacement and unemployment) of globalisation on men, and the perceived positive impact it has for women, offering women new opportunities in export-oriented manufacturing.

27 Among those who benefit are women and children of the families of rich men. Some will be able to turn this to direct benefit to themselves; among them, however, will be some whose economic independence is decreased by this relationship, i.e. those held hostage by the wealth of male relatives.

dependants. The poor can be described as a group with no surplus income, and what income is earned is spent on survival (Hynes 1999a: 46 ff).[28]

The figures on wealth (rather than income) are even more disturbing. In 1960, the level of wealth of the wealthiest 20 per cent was thirty times greater than that of the poorest 20 per cent: a ratio of 30:1. In the forty years since then, there has been a huge decline: the ratio is now somewhere between 80:1 and 100:1 (Pronk 2000: 42; McMichael 2001). Although women are more able to earn income at the beginning of the twenty-first century, their access to wealth has decreased. The expansion of transnational companies, and the concentration of wealth which has arisen from globalisation, will combine to increase these discrepancies.

The other group that is massively over-represented among the poor is indigenous peoples. In almost every nation they are the poorest ethnic groups. There are approximately 305 million indigenous peoples in the world, with around 155 million living in Asia (*The Indigenous World, 1998–99* 1999: 4–5). Indigenous peoples tend to be homogenised by the dominant cultures and are assumed to live only in some "far-away" places, therefore not having an impact on the dominant culture. There are more than a million indigenous peoples living in Europe, and more than fourteen million living in North and Central America. In South America there are nearly twenty million, and in Africa close to fifteen million. The Pacific island nations, including Australia and New Zealand, comprise more than two million indigenous peoples. These figures give little sense of the diversity of cultures throughout the world's regions, but 305 million people is not a number that can be simply ignored as irrelevant; the similar number of US citizens would not wish to be ignored.

The globalisation of monetary systems, allowing for the free flow of capital, gives an even starker picture of the movement of wealth. Henderson (2000: 64) estimates that $US1.3 trillion changes hands daily in the global market, while Anderson, Cavanagh and Lee go even further and estimate that $1.5 trillion a day is traded (2000: 33). On Tuesday, 4 April 2000, in the volatile technology stocks the mobility of money was particularly evident. "On that day the NASDAQ fell by 574 points, but it

---

28 Hynes' analysis of the distinction between men's use of income for luxury goods (among them women), and women's use of income for survival provides important insights into why context, and the use of the right categories, is important in economic analysis; see Chapter Six for a longer discussion.

also rose again by 500 points" (Cook 2000: 12 April). This day broke all the usual rules of stock trading because there was a sufficient number of investors (ironically called "wild riders") who continued to invest in internet stocks even when stocks were at rock bottom.

Mobility of money and of immaterial goods (copyright, patents, the so-called "knowledge economy") is reflected in the shift in volume of world trade, which is expanding roughly twice as fast as it was at the beginning of the 1990s. Pronk points out one of the absurdities of the trade in immaterial goods, which is that the "value of world trade has expanded faster than world production for the seventh year in a row" (2000: 42). This is only possible in a system which puts more value on the immaterial than the material. Unfortunately for women, the material remains an important part of their daily lives. The world's poorest 20 per cent are even more marginally involved in global exchange and trade, having "0.2 per cent of global credit, and participating in only 0.9 per cent of global trade" (UNDP 1993: 27 cited in Hartmann 1994: 18).

Given that the poor (and hence women) are massively left out of global trading, it is not surprising to hear women asking of free trade, "what's in it for us"? (Wichterich 2000; Hartmann 1994; Bennholdt-Thomsen and Mies 1999).

Indeed, we need to reflect on what those who have not been heard or seen already know about the current system. Those at the bottom – the poor, the marginalised, the Third World, the dispossessed – know their position *and*, importantly, they also know the position of those at the centre. Dominant Culture Stupidities are to the advantage of the marginalised, and the validity of their analysis not only needs to be respected, but also to be taken as central to all analyses of the global situation. If some of the pond is dying, the entire pond is affected.

Fantu Cheru writes that "poor people's knowledge about their own reality ... counts most" (2000: 130). But those who have access to resources, such as the designers of development programs, only rarely conceptualise "the lived experiences of poor women" (Beneria and Bisnath 2000: 174).

The project of challenging mainstream economics has come from a range of locations. The most thoroughgoing critiques are by members of the diversity matrix. Among them are feminists, theorists from the "developing world", ecological economists, Marxists and some of the young people who have been so visible at demonstrations in Seattle, Washington, Okinawa, Melbourne, Prague and who continue to protest (Klein 2000; Couch 2001). Their critiques and resistances come from an awareness of an increasing dislocation. Globalisation, with its trend toward homogenisation, is more readily noticed by those threatened with economic and cultural swamping. Saskia Sassen draws attention to this feature of globalisation when she points out that within the developed countries, those most affected by globalisation as workers are the immigrant sectors who "are not recognized as part of that global information economy" (1998: 87). They are the people whose work still relies on their human bodies (as labourers and pieceworkers), or who are involved in maintaining family and community connections, doing work such as housework and childcare which "can't be ... speeded up" (Else 1996: 26).

Economic Homogeneity and Globalisation

extreme competition diminishes the degree of diversity
in a society and contributes to social exclusion
— Louis Emmerij (2000: 57).

Globalisation is presented with a positive spin in many fora. It is seen as a system of interdependence among nations and economies, an interdependence which is portrayed as "good for everyone". Malcolm Waters defines globalisation as a "social process in which the constraints of geography on social and cultural arrangements recede" (1995: 3). This is an interesting definition, but Waters does not highlight the aspect of his definition which I regard as central to any critique of globalisation. And that is the process of disconnection, in particular, disconnection from place. The "constraints of geography" are the constraints of real life on a finite planet. As those constraints have receded, within the culture of the transnational sector, there is an overwhelming ideology that there are no constraints on anything, including what Shiva calls the "creation boundary" (1996b).

John Wiseman, citing Anthony Giddens, Tony McGrew and David Harvey, says of globalisation that it "is the best word we currently have for describing the many ways in which space and time have been compressed by technology, information flows, trade and power so that distant actions have local effects" (1998: 14). Or, as John Tomlinson describes it, globalisation is "complex connectivity" (1999:1). Keith Suter (2000) takes a more sympathetic view of globalisation which he divides into three types:[29]

- *Economic globalisation* characterised by transnational capitalism, global consumerism and mobility. The other side includes export-orientation, dispossession and exploitation of the poorest people globally.

- *Public order globalisation* characterised by co-operation between governments to combat common problems, for example international meetings on greenhouse-gas emissions, held in Kyoto (1999) and The Hague (2000), or the forthcoming Earth Summit to be held in 2002 (Dodds 2000).

- *Popular globalisation* of the sort which has galvanised political action internationally on issues such as the MAI or protests against the WTO and related institutions (Clarke and Barlow 1997).

The past years have seen an increasing number of voices raised against the *concept* of globalisation. The hype surrounding globalisation has not borne fruit; indeed, many of its promises have turned to failures on a massive scale. The earliest voices against globalisation came from the so-called Third World, but these days the voices raised come from both the rich and the poor nations, from women and from men, from environmentalists and economists, from farmers and futurists.

If there are positive aspects of globalisation, they stem primarily from the subversions of it. An example of this is the use of the internet to defeat the MAI proposal. The MAI draft document was obtained by researchers who in 1997 uploaded it on to a website. Activists from all around the world were able to read what the OECD and the WTO had been planning. Connections between interested individuals and organisations made it possible to politicise and publicise the text of the MAI. By the time ratification of the proposed treaty approached its deadline (21 October 1998), too many people in too many countries were aware of its existence and protested its impact on a whole range of domestic policies and programs. Thus it was defeated.

---

29 I touch on each of these three types of globalisation, but it is the disparities in access to resources and power between the transnational sector and the diversity matrix under the heading of economic globalisation that are my major concern.

Interdependence could become a strength, but only if that inter-dependence is carried out with respect and sensitivity to other peoples' knowledges and positions.[30] The global sweep of US culture through the agency of McDonald's, Coca-Cola and Microsoft is not a good place to start; indeed, these commercial monocultures will have to be rolled back. The unregulated free-market approach will not work any better than the unregulated dog-eat-dog approach. There are too many victims.

In Berlin in 1992, as the lifestyle of western Europe exploded into the culture of eastern Europe, cigarette companies took advantage of this new business opportunity. As we saw in Chapter Two, the new cigarette brand, West, was promoted with an ambiguous image of, on the one hand, decadence, on the other of international jet-setting youth culture. This, the beginning of globalisation in eastern Europe, is the beginning of what Fukuyama imagined would become a universal model, a "fundamental process at work that dictates a common evolutionary pattern for *all* human societies – in short, something like a Universal History of man-kind [*sic*] in the direction of liberal democracy" (1992: 48).

Globalisation affects everyone. Almost no one in the early years of the twenty-first century is unaffected by markets. But some groups – women, the rural poor and indigenous peoples – have more recently become dependent on markets and so still have an understanding of how life could be lived without market dependence.

Rajaee suggests, rather hopefully, that globalisation can provide us with the challenge of imagination, of rethinking priorities (2000: 130). But this is so only if the over-employed do not work themselves to death, kill the environment, and allow many millions of people to starve for want of basic human needs. Further, change requires a total challenge to the framework along the lines of Cheru's decolonising of "the imagination" (2000: 123). In addition, what we need now is a new philosophy which redefines "the economic responsibility of the state and the social responsibility of the business community" (Emmerij 2000: 58), one which takes seriously "the concept of accountability" (Plahe and van de Gaage

---

30 Hernando De Soto puts forward this view in his analysis of why the poor never benefit from capitalism. As he suggests, the powerful will need to see the world from the perspective of the powerless (2001: 201–204). My worry about De Soto's project is that it could become just another way of co-opting the poor and other members of the diversity matrix.

"Gobbleisation" represents a contrary view. This image and the one on page 111, represent the different perspectives of the transnational sector and the diversity matrix.

2000: 240) on the part of transnational corporations. For without such a new philosophy, those who hold power will continue to do so, since the one-size-fits-all politics leaves out the needs of the smaller nations and cultures and anyone marginalised by powerlessness.

In its current form, globalisation falls into what John Stuart Mill called "the tyranny of the majority", where "majority" is read as access to wealth, resources and power rather than as the number of people. Martin and Schumann coin the term "the 20:80" society to describe (1997: 1) the society in which 20 per cent of the world's population owns, exploits, and has access to 80 per cent of the world's wealth, resources and power. Plahe and van de Gaage in their preparatory report for the Earth Summit in 2002 on transnationals claim that transnational companies "control two-thirds of global trade and investments" (2000: 229).[31] As Wiseman writes, globalisation thus has

---

31   These figures are based on the UN *1999 World Investment Report*, United Nations Publications.

deeply disturbing consequences in relation to capital formation and productive investment, the distribution of wealth, work, income and power, the integrity of local cultures, and the sovereignty of national democratic decision-making processes (1997: 73).

The issue of national sovereignty[32] is a critical one, and at odds with the focus on export-orientation which occurs at the expense of domestic markets. The orientation toward export has a number of results; it makes it possible for:

• people to work and produce cash crops – and still starve
• labour to be exported, either in the conventional industrialised sense, or in the sense in which women's bodies are sexualised and exported
• people, out of sight and out of mind, to be exploited for the benefit of people in wealthy nations
• the IMF to impose unrealistic, ineffective and cruel structural adjustment programs on poor people in poor nations
• local cultures, traditions and knowledge to be appropriated and swamped by rampant American culture.

Export is presented as a panacea for economies in which budget deficits are greater than surpluses. Export, it is claimed, will help service the national debt and will contribute to the country's balance of payments. While all of this might work in the framework of decontextualised neoclassical economic calculation, no consideration is given to the inputs required to create an export-based economy, nor of the sacrifices expected of the domestic economy in order to sustain exports.

The dominating global ideology is one in which the "rights" of capital take precedence over the "rights" of citizens and the nation states which represent the citizens' needs. As Colette Guillamin argues, the powerful do not ask for rights; they simply take them without "anyone's authorization" (1995: 251). There is an interesting parallel here, on an international scale, with industrial relations. In the 1990s, Australia moved toward a system of Enterprise Bargaining, which was put in place in spite

---

32 Sovereignty is to globalisation as identity is to postmodernism. Globalisation does not respect sovereignty, and tends toward the "transgression" of borders and boundaries in much the same way as post-modernism treats identity. See also Peterson (1996).

of considerable opposition from some unionists.[33] In this instance the "rights" of employers (read capital) take precedence over the "rights" of workers and the unions which represent their needs. When rights language is used on behalf of the powerful, it tends to lead toward unjust behaviours and outcomes. Enterprise Bargaining ignores the differences in power between employers and workers. In the international arena similar forces are at work.

The Washington Consensus,[34] a group of powerful CEOs, government bureaucrats, media and academics, has been pushing the ideology of free-market economies since the 1970s (Clarke and Barlow 1997: 14–15; Chossudovsky 1998: 178–180). A philosophy which champions the rights of powerful corporations (see Appendix, Table 1). The point it has reached is the globalisation of this ideology. The monocultures of colonial cropping have moved into the monoculture of political ideology. The New World Order. One Nation. Sameness. Homogenised. Universal. Context ignorant. Conformity. According to Clarke and Barlow, this represents "A single world view. It is, quite simply, the globalization of an ideology, a world economic order designed by and for capital exporters" (1997: 15).

The debt which has accumulated in the Third World over the past couple of decades is directly attributable to the enforced changes made by nations to their economic systems.[35] Countries all over the world shifted their focus from sustenance to cash-cropping and satisfying the export market. This allowed the entry of capital into agriculture, turning it into agribusiness. The investment of foreigners and transnationals in the economy meant that local businesses had little chance to compete.[36] South-East Asia, which initially managed to dodge some of the worst

---

33 Enterprise bargaining is having a detrimental effect on women, and the gap between women's and men's wages, which narrowed during the 1980s, is widening again. For an early critique, see Scutt (1992); also Edwards and Magarey (1995).

34 The Washington Consensus was "Originally created by David Rockefeller, chairman of Chase Manhattan Bank, and Zbigniew Brzezinski, who would become national security adviser to U.S. President Jimmy Carter, [and] grew to include 325 top leaders, CEOs, government bureaucrats and members of the media" (Clarke and Barlow 1997: 14).

35 For examples of how this has worked, see Chossudovsky (1998); Matsui (1999); Sparr (1994); Dalla Costa and Dalla Costa (1995); Vickers (1991).

36 For a view on what the locally based businesses and organisations think about food security, see South Asian Workshop on Food Security (1996). See also Chapter Seven.

aspects of global restructuring, is now in the throes of adapting to the demands of the global economy (Brain 1999: 171–212).

The push from the IMF and the World Bank, up to the time of the Asian economic crisis in 1997, was that other economies in the so-called Third World would be able to emulate, and possibly even outpace, the western growth patterns by opening their domestic markets and moving toward production for export. The dropping of tariffs by Third World economies allows for greater "penetration"[37] of goods from North America and western Europe. Chossudovsky argues that the redirection of self-sustaining agriculture to cash crops and export-oriented crops – not food crops but coffee, cotton and cattle-feed – creates a vacuum in the domestic market which is filled by imports of commodities and consumer goods from the USA, the European Union (EU) countries and Japan (1998: 157). The creation of new export markets for wealthy nations is an advantage to the developed nations. But it is not promoted to the developing nations in this way; rather, they are informed that the developments will offset the balance-of-payments crisis for their country. This process might work, if only one developing country were to engage in this process at any one time. However, with the volume of exports increasing across a whole range of countries, the value of those exports diminishes. Third World economies have the most commodities to sell, and when a host of structurally adjusted countries simultaneously move toward exporting their produce rather than selling it to the domestic economy, there is an over-supply, and prices fall.

The goods imported by the elites of Third World nations are frequently non-essential goods such as Coca-Cola, McDonald's, branded fashion items, and pharmaceutical products which are often too old or dangerous to sell in the home markets of the developed nations. In return, the Third World nations export food and raw materials to the European and North American markets, thereby reducing the amount of arable land available for sustainable and essential food products for their own people.

Labour restructuring is also a feature of export orientation. The restructuring can be the result of bringing in expensive new machinery; or replacing some workers with others; or moving production centres from

---

37 I dislike the term "market penetration", but use it intentionally here because of its connotations of violation and violence.

place to place according to profit margins, a kind of serial displacement. The factory systems that used to operate in industrialised centres were predominantly based in large cities and relied on primarily male labour, protected to some extent by old-fashioned active trade unions. The new export processing zones tend to be located outside metropolitan centres. One result is that they are therefore outside support services and metropolitan infrastructures; some are located on borders – either literally or near ports. Wherever they are located they rely on a labour force which is "female, very young, and with little or no work experience" (Cravey 1998: 6).

A further "adjustment" to the practices of the owners of capital is that in export zones, including the Mexican *maquiladoras*, environmental regulations are relaxed; this results in a much higher turnover of the workforce due to unhealthy work practices and high rates of injury. These are the adaptable and flexible women, who have "less disposable income, spending more on transportation and food than non-*maquiladora* households" (Cravey 1998: 14). Their homes are often temporary; the extreme of this is represented by homes made of cardboard boxes to which the *maquiladora* workers are reduced (*Foreign Correspondent* 1998). The level of poverty experienced by those *with* jobs is not only heartbreaking; it breaks all the promises of a better life propounded by the purveyors of globalisation.

Free-trade zones and export processing zones are likely to increase in number under the multilateral WTO rules. These zones are specially designated economic areas where transnational companies base their production, unfettered by regulations on work practices, taxation or environmental controls. The enclaves are open only to the people who work there, guarded by security services and in many cases surrounded by high fences. They are the work version of the walled communities.[38] Safe, sterile, and all the same. But they are not necessarily safe for workers, because health and safety provisions are not abided by. Child labour is common, and high levels of toxic waste are found. The *maquiladoras* of

---

38 This is a relatively recent phenomenon in contemporary cities. They exist in Los Angeles and Houston. I am reminded of an Eric Clapton song I heard in the 1970s about the effects of the plague on a seventeenth-century city. Fear, however, kept the walled inhabitants still starving inside their walls well after the plague had vanished from among the poorest who lived outside its walls. For a view on cities which use diversity as an organisational principle, see Rogers (1997: 25–63).

Mexico and Central America, for example, are very profitable enterprises, but the living conditions of workers, who are bussed in daily, are appalling.[39] The corporations pay no taxes[40] or very low taxes, and contribute only a small percentage of what – given their resources – they should be returning to the local community. Indeed, it is easily argued that they are damaging these communities.

Such conditions prevail in every country where export processing zones draw in foreign capital. The zones displace large numbers of people, in some instances alienating large tracts of land. In the Philippines, for instance, 40 per cent of the total land area has been set aside for leases to mining companies (Clarke and Barlow 1997: 100–101). Tax holidays are offered to investors,[41] local environmental laws are waived, and labour unions are generally illegal. The host-country government, usually composed of the country's rich and powerful elite, distances itself from all regulation of activities in export processing zones, trading the health of its own people for the investment of foreign capital. The money required to build the infrastructure for the use of foreign capital outweighs the profit made from the companies' activities.[42] Swasti Mitter points out that from 1973 to 1982 in the Philippines, total profit from the export processing zones was $82 million, but the cost of inputs was $192 million (1986: 68). This is not an isolated case. With young women making up the highest proportion of workers in these zones, precisely because they are flexible and cheap, the impact of globalisation is falling most heavily on women.

---

39 See also Mitter (1986: 43–54) who describes the working conditions for women in export processing zones in Malaysia, Sri Lanka and the Philippines.

40 An example is an advertisement run by the Ghana Export Promotion Council. It outlines some of the benefits for investors in the Ghana Free Zones Board and "Gateway 2000" Project. "Duties. 100% exemption from payment of direct and indirect duties and levies on all imports for production, and export from the free zones. Taxation. Free-zone enterprises are granted 100% exemption from income tax on profits for 10 years, after which the tax rate shall not exceed 8%" (GHFB 2000: 12).

41 On a trip to Bangladesh in 1993, travelling on Bengal Airlines, I saw advertisements in the airline magazine informing potential investors that they would receive a ten-year tax holiday.

42 Mitter (1986: 68) points out that from 1973 to 1982 in the Philippines, the total profit from the export processing zones was $82 million, but the cost of inputs was $192 million. This is not an isolated case.

The process of orienting an economy toward export is one of disengagement, dislocation and displacement. Domestic production is *disengaged* from its internal market; people are *dislocated*, perhaps even exported, in order to fill the jobs of mobile capital; and "pre-existing productive systems" are *displaced* in the competition for a position in the global marketplace (Chossudovsky 1998: 17).

Building domestic economic strength is important for developing countries, as is building democracy from the inside – not as dictated by IMF structural adjustment programs, since these have economic content but little social content. In order to change the situation, those in the diversity matrix need to identify and work toward long-term and sustainable economic and social goals. This means that the resources needed to achieve these goals have to be worked out, as do the practicalities of how to mobilise such resources.

In summary, the process of globalisation occurs as follows:

- *appropriation* of land, resources, knowledge, biodiversity, bodies and body parts, parts of genes
- *incorporation* of appropriated resources and knowledge into a western legal framework of property rights, knowledge systems in universities and the US system of patents through the TRIPs regime as legitimised by the WTO
- *commodification* and privatisation of the products or systems incorporated into the western system
- *export* of whatever is exotic to another location: material goods, patents on biotechnology promoted as "solving world hunger"; export of inappropriate knowledge systems such as the Green Revolution and the gene revolution (usually called "technology transfer"); export of exotic genes into cells, creating new transgenic organisms
- *dislocation*, displacement and disconnection from the local.

All of these steps in the process lead to increasing *homogenisation* and are built on a system of inappropriate universalism. They are appropriative, lead to poverty and dispossession, and foster the increase in power and accumulation of wealth in the hands of those who already possess it.

Decolonising Economics

Neoclassical economics and the relationship of colonisation which preceded it are based on a number of assumptions:

- *progress*: that there is a linear development in cultures and that western/ European cultures represent the most progressed form of culture
- *universalism*: that western/European culture can and should be transplanted and, if necessary, forcibly imposed all around the world
- *abstraction and reductionism*: that economic activity takes place in a vacuum and the creation of value is related solely to the optimal price which is determined by the market
- *decontextualisation*: that economics and individual transactions can be stripped of context and relationship with the real social and natural worlds.

Critiques of colonisation have much to offer our understanding of globalisation. The analysis of colonisation has come from many quarters, beginning with thinkers such as Frantz Fanon (1961) and Paolo Freire (1972) and continuing today with the voices from peoples around the world (Mies 1986/1999; Ani 2000; LaDuke 1997; Gunn Allen 1998; Tuhiwai Smith 1999; Langton 1998; Atkinson 2002). Many of these writers have linked the colonisation with the growing power of corporate globalisation. Mainstream economists have jumped on the bandwagon of neoclassical economics as oriented toward profit. But economics can be understood much more broadly than this. The theories of neoclassical economics can be, and have been, used to support the growth-oriented economies (including corporate economies, see Appendix, Table 1). The USA and Western Europe are the models for neoclassical economic theories, but as Maria Mies (1986/1999) has argued, their growth resulted from the free use of the resources, the land and the labour of colonised peoples, and the free labour of women.

Maria Mies (1986/1999) was one of the earliest to identify how women are used in this global system. She has since gone on to propose ways of resisting corporate power, many of which build upon systems of subsistence developed by poor people. Martin Khor, in his critique of the global economy and its impact on the Third World, points out that:

Economically, financially and technologically, Third World countries were sucked deeper and deeper into the whirlpool of the world economic system and consequently lost or are losing their indigenous skills, their capacity for self-reliance, their confidence, and in many cases, the very resource base on which their survival depends (1996: 48).

This loss is represented by Vandana Shiva as the "empty earth syndrome" (2000b: 25–26), which she attributes to colonisation and to the imposition of monocultures: agricultural, industrial and intellectual. These concepts have been widely discussed in the theories produced by those on the margins. Gilligan (1982) distinguishes between the generalised and the concrete. Guinier *et al.* (1997), writing about educational practices in US law schools, challenges the ideal of all lawyers "becoming gentlemen" as representing another form of the universalising principle. Gunn Allen (1998), Ani (2000), Tuhiwai Smith (1999), Wittig (1992), Anzaldúa (1987), Lorde (1984) and a host of others have proposed looking at the world through a lens from the margins. All locate themselves: particularising, contextualising and concretising their theoretical positions. It is this kind of critique that is now needed in economics.

Economic globalisation has used the notion of progress to justify the practice of universalising western-oriented trade systems. Among the practices put in place have been the Green Revolution, which destroyed local systems of farming and hooked farmers into the trade in pesticides and fertilisers; fishing as an industrialised activity, using huge nets, explosives and the practice of over-fishing that has denuded fishing stocks for the people most reliant on the sea for their existence; clear-felling of forests, which dispossesses indigenous peoples of their lands. Globalisation, through its disconnection from the local, ignores biodiversity as well as the needs of native animals, and replaces natural forests with plantations.

In the urban areas, global companies move in their production arms, especially for products that are hazardous or labour-intensive; they develop the export processing zones, which are disconnected from the surrounding community in as many ways as possible.

In regions inhabited by indigenous peoples and peoples who are culturally marginalised within the mainstream (Romany peoples, the

Dalit and other "untouchables" within the Indian caste system, as well as exiles and refugees), the continuing practices of colonisation are exacerbating dispossession and poverty. In the global economy this takes the form of bioprospecting and theft of knowledge under Trade Related Intellectual Property rights (TRIPs). Like the free use of land, labour and resources under colonisation, the free use of intellectual property parallels the colonial relationship. Freedom of movement is presented as a good thing for the mobile elites while detention camps are built to hold poor people who cross borders. The systems of colonisation continue with the destruction of environments and cultures through mining, deforestation and the new products of global consumerism.

What is required is a systematic decolonising of economics. Such an economics would focus on biodiversity rather than profit, and take account of the diversity matrix: women, indigenous peoples, the poor, the marginalised, including lesbians,[43] the disabled and refugees. The process of decolonising will need to involve a massive shift in thinking and behaviour at the individual and institutional level.

In order to get a sense of what steps have to be taken to decolonise economics, I will now look at critiques by feminist economists and ecological economists, both of whom are providing roadmaps for the changes that might take place.

Feminist Economics

In this chapter I have already looked at many of the features of neoclassical economics and globalisation which are criticised by concerned feminist economists. A feminist agenda for change would require at least acceptance and acknowledgement that:

---

43 Lesbians have significantly lower incomes than gay men, and Hyman indicates that income for lesbians working full-time is also lower than that of heterosexual women. The US study found that "lesbians working full-time earned $US15,056 on average against $18,341 for heterosexual women, $26,321 for gay men, and $28,312 for heterosexual men" (Badgett, cited in Hyman 2001: 121). Lesbian income is reflecting the general tendency for women's incomes. This does not mean there are not exceptions, and that a proportion of lesbians benefit from being two-income partnerships without dependants. The evidence from New Zealand suggests that lesbian couples living together without children have higher income than their heterosexual counterparts, but when children are added to the equation, there were simlar incomes for lesbians and heterosexuals alike (Hyman 2001: 121–122).

- all people are in this together, and that the world is finite and connected
- while we have collective interests, they are also diverse
- as with other group organisms, ecosystems, and collectives, when one part is over-exploited and sickened, the rest of the organism is at risk (Ho 1998)
- power predisposes people to misuse it, unless it is regulated by social principles and sanctions
- diversity is a co-ordinating principle which allows for group survival
- respect and dignity are important elements in enhancing the well-being of humans
- the production of wealth as an ultimate aim is irrational, and the well-being and sustenance of life and culture have a higher priority
- alternatives to the male monopoly on life already exist.

In 1986, Maria Mies proposed an alternative economy.[44] Arguing from a feminist perspective, she suggested that the most important principle is "Autonomy over our bodies and lives" (1986: 222). Moving from the personal and the local to the broad view, Mies argued that such a basic change would reduce violence on both the individual and institutional levels. Connecting the violence of men with the violence of capitalist patriarchy, Mies argues that abandoning violence is the first step in abandoning exploitation. Like Susanne Kappeler (1995), Maria Mies argues firmly that men take up a sense of responsibility, and further, that men must begin to participate in the legal[45] informal economy: the unpaid and unrecognised economy (1986: 222).

Moving outwards toward global institutions, Mies makes a plea for autarky, a largely self-sufficient economy, one which emphasises self-sufficiency while still engaging in trade for goods it cannot reasonably produce itself. She recognises that such a shift would result in "a contraction of world trade and of export-oriented production" (1986: 220),[46] but argues that it would significantly reduce exploitation and

---

44 First published in 1986, *Patriarchy and Accumulation on a World Scale* was reprinted with a new introduction in 1999.

45 I do not mean the illegal informal economy in which men play a large role. The illegal informal economy includes prostitution and pornography, smuggling of drugs, people, and illicit arms.

46 It might also result in the reduction of the unnecessary spread of diseases directly caused by large-scale transporting of livestock for the production of meat (BSE and

non-reciprocal relations between nations. She also argues for a reduction in the "gap between production and consumption" (1986: 221) and for development of the relations between producers and consumers. From more recent writings, reduction in waste and taking responsibility for solving the problem of waste has become another important aspect of an alternative economy for Mies.[47]

In many ways Mies' analysis pre-empted the issues subsequently raised by other economists critical of the prevailing economic paradigm.[48] Among them are issues raised by ecological economists (O'Hara 1995; McMahon 1997; Goodland and Daly 1993; Martinez-Alier 2000), and by writers such as Vandana Shiva (1997) and Rudolph Bahro (1984), who distinguish between poverty and subsistence. As Shiva notes:

> It is useful to separate a cultural conception of subsistence living as poverty from the material experience of poverty that is a result of dispossession and deprivation. Culturally perceived poverty need not be real material poverty: subsistence economies which satisfy basic needs through self-provisioning are not poor in the sense of being deprived. Yet the ideology of development declares them so because they do not participate in the market economy, and do not consume commodities produced for and distributed through the market *even though they might be satisfying those needs through self-provisioning mechanisms* (1989: 10, emphasis in original).

Neoclassical economists regard participation in the market economy as essential. Indeed, it is one of the major assumptions of neoclassical economics centred around the idea of the "rational man" who compares prices only and never engages in altruistic economic behaviour. For those seeking ways of decolonising economics, the spaces provided by remaining outside the market economy are precisely those which offer

---

foot-and-mouth disease are two examples), or of the contamination of wild types from GM crops through transnational companies that have run trials on crops and not followed locally imposed guidelines (Monsanto in Tasmania).

47 See Bennholdt-Thomsen and Mies (1999) for a discussion of waste treatment.

48 I note with interest that in the same year, 1986, Flora Nwapa was publishing her poem of praise to the cassava crop. She wrote "You, Mother Cassava/You deserve recognition/You are no cash crop/But you deserve recognition" (1986: 43). See also Chapter Five.

the most hope for achieving changes in practice. The market economy is primarily western and modern in its orientation, and because of the ways in which power is dispersed from the western economies to former colonies, it tends to draw men into the market economy more quickly than it does women. Other marginalised peoples such as refugees and indigenous peoples are also less likely to be entirely dependent on the market economy for their sustenance. Even women from within the western and modern societies "lag" behind men in their participation, because they are more likely to engage in part-time or unpaid labour. The rhetoric of market-economy participation is that anyone anywhere can participate in the market economy; the reality is that it takes much more effort for those outside the market economy, or for those who live inside an extra-legal context. De Soto carried out research into how long it takes in Peru to set up a formal business. For lawyers it took a matter of days; for the poor it required "over three hundred days, working six hours a day" (2001: 202).

As previously mentioned, the "failure" of women to join the market economy and participate in countable activities was highlighted in Marilyn Waring's book *Counting for Nothing* (1988). Although not the first to criticise the UN System of National Accounts (UNSNA), her book popularised these ideas and made women aware of the social and economic impact of such figures.[49]

Waring argued that women are structurally disappeared from economic figures because of the way in which the UNSNA figures are collected. Drawing on examples which I will discuss in later chapters, the uncounted work includes:

- all subsistence work carried out by women (farming, gathering from forests, fishing, gardening, collecting, hunting)
- giving birth without the assistance of IVF or other designer and so-called (re)productive technologies; breastfeeding rather than substituting infant milk formula
- working as a carer within the family in an unpaid capacity (includes teaching, nursing, and administrative and financial skills)

---

49 For other analyses of the valuation of women's work and productivity, see Ferber (1982); Bergmann (1986); Folbre (1994). For a good summary of the issues, see Mayhew (1999: 732–737). In some countries, subsistence agriculture is imputed into GDP.

- voluntary work carried on outside the family
- housework, including sewing, cooking and maintenance
- any work which does not result in payment or is done on the basis of reciprocity (mutual sexual relations, community arts, helping to fix the neighbour's car in return for a meal).

As Waring points out, the result is that women are largely left out of the economic cycle.[50] And yet, without the above work, the world would come to a standstill. Women are, as Bennholdt-Thomsen and Mies point out, engaged in work the aim of which is *life*, rather than the production of capital (1999: 20). Because only "public" market activity is included, prostitution is considered to raise the GNP. Janice Raymond makes the point that in 1998, Belize "Recognized prostitution ... [as] a gender-specific form of migrant labour that serves the same economic functions for women as agricultural work offers to men, and often for better pay" (1999: 2). Waring comments that, when she sees Thailand listed as a growth economy, she wonders "what percentage of that might be attributed to the international drug trade and what percentage to the sexual slavery of women" (1988: 124). Kevin Bales, in his recent study of global slavery, estimates the value of sexual slavery to the Thai economy to be more than $US1.85 billion annually (2000: 57). The export of domestic workers from poor countries to rich countries has also become a lucrative earner, with the Philippines earning around $US3 billion annually, money that is sent home from abroad by mostly female workers (Matsui 1999: 47).

Waring goes yet further with her analysis. Realising that anything which is accounted for as free would also not show up on the UNSNA, she asks, "And what of mother earth?" (1988: 26). The theft of lands colonised by Europeans, including the resources on that land – much of which remains in the hands of the colonising governments – is not accounted for. A hypothetical example using the same principles would

---

50 Children, too, and their needs, tend to be left out of such analysis. They are also assumed to be economically inactive and dependent, a scenario a long way outside the experience of many children around the world, including children in rich countries. Their work is rendered invisible by the same forces that render women's work invisible. It is usually based in the domestic sphere, and may be unpaid or paid at a very low rate.

have the following pattern: cell lines stolen from indigenous peoples in order to create new patents on life would remain uncounted, but if the perpetrator were sued, it would then become countable.

The UNSNA relies, writes Waring, "on inducing fear (of, for example, the unknown or uncontrollable)" (1988: 37). And, I would add, of the wild. This can be readily shown in looking at colonisation, from nations, to resources, to women, to children, to culture, to the molecular level. In each case, capital has access to a large amount of free resources – land, raw materials, wildlife, plants, people, cells – and because it is "free" (not recognised as being worth paying for by the powerful) the return on the investment is significant. The UNSNA itself has become a further tool of colonisation. Developed for western economic systems, it invisibilises enormous amounts of unpaid work in the legal informal sectors of western countries, as well as in the developing countries where reciprocal and subsistence economies play an even more significant role. Waring notes that "Papua New Guinea is one country in which production outside the market is so large and the national price system so imperfect that the *existence of a national income in money value is open to challenge on conceptual grounds*" (1988: 84, emphasis in original). This is true also for the vast majority of indigenous peoples' economies (with the exception of those who have started casinos or agreed to royalty payments for the exploitation of resources).

Another perverse twist of economic calculation is the way in which pollution, environmental destruction and war become assets and growth indicators in the UNSNA. The clean-up of oil pollution in Iraq and Kuwait caused by the military during the Gulf War in 1991, for example, is counted in the UNSNA as productive. But the loss of Socotra cormorants and fish, as well as the threats to endangered species such as dugong, the Siberian crane and green turtles, is not a countable loss (Waring 1988; Bertell 2000).

Likewise, carcinogens in the environment (Bertell 1985; Steingraber 1999) create work for research scientists, pharmaceutical companies and medical institutions. War reduces unemployment by creating work in the military, in munitions factories, in intelligence, in the computing industry, and much more. Vandana Shiva summarises this process: "The patriarchal creation boundary allows ecological destruction to be perceived as creation, and ecological regeneration and creation to be perceived as non-creation" (1994: 141).

Development, structural adjustment programs and globalisation are pulling the wild elements – women, indigenous peoples, artists – into the market economy. Activities which might previously have remained outside the purview of the global economy are slowly incorporated and appropriated. Ecotourism, for example, brings cash and culture into remote areas;[51] reproductive technologies make women's bodies productive in the market sense (Klein 2001); bioprospecting draws knowledge capital out of the hands of peoples with long traditions of medicinal use.[52]

Waring's analysis is now more than a decade old, and it has been an important addition to economic theory. But it has also been co-opted,[53] and, as indicated above, efforts are being made to draw more and more of the wild elements into the market economy.[54] Cheru (2000), Khor (1996) and Faraclas (2001) argue that remaining outside the market economy can be regarded as a resistance to global economic norms. The problem is that economics is only a partial picture. Not everything can be measured, and in an economically sane system one would not want to measure everything. This challenge, a paradox, cann I think, be met by wild politics.

A different feminist approach to economics is taken by Susan Donath (2000), Julie Smith (1999) and Prue Hyman (1999). They look at the "other economy". Donath shows how it is not just difficult, but almost impossible, to incorporate children into economics, and she suggests that

---

51 See Chapter Four for a fuller discussion of ecotourism; see also Te Awekotuku (1991); Thaman (1994); McLaren (1998).

52 The neem tree is an interesting example here. A quick search on the internet brings up many more commercial sites than information sites, and they are based in a number of countries. For further information, see Shiva and Hollar-Bhar (1993, 1996); Shiva (2001d: 63). For a general discussion of these issues, see Hawthorne (2001a).

53 Waring, in a talk first given in 1991 and published in 1994, is aware of this problem, and criticises ecological economists for ignoring the work of feminist economists whose theoretical work preceded the critiques of ecological economists. The worries she expresses are similar to those I have about the concept of "natural capitalism" (see my discussion in the next section of this chapter).

54 Bennholdt-Thomsen and Mies give an interesting example of Kenyan women's resistance to export orientation and to incentives offered by the IMF to draw women into the market economy (1999: 214–217). Waring was aware of this danger. She writes in her epilogue: "if … [it] can be number crunched, economics will colonise it with impunity" (1988: 263).

the "other economy is concerned with the direct production and maintenance of human beings". She recognises that this area lies outside "the market behavior of independent, competitive beings"; her language suggests that for her the mainstream competitive model is not problematic. My argument is that production is not the point (2000: 116). Being is. I am arguing that the profit motive which is the driving force of western capitalist production should be replaced by the biodiversity motive. Maria Mies' concept of "life" (1999: 20) as central to economics is in keeping with this vision, and any challenge to neoclassical economics will need to shift its focus from doing, and from money and production to being.

Even those economists who count the relationship between parents and children as productive and part of economics, relate it to utility. Gary Becker, for example in his new household economics, refers to altruism in the context of parents and children having "utility" (1995). This begs the question of life as a "utility" for others or for the economy. As I have argued earlier a liberal utilitarian approach goes counter to the arguments developed here.

Julie Smith (1999), in a paper which takes up Waring's idea of countability, suggests ways of counting the value of human milk supply, and Vandana Shiva (2000a: 58) has suggested counting the value of cow dung.[55] In part, this is a way of making the invisible role of women in the "production of human beings" visible, or demonstrating the role of cattle in increasing soil fertility and thereby its value. Its shortcoming is that it continues to use the neoclassical model of monetary value, rather than a focus on being. Waring (1994) argues that counting the value of transactions through market indicators is the easy way out, and replicates the same process of power and reductionist sources of knowledge.

Prue Hyman (1999b) asks whether the low wages paid to child-care workers and high wages to those who manipulate the futures market really reflect the respective value or productivity of these different jobs.

---

55 "Indian cattle provide more food than they consume, in contrast to those of the U.S. cattle industry, in which cattle consume six times more food than they provide. In addition, every year, Indian cattle excrete 700 million tons of recoverable manure: half of this is used as fuel, liberating the thermal equivalent of 27 million tons of kerosene, 35 million tons of coal, or 68 million tons of wood, all of which are scarce resources in India. The remainder is used as fertilizer" (Shiva 2000a: 58).

She argues for reconceptualising dependence and interdependence so that the figures represent the contribution made by almost all adults and most children (Hyman 1999a).

What is interesting about Hyman's work is the way in which she pushes at the boundaries of economics, and her economic theories tend to take account of the specificities of locale and group (her focus has been, variously, Maori peoples, lesbians, women, and children). This approach is in stark contrast with the generalised approach of mainstream neoliberal, neoclassical economics. Among the groups she examines are lesbians, and the economic contribution of lesbian businesses and community activities. Hyman challenges the view that lesbians are all g/luppies (gay/lesbian upper-class yuppies), and points to the role of altruistic behaviour within some lesbian communities (2001: 119, 124).

On alternative economic systems, Hyman looks at the concept of unpaid exchange. This is known variously as barter, Green Dollar schemes (New Zealand), Local Economic Trading Schemes (LETS) in Canada, Australia and Britain, Time Dollars (USA), and, in one instance, LESY, a lesbian community green dollar scheme based in Adelaide, Australia (Young: 1991). The purpose of such schemes is to change the social structure to one of reciprocity.

But even such systems are subject to oppressive forces of the culture. In 1994, an Australian organisation called Bartercard was drumming up business. They approached me to enquire whether I might be interested in joining the scheme. It seemed like a good idea. The salesperson proudly informed me, a few minutes into her spiel, that they could even supply an "escort service". Bartering prostitution is no better than selling it for money. Clearly, Bartercard had not considered the exploitation of women an issue. It appears that many good alternative ideas can be readily co-opted by the dominant culture. Just as counting unpaid work can prove counterproductive, bartering services can be oppressive.

Like the feminist economists mentioned above, I am suspicious of many aspects of neoclassical economics. Like Nelson (1996), it is clear to me that economics is due for an overhaul which challenges the sexism inherent in many of its principles, and in many of the policies which erupt from that base. Like Mies, I believe that the possibility of supporting oneself through one's own productive labours is an attractive idea, as it seems to short-circuit the accumulation of money and prioritise other, more humane, elements. But I am concerned that the practicalities of this are immense, and particularly for those living in increasingly urbanised environments. Like Waring, I want women's work recognised, and I want it to be possible for indigenous peoples to maintain their knowledge base and culture through the valuing of their resources. But I am wary that for both women and indigenous peoples, counting is just the first step in appropriation. Like Hyman, I am keen for everyone to receive fair wages, or for them to be able to operate in a work exchange environment, thereby reducing our dependence on money exchange. But I continue to worry about how this will be implemented, given the way in which the example of Bartercard shows its potential flaws.

In summary, there are two competing forces at work in feminist interpretations of economics. At the liberal end, there is a push to argue that women should become more and more active in the market economy. In part, this can be achieved by changing the accounting structures, or by paying women for their currently unpaid work. This liberal view accepts globalisation as a positive force for women.

A more radical outlook is the one which resists globalisation and argues instead that some women, and some indigenous peoples and some others in the diversity matrix, are already living in an alternative economic system, and have much to offer those who are caught up in the market system. This view, if it is long-term and takes biodiversity as its inspiration or driving force, is the direction in which I would argue economic theory should go. In order for this to occur, the connections between economics and ecology need to be highlighted.

Two of the difficulties in moving to a different economic system are force of habit, and lack of understanding as to what counts as a fair deal. As so many transactions in western economies are falsely valued, it requires looking again at how values are structured. Is an hour of advice from a lawyer worth so much more than an hour of childcare? "Deinstitutionalising the exchange relationship" will take time (Mackenzie 2002: pers. comm.).

Ecological Economics

Two terms need to be distinguished here: environmental economics and ecological economics. Environmental economics is a branch of neo-classical economics, that is, it uses the same principles and assumptions of neoclassical economics as outlined above and applies them to environmental issues. It considers issues such as climate control, conservation, pollution. It focuses on the "sensible allocation of resources" (Gilpin 2000: 20), and takes up issues such as carbon taxes, environmental taxes, the use of economic instruments in biodiversity trading and waste disposal. Ecological economics,[56] by contrast, does not use neoclassical economics as its foundation.[57] Instead, it regards "the economy as being within the global ecosystem with critical interdependence" (Gilpin 2000: 87). Ecological economics therefore takes account of reciprocity, interdependence, and of sustainability of the economic system, as if it were an ecosystem.

In this section, I look at critiques of the neoclassical economic framework and globalisation by ecological economists. I do not discuss environmental economics because it is already a part of the global system and its perspectives are too frequently used to justify globalisation and excuse its negative aspects. For example, environmental economists do not regard sustainable development within a western framework as problematic provided the development does not have superficially negative consequences for the people engaging in it. The concept of "development" is not considered "problematic" by environmental economists, although it may result in moving economic activity out of women's hands into a more market-driven activity performed by men.

By contrast, for many ecological economists, "development" is inherently problematic (Norberg-Hodge 1996a: 40) since it assumes that "progress", in the western sense, is a positive outcome. In addition, sustainable development is based on the neoclassical economic principle of "growth", although it is more likely to be talked about in terms of "sustainable growth".

The notion of limitless growth has been under attack since the 1970s when Donella Meadows *et al.*, in *The Limits to Growth* (1972), first developed a thoroughgoing critique. The concept of "development" builds upon the idea of "progress", which Marimba Ani (2000) identifies as a specifically western concept. Joni Seager refers to it as the "train of

---

56 The journal, *Ecological Economics*, founded in 1989, is an important forum for discussion of the principles of this discipline. For a useful discussion of neoclassical economics and ecological economics, see Söderbaum (1992). The head-on collision between neoclassical and ecological economists is discussed in *Ecological Economics 22* (3).

57 Marilyn Waring (1994) argues otherwise.

progress" and comments on the mechanism of distancing which corporate leaders engage in to avoid responsibility. It is not, she argues, "inevitable", and not a "necessary, no-choice-about-it side effect" of industrialisation, but a "decision" taken by corporate, political and military leaders (1993: 72). These two concepts – growth and progress – are central to the idea of development. They are in direct opposition to the notion of sustainability which relies on long-term planning, reciprocity, connection, and responsibility. There can be no such thing as "sustainable growth" (Daly 1999a: 285). "Sustainable development" also makes no sense since growth is a part of development. Development within the context of international institutions is subject to outside agendas. So, in the 1990s, women became a focus of development programs in a move can only be regarded as a "continuation of the process of colonisation" (Shiva 1997: 2). In recent years, development projects have targeted indigenous communities. Are bioprospectors behind these new agendas for indigenous development projects? Is it, as Shiva points out, that "nature and women are reduced to being resources" (1997: 6)?

Martinez-Alier claims that "ecological economics is transdisciplinary" (2000: 148) and that complexity and context sensitivity are critical in measuring economic indices:

> As ecological economists we should also be interested in the processes of social perception of externalities, and in the processes of social evaluation linked to the selection of indicators and targets. For instance, an index of loss of natural biodiversity would be human appropriation of the annual biomass net production (2000: 150).

Like a number of other ecological economists, Martinez-Alier recognises the importance of an ecofeminist perspective in attempting to find ways of envisioning the future. This is in contrast to the environmental economists who simply ignore feminism and ecofeminism (Alan Gilpin's textbook *Environmental Economics* (2000) does not list ecofeminism in the index).[58] Martinez-Alier imagines a 2025 future not very different from

---

58 Among ecological economists, the inclusion of feminist economic analysis is something that has shifted a little in the past decade. The first book on the subject, *Ecological Economics* (Costanza 1991), included forty-two men and three women, and all but one were from Europe or the USA.

that of Rokeya Sakhawat Hossain in *Sultana's Dream* (1905), in which one could combine urbanisation with "gardens and local recycling of waste, with local water collection, with intermodal walking–bicycling–public transport systems, with local supplies of energy and bioclimatic architecture, and with patterns of different sorts of local work and entertainment". Martinez-Alier goes on to discuss Local Economic Trading Schemes (LETS), low-input organic agriculture, reciprocity, and redistribution and working outside the market (2000: 171).

Meanwhile, feminist ecological economist Martha McMahon points to the separate, detached individual whose "psychic, political and economic experience is organized through experiences of being set off from others" (1997: 164, 166). She argues that the view of "economic man", prevalent in neoliberal economies, reflects precisely the characteristics of "colonising man". Ecological economics, she suggests, "must be able to theorize relationship adequately" (1997: 171). Economic man has never been good at relationships, seeing everything as an exchange for the purpose of self-interest, so this challenge alone will take some time to work through. It will, for example, have to tackle "the relationship between environmental degradation and the distribution of wealth and power". But it is women and children, who comprise the majority of the world's poor, who are most affected by the economic systems in place. Martha McMahon (1997), along with theorists such as Ynestra King (1981a), Val Plumwood (1996), Catriona Sandilands (1999), and Lee Quinby (1994), acknowledges the universalising tendency of neoclassical economics and of the individualised "economic man" who is central to the theory; and like Joni Seager (1993), and Vandana Shiva and Maria Mies in *Ecofeminism* (1993) these writers draw on very particular examples to discuss the ways in which ecofeminists have engaged with economics and the forces of globalisation.

An interesting convergence appears to be occurring in the discipline of economics among those who challenge the neoclassical fundamentals. There is an overlap of views with those who are working in a range of other fields, including women's studies, indigenous knowledge and rights, ethnoecology, anthropology, and critics of globalisation (although many in these fields continue to ignore issues of economics). Just as some aspects of feminist economics have been appropriated, a similar process is at work in the area of ecological economics.

There have been some recent challenges to the conventional structure of capitalism on the basis of free markets, competition, growth, importance of high standards of living (high consumption), and at best, only moderate consideration of the health of the environment and the long-term sustainability of the environment. "Natural capitalism" refers to commodifying and profiting from "natural capital" (Hawken, Lovins and Lovins 1999: 9) and the authors refer to the centrality of living systems. This is a good beginning; however, the model puts too much focus on the possibility of making money out of these newly designed systems based on biology. And despite some interesting ideas and concepts, there is not enough emphasis on social responsibility, nor is there any obvious understanding of respect for indigenous knowledge systems. The implication is that capitalism with a new face will be okay. But will it?

Natural capitalism falls short in its aims because it puts too much emphasis on money, and continues to promote profit, rather than biodiversity, as the driving force for its acceptance by business. Maria Mies highlighted this kind of theoretical practice in her epigraph to an article in 1983: "New wine must not be poured into old bottles" (1983: 117).

Apparently for the authors, promoting America's interests is not problematic. They cite Christopher Warren: "addressing natural resource issues is frequently critical to achieving political and economic stability, and to pursuing *our* strategic goals around the world" (1999: 21, my emphasis). As mentioned earlier by Shiva, commodifying "nature and women" and other free elements (such as knowledge) and reducing them to "resources" (1997: 6) results in increasing the spread of globalisation and benefiting the transnational sector at the expense of the diversity matrix.

The authors also pretend to be politically neutral, suggesting their ideas will appeal both to conservatives and liberals. Natural capitalism shares much with another new term, "natural economics". This is transnational business planning that takes into account the environmental impact of its industries and assumes that every country in the world should have the same environmental standards. These environmental economic appropriations of ecological economics are rather like the gender appropriation of feminist economic concepts. Similar appropriations are occurring in advertising. A recent Deutsche Bank advertisement reads:

Local Knowledge and Global Expertise.
Deutsche Bank: commitment to the capital markets in Australasia.
(*Australian Financial Review* 29 May 2000: 11).

The appeal to the local–global axis is a new move in advertising, and suggests that we will see considerably more cooption and appropriation of activists' ideas in the future. From the ecological economic side, there is an increasing attempt by some theorists to make ecological economics more market-friendly. Habitat becomes a commodity (Merrifield 1996: 219), local knowledge becomes a source of profit for global pharmaceutical companies (Shiva and Holla-Bhar 1996; Brown 1994), "diversity" becomes a marketing slogan for Generation-Xers (Klein 2000: 111) and tourism becomes the latest path to paradise for culture-hungry consumers (McLaren 1998). And, as we have seen, capitalism becomes "natural" (Hawken *et al.* 2000). Linking these ideas to my own vision for the future, the environment, natural remedies, diversity and ecotourism might seem to be obvious contenders for the appellation "wild", but if peoples' lives and livelihoods are destroyed in the process, if means are not consistent with ends, then these "new" theories are just a variation on the old theories which underpin western cultural assumptions and practices.

Indeed, it is now quite possible to speak about biodiversity and profit in the same breath. Katrina Brown characterises conventional utilitarian economic measures as those which believe that a "decline in biodiversity represents a potential reduction in future stock value, dividends and profits" (1994: 735; see also Gowdy 1995: 184). An analysis which understands the instrumental value of medicinal plants in this way, and which sees biodiversity conservation as relevant only to the calculation of GDP, does not satisfy my criteria for a wild politics. Such an analysis encounters no difficulty with privatising knowledge through patents and intellectual property rights, thereby entrenching the neoliberal grip of globalisation (see Chapter Seven for more details).

Helena Norberg-Hodge (1996b), drawing on her experience of living with the Ladakhi people of Kashmir, relates the ways in which an economy, self-sufficient in the 1970s and proud of its achievements, has become dependent upon imported foods, educates its children with a Eurocentric curriculum, and is suffering from an economy being dismantled by globalisation. "Development" has not been good news for the Ladakhis. Interdependence has become dependence: a personal sense of dignity and responsibility has been replaced by a powerlessness and passivity. The Ladakhis, like many other peoples around the world, have been pulled into a system which has no respect for their knowledge and traditions. I would argue that not only small remote communities are undergoing this change, but large numbers of people are, who previously have managed to remain outside, or at least partially outside, the market economy. Among those affected are many rural people: ordinary farmers who might exchange a day's work for some tractor part or half a slaughtered cow; the unemployed, the disabled or pensioners on fixed incomes who volunteer at the local senior citizens' or community centre; children whose labour might help support the family's food supply; and women, many of whom fall into the above categories, and many more who participate in a range of unpaid activities in and outside the home. They are all threatened with further loss of autonomy.

The question is: where to from here? How can the concerned citizen move into a future which encompasses both the local and the global without using these terms as glib slogans that mean little in the structure of everyday lives? Can the citizen realistically bring about respect for the specificities of experience and locale while at the same time remaining aware of the common good? How do we learn about different ways of knowing and living without appropriating the knowledge and traditions of the poor, indigenous, women and other groups marginalised by the dominant economic and political systems? How does each one of us maintain our connections without losing our diversity, or having it appropriated?

Toward a Wild Economics

Among those working in the cross-over area between feminist and ecological economics, it is the work of Sabine O'Hara (1995a, 1995b, 1997) which I have found the most thoughtful and open to the possibilities of a very long view of sustainable society, and the development of a wild politics. O'Hara identifies three feminist concepts that she places at the centre of her thinking around ecology and economics: concreteness, connectedness and diversity (1995a: 530). This shares much with the features I have already spelt out: local and particular (concreteness), connection, context, relationship, reciprocity and responsibility (connectedness), and diversity and biodiversity.

Sabine O'Hara suggests that the attempt to "analyse bio-diversity or socio-diversity from [a] market-centred perspective would be a contradiction in terms" (1995: 33). She looks instead to what might be the essential features of an economics which puts bio- and socio-diversity at the centre. She comes up with a number of features which are all located and which tend in the direction of specificity in contrast to the universalising tendencies of globalisation. That is, concreteness is more important than abstraction, particularisation more important than generalisation, relationship more important than distribution; and specificities of conditions, time and the limits of mortality and growth are all critical to such an economics.

It is impossible to think about feminist economics or ecological economics without considering context. Women's work relies heavily on context, on knowledge of the local environment and on connections. These connections have been used to develop new models for women in the developing world: the Grameen Bank in Bangladesh has been successful because it works in small communities in close contact with real women, taking into account their personal circumstances (Holcombe 1995); likewise, the Ecowoman network provides information on women's traditional knowledge, fishing, permaculture, health and human rights for Pacific Island women through its workshops, events and newsletters. Ecowoman draws on the detailed local knowledge "women have always possessed ... of the species and ecosystems which surround them, and which make up the bioregion they inhabit" (Ecowoman 1997: 1). A global economy loses its way because it is disconnected from local bio-regions and from the needs of the people who live there. It fails because the relationship between the producer and consumer is attenuated. A global economy also fails to recognise that without the sustaining functions of women, communities all around the world would disintegrate. What would happen if women didn't feed, bathe and talk to their children? A global economy never grounds its practices in the daily details of maintaining and sustaining life. A world in which clothing was never washed would be itchy and uncomfortable; a world in which relationships were not maintained would be wracked by anarchy of the worst kind. It is, after all, the small household chores that keep the house standing. None of this work is counted in the global economy unless it is performed for pay.

Efforts have been made to count the invisible work and products women contribute to. For example, the contribution of human milk to the Australian economy has been calculated to have a combined value of approximately \$A2.2 billion in 1992 (Smith 1999: 80) and is valued at around 0.5 per cent of GDP. But as indicated above, counting doesn't change the system, although it does go some way toward acknowledging its importance for the economy. Julie Nelson claims that neoclassical economics has assumed that this background, informal sector – women and nature – will take care of itself (1997: 156), while Christa Wichterich points out that "the market economy externalizes the cost of its own reproduction by entrusting this to women as a labour of pure love" (2000: 98). Nelson also reminds us of the etymological connection between the words "ecology" and "economy": both come from the same root as the Greek word for household and housekeeping[59] (1997: 156, 161).

Just as feminism has insisted on the connection between the personal and the political, ecology cannot extricate itself from ecosystems and context; indigenous systems of knowledge rely heavily on the specificities of location and cultural tradition. This integral system of connectedness is what feminists, indigenous peoples and ecologists are bringing to economics. It comes with a number of other important elements that Sabine O'Hara lists as "reciprocity, mutual support, respect and awareness of the context of human sociality within the larger ecosystem [which] form key concepts of a contextual economic system" (1995: 37).

In 1984, I had the privilege to meet a number of indigenous women from Central Australia at the Fourth Women and Labour Conference in Brisbane.[60] What this group of women showed me in the course of the weekend had to do with balancing the importance of the group, and supporting its weakest member. Their ability to acknowledge my context and theirs and thereby create a connection of understanding was extraordinary. I felt I had participated as a group member in a way that was beyond my experience. O'Hara captures my experience. "In ecosystems, no part of the whole is unimportant. No member is, or can be, excluded from participation in the interconnected whole" (1995: 37).

---

59 Liddell and Scott (1986) translate οικοσ (oikos) also as housewifery.

60 The manner of our meeting came about through a discussion over knowledge claims. I was presenting a paper which turned out to be controversial. The women from Central Australia, even though they were critical of the paper, nevertheless spent time discussing the issues with me and supporting me through a difficult conference.

Among this group of women, there was a sense of both participation and interconnectedness that was new to me. It is this sense of participation I have in mind as a way of approaching economics. It means putting issues on the table, not hiding externalities in low prices, and above all, it means sharing knowledge. Any new economic system will have to increase opportunities for participation, because without doing so we can expect to see more intense confrontations between those who are for and against globalisation.[61]

Sabine O'Hara names place as a further feature of an economics which puts biodiversity at the centre. Displacement is a feature of all societies functioning within a neoclassical economic paradigm. And, as we saw earlier under globalisation, the "constraints of geography ... recede" (Waters 1995: 3). Globalisation, once again, builds on the heritage of colonisation which relies on displacement, both of the colonised and the coloniser. At the time of colonisation, Britain developed a system of so-called public schools (many of them boarding schools) to which future colonisers were sent. There they learnt to disconnect from the place where they had grown up because the imperial system required that they spread "civilisation" to the colonies. This system is still in place and was used in Australia by rural people who lived too far from the centres of education. I was sent to such a boarding school, displaced from the place I still call home. The poorer members of society experience itinerant work, migration, exile and fleeing as a refugee (either to urban centres or other countries) as important aspects of the economic system.[62] In the global economy, making it easy for goods to cross borders means that the same stores, the same hotel chains, the same systems operate all over the world. This suits the neoclassical economy for which place is considered

---

61   The S11 protest against the World Economic Forum in Melbourne (11–13 September 2000) was one of many such confrontations in different countries around the world, following the Seattle protests against the WTO in November 1999. Most of the protesters were well-informed, literate, internet-connected and customers of global corporations. They/we were able to see how people in poorer nations are exploited for the convenience of those in the richer nations. They/we were also concerned about the ways in which food produce is increasingly disconnected from them/us through research and development of seeds, genetic modification and industrial farming, and the way in which ordinary people are dissuaded from participating actively in the economy.

62   For a discussion of migration and globalisation, see Sassen (1998).

irrelevant. But for a wild economy, place matters. The Seikatsu Club's relationship between the consumer and the producer would be standard (see Chapter Six, and Bennholdt-Thomsen and Mies 1999: 131, for more on the Seikatsu Club). In Canberra a biodynamic butcher, Richard O'Dell, procures meat from a single source – a farmer, Ron Ward, from the nearby town of Cootamundra – and as conditions fluctuate for his supplier Ward, so they fluctuate for the consumer. O'Dell speaks about the importance of his relationship to the supplier and their commitment to one another, and also about the state of the animal killed for meat. This is an unusual approach for a butcher to take, and raises many questions about the system of slaughter that most meat consumers take for granted.[63] The point I am making here is that, even for an industry such as meat production, it is possible to change practices and put relationship at the centre. It is difficult to buy local produce in large urban centres and even in rural towns. The practices of organic and biodynamic farming entail much faster consumption times, and so the products are less likely to travel very long distances between producer and consumer. Although the number of organic and biodynamic outlets is increasing, there are not enough to supply all consumers, and they are generally more readily available to middle-class consumers who can pay the higher – and more realistic – prices.

As argued above, growth in an economic system which puts the biophysical at the centre is not limitless. It is also not without boundaries. Planting exotic trees in one country and clear-felling the same endemic tree in another is one of the absurdities of a disconnected system of economics. Likewise, feeding meat to herbivores (cattle feed before the British BSE epidemic) represents disconnection from the process of production. In spite of BSE, these practices continue in the USA. Similar practices can be seen in industrial farming, fishing,[64] and forestry around the world. A recognition of limits would involve creating an economy in which "each gives as much as, or more than, she takes" (Hawthorne 1993). It would have to include the cost of so-called externalities in the

---

63 Patrice Newell also discusses the importance of developing relationships with the local abattoir and butcher (2000: 28–29); for a different view on the politics of meat production and consumption, see Carol Adams (1990).

64 The industrial growing of prawns (shrimps) in areas which have been prime rice-farming land, now under threat from salination caused by prawn farming, is one such absurdity, see Wichterich (2000: 74–78).

price of goods sold. The externalities in, say, the production of a piece of paper would involve the cost of destroying plants growing near the felled tree as well as its replacement cost, the cost of transport, of milling, of chemical treatment during production. On this basis, a piece of paper coming from the burning forests of Indonesia[65] would cost much more than a piece of paper produced in a sustainable way. This would be so because externalities can be costed in the time it would take to regrow Indonesian forests. The time taken will be much longer and involve many more resources to fix the damage (if it can be fixed).

In the new global order envisaged by transnational companies, time, like place, is an irrelevance. With instant email and internet contact, time zones are only a small glitch; the global traders can use them to their advantage as they gamble on stocks and shares across time zones, even at night. International air travel is a bigger glitch, but most centres of trade are reachable within twenty-four hours. Time is flattened in the neo-classical system, but as anyone who has ever watched time-phase photography knows, time is forever changing in dynamic systems. The homogenising of time and place arises out of a philosophy disconnected from the real world and its cycles of growth, change, decay. Instead, we get a looming catastrophe, a flat horizon and instant gratification.

Feminism, ecology and indigenous knowledge systems build on and acknowledge complexity. They connect the personal, the system, the local, to the biophysical realm and to culture.

Economic theory, in order to be consistent with the principles of wild politics, would have to take as a central proposition its obligation to our children: intergenerational sustainability. I do not mean five years, or even fifty, but rather a time frame of many thousands of years. In July 1984, Lilla Watson presenting a keynote speech on "Aboriginal Women and Feminism" at Australia's national Women and Labour Conference, pointed out that for Aboriginal people the future went as far forward as it went back. She argued that Aboriginal people had a 40,000-year plan.[66] What I

---

65   Choong Tet Siu (1997: 42), citing the World Wide Fund for Nature, suggests that it could take up to 100 years to reforest the 40,000 to 60,000 hectares of destroyed forest. Some things, however, might never recover, among them Sumatran tigers, orang-utans and elephants.

66   Research since 1984 indicates that Aboriginal people have been in Australia for at least 70,000 years, possibly 100,000 years.

have in mind is a world something along the lines of Lilla Watson's 40,000-year plan. By envisioning a future of this length, it becomes essential to consider how resources – renewable and non-renewable – can be maintained, as if permanently.

We do not have examples of this in the west, and the model is incompatible with a market-driven view of the world, which encourages individuals to make decisions for short-term advantage (Gowdy and McDaniel 1995: 185). There are examples in the indigenous world. Such a vision also assumes sustainable approaches to life – production and consumption – and assumes that they can be maintained over very long periods of time. One model, which has sustained fragile desert environments for millennia, is that used by indigenous peoples in Central Australia. Bell (1983/2002) describes the rituals used by Kaytej women in the maintenance of the environment. The rituals are a central part of social organisation, and part of the religious life of the community. But they also have an economic function, in that they predispose every member of the society to preserve, maintain, and take responsibility for particular areas of land. Western culture, if it is to move in the direction of long-term sustainability, would need to find some mechanism akin to these rituals and alter its system of land tenure. A culture inspired by biodiversity could begin to move in the direction of this level of responsibility for the environment.

In proposing a different approach for economics, the emphasis has to shift from the decontextualised world of perfect information represented by neoclassical economics. Instead, relationship is central, as is a sense of connectedness which takes account of real needs, rather than consumer needs generated by marketing. A decolonised wild economics would be grounded in a sense of place, and in the maintenance of the environment – including land, biodiversity, and non-renewable resources – to such an extent that it would not be difficult to imagine it remaining in a sustainable state for many thousands of years.

The global economic system has its parallels in the western legal framework. Again universalisation and disconnection come to the fore. But indigenous systems of land challenge these notions. Firstly, they challenge the western system of land tenure; secondly, they insist on relationship and responsibility as central to land tenure.

CHAPTER FOUR

LAND AS RELATIONSHIP
AND LAND AS POSSESSION

> *Indigenous peoples' role in conserving biodiversity has*
> *been consistently underestimated. In large part this is due*
> *to the failure to appreciate the anthropogenic (i.e. human*
> *created) or humanized (i.e. human-modified) nature of*
> *apparently pristine or "wild" landscapes. But scientists*
> *are increasingly discovering that what they had thought*
> *were wild resources and areas are actually the products of*
> *coevolutionary relationships between humans and nature*
> – Darrell Posey (1996: 6).

Land as Resource or Relationship?

Attitudes to land, the connection or disconnection between land and its people, and the ways in which land is passed from one generation to another, tell us a great deal about the basic institutions of a particular culture. An example is the difference between the individualised ownership of land in western culture, as opposed to collective responsibilities for land in many indigenous cultures.

I argue that regarding land as a commodity, as a utilitarian resource, will not ensure the very long-term sustainability of land which Lilla Watson's (1984) 40,000-year plan presupposes. I suggest, instead, that western culture needs to shift its perception of land as something useful and profitable, to the view that the land is a living entity with which one has a relationship, and for which we are all responsible and from which we all benefit.

Wilderness

In the mind of the general public in western countries, wilderness is an area untouched by human habitation, and most public agencies take this view.[1]

---

1   For a challenge to this view, see Collard (1988); Wright (1991); Langton (1998).

The protests at the World Economic Forum in Melbourne from 11 to 13 September 2000 brought together many individuals and groups from the diversity matrix. The Melbourne Jabiluka Action Group expressed their support for the Mirrar people of Arnhem Land, who had been protesting against the uranium mine on their land for many years (see also note 2 this chapter).

National Parks, on the whole, are protected areas. They are protected from certain human activities (farming and mining[2] are usually excluded) and from non-native animals, and introduced plant species are kept at a minimum. Such a view exemplifies the separation of nature and humanity in the western approach to wilderness.

> A park is a managerial unit definable in quantitative and pragmatic terms. Wilderness is unquantifiable. Its boundaries are vague or nonexistent, its contents unknown, its inhabitants elusive. The purpose of parks is to use; the earmark of wilderness is mystery. Because they serve technology, parks tend toward the predictable and static, but wilderness is infinitely burgeoning and changing because it is the matrix of life itself (Drew 1999: 73).

It is certainly the case that "wilderness parks" are a contradiction when the above definition is applied. Drew separates the wilderness from humanity, removing it from all contact with human existence, and this is emblematic of how non-human players in the world are separated out from humanity. The concept of wilderness is a construct of the western imagination, and separating out "wild lands", making them free of human endeavour, is suggested as a solution by environmentalists.[3] Some argue that the problem of the western construction of nature is that it places humans at the centre – it is anthropocentric[4] (Mathews 1994:

---

2   An exception to this is the Rio Tinto Jabiluka mine on Mirrar land in Arnhem Land. (See the Mirrar website: http://www.mirrar.net/indexer.htm, accessed 16 August 2000.) For further information on uranium mining and the Mirrar people, see Katona (1997). The mine was closed in 2000.

3   Gowdy and McDaniel (1995: 188) suggest this, although they do limit it to making the lands "essentially free of economic exploitation". It is not clear whether their definition includes the economies of indigenous or traditional peoples who contribute to the maintenance of the ecology. I am not opposed to restoring lands, and removing environmentally destructive elements; however, I do think that why and how we do this is as important as the doing of it. For example, a survey undertaken by Greening Australia showed that simply replanting trees without attention to which trees are planted into which locale, is not only expensive, but also less effective than preserving remnant growth. So to argue for land clearing on the grounds that trees can be replanted is spurious (Murray and Willis 2001). I am also against further dispossession of indigenous peoples on the dubious grounds that everyone else will benefit.

4   Critics of western culture, among them Ramachandra Guha (1989), argue that the anthropocentric view which focuses on preservation of wilderness areas is, as Shiva (1993a) would argue, a local tradition and peculiar to American environmentalism.

37–40),[5] but my argument is that anthropocentrism requires separating humanity out from the biophysical world and creating a hierarchy in which human beings are at the pinnacle. Anthropocentrism allows "deep ecology" thinkers to remove people altogether (Naess 1998), thereby ignoring the relationship between people and the land which has persisted for many thousands of years before people separated from the land and nature, and began destroying it. Separation and disconnection are the processes which allowed anthropocentrism, and the domination of nature by humanity, to flourish as conquering philosophies.

In recent years there has been a gradual recognition that indigenous inhabitants have had a long-term impact on the environment. In order to maintain that environment, or alter it in some cases, the continued relationship between people and land is what creates the possibility of long-term sustainability. Some researchers have suggested that indigenous peoples contributed to the destuction of the mega-fauna (Flannery 1994) or forests (Diamond 1991). After changes were made to Land Rights legislation in Australia, some National Parks (Uluru, Kakadu, Nitmiluk and Gurig are the oldest) were returned to their traditional owners and are now run by boards of management which include traditional indigenous owners. In many areas the traditional owners continue practices such as mosaic burning, hunting of native animals, harvesting and gathering traditional foods, medicines, and other products, as well as maintaining ritual connection to the land.[6]

The entry display board at the Nitmiluk Visitors Centre in the Northern Territory has the following notice:

Nitmiluk is not a wilderness.

It is not pristine or untamed: it is a human artefact. It is a land constructed by us over tens of thousands of years – through our ceremonies and ties of kinship, through fire and through hunting over countless generations of our people the Jawoyn … Nitmiluk is now fenced by lines on a map but remains

---

5   Freya Mathews does, nevertheless, point to the advent of separating out the "wild" and the "tame", allowing for no such thing as "wilderness" during the Neolithic (1994: 45). Val Plumwood (1996) gives a more satisfying analysis of the process of separation.

6   Langton (1998: 58) points out, however, that "the management regime imposed by the managing government overrides Aboriginal land use through zoning, regulations and other devices."

an indivisible part of our traditional lands, linked through our ceremony and our law.

Once again we are able to care for our country – not as *terra nullius*, or an empty land; not as an untamed wilderness – but as a part of a living heritage that forms a basis for economic and social independence for our people (cited in Langton 1998: 34).

Wayland Drew's binary definition, quoted above, does not reflect the complexity of the relationship between indigenous peoples and the land. It is instead a simplistic idea of "man" against nature, wilderness as challenge, as mystery. Indigenous knowledge and understanding of the land invalidate the notion that "the earmark of wilderness is mystery" (Drew 1999: 73). The epistemological separation required by this is the hallmark of western knowledge, not of indigenous knowledge systems, since indigenous peoples know the so-called mysteries of the "wilderness". They are mysteries to the western mind because the western mind has not stayed long enough to know.

The idea of wilderness emerges from a craving of urbanised peoples who look toward nature as a healing experience, and to some extent with fear. Such fear creates wilderness "theme parks" where wilderness can be safely encountered, for example, Yellowstone National Park, USA. Of course, such experience is only necessary in a culture full of dis-ease. Preservation becomes necessary only when the culture is intent on destruction. In the Trombetas River zone of Brazil, the Brazilian environmental agency IBAMA made an unholy alliance with mining interests to declare the zone inhabited by indigenous peoples a "biological reserve" (Acevedo and Castro 1993 cited in Martinez-Alier 2000: 155), thereby preventing the indigenous peoples from continuing their traditions and usual ways of life. This conflict between western conservationist ethics and the indigenous owners is interestingly expressed by Peter D. Dwyer in a work purporting to reflect on the issues. He writes:

to [western] conservationists, the environment is disengaged from human life, from "culture", and perceived as "natural". In cases where indigenous perceptions concede of no such contrast the inevitable impact of these co-operative programs can be described only as conceptual hegemony (1994: 95).

There are several problems here. Firstly, this view of western conservationists is a very masculine and mainstream view: it suggests that disconnection is the norm. It would be contested by ecofeminists and many ecological activists. Secondly, it suggests that indigenous peoples are *incapable* of making such a contrast. Indigenous theorists, however, suggest that they are not incapable of abstraction or separation, but rather that their worldview insists that responsibility to the communities in which one lives is important. They also argue for the development of "global indigenous strategic alliances" (Tuhiwai Smith 1999: 108).

Marcia Langton goes even further in her analysis of wilderness, arguing that the "popular usage of the term 'wilderness' in Australia has had the effect of denying the imprint of millennia of Aboriginal impacts on, and relationships with, species and ecologies in Australian environmental history". At the same time the uninformed public has unrealistic expectations of "a pristine environment without 'human' impacts and of an indigenous population living in pre-colonial circumstances" (Langton 1998: 18, 31). The western knowledge, legal and corporate systems undermine the traditions and perspectives of indigenous peoples. Land is the primary interface between these competing systems, while discrepancies in power – particularly violence, reward and systemic power – ensure maintenance of the western status quo. Haunani-Kay Trask connects the ways in which industrialists and those fighting for wilderness approach nature.

> Even the ecological/wilderness approach remains within the view of nature as a resource for humans. The only difference between this view and the industrialists' view is that the former fights for preserves and wilderness areas. Philosophically, however, the Earth is still seen as a resource (1986: 183).

Indigenous peoples who follow a hunting and gathering regime do not need to invent wilderness; rather they create mechanisms of responsibility and rights toward the land and ways of maintaining their relationship with it. When agriculture is "invented",[7] human relationships change. And their

---

7   I do not mean to imply here that this happened suddenly or is an identifiable event. The "invention" of agriculture represents a shift in the relationship of humans to the land, to food storage and to ownership. There is a continuum between hunter-gathering regimes and incipient agriculture, with the two often co-existing.

relationships with land, water courses, animals and plants also change. Efforts to control "nature" arise, and people begin to live on the land, rather than in it. However, agriculture does not have a necessary connection with domination (Mathews 1994 posits that it does), although Jared Diamond, in the tradition of Rousseau, argues that social inequality might have its origins in agriculture (1991: 169 ff). There are many ways to farm: some farmers respect natural cycles and processes, some do not. Indigenous farmers, organic farmers, farmers using traditional techniques of land cultivation[8] can work in sustainable ways; contemporary farmers can also farm sustainably (see Chapter Five for more details).

Max Oelschlaeger, in his massive work *The Idea of Wilderness*, traces some key steps in the development of the concept. He makes it clear that there is no need for such an idea among those who live in relationship with the land. The Paleolithic peoples, for instance, made no such distinction: "home was where they were and where they had always been. They could not become lost in the wilderness, since it did not exist" (1991: 14).

But even more important in the development of the idea of wilderness was the western scientific alienation of its knowledge systems from everyday life: Francis Bacon (1561–1626), René Descartes (1596–1650) and Isaac Newton (1642–1727) are key figures in this cultural shift.[9] Deforestation on a huge scale was a precursor to the Industrial Revolution in Western Europe (Schama 1996: 45–53) just as in earlier centuries, deforestation accompanied the development of agricultural peoples across Western Asia, the Middle East, Northern Africa and the Mediterranean (Diamond 1991). Similar processes may have occurred on Easter Island and among the Anasazi people of New Mexico (Diamond 1991: 302).

In the "Enlightenment" period, the ideas of Bacon, Descartes and Newton began to dominate the culture of the elite. They began a process of disconnection and universalisation which is still in progress, still

---

8   Being an indigenous or traditional farmer is also no guarantee of sustainability. For example, the slash-and-burn farming technique can be quite destructive, although its destructiveness has increased with encroachments on available land areas by colonists, thereby decreasing the area of land for indigenous use and increasing the rate of burning cycles. Colonisation and the "Enlightenment" have much to answer for.

9   Margaret Wertheim comments that the "very homogenization of space that is at the heart of modern cosmology's success is also responsible for the banishment from our world picture of any kind of spiritual space. In a homogeneous space only one kind of reality can be accommodated" (1999: 151).

spreading across the world into places and cultures which have had just on fifty years since first contact[10] (Diamond 1991: 202–204). Alongside the idea of Adam Smith (1723–1790) that "consumption was fundamental to human well-being" (cited in Oelschlaeger 1991: 92), western culture has created the need for an idea of wilderness. To the "Enlightenment" thinker, "the wilderness condition was something repugnant in which human beings lived mean and savage lives" (Oelschlaeger 1991: 93).

Not surprisingly, the development of the idea of wilderness occurred in North America, which during the eighteenth and nineteenth centuries was becoming rapidly "humanised". In Europe and Asia this shift had occurred much earlier, so the change was more difficult to detect. In North America, the two worlds, "humanised" and "wild", still existed, but the latter was fast disappearing. It was in this setting that Henry David Thoreau (1817–1862) and John Muir (1838–1914)[11] developed their ideas. Thoreau's writings explore both the ideas and practice of wildness.[12] He was interested in the ways of "Indians" and in experiences of living face to face with nature. In the end, his work also led him to believe that wildness and culture were inextricably linked. Society, he argued, "is endangered when wilderness is destroyed" (in Oelschlaeger 1991: 165). Although his work connects nature, wildness, society and creativity in some interesting ways, it remains permeated with Enlightenment assumptions of access to solitude and nature for the privileged, so that "man", the real man, the Wild Man (Bly 1992: x) can "find his connection to the universe" (Gunn Allen 1998: 60). A vision of where society at large might go in the future must extend beyond these assumptions, take more account of complexity and diversity, and acknowledge the ways in which power influences what we know and what we take account of. All the same, Thoreau's refrain, "In Wildness is the preservation of the World" (1862/1962: 224) is worth contemplation.

---

10 Jared Diamond is here referring to the Grand Valley of the Balim River in Papua (West Papua). The valley was peopled by around 50,000 Papuans and remained unknown to outsiders until 1938.

11 John Muir (1838–1914) was instrumental in the establishment of America's Sierra Club and in contributions to the development of National Parks. For more on his life and works, see Oelschlaeger (1991: 172–204).

12 Like many other theorists there is a disjunction between Thoreau's writings and his life practice. Although he lived in a cabin by a pond, his existence there could not be described as self-sufficient.

Dave Foreman of Earth First! and Arne Naess, who developed the idea of "deep ecology", are the contemporary inheritors of the ideas of Thoreau, Muir and Aldo Leopold (1887–1948). Foreman, for example, writes, "The preservation of wildness and native diversity is *the* most important issue" (1998: 359; see also Naess 1998). But the problem with these contemporary idealists is that, like Dwyer, they demand that people are insignificant in the world of wilderness. "Wilderness fundamentalism" (Foreman 1998: 358) is not the answer; nor do I believe that Foreman's concept of the eco-warrior[13] useful in a world already dominated by human (masculine) aggression. This is evident in his opportunistic use of gender pronouns. At the moment of writing about warriors, Foreman suddenly changes the gender: "A warrior recognizes that *her* life is not the most important thing in *her* life" (1998: 363, my emphasis). Ironically, by shifting gender at this moment, he restates a truism of so many women's lives now and in the past. It becomes not the revolutionary statement he intended, but one that simply upholds the old male-dominated order. In this instance, *she* is now supposed to sacrifice *her* life, not for family, husband or country, but for "the millions of other species" and the earth itself.

Deep ecology was developed by Norwegian philosopher Arne Naess in the early 1970s. Superficially it appears to share much with feminist writing on ecology with its "non-hierarchical thinking" and "celebrating the interwovern connectedness of all of us" (Seager 1993: 230). Some early feminist works pointed also to the importance of connective systems (Griffin 1978), biophilic thinking (Daly 1978) and the world as organism (Merchant 1980). But the two theories diverge when it comes to understanding the politics of selflessness and of giving up an "independent existence" or merging with the natural world (Seager 1993: 235). I have no argument with ecocentrism, or dispensing with anthropocentrism; however, a blithe disregard for women – and women's knowledge – as if women were not part of the connected web, falls short of a feminist vision of an ecologically centred world. In addition, setting aside large tracts of land, dispossessing those who have maintained them for millennia, so that

---

13   Again here there are echoes of the masculine romance of the Wild Man. But the Wild Man, as represented in the works of these western eco-warriors, does not appear to have that deep sense of responsibility and reciprocity which is essential for a long-term sustainable relationship as that suggested by Langton (1998), Gunn Allen (1998), Bell (1983/2002) and Watson (1984).

a few privileged western men and women can enjoy the solitude and mystery of wilderness, is unjust. Even if these appropriative moves are justified on the grounds of protecting biodiversity, the impetus denies the dynamic relationship between people and biodiverse environments. As Val Plumwood has so cogently argued, deep ecology[14] is entwined in its nineteenth-century rationalist philosophy in which universalism (another word for colonisation) is central; in which objectification and detachment are privileged; and in which utilitarianism often supplies the justification for acts with severe consequences for those outside the privileged group. Deep ecology also ignores the problem of human responsibility in relation to the biosphere. In the process of merging with nature, there is no recognition of the importance of human actions in shaping the environment. Susanne Kappeler argues that an important step in making change takes place when others are taken seriously. As she writes, change "would require a view of people which takes seriously and reckons with their will, both their will to violence and their will to change" (1995: 5).

In a culture in which the *utamaroho*, the inspiration, were biodiversity, taking the will and the actions of others seriously would be integral to the functioning of culture. As a result, separation of the wild from the human would cease to be necessary as a means of protection. It is, as Bengali feminist Rokeya Sakhawat Hossain argued in 1905, like enclosing women in harems, while the men remain free to do whatever they like (1988: 9). In the case of land, the wilderness is separated, fenced in by lines on a map (as at Nitmiluk), and only accessible to the privileged of the world.

---

14 See Val Plumwood's analysis which focuses on the connection between rationalism and deep ecology including discussion of universalisation, of disconnection through merging, colonisation and transcendence (1996: 163–168). For other critiques of deep ecology, see Salleh (1984, 1992); and Cuomo (1994).

Land

> *Ancestral activity in country provides a metaphor for*
> *relations between the living: the comings and goings of the*
> *dreaming animate the landscape, infuse it with significance,*
> *and provide paths along which links between living people*
> *may be traced. Each individual has a unique complex of*
> *relations to land, its sites and dreamings, but it is the*
> *corporate nature of interests in land which is emphasized*
> — Diane Bell (1983/2002: 137).

"Land" is a word redolent of meaning. It conjures images of home or of fear; of possession and dispossession; of the body, journeys and pathways; of nature gone wild or of civilisation and cultivation. At which end of these continua your thoughts fall will depend on your origins, your culture – rural or urban, indigenous or immigrant.

Humans have fought over land for millennia. As one group moves into another's territory, aggression manifests, unless the incursion is accompanied by the mingling of families, or an agreed system of sharing of land between the inhabitants.[15] In recent centuries the shifting ownership of land has progressed at an alarming rate, with a complex weave of cause and effect interacting as mass dispossession. From discovery and invasion to colonisation, mass slaughter, mining, fishing, tourism and industrial farming, the outcome has been flight to urban centres with its concomitant alienation, increased crime rate, and inhuman poverty through crowding.

In Europe, at the beginning of the Agricultural Revolution, the poorest people were dispossessed through the enclosure movement:[16] the fencing of huge tracts of land previously used by local people. The enclosure movement prevented hunting, stopped gypsies and villagers from crossing the land and made it impossible to agist animals in times when feed was short. The rich had more space to enjoy and were able to

---

15   The Yolngu of Arnhem land in northern Australia have a land tenure system which allows extended families to have access to coastal land and resources as well as inland areas and resources. For details on this, see Williams (1986). All Aboriginal land-tenure systems have mechanisms for sharing, succession and co-management. Relationship, responsibility and rights are key features.

16   "The English Enclosure Acts of the 1500s and 1600s marked the beginning of the assignment of exclusive rights to the natural world" (Wilson 2001: 290).

truly possess the land. In Scotland the clearances[17] removed shepherds and farmers from the land; in Ireland the potato famine did the work through starvation and mass emigration.

This approach to land was continued as European countries colonised the New World. The New World was filled with peoples who had a different relationship to land. Many of them shared a particular stretch of land in much the same way as Europeans had in earlier times.

Carolyn Merchant, in her discussion of the mechanistic view of nature which results in domination, identifies "a set of ontological, epistemological, methodological, and ethical assumptions about 'reality'" (1999: 164–165). In summary, she enumerates them as:

- nature is made up of discrete particles
- sense data are discrete
- the universe is a natural order, maintaining identity through change, and can be described and predicted by mathematics
- problems can be broken down into parts, solved, and reassembled without changing their character
- science is context-free, value-free knowledge of the world (Merchant 1999: 165).

Significantly, separation, disconnection and abstraction are entrenched in all aspects of the mechanistic approach to nature. Merchant's analysis within the discourse of ecology echoes the concerns of Ani (2000), Bell (1998), Shiva (1989) and Tuhiwai Smith (1999).

Another feature of the disconnected European worldview is evident in Australia. The inability to "see" that other peoples inhabited the land led to the proclamation of the areas settled by Europeans (primarily the eastern seaboard) as *terra nullius* (see Langton 1998; Reynolds 1990; Plumwood 1994: 77; Salleh 1997: 119; and Chapter Two). Probably around a million people inhabited the land and held heritable rights to it through a complex system of ownership, but this was ignored.[18]

---

17 Guy Hand points out that the English "called the native Highlanders 'savages' (from the Latin root *silva*, meaning forest) … As forest disappeared, so did the very words to describe them" (1999: 137–138). Once the forests had been cleared, "landlords realized sheep would be more profitable than tenants on the now bankrupt Highland soil" (1999: 138).

18 The struggle for recognition of Aboriginal ownership continues. Formal recognition of Native Title was first achieved with the Mabo decision in 1992 (Bartlett 1993); the Wik

The doctrine of *terra nullius* was also used in Africa (Salleh 1994: 77). It allowed Europeans to dehumanise people (sometimes counting them as a part of the "wild life"), and to invisibilise all resistance to colonisation. The doctrine of *terra nullius* arises from a deeply racist view of the world. In Australia, Africa and elsewhere, indigenous peoples were dispossessed, massacred, educated into the colonisers' ways, and moved on to land considered useless, where they lived on reservations and missions. Like the land, they vanished epistemologically and became construed as "the race on the brink of extinction".[19] Until, of course, valuable minerals or other natural resources were discovered.

> In Aboriginal Australia people and land were united in ways that are difficult for outsiders to grasp. Access to land was vital for the maintenance of both body and soul. Food and water were necessary for physical survival but land was far more than an economic resource. People were tied spiritually to a particular locality; this was their "country", "home" or "dreaming place", a tangible link with the ancestors who had lived and died there and with the Dreaming beings who originally created the territory. Through such links people derived a sense of belonging, of identity and of oneness with the living world (Dingle 1988: 9).

---

and Wik-Way people of Cape York Peninsula achieved recognition of their exclusive ownership over 6000 square kilometres of land on 3 October 2000. However, 21,000 square kilometres of land remain in dispute and are currently under leasehold by seven pastoral and four mining companies (Pryor 2000: 5). Many other Native Title claims remain outstanding throughout Australia. Claims for Native Title recognition have been made over the last three decades. Between 1968 and 1971 the Yolngu fought the first land rights battle in the courts; they lost, but in 1976 the *Aboriginal Land Rights (Northern Territory) Act* was enacted, enabling Aboriginal title to Aboriginal Reserves in the Northern Territory and the ability to claim vacant Crown land (Williams 1986: 19).

19 This is exemplified in works such as Daisy Bates' *The Passing of the Aborigines* (1938), which was one of the most widely read books on Aborigines in Australia from the 1940s to the 1960s and influenced many of the views of that era. Her influence can still be seen in the views expressed by right-wing politicians such as Pauline Hanson. The Prologue of Bates' book is entitled "A Vanished People". Nor is this view entirely a thing of the past. It continues in works such as Berndt and Berndt *A World That Was* (1993). The implication of the title is that the culture no longer exists. See Bell (1998) for a challenge to the view.

The perceptual shift from *terra mater*[20] (mother earth) to *terra nullius* reflects both a political shift and an ecological shift. On the one hand, *terra mater* represents a perspective which views the earth as abundant, as ever fruitful, as represented by Aboriginal people in the statements which indicate a relationship between self and land as intimate, and as connected. The well-being of the one is reflected in the well-being of the other, and land is considered a partner in survival. In this system, humans and land replenish one another. On the other hand, *terra nullius* represents a perspective which sees earth as empty, unused, as wasteland, as a resource to be plundered, as resources which must pay their own way.[21]

In an interesting legal sleight of hand, there are very different requirements of residence for Native Title claims and Crown Title claims. Connection to land is an essential requirement to prove Native Title under the Mabo ruling. This is expressed legally as "traditional title is rooted in physical presence" (Toohey J Mabo (2) at 188 cited in Kauffman 1998: 9). The High Court in a New South Wales case said that Native Title claimants are required to prove that they have not "[ceased] to have a requisite *physical* connection with the land" (*Coe v Commonwealth* Mason CJ (1993) 38 ALJR 1, especially at 42–45 and 51–52). By contrast, the western system of land tenure has no such requirement imposed upon it. The British Crown was able to assert sovereignty over land it had neither seen nor occupied. Connection might be a sufficient condition (as in the case of mining claims, or squatters) but it is not a necessary condition. With Native Title, physical connection is codified as a necessary condition.

---

20 By using this term I do not mean to imply that the earth is "our mother" with all the contradictions and blames that incurs. More to the point is the fact that the earth is living and in relationship to those who inhabit it. For an excellent critique of "the earth is our mother" syndrome, see Seager (1993: 219–221). As Seager points out, "mother earth" is not here to clean up after us and take humanity's abuses! It also lets the abusers off the hook, for if we are "her children" we are accountable or responsible.

21 Such a view allows one to "choose" only between two negative options. Marilyn Waring compares the case of the construction of a dam which would kill wildlife against a concept called "Wildlife Fish User Days". She concludes that these two pseudo-alternatives simply allow one to weigh "one market utility – namely, a silt-producing, ecologically-damaging, 'productive' dam – against another – namely, income from the legitimised violence of men against animals, euphemistically called leisure" (1988: 216). Waring cites this example as the conclusion of a survey of leading conservation strategists from sixty-five nations (1988: 215).

A further example of the distinction between indigenous views of land and western views is that in western law, not only the Crown but also an individual owner does not have to have any connection with the land. In western law, an owner can purchase land without living on it, or maintaining it; an owner can own without even knowing where the land is. Such a disconnection from land is increasing, and the internet is playing an important role through land sales by image only (Dunlevy 2001: 2).²² The epitome of disconnection is that property investment through urban development, mining and agriculture can be a part of the portfolio of anyone who has a superannuation policy or share portfolio. Disconnection from real estate is becoming a disconnection from reality.

Marcia Langton points to an interesting legal clash between agriculture and hunter–gatherer systems. She writes:

> The main proposition in British law which supported the *terra nullius* fiction was that land subject to agriculture was owned, while land subject to a hunting and gathering regime was devoid of human laws which could be recognised by the Australian judiciary (1998: 31).

In a society where people work with the land, such a view is impossible. Aboriginal women, for example, when foraging, would intersperse work, recreation and child-minding. "The aim was to collect enough food for their family for the day with *the minimum expenditure of effort*" (Dingle 1988: 12, my emphasis). In other parts of the world, as agriculture developed, and perceptions of time became linear rather than cyclical, people's perspective on land and nature shifted too, and "nature was conceived of as valueless until humanized" (Oelschlaeger 1991: 31). The *terra nullius* perspective strips the earth of all possibility of the sacred. Eve eats of the apple in spite of the sacred prohibition; Tiamat is dismembered (Daly 1978: 107–112). Denoting a living being or place as sacred has resulted in preserving regions of biodiversity, and has also been a means of ensuring that particular species are not over-harvested. This has happened in India (Shiva 1993a: 89), in the cultures of Native America (LaDuke 1999: 1), among indigenous Australians (Bell 1984,

---

22 Deborah Bird Rose (2000: 218–235) discusses some of the distinctions between western and indigenous views of land.

1998; Williams 1986); indeed, it is something which appears in most religious traditions of the world.[23]

It is easy to identify indigenous and traditional cultures which can be characterised as promoting a strong sense of place and relationship to the land and which furthermore encourage the sharing of resources. My exploration also includes a search for whether this ever happens in European-based systems of land tenure.

Dealing with Waste

In the 1950s, in rural New South Wales, all of our home waste was recycled. The food scraps were fed to the chooks, who recycled them into manure. The chooks ran free in the paddock behind the chookyard, where the house cow also grazed. They returned the scraps to the family as free-range eggs (although none of us knew that term then: it was not necessary in our world to make the distinction between battery and free-range). The newspapers were stacked into piles, and once every six months we children were conscripted into carrying armloads to the car. They were delivered to the butcher who used them for the outer wrapping layer on his meat sales. Other paper products were burnt in 44-gallon drums, or were used to start fires in the open fireplaces. Bottles and cans were separated into two 44-gallon drums. The bottles were recycled through the local soft drink bottler, while cans were burnt and buried. Local government provided no recycling services, but everything was reused, whenever possible. Clothing was passed down and made over; children's toys were passed on to others. Even unsuccessful presents and trophies were stored and eventually diverted as gifts in other contexts. Children were drawn into the recycling process, and since all soft drink bottles had a small return deposit (sixpence), we became assiduous recyclers at an early age. The commodification of everything has made such recycling more and more difficult in the western world; since last year's brand name is not this year's, the fast pace of obsolescence means that re-use becomes insulting. Poor people in many countries still pursue these ways. But for how long?

---

23   The literature on religious traditions is too numerous to list here. A good test for the reader is to think of their own religious tradition and consider places and species which carry the term "sacred". In the Christian tradition, for example, the Church of the Holy Sepulchre in Jerusalem identifies one such sacred place, connected with rocks. Sacred olive groves are frequent referents in the Biblical literature.

Can we turn around our attitudes in time to catch up with them?

In a similar vein, Maria Mies and Veronica Bennholdt-Thomsen tell the story of the German village of Eifel (1999: 141–143). Fifty years ago it was a self-sufficient village with forest nearby, and commons which straddled roads and lay between blocks of private land. The commons were maintained by each household of the village which contributed its share through work performed as a reciprocal service to the community. The communal work was offset by access to the resources of the commons such as firewood and grazing rights, and the poorest villagers were able to use the village land. As Mies and Bennholdt-Thomsen write, today the thirty-two peasant families have been reduced to two.

> The village commons have either been privatised or are being leased out to a few big farmers who buy or lease all land. The only commons still left is the village forest. But the system of free communal labour has been totally abolished and replaced by wage labour (1999: 142).

The greatest irony is that land which was previously sustained through communal labour and grazing of animals on verges has become a source of "green waste". And because the commons are so reduced there is no-where to recycle organic matter, and so waste is transported to Thuringia in the former East Germany to be composted. The expense of this proce-dure results in large village debts which cannot be serviced.

"Freeing" the Land, Enclosing the Commons

The decreasing access to commons as land is analogous to the decreasing access to other kinds of common property: natural resources, plants, genetic resources, knowledge. The privatisation of the commons is occurring, through a process of "violent intrusion, enclosure, division, fragmentation, segregation and then hierarchisation and centralisation to get access to the resources that are still controlled and used by local communities as commons" (Bennholdt-Thomsen and Mies 1999: 144). Only those with a pre-existing sense of community and common good are ready to resist such incursions.

The "freeing of land" which is promoted by the World Bank and other agencies intent on development at any cost, is, in fact, intended to tie up the land for private "productive" purposes. A strong system of communal ownership of land, such as that among indigenous Australians or in Papua New Guinea (Faraclas 2001), means that free capital cannot plunder the resources readily. Indigenous Melanesians in New Guinea, the Solomon Islands and Vanuatu, as Nicholas Faraclas points out, are among the few peoples whose nations have not yet moved toward the liberal western notion of ceding property rights to the state. He notes that more than 90 per cent of the national territory has not been "registered under 'western'-style land legislation" (2001: 68). He suggests that the maintenance of traditional communal rights is playing an important part in providing alternative models to globalisation.

The "freeing" of land for private property is analogous to the enclosure of "global commons". But there can be no such thing, since "commons *presuppose a community*" (Bennholdt-Thomsen and Mies 1999: 152). A community has a history over time, and a location in place. Further, the way in which the word "freedom" is used presupposes a free-for-all without responsibilities. This is this same use of freedom as in Garret Hardin's famous article "The Tragedy of the Commons" (1968) which creates an intellectual furphy: that freedom is about maximising one's own personal good without regard to the greater common good (see also Roy 1999). This idea resembles the neoclassical economic vision of "economic man". It is about appropriating, universalising and standardising the local. This notion is in stark contrast to the kind of freedom, identified by Shiva and others, that the maintenance of cultural traditions has enabled conservation, for example, via the continuation of sacred traditions, sacred groves, sacred sites and similar prohibitions on destroying the local ecology. The women of the forest in Papua New Guinea described by Mogina (1996) are also maintaining simultaneously culture and ecology; in India the knowledge of neem and its uses through Ayuvedic medicine has ensured the protection of neem trees (Shiva 2001e). Freedom as defined by Hardin and the proponents of globalisation amounts to "dismantling the commons" (Fairlie, Hafler and O'Riordan 1995: 50). Such "freedom" is perpetuated through an export-oriented privatisation which moves people out of self-sustaining relationships into the market economy. The result is systematic over-exploitation of the environment and its resources because the relationships of responsibility and reciprocity break down once the commons are dismantled. Hardin's model of the commons is based on an individualistic view of the world; it is more characteristic of the western system than of an interconnecting web of relationships between individuals and between communities that tends to protect resources rather than run them down. Fairlie, Hafler and O'Riordan, writing about the fishing industry, point out that when

> rapid resource depletion has occurred in commons regimes, it has been occasioned, in most cases, not by brute competition within the community, but through interference from outside the community, most frequently from a market economy which neither recognizes nor respects the often subtle rights and responsibilities by which the commons has been managed (1995: 60–61).

The reciprocity of German peasants, the sacred duties of Aboriginal people who "look after country", and the common good argued for by Arundhati Roy (1999), resemble the concept of a land ethic identified by Aldo Leopold.[24]

> A thing is right when it tends to preserve the integrity, stability, and beauty of the biotic community. It is wrong when it tends otherwise (in Oelschlaeger 1991: 238).

The Narmada Valley Development Project in India, funded by the World Bank, threatens to do just that, as it "will alter the ecology of the entire river basin of one of India's biggest rivers" (Roy 1999: 33). With four proposed dams along the river's length, it will displace millions of people. Fifty-seven and a half per cent of the displaced people are Adivasis, the indigenous people, and the Dalits add further to the displacement figures. Once again, the poorest people pay the biggest price. As Roy points out, "India's poorest people are subsidizing the lifestyles of her richest" (1999: 21). Other rivers are also under threat. In Malaysia in 1996, the proposed Bakun dam on the Balui River in Sarawak was given the go-ahead. Apa Bagie, head of Mothers Against Bagun, in speaking against the submersion of 690 square kilometres of forest and farmland, said she was not interested in compensation: "We just cannot be separated from it … we just want our land and we want to preserve our culture" (Roodman

---

24 Aldo Leopold was the founder of the Wilderness Society in the USA, and the author of a number of influential books, among them *Sand Country Almanac* (1948) in which he writes extensively about the land ethic. For a discussion of his life and works, see Oelschlaeger (1991: 205–242).

1996: 8). And in Vietnam, it is the Mekong River, "one of the world's last great rivers that still runs relatively free". Plans include damming the main stream of the river and a number of its tributaries, "all in the name of economic development" (Simon 2000: 9). The salient question is whose economies are going to be developed through this intervention? What will happen to the fisherpeople who depend on the river for their livelihood? Will the dam wall become a site for a major highway, thereby also threatening the integrity of the forest? What will be the bottom-line return for the investors in this project?

Feminist Conceptions of Land

Mary Daly uses the title of her book *Gyn/Ecology* to point to "the complex web of interrelationships between organisms and their environment" (1978: 9). Susan Griffin's *Woman and Nature* was published in the same year, and like Daly, she finds it necessary to move into a poetic style, "writing associatively, and thus enlisting my intuition, or uncivilized self" (1978: xv). In the section called "Land", Griffin writes:

> He broke the wilderness. He clears the land of trees, brush, weed. The land is brought under his control; he has turned waste into a garden. Into her soil he places his plow (1978: 52–53).

Here the identification of women and land is clear, and Griffin's prose picks up on this identification, slipping easily from land to body and back to land again. Although not a surprising identification, the theoretical position taken by Griffin and Daly reflects their attempts to move beyond anthropocentrism and the instrumentality of a male-centred universe. They both argue that what is bad for the earth is bad for women, and vice versa. They also argue that exploitation of the land is accompanied by exploitation of women, and that masculinist perceptions of women and their bodies often reflect similar views of land and nature. This view has been extended by numerous ecofeminist theorists since that time (see Merchant 1980; Collard 1988; Shiva 1989; Diamond 1994; Salleh 1997; Plumwood 1996).[25]

---

25 For a contrary view, see Biehl (1991). Biehl, however, misconstrues the parallels between women and land as "biologically fixed attributes" (1991: 25). I am not arguing for an essentialist identification between women and land, or the land as mother, but rather for an acknowledgement that patriarchal and capitalist systems, in their push for a univer-

Carolyn Merchant examines the historical views that western culture has entertained, from the world as organism to the world as machine, or more recently as a system to be managed. She writes at length about the organic metaphor as a central symbol within European culture until the sixteenth century, and the subsequent ontological shift that occurred with the move toward a scientistic framework during the "Enlightenment". This framework has now been replaced by the more recent shift toward information systems that has come with the digital age at the end of the twentieth century. Andrée Collard, in a work which owes much to Daly and Griffin, takes the ecocentric world for granted; she despairs that the main purpose for wildlife conservation has to do with preserving enough wild animals for men to hunt (Collard 1988: 155; see also Waring 1988: 216). The functional purpose of ecological preservation, with its reliance on reductionist rationality and economic measures, is reminiscent of the nineteenth-century approach to conservation and preservation. Functionality assumes an anthropocentric utilitarian attitude toward nature.

Vandana Shiva (1989: 41) uses the symbolism of *terra mater* – the Great Mother, Gaia in the Greek tradition, *Prakriti*[26] (nature) in her Indian tradition – as a core metaphor for her approach to land, a concept which appears in many cultures around the world. In the Ngarrindjeri worldview, the root forms of the words "land" and "body" are related. The word for "land", *ruwi* (sometimes written *ruwe*) shares the same root as *ruwar*, "body" (Bell 1998: n.3, 622). When earth and body are connected in these ways, it becomes crucially important to take account of the consequences of one's activities in relation to land. As Shiva writes, "[the] partnership between women's and nature's work ensures the sustainability of sustenance" (1989: 45). What this view suggests is not that there is a crude identification between the concepts of "woman", "body" and "land", but that work, life and sustenance are aspects of relationship between these concepts. They are metaphors that are useful in concentrating symbolic connections.

The connection between women, colonisation, the land and the body has been referred to many times (see also Mies, Bennholdt-Thomsen and von Werlof 1988). An early example comes from Robin Morgan in an essay first published in 1974. She writes:

salising and utilitarian approach to both women and the land, demean both in similar ways.

26 Shiva (1989: 39) adds that the nature of Prakriti is "activity and diversity".

Women are a colonized people. Our history, values and (cross-cultural) culture have been taken from us – a gynocidal attempt to manifest most arrestingly in the patriarchal seizure of our basic and precious "land": our bodies (1977: 161).

Irene Diamond (1994) also takes up the notion of body and earth as connected in her chapter "Our Bodies, Our Earth".[27] The idea of consequences is an important trope in her analysis of feminism and ecology. Acknowledging consequences means acknowledging connection and responsibility. That one's actions have consequences is something that is less apparent to the most powerful, and many industrialised and commercialised activities are carried on as if there were no consequences. As argued earlier, the most powerful are frequently insensitive to cultural nuances, especially to the cultures of those in the diversity matrix. Dominant Culture Stupidity itself has consequences.

Ariel Salleh, in an analysis that touches on many issues raised in this book, highlights the importance of complexity. She shows the new ways in which "corporate colonisation" has an impact on women and indigenous peoples, for whom "the semantics of self-determination is annulled by the thrust of white men's science beneath their very skins" (1997: 193). She characterises the eurocentric view of *terra nullius* in respect to land as 1/0. This is, she argues, much the same as the relationship of men to women, of eurocentric cultures to the other. These relationships can be expressed as "what has standing (A) and what does not (notA)" (1997: 35). Salleh goes on to say that psychoanalytically this could be expressed as "since Man has one, he is 1. When you look at Woman, you see only a 0, a hole, a zero. She is ... a lack" (1997: 36). Freud notwithstanding, Salleh's point is useful symbolic shorthand which allows for analogies to be made between how the different members of the diversity matrix are treated in similar ways, and experience similar kinds of dispossession, although the particular instances might appear superficially different. The analogy to be drawn here is that men/women are in a 1/0 relationship; that European systems of land equal 1; *terra nullius* equals 0. Again 1/0. Europeans equal 1; indigenous peoples 0.[28]

---

27 This chapter title also has resonances of the iconic volume, *Our Bodies, Ourselves* produced by the Boston Women's Health Collective.

28 An interesting variation of this 1/0 binary opposition/scoreboard appeared in the media a day after President George W. Bush sent missiles into Afghanistan (Wolpe 2001: 19).

Val Plumwood, in a similar vein, refers to the importance of "special relationships" and indicates that within the ambit of these special relationships are those with "particular animals, trees, and rivers that are well known, loved and appropriately connected to the self" (1996: 159). Her critique also takes in a critical examination of the universalist assumptions of liberal rationalist philosophy and the ways in which these intersect with deep ecology.

These few selected feminist approaches to land give a sense of the direction of feminist thought on this topic. Feminist analyses have been further extended by those of scholars from a wide range of cultural backgrounds, including indigenous scholars and scholars working with indigenous peoples for whom battles around land ownership and residence have become central to the understanding of indigenous politics.

Indigenous Conceptions of Land

What the Indians are saying is that ... Wilderness is not an extension of human need or of human justification. It is itself and it is inviolate, itself. This does not mean that, therefore, we become separated from it, because we don't. We stay connected if, once in our lives, we learn exactly what that connection is between our heart, our womb, our mind, and wilderness. And when each of us has her wilderness within her, we can be together in a balanced kind of way
– Paula Gunn Allen (1998: 61).

Many indigenous peoples speak of land and being as inextricably inter-twined. Land is the first thing to be named, travelled across, sometimes transformed, and sacralised. The symbols which make up the universes of many indigenous peoples are dependent on land, emerge from the land, or re-merge with land and, in this way, with the people of *that particular land*. Indigenous conceptions of land are characterised by a particular relationship with specific ecological regions. The particularity of indige-nous knowledge and its relationship to the environment can make it difficult to write about in general ways, and it is not my intention to homogenise indigenous systems of thought. However, I have used the

---

The article was entitled, "Scoreboard: globalisation 1, terrorism 0". An advertisement for Alfa Romeo cars in December 2001 on a Melbourne freeway reads "Italy won, Germany nil". The market, global sport, and politics are interwoven. Such scoreboard mentality maintains the illusion that globalisation can be equated with winners.

word "indigenous" throughout in instances where it is more important to make a general observation than to particularise a specific instance.

The term "relationship" implies a connection; it implies a dynamic between two or more entities. In the case of the indigenous relationship to land, there is a notion of reciprocity which involves responsibilities on both parts. The responsibility of the people is to look after and maintain the health of the land; its health as an economic resource also includes its cultural and spiritual health. As Gloria Anzaldúa points out, the word "responsibility" implies an "ability to respond" (1987: 20). Responsiveness, reciprocity and respect combine in Central Australian Aboriginal approaches to land.

Diane Bell, writing of the Kaititj (Kaytej) women of Central Australia, distinguishes sharply between the conception of "country" held by Kaititj women, and that of the European system of land tenure (1981: 356). The Kaititj notion of country is located firmly within a metaphysical system of knowledge, one not tied to individual ownership, but rather to spiritual continuity which includes the well-being of the land itself. Within this system, different women and men take responsibility for different areas of country in a way reminiscent of a mosaic or patchwork. Bell notes that "Country is both a basis of identity and an analogy for emotional states" (1981: 352). In her later work on the Ngarrindjeri and the people who live in the Lower Murray region of South Australia, she extends this idea, pointing to the common Aboriginal "moral relationship of people to land" and, in the case of the Ngarrindjeri, "the power of individuals through their *miwi* [feeling located in stomach, soul substance] to know a relationship which is at once visceral and intellectual" (1998: 268). The visceral response is one that Sarah Milera experienced as preparations for developing a bridge site to connect Hindmarsh Island to the mainland were made. "When they drove the pegs into the ground I felt a spiritual wounding ... they rushed me to hospital ... when you get a spiritual wounding no medicine can help you" (Bell 1998: 267).

For the Kaititj of Central Australia, the relationship of people to the land occurs through rituals of reciprocity. The rituals are the social glue, but they also bind[29] people to particular stretches of country, land which

---

29 The word "religion" comes from the Latin *religio-*, meaning obligation, a bond between humanity and deities.

entails maintenance through ceremony. For the Ngarrindjeri, funerals have become a contemporary means of maintaining cross-community connections, which at one time would have been maintained through a range of ceremonies (Bell 1998: 307).

Nancy Williams (1986), in her study of land and the Yolngu of Arnhem Land in Northern Australia, writes of the ways in which story, land and people are connected. Each community/clan/family is associated with a particular narrative, and these in turn link to other narratives. Together they weave a web of relationships which span the larger "people" or territory. In a similar way, the Ngarrindjeri women are engaged in weaving baskets that "shape the Ngarrindjeri world ... [with] diverse strands" (Bell 1998: 83). And as Diane Bell points out, this is what many women, in cultures from South America to Arnhem Land, do (1998: 87–89).

Land has become the pressure point between the worldviews of indigenous peoples and western jurisdictions of land.[30] The Yolngu of Arnhem Land, for instance, continued to believe that the land they lived on was theirs, in spite of the European legal rules pertaining to ownership. Since in their view, their traditional law was binding to them, there was no need to alter their view. At least, not until mining and exploration threatened their way of life, resulting in the fight for the first Australian land rights court case (1968–1971). There are numerous indigenous expressions of the connection between people and land. Mowaljarlai, from the Kimberley region, says, "[the land] acts for the people and their imprint is still there" (Mowaljarlai and Malinic 2001: 192), while Doug Campbell, from Yarralin, near Victoria Downs, says, "The Law is in the ground" (Rose 2000: 56).

In Papua New Guinea, where 97 per cent[31] of all land is customarily owned (Rakova 2000: 8), customary law and the introduction of new laws framed through western conventions are in conflict. In 1992 the PNG government proposed that "landowners register their land and get the government to look after it" (Rakova 2000: 9). The proposal failed. Ursula Rakova sums up the attitude indigenous PNG peoples have to land:

---

30   For instances of conflict between indigenous peoples and western institutions such as governments and corporations, see Pryor (2000: 5; Australia); Bellos (2000: 12; Brazil); Coburn (2000: 13; Mexico); Rakova (2000: 8–9; Papua New Guinea).

31   By contrast, in Hawai'i "Forty-one landowners own about 95% of the land" (dé Ishtar 1998: 11).

We really treasure the fact that the land still remains with us. To us land is something that we cannot part away with, and is not a saleable commodity (2000: 9).

Similar intellectual frameworks exist for indigenous peoples in North America. "Where the natural world ends and the human world begins there you will find the Seminoles"[32] (LaDuke 1999: 27). "The people and the land are inseparable" writes Leslie Marmon Silko in her discussion of an urban Yaqui village situated in the city of Tucson (1996: 85). She notices that even within an urban setting the rhythms of traditional life continue and a sense of community connected to their locale remains a part of the inhabitants' approach to life. The daily rhythm and the seasonal rhythm of life are important to people who have not embraced the technologies of the electric light, heating and air-conditioning.[33] The seasonal shifts are evident in Hugh Brody's study of the trails and maps of British Columbia Indians in Northwest Canada (1981: 146–177). The land is imbued with meaning, with connection to the seasonal rhythms of animals,[34] plants,[35] and stars.[36] The connection between nature and human culture becomes so intertwined that the land may be said to speak or sing.

Land as Possession

Ownership of land, in the European tradition, has shifted from one of collective ownership, in pre-agricultural Europe, to one of royal

---

32 The Seminoles' traditional land is in the state of Florida, taking in the Everglades, Lake Okeechobee and Big Cypress Swamp.

33 In my view, it is not a matter of romanticising what used to exist over our contemporary lifestyles. I know from my own experiences of "going bush" for weeks at a time that the rhythm of day and night, the awareness of moon, stars and sky change when one lives more closely *with* nature.

34 In the state of Oregon, the Tygh people maintain a relationship with the salmon, while in the Mid-west, buffalo are considered older brothers (LaDuke 1999: 2, 139).

35 Even with introduced species, such as the dandelions in the Ngarrindjeri territories, traditions accommodate to the changes in the landscape wrought by white people (see Bell 1998: 574).

36 The appearance and disappearance of the constellation of the Seven Sisters, the Pleiades, connects to ritual for many peoples, among them the Ngarrindjeri (see Bell 1998: 578). Likewise, the Morning Star (Venus) has religious connotations for the Yolngu of Arnhem Land, and also for early Christians of the Middle East (this remains in Catholic tradition as Stella Maris).

ownership, where the King owns the land and all that he can see is royal, real, real estate, (Frye 1983) to private ownership by rich individuals of the aristocratic class and later the merchant classes. In the late twentieth century the shift was to corporate ownership in which the transnational sector owns and controls large tracts of urban and rural land. Property as ownership[37] arises from eighteenth-century liberal views of property rights as preserving liberty (Dodds 1994: 49; 58). Although it is clear that it is the liberty of masculine and wealthy individuals that is preserved under this regime, the system of power which supports corporate owner-ship has changed little. It holds sway in spite of challenges to property rights through Native Title and other claims.

The European ownership of the world began with colonisation where land was either claimed for the Crown (or the Pope) or declared "unowned", "empty" (as in Australia and parts of Africa) and thereby appropriated. Land was then put to use in ways deemed best for the European economy. As Ursula Rakova says of the appropriation of land in Papua New Guinea, "We know that where land was forcefully passed away to companies, consequences have happened" (2000: 9).

The consequences of a worldview driven by the idea of land as pos-session can be seen throughout the world in a range of industrialised and disconnected uses of land and the people:

- Plantations: The development of plantations went hand in hand with the spread of slavery. See Patterson (1982) on slavery in the USA. Australia did not escape this blight: indeed; as slavery was winding down in other parts of the world, Kanak people were being captured from Vanuatu and sold as slaves to the owners of cotton, and later sugar, plantations in Queensland. See Bandler (1994: 11–12).

- The milling of timber on a grand scale: Merv Wilkinson (Loomis 1995: 9) provides figures for the forestry industry in British Columbia, Canada. "The Department of Forestry claims that in 1988 the forests grew 74 million board feet during the year. The cut during that year was 90 million. I have heard that the more correct figure is 108 million. Is there any worse 'deficit financing' than that?" Levels of deforesta-tion globally are causing enormous long-term destruction to

---

37 For a brief and incisive critique of western property laws versus traditional African approaches to "property" and their impact on women, see Majeke (2001).

biodiverse regions of the world. In Brazil, it is estimated that during the 1980s the number of hectares deforested ranged from 1,013,000 to 3,000,000 (see Kolk 1996: 68, Table 2.2). Deforestation has continued in Brazil, and also in South-East Asia (Siu 1997).

- The mining of gold and diamonds: Examples include the use of Black workers in gold mines under Apartheid in South Africa (Richardson and Van-Helten 1982); war in Angola which has been fuelled by diamonds (Global Witness Report 1998); the use of children as slaves in mines in Niger (Jennings 1999).

- The mining of phosphates: Nauru, once the "richest nation per capita in the world" (Niesche 2001: 28), is a small island nation in the Pacific Ocean (area 20 square kilometres, population 7000) whose entire ecosystem has been destroyed by the mining of phosphates by the British Phosphate Commission for farmers in Australia and elsewhere in the western world. Post-war farmers such as my parents benefited from the Australian government superphosphate bounty in the 1950s and 1960s. But Nauru is now paying the price with a landscape that resembles a war zone and with extreme poverty. Australian farms are also paying another price with increased soil acidity and, in inland waterways, blue-green algae blooms (Vanclay and Lawrence 1996). In 2001, Nauru, for a price, entered the market for "processing refugees" for the Australian government. Refugees are being commodified, and used to earn desperately needed foreign currency for a bankrupt Nauruan government.

- The mining of copper: The BHP-owned mine at Ok Tedi in Papua New Guinea has been the subject of protest and lawsuits due to its ecological destruction of the Fly River.[38] Wep Kanawi, the PNG Country Director of Nature Conservancy, says that the mine has "destroyed over 1000 square kilometres of wetland and virgin forest"

---

38 BHP continued to deny that it would close the Ok Tedi mine (Gale 2000: 2), but by August 2001, after it had become BHP Billiton, it announced that the mine would close. The devastation of the Fly River ecology has been enormous, but the mine contributes 10 per cent of PNG's gross domestic product. BHP Billiton has decided to put its 52 per cent "equity into a trust fund to be managed by the landowners affected by the damage caused by Ok Tedi" (Counsel 2001: 5). In terms of sustainability, this barely makes up for the long-term damage caused by the company. For further information, see http://forests.org/pngforest.html. For the impact of copper mining in Irian Jaya, see Richburg (1998: 25).

and the destruction of "all life in the river, and all the arable land close to the river [has affected] ... about 100,000 people (Green 2000: 13).

- The building of factories where dangerous substances are manufactured: The 1984 gas spill at Bhopal, India, resulted in the poisoning of thousands of people living around the pesticide plant. Owned by US company Union Carbide, the spill brought to the attention of the public the systematic manufacture of toxic substances in poor countries and the dangers it posed to poor people (Reich 1991: 98–139).

- The creation of wastelands through dumping of wastes: The people of Saipan Island in the Northern Marianas protested locating military installations in their forest where there are birds "that you only find on Saipan and Rota" (Chailang Palacios cited by dé Ishtar 1994: 92). In Hawai'i, the local people complain about the intensity of military activity, including "nuclear waste from submarine reactors in Pearl Harbor (which was once a very rich fishing area)" (dé Ishtar 1994: 113).

- The imposition of military sites in which sacred landforms are blown up and the ecology polluted: The Kanaka Maoli, the people of Hawai'i, have protested the establishment of Kaneohe Marine Corps Base on the "sacred peninsula of Mokapu where, we believe, the first Kanaka Maoli was created (dé Ishtar 1998: 10). This is akin to locating a military base in the Vatican.

These processes have been repeated on the human body,[39] which has also been colonised and appropriated over time. The latest form of colonisation of the land and of the body is through the process of bioprospecting: the theft of resources from the land, the privatisation of the resources through the imposition of US patents, and the commodification of the products by the pharmaceutical industry. On the human body, the colonisation has occurred through research conducted under the guise of the Human Genome Project or its sister program, the Human Diversity Genome Project. When Australia was colonised, the body parts and skulls

---

39 The flushing and harvesting of women's eggs in reproductive technologies is one such
    example with a direct effect on women's lives. See Klein (2001) for an analysis of how
    women's bodies are being globalised. For critiques of reproductive technologies, see
    Arditti *et al.* (1984); Corea (1985); Klein (1989a, 1989b); Akhter (1992, 1995); Rowland
    (1993); Raymond (1995).

Nuclear waste is dumped on indigenous lands in Australia (and elsewhere). Anti-nuclear activists protest environmental and cultural destruction, linking damage to the artesian groundwaters to dispossession of indigenous lands.

of Aboriginal people were "collected" by eminent nineteenth-century scientists who saw nothing wrong with the practice. The practice continues, albeit on a level which cannot be perceived by unassisted human sight. Molecular colonisation (see Chapter Seven) continues the practice of the colonising of human bodies, which in turn reflects the earlier practice of colonising the land and culture of non-European peoples, of the diversity matrix.

A similar process is at work in areas where "deterritoriality" occurs. The ultimate in "separation between self and nature" (Kuletz 1998: 7), deterritoriality allows increasingly large tracts of land to be sacrificed in order to maintain the global system of power. Not surprisingly, many of the areas chosen for sacrifice are lands which have belonged to indigenous peoples for millennia. As these lands do not represent a sovereign nation under the terms of western definition, they are vulnerable, in a legal sense, to misappropriation. Comparable to *terra nullius*, and as Valerie Kuletz points out, representative of the play of nuclear politics, it is native lands which are most likely to be subjected to deterritoriality. Kuletz is writing of the American southwest, but in Australia, in the Pacific Island nations, in the vast stretches of Siberia, the same process is at work. These are lands intimately woven in with the lives of indigenous peoples, known to their inhabitants in the way in which some people know their own bodies. They have been used to test nuclear weapons, to develop military strategies, and now they are slated for nuclear-waste dumps. An international corporation, Pangea, has proposed an area of the Pilbara in Western Australia as a suitable site for nuclear waste. This is one of a series of violations against indigenous communities in Australia, from testing on Maralinga lands in the 1950s and 1960s to mining of Mirrar land at Jabiluka, and in the Western Desert and Pilbara regions. The traditional owners of the area include "a number of Aboriginal communities, among them Jigalong, Pangurr and Cotton Creek. This region is the traditional homeland of the Martu (Western Desert) people, and there are still significant numbers of people living in this area … further south [are] the Bidjandjadjara people, who were very angry when Pangea flew a media crew onto their reserve without first seeking a permit" (ANAWA website 2001).[40]

---

40 www.anawa.org.au/waste/traditional.html.

Tourism: Land and Wilderness as Commodity

> *Tourism promotes the same colonial tendencies that*
> *agricultural export companies, missionaries, and others*
> *perpetrated in earlier centuries. Colonizing is not new,*
> *but tourism development as a form of colonizing is*
> *new and growing at tremendous rates*
> – Deborah McLaren (1998: 70).

Helena Norberg-Hodge (1991), in her study of the Ladakhi people of Kashmir, found that tourism turned what had been cultural pride and personal confidence into a sense of worthlessness, poverty and disconnection from their histories and traditions.

Ngahuia Te Awekotuku found that tourism tended to emphasise stereotypical notions of female "exotic sensuality" (1991: 91) that cluster around Polynesian women. In these settings, the host people, their culture and their environment become "bits and pieces to be isolated and manipulated for a few people's personal profits" (Thaman 1994: 191). The women of Guam have suffered the combination of all these aspects of tourist colonisation, and with the development of resorts along the island's best beaches, the prostitution industry has gained a foothold to cater for "Japanese, American and Australian businessmen" (dé Ishtar 1994: 75). The connection between prostitution and tourism is well known, and its impact is felt most immediately by women, children, and adolescent girls and boys.[41] In such circumstances, people lose their connection with their bodies and sense of self-worth; they lose also their connection with their land and culture; they are alienated from it by the promise of the elusive material rewards of western capitalist culture. Chailang Palacios, from the island of Saipan, makes the connection clear:

> [Tourism] is not really helping the economy – most of the money goes back to Japan. The tourists bring money but psychologically, socially, it is destroying the people. Half of the Chamorro, they lease their land for fifty-five years to the Japanese, so now they are landless. The land is bulldozed for hotel. There is no land to get back (in dé Ishtar 1994: 85).

---

41 For further discussion of the combined impact of tourism and prostitution, see McLaren (1998: 87–89); Bales (2000: 34–79), on Thailand; Hughes (1999: 157–184), on internet prostitution; Matsui (1999: 114–116), on prostitution of aboriginal women of Taiwan. For an insightful analysis of the prostitution industry, see Jeffreys (1997).

Just as land is appropriated (whether by theft, lease or imposition of military [42] or corporate structures) so too is culture. An example is the *hula* ceremony of Hawai'i, a ceremony about peace and fertility in which the elements of sea water, sacred stones and plants are brought together with singing and dancing. But the hula hoop known to most western peoples is the playground hoop, the circus hoop of entertainment. It represents what I have called elsewhere "the politics of the exotic".[43]

Tourism has become just another way for the wealthy, mobile westerner to appropriate yet another corner of the earth. Tourism is based on "cultural voyeurism" (Hawthorne 1989) and on a psychic separation of one's own culture from the culture visited. The tourist, like the wilderness visitor, can never stay long enough to understand the "mysteries" of the place visited. Indeed, these days it is possible to travel to other countries and experience the local culture as nothing more than an exotic backdrop to a homogenised and sanitised western lifestyle in resorts which accept US dollars and sell the same resort labels and commodified experience throughout the world. In these places, culture is commodified, the local people turned into objects, and the best places bulldozed for resorts or shopping centres catering to the tourist consumerist "needs". A mono-culture which replicates western fantasies of (mostly) tropical paradise is created, and the locals learn to speak English. Tourism is justified on economic grounds: "tourist expenditures ripple throughout the local economy, through transactions from laborers to local markets, benefiting the whole community" (McLaren 1998: 31). But Deborah McLaren goes on to point out that, in fact, because of "leakages", very few of the tourist dollars spent remain in the community. This is particularly so when resorts and tourism companies (in transport, entertainment or accommodation) are owned by overseas companies, and in particular when they are part of a transnational corporate chain. McLaren states that "where leakages are up to 80 or 90 percent ... [it] can be a recipe for disaster with respect to international balance of payments for a small, underdeveloped country" (1998: 31–32).

---

42 See Torres Souder who writes on the military colonisation of Guam "the choicest lands – extending from Tarague in the North to Orote in the South – were taken without just compensation for the 11 military bases that now grace our tiny homeland of 212 square miles" (1994: 194).

43 For an in-depth discussion of these issues, see Hawthorne (1989).

But what about ecotourism? The new tourism, promoted as "take only photographs, leave only footsteps", suggests that the old appropriative tourism is a thing of the past. The new eco-friendly tourists are keen to see the "real" places, the unspoilt places.

The rise of ecotourism in the last decade is a symptom of western culture's malaise. And although most ecotourism providers mean well, such an industry is possible only in a culture where alienation from nature, from the daily, seasonal, annual cycles, is the norm.

The ecotourism industry has many critics. The most vociferous of them are indigenous peoples whose traditional lands, waters and cultures are exploited in the name of ecology (Te Awekotuku 1991: 73–105; Thaman 1994: 183–191; dé Ishtar 1994). The double bind is that many of these peoples rely on the income from ecotourists to sustain a foothold in the contemporary world economy. Where once they were self-sustaining, in the best sense of the word, now with ecological pollution and dispossession of large tracts of land, the economy has shifted to one of dependence on outsiders. Such a compromise on the part of indigenous peoples can be seen as comparable to the participation of women in the workforce. Participation in the economy does nevertheless provide an income for survival. This does not change the fact that it is the export of experience as a new commodity to sell to outsiders.

The indigenous owners of National Parks such as Gurig National Park in Arnhem Land conduct tours for visiting tourists, usually sharing information on traditional uses of plants. But even in these places, the greatest beneficiaries of National Parks are non-indigenous Australians and foreigners. As H. C. Coombs has pointed out, the intimate connection with the land which they have sustained for millennia

> is progressively being denied to Aborigines, denied by their alienation from the land, by their compulsory incorporation into a commercial economy and by the imposition, on them and their children, of an alien pattern of education (1996: 39).

Wilderness, itself, has become a commodity to sell. Aldo Leopold recognised this back in 1937 when he alerted ecotourists to the fact that "all conservation of wildness is self-defeating, for to cherish we must see and fondle, and when enough have seen and fondled, there is no wilderness left to cherish" (in Oelschlaeger 1991: 228).

McLaren makes a list of some of the places spoilt by ecotourism through the clearing of land, the development of dams and airports, as well as such seemingly innocuous things as "golf courses, ecoresorts, ecocondominiums, ecolodges, ecomarine parks, and ecoranches". Among the places listed are resort developments in Costa Rica; the sheer number of people visiting the ecologically delicate Galapagos Islands; the building of a hydro-electric dam in Sarawak to cater to the energy needs of tourists; and the building of golf courses on land previously used for agriculture or forestry (1998: 105–108).

Adding the prefix "eco-" to tourism has not brought about deep change. What would be required for a wild politics ecotourism would be turning around the reasons for tourism and ecotourism. Fundamental to a revisioning of tourism is respect for the people whose homeland the tourist is visiting. Such respect is not engendered by transnational corporations buying up the land and redeveloping it for the wealthy, mobile elites. Local communities need to have the controlling say in how tourism can be structured. Locally owned accommodations and services and a decentralised industry are basic to the restructuring of tourism. A willingness by travellers to engage with the local cultures encountered is another important pre-condition. Beyond these structural changes, a more fundamental issue has to be addressed: to scrutinise the reasons for the "need" for so much tourism on the part of the privileged.

The solution, I argue, lies in recognising the possibilities for "wildness" in all locales, not just in those separated out as special and called National Parks, wilderness areas, exotic paradises, or world heritage areas. The entire globe is a world heritage area, and unless we begin to think of it in this way, vast areas will become uninhabitable by humans and other species.

Separation, distancing – and declaring only some places special – is the crux of the problem. I believe that the wild is in all of us, in our gardens, in laneways, in the canopies of trees, in city creeks, in marshlands and mangroves. The health of these niches is a good indicator of the health of the larger ecosystem. Separation in this way is analogous to declaring certain endemic plants to be weeds. Not because they are noxious in the environment, but simply because a use for them is unknown, as if all plants had to have a human purpose. Such a thought is unthinkable if the ecosystem is at the centre of politics.

Likewise, it is possible to commodify the wilderness by filtering it through the products of the global market, from feather-light tents, to fabrics made from Coca-Cola bottles, to the latest gear for the mountaineer or walker. With such commodities at hand, the experience is less likely to be one of hardship, of battling against the elements, or even simply of living with the elements over a long period of time. Most wilderness experiences on offer are for a limited period of time, from a couple of days to a few months. Rarely does the experience extend to a complete cycle of the year. This is at great odds with the real-life experience of many of the earth's contemporary peoples and most of the world's people only a few centuries ago. The commodification of this experience has become possible only because indigenous peoples have been disconnected from agriculture and dispossessed of land.

Urban Land

It is relatively easy to see how wild politics applies to rural land, to land which once belonged to indigenous peoples, to land which borders coastlines and rivers. But what of urban spaces? What of the land which comprises the streets we walk along, the lanes we inhabit, the freeways on which we drive; the industrial, commercial and residential land in which most of the world's people now live their lives; and the public spaces in parks, riversides and so-called "vacant" blocks? Globalisation and the concentration of resources in the hands of giant corporations are removing more and more urban spaces from public ownership. Industrialisation in cities has been in progress for much longer, and the impact has been significant, with pollution at crisis levels in many cities, especially the mega-cities in poor countries.

In rich countries, a number of interesting developments are occurring which affect the way in which public space is used, and how it is delimited. Naomi Klein suggests that we need to "un-brand" the space which has been occupied by the corporate forces, and that street culture has provided designers who advertise in *Vogue* with ideas which they have appropriated (2000: 81). Christian Lacroix admits that "very often the most exciting outfits are from the poorest people" (cited in Klein 2000: 73). In a similar move, inner urban spaces are being appropriated for the use of brand advertisers, whether it be Levi's massive ad campaign in Toronto, or the Nike swoosh branding of "resurfaced urban basketball courts", where

Nike pays nothing to advertise, and instead "files the cost under charity" (Klein 2000: 37, 75).

If these same street people, however, want to shop in exclusive outlets, they may find themselves evicted, or locked out altogether. Universal Studios owns a shopping complex in Los Angeles called CityWalk. Here "'Boisterous activities' are forbidden [as are] ... wearing clothes 'likely to create a disturbance' ... and any 'expressive activity without the prior written permission of the management'" (Beckett 1994: 35). Los Angeles is also the home of private-gated residences. Park La Brea, near Hollywood, was one of the earliest developments (Beckett 1994: 37); near Melbourne, Oaklands Park development is under way (Franklin 1998: 13). Others, such as the marina developments on Hindmarsh Island, South Australia, and at Port Hinchinbrook in far north Queensland, have provoked heated public protest.[44] Such developments are in stark contrast to highly accessible city markets which encourage the "diversity, vitality and humanity of everyday city life" (Rogers 1998: 24).

Although modern cities tend in the direction of anonymity and disconnection, this is not an unavoidable ingredient of city planning or of city life. As Richard Rogers points out, the "emphasis is now on selfishness and separation rather than contact and community". He goes on to suggest that cities should be "viewed as ecological systems and this attitude must inform our approach to designing cities and managing their resources" (Rogers 1997: 10, 30). Some interesting correlations are apparent in the ways in which cities can be structured, and the ways in which rural land use is now also structured. The monocultures typical of rural land tend to be replicated in cities so that the places where people work and pursue leisure are separated from one another and from domestic living spaces. They could instead be incorporated into a series of small areas comprised of relatively few (several thousand) people. Instead of having concentrated urban functions, the city would be "compact and polycentric" (Rogers 1997: 168). Countryside and city

---

44 The Hindmarsh Island development has been subject to protest because it breaches sacred sites of indigenous Ngarrindjeri women (Bell 1998); Port Hinchinbrook has been developed at the expense of mangrove swamps and sensitive environmental habitats. On visiting both sites, I found the two developments to be almost interchangeable in their physical appearance. This was the case architecturally, as well as in the landscaping of waterways and greens.

would overlap and proximity would be maximised. The latter is more like a mixed-farming model with its integration of systems and crops.[45] On a reduced scale, similar principles can be applied to an individual residence. There are numerous examples now of the house which circulates the energy it uses, energy which can return to the grid – whether it be water, sewage or electricity – instead of always drawing energy out of it in only one direction (Mobbs 1998). Through use of networks of decentralised power generation and waste recycling, the mixed-use model can be further intensified without producing excessive amounts of wasted power or creating waste which cannot be adequately disposed of (Rogers 1997: 51). Decentralised or polycentric systems are less prone to violence internally and considerably less vulnerable to external attacks such as that of 11 September 2001.

As in other areas discussed in this book, the principles of diversity, of connection, context, responsibility are important in developing housing systems which will work to create vitality and community, "familiarity and surprise" (Rogers 1997: 15). By creating a mix of activities, the society can move away from the monocultures of large-scale, context-stripped and unaccountable activities, and thereby generate a level of citizen engagement, participation and responsibility that is currently lacking. Diversity is also increased. With such a system in place it would be unthinkable to allow large corporations to brand public spaces or pollute the environment in a myriad of ways. It would be equally unthinkable for individuals not to be responsible for the sustainable disposal of waste, or to create enclaves where violence breeds out of control.

Veronika Bennholdt-Thomsen suggests some basic principles which can be applied, not just to local communities, but also to the WTO. Her list reads:

Priority is given to the useful, to what is needed.

Small has priority over big.

Personal relationships are better than anonymous ones.

Decentralized solutions are better than centralized ones.

The local takes precedence over the international (2001: 224).

---

45   See Rogers (1997: 39) for diagrams. Compact mixed-use nodes reduce journey requirements and create lively sustainable neighbourhoods. Jane Jacobs was one of the earliest critics of how large cities are structured (1961, 1984).

Bennholdt-Thomsen argues that developing an urban "'economy of daily well-being' has very little to do with money but a lot to do with human care and human contact". Moving away from abstracting people, she recommends regarding human encounters "as a value in itself" (2001: 217). Her list distils many of the ideas which have been developed in this book.

Urban Land as Wild Space

The experience of wilderness, of tourism based on the exotic (Hawthorne 1989/1990), is not the only way to experience the natural cycles of life. Gardening, even in the most crowded urban conditions, can create such an awareness. H. Patricia Hynes, in her research on inner city gardens in the USA, points to the way in which

> Community gardens create a relationship between city dwellers and the soil, and instil an ethic of urban environmentalism that neither parks nor wilderness – which release and free us from the industrial city – can do (1996: xv–xvi).

The city garden also maintains the connection with the local; indeed it intensifies local connections and creates a sense of worth when previously there might have been only rubble, rubbish and vacant or unuseable and unfriendly open space.

The long-term possibilities of urban gardens as a source of economic viability are recognised by Bernadette Cozart. Cozart, an activist in the Greening of Harlem Coalition, has this to say:

> When I look at Harlem, I see a community ready to burst forth. I see vacant lots as sources of jobs. I can see growing vegetables and herbs and going all the way from seed to shelf. In specialty shops, you see all kinds of delicacies. I envision watermelon rind jelly, tomato preserve, and "cha cha" with labels that say "grown and made in Harlem" ... Add the beauty of nature to Harlem and give kids who've only known New York City as concrete and steel the chance to get to know nature ... we have to figure out a way to bring nature to the city (in Hynes 1996: 31).

Cozart's vision extends beyond gardens to the greening of cities everywhere, turning vacant blocks into "farms, tree and shrub nurseries" (in

Hynes 1996: 31). Jacqueline Leavitt and Susan Saegert (1990) in their study on community households in Harlem, discovered that the people most interested in transforming the inner city were "mainly women, often elderly ones, who ... had strong ties with other tenants and great affection for their neighborhood" (cited in Hynes 1996: 19). Their participation in the informal economy of the community and their attachment to their locality were important factors in the leadership role women have played in the development of inner urban gardens.

New York is not the only city to prompt such developments. In Detroit, a group of African American women who call themselves the Gardening Angels have begun to develop inner city gardens. Since 1994 they have created more than 100 gardens (Mies and Bennholdt-Thomsen 1999: 135). As Maria Mies and Veronika Bennholdt-Thomsen point out, their vision is of

[a] city independent of the investment decisions and the money of big companies which have no responsibility for, and no loyalty to, the people. They want to build a local economy based on the principles of autonomy, self-help, and the creation and furthering of communal principles (1999: 135).

In Tokyo, a group calling themselves the "Yabo farmers" (wild farmers) grow rice, vegetables and other grains communally, as well as raising small farm animals such as chicken, pigs and goats, on land set aside for construction, but not yet built upon. Their rationale for this farming practice is to make cities arable and to resist the neoliberal model upon which Japan's economy is based. Japan is a long way from being self-sufficient in food, even needing to import rice from countries such as Thailand and the USA (Mies and Bennholdt-Thomsen 1999: 137). Those involved in urban farming are employed in a wide range of occupations, including computing and communications, as well as single mothers and office workers.

Christa Müller, in Göttingen, Germany, researched the way in which refugee women have participated in the International Gardens project. The project has enabled women (from Bosnia, Kurdistan, Sri Lanka, the Persian Gulf and ten other nations) who felt dislocated and missed their gardens, to "put down roots" for the future. Developing relationship, a sense of reciprocity, as well as enabling the women to give some of their skills to the new community, allowed them to move away from being recipients of social welfare, which in turn meant "being able to free themselves from their reduced status as refugees" (2001: 190, 198). The gardens also encouraged cross-cultural communication and socialising through sharing knowledge of plants, planting techniques, even the simple act of finding familiar herbs.

Urban arability shifts the location of agricultural production from farms located outside the city (once again separated), often very long distances away, to the city itself. Urban arability changes the balance between production and consumption, and potentially creates a connection to the means and place of food production. City food co-operatives have used a similar principle of maintaining the connection between producer and consumer. I resist the notion that a land ethic or experience of connection to the land is only possible in a rural setting, or demands that vast uninhabited regions of wilderness are the only option. City gardens show how it is possible to combine urban intelligence with existing land intelligence.

Steps to Developing a Wild Politics of Land

The application of wild politics to land demands profound changes in the western approach to living. It entails taking on a much greater responsibility for the environment than is expected from those in the western tradition. In indigenous cultures, however, this is not an unusual approach.

I do not assume – or romanticise – that previous generations have always lived sustainably. There are many early examples in the literature of deforestation, desertification and starvation as a result of over-plundering of natural resources (Diamond 1991).[46]

Mies and Bennholt-Thomsen suggest that the starting point for a new awareness of commons is waste. As they note:

---

46 Flannery (1994) makes similar suggestions about the impact of indigenous peoples in Australia and Aotearoa/New Zealand. However, Langton points out that Flannery's "provisional chronologies" are used by "provincial governments and their neocolonial parks and wildlife services to deny Aboriginal people access to, occupation and use of conservation areas, including areas which they own under Australian law" (1998: 53).

In a commons regime [production and consumption] are not two separate economic spheres but are linked to each other. Production processes will be oriented towards the satisfaction of needs of concrete local or regional communities and not towards the artificially created demand of an anonymous world market. In such an economy the concept of waste, for example, does not really exist. What can be consumed and whose left-overs cannot be absorbed within such a distinct eco-region cannot be produced. Such a "moral economy" of a particular region requires, this is evident, a community which feels responsible to sustain the regenerative capacities of the region (1995: 13).

Waste thus becomes a "negative commons" (Mies and Bennholdt-Thomsen 1995: 15), something for which everyone is responsible. Being responsible for our waste is a beginning for being responsible for what we produce and what we consume. This change would indeed begin a moral economy.

Extending this principle into the international arena would change the way in which toxic wastes are dealt with. If toxic wastes are internalised, so that the producers of the waste have to live next door to it, the chances of reducing the risks to the local populace are much greater (Daly and Goodland 1994: 80).

Twenty-first-century urban people are no longer Paleolithic nomads whose sense of value relied on portability, although if the modern ecotourist is any indication we could move toward

the hunter's ascetic conception of material welfare: an interest only in minimal equipment, if that; a valuation of smaller things over bigger; a disinterest in acquiring two or more of most goods; and the like. Ecological pressure assumes a rare form of concreteness when it has to be shouldered (Sahlins 1972: 33, quoted in Oelschlaeger 1991: 14).

This challenge to materialism is picked up by Patricia Grace in a humorous short story, "Ngati Kangaru". It tells the story of a summer resort, unoccupied in the cooler months, which is repossessed by Maori to house cousins returning from Australia. Using the tricks of the trade developed by nineteenth-century colonisers, Billy and his cohorts are "Reclaiming a moral wilderness" (Grace 1994: 34) by occupying unoccupied land and dwellings, and renaming all the features. The deeds to the titles have been signed over by tramps, the unemployed and anyone without a stake in the property. By the time the official owners arrive for their annual holidays, it is too late. The land has been returned to its original owners. Grace uses the motif of over-consumption to great effect in this story of reconciliation (to the satisfaction of the indigenous owners) and reclamation. She makes her point by applying the same rules of possession to the colonisers and capitalists as they used against indigenous peoples. Confronted by reversal of power relations, it becomes quite obvious how unjust the original dispossession was.

Reclamation is also the goal of the inner city gardeners documented by Patricia Hynes. The garden, according to Michael Pollan, represents

> [the] "middle ground between the wilderness and the lawn" [and] may "suggest the lineaments of a new environmental ethic … and help us out in all those situations where the wilderness ethic is silent or unhelpful," or where the experience of wilderness is unaffordable and inaccessible (in Hynes 1996: ix, quotation marks in the original).

Like the reinvention of the commons described by Mies and Bennholdt-Thomsen, Hynes describes how the urban gardens are built on work done "by the community, for the community, at no cost to taxpayers" (1996: 23). As community leader, Lorna Fowler, explains:

> Their ecology is predicated not on wilderness without people but on a mutuality between humans and nature; their economy is predicated on traditional finance, sweat equity, barter, and non-monetary sources of wealth such as networks, good will, generosity, altruism, plant lore, and horticultural expertise (in Hynes 1996: ix).

Ironically, while inner city gardens are being developed by the poorest communities, the wealthy are taking a different route. They are moving into gated compounds (Franklin 1998: 13), shopping in private shopping malls (Beckett 1994: 34–39), or remaining at home and doing it all virtually (Boyer 1996; Mitchell 1995). The result is the "destruction of public space" (Beckett 1994: 39), rather than the restoring of hope (Hynes 1996: viii). Homogenisation, and the exclusion of all wild elements (unruly teenagers, the poor, or people who look different because of colour, ethnicity, dress) means that such places become sterile refuges, prone to authoritarianism and conformity. They are based on a view that regards difference as a threat, that fears diversity, and that condones ideologies of power such as sexism, classism and racism (see also Williams 1991: 44–51).

The tendency, across rural and urban land, is for greater and greater concentration of land to be owned and used by fewer and fewer people. In cities, it results in the privatising of public space, and the branding and marketing of city architecture and of events (Klein 2000). In rural areas, it results in the privatising of the means for using public or private space. Resorts claim the best beaches,[47] ecotourism companies claim trails and pathways into remote areas, and farmers are faced with the privatising of germplasm and seeds.

These activities of the global corporate sector depend on the assumption of ownership. Beginning with the ownership of land, the concept of ownership has shifted to include people, products, cell lines, intellectual property, space, and experience. Challenging the concept of land ownership, in the sense of private ownership, would have far-reaching consequences. If biodiversity were the inspiration of the culture, would such ownership be possible? Or could the cultural focus shift in order to bring forward the transience of human time, and the creation of a "moral economy" (Mies and Bennholdt-Thomsen 1995: 13)? This would involve acknowledging collective responsibility for maintenance and sustenance of the land, and all that arises out of it. If each of us were to give more than we take, that alone would change the balance of survival of all on the planet.

---

47 In the USA where the privatisation of public lands has a long history, the development of the California Coastal Trail has run into resistance from rich private individuals who "oppose the use of easements on their properties" thereby preventing ordinary citizens from walking on the beach (Booth 2001: 11). From personal experience, I found it shocking that I could not get to the beach in California because of widespread privately held land. Australian beaches remain largely public land (major exceptions include land occupied by the military, dockland areas, and some resorts).

CHAPTER FIVE

FARMING, FISHING AND FORESTRY: FROM SUBSISTENCE TO TERMINATOR TECHNOLOGY

The diverse, context dependent and evolving
nature of biological systems does not
lend itself easily to standardization
– Sabine O'Hara (1997: 150).

My childhood was filled with the contrasting cultural shifts of the 1950s. The pantry of my aunt was filled with preserved fruit. When plums were weighing down the branches of the tree, they would be bottled. As each fruit came into season, it would be added to the collection in the pantry. During winter, the family ate their way through the stock of food until the next season came round again. My aunt also knitted for her children, sewed, cooked up feasts, and created a self-sustaining garden filled with vegetables, fruits, chooks and a menagerie of other animals. My mother knew how to bottle fruit, but our pantry was filled with tinned apricots and peaches from the nearby cannery. I don't recall ever seeing my mother knit; she sewed just often enough to prove that she was quite adept, and she hated cooking. She raised poultry, milked the cow every morning, was a fine horsewoman, and skilled at working the dogs when it came to moving sheep. Unlike many other farm women of the era, my mother had finished her housework by 10 a.m. I now recognise how it was that she achieved this. Her interests lay outside the household. She had a wool classer's certificate and an endorsed truck licence. She spent time "up the paddock". Soon after marrying my father she bought land; she reconciled the monthly and annual accounts; she planned and discussed with my father which paddocks should be planted and which left fallow. She was well known for holding just about every office-bearing position in local community organisations, and was active in politics. She spent a significant amount of time "being there" for friends, family and people in the local community. And she read voraciously.

Farmers protest against genetically modified organisms at Melbourne's S11 rally, September 2000.

My aunt was continuing the culture of her mother, and her mother before her. My mother was breaking out, using the new appliances – which my aunt also cherished – consuming the goods on the shelf and moving in the direction pointed to by the post-war economies of the West. They were two responses to the time, each had its strengths and weaknesses. Each represented a transitional phase, but a difference in focus. My aunt sustained her household with home-produced goods. My mother, while engaged in some of this work, shifted her focus to the larger world outside the home. But both agreed on one thing: *women don't work*. And certainly, not for pay.

Women's contribution to the economy as primary producers has long been neglected. It is only with the advent of the international women's movement, and feminist challenges to how work is counted (Waring 1988), that the real significance of women's contribution has been made apparent. Figures produced by the Food and Agriculture Organisation (FAO) in 1995 suggest that women produce 50 per cent of the world's food. In some parts of the world, women's contribution to primary production and food rises to 80 per cent (Karl 1996: 7, 8). Women are producers in the agricultural sector, as well as playing a significant role in forestry, and small-scale fisheries. Because much of the work performed by women is small-scale, often domestic, and oriented toward satisfying local needs with local products, it is often women who are best placed to notice environmental degradation. Women play a crucial role in maintaining biodiversity, both as active conservers of ecosystems and as activists in preventing environmental damage.

Farming in Kenya and Nigeria

Just as women like my mother in 1950s Australia were drawn into the transitional world between paid work outside the home and being homemakers within it, women in countries around the world are still facing a transitional world. They work, but their work is often neither seen nor counted.

Scene: A male extension agent is talking to a Kenyan farmer in 1979 about how to improve his maize yield. In the background a woman is unobtrusively weeding low plants between the rows of maize. The agent is telling the man to increase his yield by planting pure stands of maize, but much of the family's nourishment comes from the beans the woman farmer is weeding, unnoticed by the extension agent (Robertson 1997: 259).

The Green Revolution attempt to plant high-yielding varieties of seeds in monoculture cropping was a failure (Shiva 1991), and Claire Robertson's example highlights some of the differences in approach. This scenario can be reproduced in countries around the world, in the so-called Third World, as well as among poorer farmers in the west.

Cassava in Nigeria and beans in Kenya are associated with women. Women plant them, tend them, grow them, harvest them and cook them in a variety of ways. What follows is the story of these two grains, of women's farming practices and how the fate of these crops "under and after colonialism resembles that of women" (Robertson 1997: 262).

It was Flora Nwapa's poetry that first drew my attention to cassava. I heard her speak about her book *Cassava Song and Rice Song* in 1987 at a conference of women writers from around the world. I was struck by the force of the story she had to tell, and that she had chosen to do it through two long poems.

"Cassava," explains Flora Nwapa, "is a woman's crop; only women plant it in Nigeria. It is *infradig* for a man to plant cassava, but he eats it, yes, he eats it. When he becomes affluent, he is ashamed of eating it. Cassava is not only used to prepare different kinds of foods, it is sacred to women. It has supernatural power" (Hawthorne 1987: recording Israel Radio).

Nwapa goes on to explain that she grew cassava during the civil war, and it helped her to survive. And cassava has many symbolic connections to women. The stems of the plant were used in resistance to British colonial domination, in what is called the Women's War of 1929 (1986: 40). Traditionally, it is planted by propagation, and can be harvested easily, even pulled from the ground by children (1986: 19).

> Cassava alone can sustain us
> Cassava is a merciful crop
> It is a crop that tolerates
> Any type of soil
> It is a crop that
> Does not need much attention

You clear the soil
You plant the stem
You weed the farm just once
You wait for the harvest
And what can you not do
With mother cassava? (1986: 69–70).

Flora Nwapa praises cassava, not just for its ease of cultivation, but also its efficiency and efficacy as a healing plant.

We plant your stem
Throughout the year
We clear the farm
Only once a year.

In a short time
You grow very big
In a short time
You are ready for harvest

You make no fuss
You are most humble
You are most kind
To your children

We used your leaves,
in the gruesome war.
We used your leaves
For making soup.

So our children
Were saved
Saved
From the deadly disease

Great Mother Cassava
Bear with us
Henceforth
We shall sing your praise (1986: 3–4).

In "Cassava Song", Nwapa details the many ways of preparing and cooking cassava. She praises it for its versatility, acknowledging that it takes quite some preparation, but unlike other foods such as yam "You remain unspoilt/For days" (1986: 16).

The versatility of cassava includes producing soft food for young children, side-products such as starch from the drops that fall from the bag in which it hangs, and *gari* which "drive[s] away constipation". And cassava "Fills your stomach/With solid food" (1986: 12, 19–20, 22, 36).

Currently there are efforts to propagate cassava from seed, rather than using the traditional vegetative method. The seed used is called true cassava seed (TCS) and the efforts put into the research are justified on the basis of its potential "to reduce virus build-up in vegetative material" (Iglesias, Hershey, Calle and Bolaños 1994: 283). This, at first, appears to be a positive step, but on reading the full article, it becomes clear that there is another agenda.

The authors acknowledge that the vegetative propagation produces plants with good "plant architecture" and that such plants are good for "intercropping" (Iglesias *et al.* 1994: 284). In the research strategy suggested at the end of the article, the authors state that "root yields from TCS are comparable with yields from vegetatively propagated cassava *under optimum management conditions using selected progenies*" (1994: 288, my emphasis). Further, they write "Reduced early vigour and late branching in crops grown from TCS may impose certain restrictions in terms of cultural practices"; and "One of the principal limitations to the acceptance of TCS by cassava processors [women] and consumers would be the increased variation in root quality. Variable quality would probably be acceptable in industrial markets *but not where roots are to be used for fresh consumption*" (1994: 288, my emphasis).

Intercropping is basic to African farming techniques, and has been shown to be the most sustainable approach to farming (Shiva 1993a: 50, 56, 58). Growing conditions in Nigeria are not always ideal, and management practices – those unmarked western scientific labels – will not necessarily be the same as those practised by these researchers. The authors do not elaborate on what cultural practices might need to be restricted. Certainly the record of such restrictions is not a glorious one in the history of colonisation. And finally, they are prepared to push a technology which compromises the nutritional quality of the root for people who are sorely in need of a regular source of food they can eat "Every day of their lives" (Nwapa 1986: 42).

On the last page of the article, the agenda finally becomes clear. "Eventually propagation by TCS will *facilitate mechanization of crop management activities*" (Iglesias *et al.* 1994: 284, my emphasis).

Obviously, research is useful in creating a higher probability of success with agricultural staples, but to ignore the traditions, in order to get a compromised quality, just to "facilitate mechanization", is too high a cost. Resources would be better spent researching why women use the methods they do, and, with their participation, looking for ways of reducing viral problems and increasing yield that are useful to those who grow the crops. To carry out research in a "virus free area" (Iglesias *et al.* 1994: 288) is unrealistic, and disconnects the plant from its growing context.

Unlike the authors of this article, I do not believe that this experiment shows "considerable potential" (Iglesias *et al.* 1994: 289). Rather, it has the hallmarks of many other agricultural interventions from the west, namely, imposing decontextualised systems which benefit agribusiness, not the farmers engaged in growing and harvesting crops.

Cassava is not only a nutritionally useful crop, but is also being used to assist in the conservation and improvement of the environment. Gbadegesin discusses the connection between the increasing number of female-headed households in the Olokemeji area of Oyo State, Nigeria and the "cultivation of less nutrient-demanding crops such as cassava and yam" (1996: 115). The research also demonstrates the connection between structural adjustment programs (financial liberalisation, privatisation, exchange-rate adjustments and reduced tariffs), and the migration of men out of rural areas to urban areas. When male householders return, they turn their energy toward growing cash and export-oriented crops. By contrast, the women tend to conserve and improve the environment by engaging in "tree planting along farm boundaries and on degraded farms, for fuel and other purposes" (1996: 117, 119). Indeed, the women complained of male villagers embezzling wood obtained from communal tree-growing projects.

Cassava, alongside other mixed farming regimes in Nigeria, provides villages with a reliable nutritious crop which also contributes to environmental sustainability.

In Kenya, the Kikuyu women have faced similar challenges with different crops. Traditionally beans have played an important social, nutritional and ritual part in women's lives. Beans have continued to be important, but the kinds of beans grown have shifted from the traditional njahe beans to green beans in a developing export economy, and more recently under IMF imposed structural adjustment programs, to coffee beans.

> Beans are a women's crop, a women's trade commodity, and preeminently a women's food ... Njahe are small round black beans with a white cap on them which have special significance for the Kikuyu. They are intimately associated with women, especially women's reproductive functions (Robertson 1997: 262–263).

Kikuyu women eat beans at significant periods in their lives: prior to clitoridectomy,[1] during marriage negotiations, during pregnancy and after childbirth, and again after menopause. Beans are very high in protein content, higher than other grains, and nutritionally complement other foods traditionally eaten by the Kikuyu, such as millet and maize. On the negative side, economically speaking, they take a long time to grow, and the cooking time is also long. But symbolically, this gives them extra potency as they require attention, nurturing and an ongoing commitment to their cultivation.

> Beyond material issues here is the symbolic assertion of white over dark, which was applied not only to skin color but also to European food preferences in beans and maize (Robertson 1997: 261).

So, what does it matter if a crop with symbolic associations to women, and a wide acceptance as a food source, is replaced by exotic plants? And what is the problem if production methods change with the introduction of new knowledges through colonisation? Should one not assume that with progress some things fall by the wayside?

The problem is that knowledges are never neutral. It seems strange to me that a bean can be replaced simply because it is black. But the

---

1   For an evocative portrait of a young Nandi woman's life in Kenya, including traditional rituals and farming practices, see Jane Tapsubei Creider (1992).

association of njahe beans with the indigenous people did not stop just at
the idea of "bringing civilisation", it was tied intimately with racist ideas of
hygiene and cleanliness. White food was better. It was cleaner. Such
attitudes affect the taste buds and ideas about what is edible and what is
not. "Purification campaigns" were also put in place. What this meant was
that the government instituted compulsory inspection of export crops to
ensure that the beans were not mixed with other varieties. Louis Leakey
in 1966 described how a farmer prepared the land and grew his [sic] crop.

When a piece of ground has been cleared and hoed and prepared for
planting, a number of different crops are planted all mixed up on one and the
same patch. No attempt is made to segregate the different crops, and no
attempt is made to plant in lines. This to the white man appears to be very
crude and unscientific. I have heard it argued again and again that if a Kikuyu
would only divide up the plot of ground that he happens to have available,
and would plant his maize in one part of it, his beans in another and his sweet
potato in another and so on, he would get a bigger yield of each of these
crops, and, moreover, a better one. But would he? (in Robertson 1997: 286).

As recent research has shown, monoculture does not necessarily produce
better yields (Shiva 2000b: 110, 114), but it does make industrialised
farming for the export market easier. However, the costs are high. In
Kenya, mixed farming of several crops as described by Leakey was more
sustainable, as soil fertility was maintained, and it reduced problems with
pests, as well as vulnerability to disease. Further, in Kenya, the shift away
from bean production has reduced the nutritional value of the foods
grown for individual, family or local consumption.

Other policies fostered by the government included a misdirected focus
on export for European markets to the exclusion of more complementary
markets in India and South America, and cheaper transport costs for privileged exotic crops such as maize. Maize (corn) is indigenous to the Americas.
It is not surprising that an exotic crop becomes the privileged crop, given
that displacement is central to the neoliberal process of globalisation.

In Kenya, maize had become indigenised after many generations of
cropping. Indigenised maize was yellow and purple, and has a high food
value. Kenya White maize was produced through hybridising Natal Flat
White maize with Hickory King, a North American variety. The growing

of maize in Kenya was not some accident, brought about by simple introduction of the seed; rather, it was pursued through government policy in order to link Kenya to international markets, and resulted in active participation of transnational corporations in Kenyan agriculture. Export, "The Almighty foreign exchange" (Nwapa 1986: 43), became the primary goal of the Kenyan Department of Agriculture.

On the whole, since colonisation and particularly in the period after World War II, the needs and preferences of the local populace have been consistently ignored. Unsellable varieties of beans do not store well and may become inedible (beans harden with storage time). By planting mono-cultures, and harvesting them all at the same time, the dietary needs of communities are not well met. Since the implementation of these policies, rates of malnutrition have increased (Humphrey 1945, cited in Robertson 1997: 283); soil fertility has decreased, male-owned export-oriented market gardens have come to dominate the industry; and the latest favoured crops include green beans, soya beans and coffee beans. Growers are subject to the fluctuations in international markets. By industrialising their farming practices, they need to spend more on inputs, such as fertilisers, pesticides, and, in the case of soy beans, they need to inoculate the soil prior to planting. These practices benefit transnational corporations, while disen-franchising those who depend on their work for their survival, and the continuing survival of the community and the environment.

By contrast, the earlier cultivation of njahe was controlled by women, grown in mixed sustainable plots, and had a much higher marketability to the local populace. As Robertson points out, "local taste prevails" (1997: 296). Furthermore, Kikuyu women's ties to their indigenous religious practices are severed; meaning is displaced; and economics and inter-national trade, along with the encumbering hierarchies and capricious tastes and values of those markets, become the dominating force.

Colonisation in Kenya introduced new seeds, new methods, and new tastes to be considered. Further enforced by policies of purification and privileged access to markets, the food economy was dislocated in favour of the exotic and export-oriented needs.[2] As Arundhati Roy says in the context of Indian farmers:

---

2   "In Africa, many countries have up to half of their arable land planted in luxury export crops, from cacao to peanuts" (Crouch 2000: 26).

People stop growing things that they can afford to *eat*, and start growing things that they can afford only to *sell*. By linking themselves to the "market" they lose control over their lives (1999: 85, emphasis in original).

With the new global economy, the effects of dislocation are amplified, women and small farmers are disempowered, genetic diversity is reduced. The myth that "biodiversity reduces yields and productivity" is spread by transnational biotechnology and seed companies, but as Shiva points out "yields and productivity are theoretically constructed terms: they change according to the context" (Shiva 2000b: 110). With dependency on seed companies and international markets, farmers are increasingly vulnerable to agricultural disasters through exposure to a wide variety of crop diseases. Ironically, they experience greater vulnerability to famine. In addition, transnationals do not respect the harvest of genetic diversity, and both biological and cultural alienation of women's traditions are heightened. The domination by European and western needs is, as Robertson concludes,

the triumph of hierarchy, and the fulfillment of agricultural imperialism. Kenyan green beans are usually picked long before maturity. Dried beans represent, rather, lateral connections, more democratic tendencies, and the potential fertility of maturity (1997: 295).

There is a pressing need for studies which are not biased toward western-style, monoculture agricultural practices, which recognise that yields per hectare are not simply a matter of measuring seeds only, but rather are based on the recognition of polyculture and "the complexity of traditional agricultural systems" (Crouch 2001: 26).

Vandana Shiva summarises the impact of what has happened to cassava, njahe beans, and a host of other traditionally farmed foods grown in home gardens (2000b: 111). She points to the systemic nature of monoculturalism in agriculture, highlighting the problems of the "development paradigm".

The Green Revolution is a prime example of the development paradigm. It destroyed diverse agricultural systems adapted to the diverse ecosystems of the planet, globalizing the culture and economy of an industrial agriculture. It wiped out thousands of crops and crop varieties, substituting them with monocultures of rice, wheat and maize across the Third World. It replaced internal inputs with capital- and chemical-intensive inputs, creating debt for farmers and death for ecosystems (1997: 107).

The industrialisation and globalisation of maize have come full circle with the NAFTA agreement.[3] Mexico exports cheap oil to the USA, but has lost its ability to export maize at a sustainable price. Instead, maize is imported into Mexico, destroying the indigenous agriculture of southern Mexico and supporting a wasteful agricultural system in the USA with all its inputs of fertilisers and fossil fuel (Martinez-Alier 2000: 158).

In Kenya, the process of globalisation has also been played out through the cultivation of another non-food export crop: coffee beans. Terisa Turner and Leigh Brownhill provide an interesting case study from the women of Maragua, located at the centre of Kenya's coffee-growing region about eighty kilometres north-west of Nairobi. Women in this region have always had food cropping rights through farming the land of their husbands. In the event of the death of the husband, women would marry other women, "thereby becoming 'husbands' with all the land rights of their deceased husbands" (Turner and Brownhill 2001: 108). Such practices ceased under the process of "decolonisation", during which time men made deals whose outcome was increased dispossession and dislocation of women. These deals involved participating in the "World Bank sponsored privatization drive of the 1990s" (Turner and Brownhill 2001: 109) through taking loans in order to grow export coffee crops. As the coffee crops expanded, they largely replaced women's food gardens, which in turn decreased the amount of time women would spend working together in groups on one another's gardens, thereby increasing women's isolation.

When coffee commodity prices dropped, women began threatening to stop caring for the coffee crops, and tension in marriages increased. But Kenya had become dependent on coffee exports. The World Bank and the IMF responded by increasing subsidies for coffee, inducing the women to

---

3   The Zapatista uprising that began on 1 January 1994 was the direct response of indigenous people to the introduction of NAFTA and its neoliberal agenda. In particular, the indigenous people were protesting against the NAFTA-inspired change to the Mexican constitution of Article 27, which hitherto had protected communally held indigenous land from privatisation or sale to foreign investors. For an analysis of the economic impact, see Martinez-Alier (2000); and for accounts of the uprising that put women at the centre, see Rovira (2000); Ortiz (2001).

remain engaged in coffee production. Thus women had to spend more time on their husbands' coffee crops, in part because of the pressure for more cash now required for services such as health and education. Women, however, began to rebel by planting "beans between the coffee trees, contrary to restrictions against intercropping with coffee". This helped to increase the soil fertility and reduced inputs such as chemical fertilisers. Eventually, women in Maragua began uprooting the coffee trees, using them for firewood, in spite of the threat of seven-year jail sentences (Turner and Brownhill 2001: 113). Women also replaced the coffee trees with food crops such as bananas, vegetables and food crops which could be eaten or traded locally. Turner and Brownhill conclude that the women's resistance to participating in coffee production represents a resistance to "an individualized labour process organized by husbands" (2001: 123); a resistance to export-orientation, privatisation, and increased dependence on the cash economy favoured by the World Bank and the IMF. The women in Maragua re-established collective work processes of working one another's food gardens, and returned to a focus on production of food for home consumption and trading within the local area.

Forestry in Europe, North America and South Asia

> *What forest bring us;*
> *soil, water and clean air;*
> *soil, water and clean air;*
> *the basis of our life*
> (Chipko slogan, cited in
> Wickramasinghe 1994: 16).

As Carolyn Merchant points out, "the legal term *forest* [was] being used to designate lands where game was reserved for kings and the nobility" (1980: 63). This was reflected in my own childhood experience. The native forest of white cypress pine (*Callitris columellarsis*) comprised a timber that had high resistance to termites and decay. The forests were cleared and used for house building, flooring and panelling, as well as for the miles of fences built to keep in the sheep. The remaining forest became for us, as children, the home of games, of cubby houses; our imaginations located every story of forests or woods in the remnants that bordered our house. No other place on the property accounted for so much joint activity. It was a place where the world of farming crossed over into culture and social life.

A forest, according to the *Oxford Dictionary*, has three meanings: "1. An extensive tract of land covered with trees and undergrowth sometimes intermingled with pasture. 2. A woodland district, usually belonging to the king, set apart for hunting wild beasts and game. 3. A wild, uncultivated waste." None of these meanings indicates that a forest "is a process of interrelatedness" (Loomis 1995: 27). What the dictionary does reveal is our attitude toward the forest.

For people living in the industrialised west, the forest has great nostalgia. It is a symbol of what has been lost. The history of "civilisation" is the history of deforestation. On the Eurasian continent and in North Africa, the western movement of peoples was accompanied by the felling of vast tracts of forest lands (Diamond 1991: 285–303). Only in places which would support few people, or which were inhospitable, did forests survive. In the northern hemisphere, Siberia, the Arctic Circle and equatorial Africa escaped destruction. As people moved across the earth's surface, habitats were destroyed: on Easter Island, deforestation led to the total collapse of the society; in the Americas, it is likely that the Anasazi and the Maya destroyed significant tracts of forest (Diamond 1991: 297–298).

In writing about the destruction of European forests, initially in the thirteenth century, and again in the sixteenth century, Carolyn Merchant notes:

The disruption of the forest ecosystem by the rise of early modern industry, coupled with the careless use and mismanagement of resources, bears striking parallels to current environmental issues and is illustrative of the fact that today's environmental crisis is not new in kind, only in degree (1983: 67).

At the beginning of the twenty-first century, this destruction continues apace. The fires which burned through the Borneo forests (ABC Television News, 28 April 1998) are likely to cause the extinction of the orang-utan in its native habitat; the forests on Vanuatu are being felled at an alarming rate; destruction of biodiversity continues on the Australian continent at the rate of about a million hectares a year (Coulloupas 1998: 3); forests which survived earlier periods of destruction are now under threat. The difference is that these are the last existing forests. It is too late for the

Lithuanian forests which once supported the bison[4] (Schama 1996: 45); it is almost too late for the forests which supported the Asian tiger and the panda; it is too late for the Tasmanian forests which supported the thylacine (the Tasmanian tiger); it is too late in too many places.

In the nineteenth century, John Muir wrote that "going to the woods is going home; for I suppose we came from the woods originally" (in Oelschlaeger 1991: 178). But for many people it is too late for this too. Their homes have been destroyed, more forests have been felled, and "timber" is planted, not according to the needs of the community, but according to the needs of the market and the export dollar.

Just as the transnational seed companies claim that monocultures increase yield (Shiva 2000b: 110), the forestry industry claims that "logging benefits wildlife" (Wolke 1999: 95). But as Howie Wolke goes on to argue, in the North American context to which he is referring, logging benefits bureaucrats. "To advocate wildland preservation is to advocate fewer bureaucrats" (1999: 99).

Roads are built for access to native forests, native forests are felled, and the needs of the market are met by planting "industrial trees", those with a long straight trunk that can be plantation-grown in "tidy battalions" (Schama 1996: 50). Exotic species are invariably chosen to fill this gap. In recent years, with women moving into research, with indigenous peoples retrieving their own traditions, their own knowledge, it is gradually becoming apparent that women have a great store of knowledge about forests, and have for generations been "thinking like a forest".[5]

Anoja Wickramasinghe, in a case study on women and forestry in Sri Lanka, relates women's knowledge of forestry to cultural factors, with women passing on through their practices

> knowledge about tree species, locations for germ-plasm, ecological niches in which each species survives best, low-cost conservational technologies, multiple uses of tree products and technologies of preparing, processing and preserving products and technologies in multiple land-use (1994: 93–94).

4   Schama comments that "because of their sacred place in the theology of the royal hunt, the ancient frontier forests had been spared the kind of industries that elsewhere in Europe, from England to Brandenburg, had cut huge slices out of their acreage" (1996: 45).

5   Max Oelschlaeger uses this phrase in relation to John Muir (1991: 198).

She argues that by recognising women's culturally developed knowledge "it would be possible to eliminate several years of experimentation and trials" (1994: 94). She makes a distinction, which reflects the experience of women in Africa, between the attitudes of women and men to trees, namely that women have a "lasting interest in tree products" and men an "interest in timber obtained through destructive harvesting" (1994: 92). This, in spite of the fact that men eat the tree products grown by women. Because timber, like rice and coffee in Nigeria and Kenya respectively, represents export value, timber programs are favoured and subsidised, ignoring the locally based needs of women. As she suggests:

> community forestry programmes in the developing world have become limited by traditions of male leadership and power. This has marginalized the women who actually practice forestry (1994: 25).

The connection between deforestation and export-orientation is not unusual. Although the deforestation of Sri Lanka began in the sixteenth century, first with Portuguese, and then Dutch colonisation, it was not until the British arrived and began clearing the land for plantations that the subsistence economy was also disrupted. Commercialisation and export-orientation prevailed, and the economy was transformed. The British were well practised in this; they had already deforested their own lands. Just as communal lands had been destroyed in Britain, so too in the colonies. Under these circumstances, indigenous peoples are forced to become labourers in the cash economy. As argued by Wickramasinghe above, men join the cash economy, sometimes migrating away from their homeland, while women tend to remain within the subsistence economy, farming, gardening, collecting and producing household goods. Women are joined to households because of the nature of their maintenance work, such as the raising of children, preparation of food, collection of water, fuel and fruits, and other kinds of domestic work. But it also gives them a continuing connection with land and place, with the knowledge of their grandmothers, and with the products of forests, trees, medicinal plants.[6]

---

6   Diane Bell's research with indigenous women in Central Australia also bears this out. She comments that during World War II indigenous men often joined the cash economy by joining the army. Women, on the other hand, "found a narrowing of opportunities" (1983/2002: 70). Women, on the whole, remained outside the cash economy during that period.

Women, especially poor women, are often accused of deforestation because of their need to collect fuel wood. But, as research by both Anoja Wickramasinghe in Sri Lanka and Farida Akhter in Bangladesh has shown, this is not the case. Wickramasinghe points out that the curing of tobacco has had a twofold impact on the forest: firstly, in the felling of trees in order to plant tobacco, and secondly, in the curing of the tobacco, which consumes much more firewood than the household needs of women (1994: 59). Further, as firewood becomes a scarce resource, it soon becomes available only from the Ceylon Tobacco Company.[7] In this way, women too, as consumers, are drawn into the cash economy. The scarcity of wood also means that women cease to make their own household utensils from plant materials, and they are further impoverished by ceasing to pass on the traditional skills between generations of women (see also Sittirak 1998: 115–133).

Farida Akhter concludes her study, *Women and Trees*, with the suggestion that the poorest families are the most productive.

[They] plant more trees utilising the minimum land which they have. They take care of plants and trees more eagerly not only because nature is their immediate source or subsistence but also because they understand the importance of trees for the environment (1990: 37).

Akhter also points out that trees are almost never cut for firewood; instead, fallen branches and leaves are used. "Destruction of trees is done by brick field contractors, traders of firewood, and the timber merchants" (1990: 16, 38).

Trees are cut, however, in a financial crisis. For poor families, such a crisis occurs on the marriage of a daughter, in order to meet the cost of a dowry (Akhter 1990: 33), or on the death of a mother who has outlived her husband. One woman stated:

It is trees which are more reliable than sons. If you have a tree you can be sure that at *nidan kal* – the time of death – the funeral cost will be met by the tree (1990: 36).

7   This is also borne out by Bina Agarwal's research on women's relationship to land in South Asia, including her comments that "appropriation and exploitation of forest lands by the State and the privatization of the commons" have been declining over the past four decades (1994: 455).

The biggest problem cited by Wickramasinghe and Akhter in women's relation to tree planting and conservation is their lack of ownership of the land. Ownership, in both Sri Lanka and Bangladesh, is held by the male head of household, and only on his death does ownership of a portion of the land pass to the woman (Akhter 1990: 25). Daughters, as Akhter points out, are regarded as only temporary residents of the household, and therefore they can make no ownership claim on anything, since on marriage, they will leave for their husband's household (1990: 21). The few women who manage to claim ownership of land are more secure and able to make long-term plans for planting of trees. Male ownership also means that with the increasing commercialisation of farming, the granting of subsidies or loans, women are locked out of credit arrangements and the chance to become financially autonomous. As with the crops mentioned earlier, women use trees for many purposes.

> Women tend trees which produce multiple products ... Food, fuelwood, fodder and organic residues for mulching are the products they are concerned with, and so the species which are best deemed either satisfy all these needs or a number of them. If one ranks species accordingly, it becomes clear that jack (*Artocarpus heterophyllus*) and coconut (*Cocos nucifera*) are preferred (Wickramasinghe 1994: 87).

> The trees benefit us in so many ways we cannot even begin to describe. Many of these benefits are not tangible. Do we see the cold breeze from the trees? The trees contribute to the rains which we need for our crops. The shadow of the tree is essential for everyone of us (Akhter 1990: 25).[8]

What becomes clear in the research on forests and farming is that there are two competing systems at work. The dominant one can be described as an isolated system. It is characterised by segregation, selection from

---

8   José Bové complains that the intensification of agriculture in France has led to the eradication of hedges, and that animals which are put out to pasture now have "no shelter from wind or sun" (in Luneau 2001: 65). Gbadegesin writes of the importance of cultivating particular species of trees in Nigeria. Among the most important reasons given are "shade for animals and human beings" (1996: 119); the second most important reason was the additional organic litter provided by certain trees which shed their leaves. Trakansuphakon (1997) writes about the importance of trees to the indigenous Karen people of the Burma–Thai border region.

above, management and ownership from outside, monoculture, belief in progress, decontextualisation, compartmentalisation, displacement, hierarchy, industrialisation, products, concentration, dependency, scarcity, external interventions, export-orientation, single use, cash, poverty, subsidies, chemical inputs, large acreage with variable productivity, and a high susceptibility to disease. Isolated systems are counted in the UN System of National Accounts. They are therefore considered real and productive. They are the system pushed by development agencies, the World Bank, the IMF and transnational companies. What they replace is an entirely different system, best described as an integrated system. To put this into a feminist framework, an integrated system shares much with Angela Miles' term "integrative feminism" (1996), a feminism informed by the principle that the personal is political, and in particular concerned with harmony between means and ends. Integrative feminism recognises particularity and diversity.

Integrated systems are characterised by participation, diversity, relationship, multiple use, dispersed selection, management by participation, involvement, complexity, engagement, context, renewability, local knowledge, and traditions. They are community-driven and result in high productivity of small acreage.[9] They are regarded as domestic and are therefore not counted in the UN System of Accounts. These systems are obscured by the more obvious, export-earning isolated systems which are "riddled from top to bottom with male decision-making and operating out of a paradigm in which 'technology' is seen as a key element." (Wickramasinghe 1994: 73).

It is too simplistic to say that the isolated system reflects men's practice and the integrated system women's, but it is evident that the more powerful members of any community tend to congregate in the first category, while the least powerful congregate in the second. In countries such as Australia, entire indigenous communities are found practising in an integrated way, but when commerce and external labour appear, men are more likely to be pulled into the market economy first.

---

9   On productivity, Shiva writes: "Yields usually refers to production per unit area of a single crop. Planting only one crop in the entire field as a monoculture will of course increase its yield. Planting multiple crops in a mixture will have low yields of individual crops but will have a high total output of food" (2000b: 110); see also Norberg-Hodge (1996c).

Just as deforestation in Nepal has had dire consequences for some parts of Bangladesh, the deforestation of Mount Sarno in Italy was directly responsible for the deaths of so many of the villagers in the 1998 mud slides (Stanley 1998: 9). In Samoa, the people of the village of A'opo are concerned that the activities of commercial timber companies are causing water shortages (Park 1994: 133). Deforestation has worldwide consequences.

Forests are places where trees dominate, but trees are by no means the only source of sustenance and survival for traditional peoples. The Karen peoples in the border region between Thailand and Burma have integrated management structures in place which are maintained with religious sanctions. For example, there are prohibitions on felling certain trees, or trees which bear a particular relationship to other trees or animals in the forest (Trakansuphakon 1997: 166). The women of Sri Lanka use a wide range of other plants, while in New Zealand, Samoa, Tonga and other lowland Pacific Island regions, the movement of birds and insects, seeds and pollen is central to the continuing biodiversity (Park 1994: 136).

Deforestation has had an ecologically disruptive effect on all land-based systems, not just in the areas immediately bordered by forests, but upstream and downstream of them, as well as across continents. Deforestation also has an impact on fisheries. This is the case in Samoa (Park 1994: 140) and along the Great Barrier Reef in Queensland, where coral growth, and hence fish health and diversity, is affected by run-off.

In sum, the impact of western culture on indigenous and traditional regimes of forest management can also be shown in that penumbra which occurred in Europe in the nineteenth century. After the bison had disappeared from Germany, along with many other species, a diversity of creatures still remained in the eastern forests on the border between Poland and Lithuania. The Lithuanian forest of Bialowieza was home to elk, bison, lynx, wild boar, reindeer, hare and bear, along with mushrooms, garlic, wild honey, herbs, leafy vegetables, fruits and nuts. Trees included ash, aspen, maple, oak, linden, willow, birch, elm, hornbeams and spindle trees, pine and fir. And they were all "jumbled together", without order. The new scientific approach shifted this regime of diversity in which the forest peoples subsisted on products of the forest, taking small game for a small licence fee, to one which was "on a more orderly footing" (Schama 1996: 49). Schama summarises the ideas of Julius von Brinken, a forester, who visited Bialowieza, Lithuania in 1820:

What was needed ... was a methodical forestry that would, over time ... bring it into some kind of proper hierarchy. Varieties would be massed together so that those suitable for one purpose, like shipbuilding, could be efficiently harvested at the allotted time, while timber more suitable for building materials would be cultivated elsewhere. In this ideal regime, the trees would be graduated in age, so that foresters would not need to wander all through the woods looking for trees of maximum maturity or whatever the designated age might be for the job. Specimens of a like variety and maturity would present themselves *in tidy battalions ready for their marching orders* (1996: 50, my emphasis).

These ideas of an ordered universe spread around the world. The great forests of Canada were floated down river, just like a naval battalion. And such ideas persist even today.

In Australia, the wild native forest is replaced by plantations. The Australian bush is not a tidy place. The native flora does not array itself in straight lines, the branches of trees writhe like dancers' arms. There is a word used by the Ngiyambaa people of western New South Wales which describes this interaction, this "beingness": *walu* represents the untamed wildness of the Australian bush, the hanging strips of bark, the scattered leaves, the "disordered" look that is so very different from the artificially kempt and ordered stretches of land that have been farmed or turned into plantations or orchards. In an area of South Australia currently claimed by the Ngarrindjeri people, a forest with plenty of *walu* is transformed into marching battalions of tall, straight, exotic and industrialised pines. Eucalyptus trees like this are unsuitable for harvesting as "timber" and are not used in plantations.

The military approach has laid waste much of the world's forest. I believe a change in the western industrialised approach is urgently needed. As forester Merv Wilkinson has stated, "Rows of trees are not forests. They represent blind stupidity and a one track mind" (Loomis 1995: 5).

It is not as though sustainable forestry has been shown to be impossible. Listening to the traditions of the people close to forests would be sufficient to show that. The fifty-year experiment that Merv Wilkinson has worked on with his "Wildwood" property in British Colombia, Canada, shows that not only is the forest sustainable, but it is possible to increase both the health and the productivity of a forest when one works with – rather than

Where native forest once grew,

The "disordered" look, or *walu*, expresses the unfettered being of wild eucalyptus trees, Fleurieu Peninsula, South Australia.

against – nature. Similarly, Bill Mollison's (1978) experiment with permaculture in Tasmania, Australia, has led the way to interrelated methods of
sustainable forestry and agriculture complementing one another. Like the
ancient art of companion planting, a nurturing approach to forestry and
farming – an approach exemplified by co-operation and interrelation, one
based on an integrative system – is a method which has a future. I contend
that monoculturalism in forestry is as negative and destructive as it is in
farming, since it increases the susceptibility of trees to disease, as well as
encouraging an uncreative and uncaring approach to the harvesting of
trees, clear-felling – and a pervasive ignorance of context and of history.

A wild politics approach to forestry would mean that the *relationship* of
everything – living beings and the non-living elements of the ecosystem as
well – in the forest would be more important than talk of economics,
efficiency, resources and incentives (Turner 1999: 123). Turner points out
that economic theory only works when "everything is abstracted into
commensurate units and common value" (1999: 125).

> Just as time is abstracted from experience and rendered mechanical (the
> clock) so it can be measured, space is abstracted from place and becomes
> property: measurable land. In the same way, trees are abstracted into board-
> feet, wild rivers are abstracted into acre-feet, and beauty is abstracted into a
> scene whose value is measured by polls. Economics reduces everything to a
> unit of measurement because it requires that everything be commensurate
> – "capable of being measured by a common standard" – its standard (Turner
> 1999: 125).

Abstractification (Ani 2000), reductionism (Shiva 1995) and universal
standardisation through context-stripped approaches are decimating the
world's forests. This is borne out even in the literature on biodiversity
loss. Edward Barbier and Michael Rauscher provide a list of "variables,
parameters and functions" (1995: 263) to model ways of using tropical
forests sustainably. But the elements which I have focused on – for production and control of water, for food, medicines, leaves, roots and wood for
producing home-made implements, and for symbolic, sometimes sacred,
uses – do not feature in their measurement. The following list contains
the elements these two authors see and account for:

the bulldozers have triumphed,

A few hundred metres from the wild trees is clear-felled devastation.
A nearby sign said "Plantation Timber – A Renewable Resource".

- tropical timber stock
- tropical timber logs extracted or commodities produced (log-equivalents)
- tropical timber logs/products exported (log-equivalents)
- domestic consumption of logs/products
- consumption of imported goods
- regeneration function of tropical forests
- deforestation rate, per unit (log-equivalent) timber extracted
- terms of trade
- social rate of discount (1995: 263).

Thus everything is measured in log-equivalents, with timber as the primary recognisable resource. If this is an indication of the thinking of those interested in the issue of biodiversity loss, I suggest we urgently need another way of thinking, a way which integrates human lives and forestry, which recognises the politics of the wild; is concerned with means and ends; and takes account of complexity, including complexity arising from relationship and markers of time. I argue that we need a model not "constructed around the ubiquitous" (Swanson 1995: 259) systems of current global institutions, but one which considers the alternatives used by women, by indigenous peoples, and by those who have maintained natural environments sustainably for many years.

Fishing in the Pacific

> *"Women don't fish" I was told in all the countries I*
> *visited in the course of my two women in fisheries studies.*
> *Yet in two of these countries there were actually women*
> *fishing on the shore outside the fisheries department in*
> *plain view – in one case women were gathering shellfish*
> *for sale, in another case they were hand-lining*
> *– Penelope Schoeffel (1995: 12).*

Interesting parallels emerge in my research across different traditional activities of women in vastly different cultures. In Sri Lanka, women use the products of the forest in ways that contribute to sustainability. In New Guinea, women pass on their knowledge of medicinal plants and contraception, as well as using the protective covering of the forest as the primary place for communicating women's knowledge between the

and the land is being planted with the introduced *Pinus radiata*.

A battalion of *Pinus radiata* in Second Valley Forest, Parewa,
Fleurieu Peninsula, South Australia.

generations (Mogina 1996: oral presentation).

In Central Australia, women hunt for small animals such as lizards, dig for roots, pick fruits and seeds. Once again, their activities have a low impact, and they continue to use the same implements, such as digging sticks, as they have done for millennia. Because women are so often accompanied by children, they concentrate on activities in which children can participate. They pick fruit, edible leaves, bark, and roots, pluck fungi from the forest floor, and hunt small animals and birds.

In Western Samoa, women visit the mangrove forests. They fish for crab in a low-impact way, which does not appear to have changed much from traditional practices. Indeed, in all Pacific Island economies, women, *and their children*, contribute 50 to 80 per cent[10] of the total fisheries production (Bidesi 1994: 124). As one writer has put it, "the basic equipment in hunting and gathering: the eyes, hands and feet" (Gina-Whewell 1995: 23). Women develop dexterity and quickness in order to catch fish or crustacea with their hands without injury. And women have a store of local knowledge about fishing: knowledge of how best to pry catch off rocks and mangroves, about the best weather conditions for fishing and gleaning, including phases of the moon, tides, and seasons (Gina-Whewell 1995; Taniera and Mitchell 1995). Women's subsistence and semi-subsistence fishing practices tend toward the low-technology end. Their tools of trade are usually "hand lines, hand nets, digging sticks, goggles and traps" (Bidesi 1994: 125). They make frequent short trips in which time is structured around other daily domestic tasks such as child-rearing and cooking. While men's activities are mostly dependent on outside resources such as fuel and ice, women go fishing in between other activities. Unlike the men's activities, women's daily fishing trips are not interrupted by expensive and time-consuming repairs to equipment which can result in

---

10   These figures reflect similar figures for land-based hunter-gatherers. Lee and de Vore (1968) estimate that women provide around 80 per cent of food provisioning through gathering, while men through hunting activities provide about 20 per cent (cited in Shiva 1989: 104). Diane Bell notes that in desert regions of Australia "it was the women who provided the reliable portion of the diet (up to 80 per cent)" (1981: 319). Bell also suggests that "women are the economic mainstay" and that their access to food resources and their right to distribute those resources in the community gives women a degree of independence, and concomitantly dependence by men on women (1983: 54–55). Turner and Brownhill state that in "Africa women do some 80 per cent of all farming" (2001: 107).

periods when no fishing takes place. While both lagoon and open-sea fishing were practised by men in the past, and both produced sufficient for sustainable and continuous small harvests, the advent of motor boats with modern fishing equipment and cooling facilities has meant depletion of fishing stocks in both environments. Depletion is a particular problem in lagoons, which are also dependent on the mangroves for the continuation of their existence.

In all these environments, the men have been drawn into the cash economy. In Kenya, as mentioned earlier, they benefit from the export-oriented growing of coffee, supported by both state and global institutions; in Sri Lanka, they work on the plantations, driving tractors, using the machinery of industrialised farming; in Samoa they are drawn into the commercial fishing industry, often fishing off-shore in motorised boats to earn cash (Tolova'a 1994: 229); in Australia, they travel in four-wheel-drive Toyotas to the hunting areas, and use rifles, or they become stockmen on the vast company-owned stations.[11] Perhaps the reason is simply that western men's culture was readily transferable to indigenous men, that women's contribution was invisible, just as it had been in the realms of the colonisers.

Worse still than the acceptance of western implements is the destructive use of the military approach to harvesting: key examples are the use of bleach and dynamite fishing in the sea, the use of insecticides on small plants, and chainsaws for felling trees on land (Tolova'a 1994: 229–230). The military approach contributes devastatingly to over-harvesting, deforestation and homogenisation of cultivation practices. The practices also respond to and create greed, dependency on cash and consumerism. Further, just as the products of men's hunting in Central Australia contribute only a little to the dietary needs of the community, in Vanuatu, women's subsistence and semi-subsistence activities account for "61–65 per cent of protein supply" (Bidesi 1994: 126), while commercial fishing contributes around 5 per cent.

The consequences of this for the world's people, now and for the future, are hugely important. I believe that it means that worldwide, many women still have access to the knowledge which can help to sustain the planet through the twenty-first century and beyond. Obviously, there are men too with this knowledge, but perhaps it is time to listen to the women.

---

11   See, for example Rosser (1987); Marshall (1988).

As cash comes to dominate daily affairs, there is a push to sell surplus produce, including women's surplus produce. But in the official figures, women's contribution is still missing. The effort by development agencies to make visible women's work sometimes simply makes the knowledge more easily available for appropriation. As in Kenya, where "more than 90 per cent of extension officers are male, and most of their support is [still] oriented towards male-dominated fisheries" (Bidesi 1994: 125).

Industrial fishing attracts large amounts of foreign investment, is export-oriented and, like forestry, focuses on one or two species. In the Pacific, tuna is the dominant catch. But just as over-harvesting and over-capitalising have destroyed forests and other fisheries, the tuna industry will not be sustainable if it continues at the current pace of development. Industrial fishers consider the resources of the oceans to be there for the taking. And since so many of the island nations are short of cash in their economies, most go along with access agreements for foreign exchange. But, as Claire Slatter points out, the sums received are paltry. She cites figures for 1988, in which year Japan, Taiwan, Korea and the USA realised $US1.1 billion in tuna catch, in exchange for a mere $US30 million in access rights (1994a: 133). Even with a renegotiation of the rights in the early 1990s, the transnational tuna industry "is laughing all the way to the bank" (1994a: 133). Their fleets have become fishing factories, and their intention is to make as much of a profit from current stocks as possible. Sustainability has not been a consideration; rather, the industry's motives are the same as those of the nineteenth-century new foresters: concentration on harvesting a single species in a single area, freezing overstocks, and grabbing whatever they can without consideration for the future.

When fisherpeople outside the USA come up with an idea for capitalising on globalisation, those same companies profiting from the exploitation of Pacific Islanders get angry, and accuse the new entrepreneurs of "unfair competition". The salmon producers from Chile are producing Pacific salmon for the Japanese and North American markets at a fraction of the cost of US-produced Atlantic salmon. Just as boys in the classroom complain of not getting enough attention when girls' needs are met (Spender 1988), the North American fishing industry is complaining of losing their privileges (*All Things Considered*, National Public Radio: 18 June 1998). In a poem reminiscent of Flora Nwapa writing about cassava, Jully Makini writes:

> You reap a harvest
>   you did not plant
> You drain my resources
>   in the name of development
> You fish in my waters
>   for bonito
> You pay me a little
>   for permission
> You process your catch
>   compressed into cans
> You pour back your waste into our seas
>   Pollution!
> Then you sell back to me,
>   at a profit
> Solomon Blue (1994: 134).

The Pacific Ocean is recognised as an extraordinarily resource-rich environment, and in terms of biodiversity it is a "marine goldmine" (Slatter 1994a: 132). The forest, too, once produced a huge diversity of species, and birds assisted in the spread of pollen across large areas of land. The ocean deeps and the off-shore seas likewise contribute to the diversity and numbers of coastal fish. With the pressure from Distant Water Fishing Nations'[12] activities, "coastal communities report that they are not catching the fish they once used to catch" (Slatter 1994a: 142). As Slatter notes elsewhere (1994b: 33), although the World Bank is aware of "the extent of environmental damage", it nevertheless admits that "because practically all likely sources of economic growth will involve more intensive use of fragile resource bases" (World Bank 1993: xv) the damage is likely to increase. But instead of proposing to reduce the intensive use, the report simply suggests that "careful environmental management will take on added importance" (1993: xv). The pertinent question here is, will the outcome benefit the local ecology, or the bureaucrats?

The pursuit of the "Almighty Foreign Exchange" in fisheries is having the same effect as it has had in agriculture and forestry. The oceans have not been exploited for as long, in the same high-pressured way, as has land,

---

12   Asian Distant Water Fishing Nations include South Korea, Taiwan and Japan.

but they too are on the verge of collapse (Food and Agriculture Organisation 2000; Pollack 1995; Culotta 1994; *Economist* 1994; Kurien 1993). Forests, farms and seas are in an integral relationship, where if one collapses, the effects cascade into the other areas.

Digitised and Globalised Farming: What the future holds

Farming is in a state of crisis. In the rich countries this has been played out in different ways. In Britain, epidemics of mad cow disease (bovine spongiform encephalopathy, BSE), followed by swine fever, followed by foot-and-mouth disease, have created nervousness among consumers and despair among farmers (Kneen 1999; O'Hagan 2001). In the USA, corn farmers who have grown many thousand hectares of genetically modified (GM) corn are finding it difficult to sell their corn on world markets (Lappé and Bailey 1998). In France, farmers protested against McDonald's, and the imposition of trade penalties against French Roquefort cheese (Luneau 2001: 4). In Australia, the deregulation of the dairy industry is having a severe impact on the survival of small dairy farmers (Dunlop 2001). The industrialisation of farming, the increasingly important emphasis on monoculture with high inputs, and high susceptibility to attack by pests or viruses, is creating a fertile ideological ground for arguing the case for biotechnology investment opportunities. These opportunities, however, will mostly benefit the large-scale industrial farms, many of which are owned by corporations. It makes small-scale farming more and more difficult, and organic farmers are under threat from neighbouring farmers who are sowing GM seeds.

Britain has been wracked by mad cow disease and the slaughter of 1.5 million head of cattle, export bans, and widespread fear of a future epidemic of Creuzfeldt-Jacob disease (CJD). The BSE crisis came about because of an ideology of production that treats animals as if they were machines. In a way reminiscent of the "high-yield" rhetoric of the Green Revolution, cows made to be more "productive", to produce more and more milk, are seen only as an udder, a body part disconnected from the rest of the animal (Shiva 2000a: 59).[13] José Bové articulates the result persuasively:

---

13 Patrice Newell notes that "there's talk about producing steaks in stainless-steel vats in laboratories, steak without cattle" (2000: 185). Feminist critics of reproductive technologies have made similar observations of women being used as "mother

A cow "pushed" to produce 8000 to 10,000 kilos of milk a year becomes much weaker, and more susceptible to all sorts of health hazards, than a cow producing 6000 (in Luneau 2001: 83).

Cows are induced to increase their "productive capacity" by injections of recombinant Bovine Growth Hormone (rBGH) manufactured by Monsanto. But rBGH works best when combined with a high-protein diet, that is, a diet composed of rendered animal protein, including protein from cattle. Cows fed in this way are denatured and decontextualised. Farmers who feed their cows meat products thereby change them from herbivores to carnivores, and into cannibals.[14] In order for this process to proceed smoothly, as if on a factory production line, cows are moved indoors and confined to feedlots (Dufour in Luneau 2001: 65). This, in turn, has an impact on other aspects of farming such as crop production. José Bové points out that in France, "more than 75 per cent of cereal production is destined for animal feed" (in Luneau 2001: 62).[15]

Furthermore, the construction of feedlots is an expensive business, and small farmers are unable to expand in this direction. As the small farmer sells to the big farmer and goes out of business, intensification continues, as does an increasing homogenisation as farms become progressively larger (Dunlop 2001: 19). More loss of biomass occurs when hedgerows (O'Hagan 2001: 50), which hinder "the movement of machines" (Bové in Luneau 2001: 65), are eradicated, resulting in biodiversity loss. Andrew O'Hagan, in his influential essay *The End of British Farming*, makes much

machines" (Corea 1985), "living laboratories" (Rowland 1993), and "bodies without women" (Klein 2001, pers. comm.).

14 Boundary crossing is a significant and widespread problem in genetic engineering (see Ho 1998 for an extensive discussion). See also Ricarda Steinbrecher: "Biotechnology promises a new agricultural revolution in which resources are no longer limited by the boundaries that define each species" (2001: 77). In his Foreword to the new edition of *The Diversity of Life*, Edward O. Wilson notes that the two biggest factors endangering species in the USA are "habitat loss, 88 percent; exotics, 46 percent" (2001: xv). These correspond to the factors I have highlighted – the development of monocultures (whether rural or urban) and the dislocation of species (including industrial farming and genetic boundary crossing).

15 I remember when my parents shifted the orientation of their farming from human food – wheat and oats – to the production of animal feed. In the mid-1960s they began to grow sorghum, millet, and maize for export to the feedlots of Japan. In later years, just before retirement, they grew sunflowers and canola. See the later section in this chapter on aquaculture and fishmeal production. See also Crouch (2001: 25).

the same point: "The pursuit of abundance has contributed to the creation of a great rolling emptiness" (2001: 34). Over-production has led to "the creation of a false economy" (2001: 45). O'Hagan traces the origins of the crisis to the technologisation of British farming during the 1950s and 1960s – the same period when the Green Revolution was occurring in India, Africa and other parts of the so-called Third World. In Britain, farmers used increasingly larger amounts of fertilisers and pesticides in the search for higher yields. The result was severe environmental damage:

> Motorway bypasses, electricity pylons, larger fields attended by larger machines, with meadows ploughed up, marshes filled in, woods and grasslands usurped by acreage-hungry crops – what the writer Graham Harvey refers to as "this once 'living tapestry'" was being turned into "a shroud ... a landscape of the dead" (2001: 45).[16]

Technologisation led to over-production. Subsidies linked not to the environment but to production have created a self-defeating vicious cycle with illogical outcomes such as "farmers killing their livestock for want of a profit, or to save the fuel costs incurred in taking them to market" (O'Hagan 2000: 23, 12). The illogic of this system springs from the features of globalisation outlined earlier: appropriation, incorporation, dislocation, commodification ("Everything is a commodity," said Nigel Rowe, one of the farmers interviewed by O'Hagan, 2000: 24), production for export, and homogenisation.

Just like high-yield variety (HYV) seeds, cattle produce false amplification of yields when fed hormones. Bové reports that "using hormones could increase an animal's weight by 5 to 10 per cent, sending a cow's value up by 500–1000 francs" (in Luneau 2001: 83).

The Australian dairy industry has undergone a process of deregulation since 1999, particularly in the state of Victoria where "only 7 per cent [of milk production] is for domestic consumption and the rest is for value-added activities and export" (Fraser 2001: 30). It is the export-orientation of the industry which is pushing it in the direction of deregulation. Deregulation is closely associated with National Competition Policy,

---

16 Compare this bleak picture to Schama (1996) on the landscape of the Holocaust, cited in Chapter Two.

which in turn is oriented toward standardisation[17] of industry in order to fall in line with WTO rules. But as Ian Dunlop argues, the economic or market-oriented approach of the deregulators does not take into account "the real lives of real people" (2001: 8). The contest is between competing systems. Those in the transnational sector are for deregulation and intensification – increased farm size, standardised product, more productive cows, transportability over long distances, and export. While in the diversity matrix, French farmers participating in intensification of farming with an orientation toward export began to see its pitfalls:

> [They] became aware of the economic and ecological madness of a system which consists of separating the calf from its mother, only to give it milk which has been collected by lorry, taken to the factory, pasturized, creamed off, dried, reconstituted, packed, and then returned to the specialist calf-breeder to feed to the calves (Bové in Luneau 2001: 139).

In Australia, Jim Scott reflects on another kind of ecological madness:

> feedlots have huge numbers of cows, resulting in concentrations of manure and effluent that need to be disposed of rather than have cows re-cycle it back to pastures naturally as they graze. Harvesting and irrigating crops for large feedlots will use up energy as will transporting milk around the country from the main dairy state, Victoria, once most coastal dairy areas in NSW and Queensland have been shut down (in Dunlop 2001: 9).

In 2001, once again, hundreds of thousands of livestock in Britain and Europe were slaughtered, this time because foot-and-mouth disease (FMD) made those animals "economically unviable" (Baker 2001: 6; O'Hagan 2001). The reason for this is two-fold. On the one hand, animals who have sores around the mouth are not able to eat, and so they lose condition and weigh less when sent to market, therefore providing a lower return to the farmer and the economy as a whole. On the other hand, and of ideological importance, countries which do not have FMD-free status

---

17   International accreditation systems, such as ISO9000, are a part of the standardisation process. ISO is derived from the Greek word, ισοσ, which means same, equal. In the context of globalisation it implies decontextualisation and homogenisation.

"risk losing their export markets to other disease-free nations" (Baker 2001: 6)[18] in the event of an outbreak such as occurred in the UK in 2001. FMD is a highly infectious viral disease. Its most obvious manifestation is the blisters, and it can also be present in manure, milk, saliva and exhaled air. When the disease is in its most acute phase, the virus is present in all parts of the body including the blood.[19] But most animals recover from FMD within a few weeks, and the symptoms have been compared with "a moderate case of human flu" (Daley 2001: 22a). The FMD crisis followed hot on the heels of BSE and swine fever outbreaks in Britain; first discovered at an abattoir, Cheale Meats, in Essex (O'Hagan 2001: 59), it was announced on 20 February 2001. Newspaper reports suggest that "swine were fed swill which included processed meat products from overseas contaminated with the virus" (Daley 2001: 27b).

The spread of FMD was accelerated by the specific circumstances of the transporting of stock in Britain. Local abattoirs deemed "inefficient" had been closed, and so stock for slaughter are frequently transported across country, and "kept in holding pens along the way" (Daley 2001: 22a). The preconditions for the spread of FMD are precisely those changes to the production cycle which have been implemented in the interests of efficiency: increased intensification of farming, reduced biodiversity, export-orientation, increased dislocation between the farm and the consumer, and multilateral trade rules that amplify competition.

Vandana Shiva observes that the "zero tolerance for disease has led to a zero tolerance for animals. Farm animals and farmers have been made the enemy. The countryside has been turned into a war zone" (Shiva 2001b: 1). Her argument suggests that an unreal expectation is placed on

---

18 "FMD is endemic in parts of Asia, Africa, the Middle East and South America, with sporadic outbreaks in disease-free areas. Countries affected by FMD in the past twelve months include Butan, Brazil, Columbia, Egypt, Georgia, Japan, Kazakhstan, Korea, Kuwait, Malawi, Malaysia, Mongolia, Namibia, Russia, South Africa, Taipei, Tajikistan, Uruguay and Zambia. The last major outbreak of the disease in the EU was in Greece last year" (www.maff.gov.uk/animalh/diseases/fmd/qa1.htm#8 12 March 2001). Other reported cases have been in France, Argentina, Turkey and the United Arab Emirates (*Melbourne Express* 2001: 2). The only known outbreak of FMD in Australia occurred near Melbourne in 1847 (Shiel 2001: 2). Other countries free of FMD are Canada, the USA and New Zealand (*Melbourne Express* 2001: 2).

19 See the website of the Ministry of Agriculture, Fisheries and Food (MAFF), UK, (www.maff.gov.uk).

living things, and this is resulting in a movement toward more and more disconnection from real life. If animals in their millions can be slaughtered for a non-fatal disease, what will this mean eventually for our outlook on people, particularly poor people who are diagnosed with a disease?[20] Our collective vulnerability to the ideological stance of perfection, immortality and transcendence is a paradox in a highly technologised society with a utilitarian approach to problem solving.

The advent of GM crops heralds a new form of intensification and disconnection in farming, and it will lead to more crises, not fewer. According to O'Hagan:

> GM crops are corrupting the relation of people to the land they live on. Farmers were once concerned with the protection of the broad biodiversity of their fields, but the new methods, especially GM, put land-use and food production into the hands of corporations who are absent from the scene and environmentally careless (2000: 54).

In Tasmania, Australia, both Aventis and Monsanto have been accused of flouting protocols established to control trials of genetically modified organisms (GMOs) (Darby 2001: 11). Twenty-one canola crops were found to be resprouting out of a total of forty-nine former crop sites.[21] In South Australia, Aventis was found to have left harvested canola "in a roadside dumpster and on the local tip" (Phelps 2000: 23; Strong 2000: 1). Monsanto has also admitted that genetically modified cotton seed has possibly entered the food chain in Australia through cattle feed (Seccombe 2000: 3).[22] In the USA, the corn industry is in dire straits due to a crisis in marketing, and consumer resistance to genetically modified foods,[23]

---

20 AIDS activists would argue that this is the end result of the misuse of patents which prevents people suffering from HIV and AIDS in Africa and other poor nations from purchasing the much cheaper generic drugs, see Oxfam (2001). Feminist critics of genetics argue that eugenic thinking has always been part of those scientists wishing to engineer "good life". The push for euthanasia further supports these claims (Klein 2001b: pers. comm.).

21 One year earlier, it appeared likely to anti-GMO activists that Tasmania would go "permanently GE-free and perhaps organic" (Phelps 2000: 22).

22 This contradicts claims that Australian farming is clean and green. Eliminating intensive farming practices, including feeding of cattle, would prevent such problems from arising.

23 "Aventis was formed early in 2000, through a merger of AgrEvo and Rhone–Poulenc.

resulting in low exports to EU countries, Australia and New Zealand where labelling and other restrictions apply (Toyne 2001).

The major defence for spending huge resources on researching and growing GMOs is that of world hunger.[24] Richard Shear gives Monsanto's perspective:[25]

> In agriculture companies such as Monsanto, Ciba–Geigy, Plant Genetic Systems and others believe that crops could be "re-engineered" to provide technology for ensuring that the world could be fed as future population demands required (Shear 2000: 34).

Aventis/AgrEvo has a similar view:

> Biotechnology holds great promise for increasing food production ... Seed is the vehicle by which this new technology will be delivered (Richer and Simon 2000: 41).

Meanwhile, representatives of the World Bank talk about "poverty alleviation":

> A large number of poor households in developing countries derive their livelihood from resource-poor areas with difficult agroclimatic conditions. Ensuring their access to technologies is therefore crucial for poverty alleviation (Lele et al. 2000: 1).

None of these quotations, nor the articles in which they were embedded, mentions that the poverty of resources in areas inhabited by these households is in large part due to the impact of colonisation, developments such

---

Bayer is now negotiating to buy Aventis, in part as a result of Aventis's troubles over Starlink corn" (Phelps 2001a); AstraZeneca was created by a merger between Zeneca and Astra; Novartis was created from Ciba–Geigy and Sandoz. The constant flux of changing names is also a useful marketing ploy, allowing the general public to remain ignorant about who is really creating the foods we eat. These companies have been called agriceuticals, a term coined by Ray Goldberg.

24 Both sides of the argument have been aired in the popular press with Scrinis (1999: 13) critical, while O'Neill published an article with a photograph captioned: "Healthier lifestyle: Genetically modified rice will help correct a severe iron deficiency for millions of people" (2001: 52). See the arguments in this chapter on Golden Rice.

25 For a critique of Monsanto's practices, see Crouch (2001: 27–29); on Aventis/AgrEvo see Schmitz (2001: 47).

as large dams and bridges, the Green Revolution, and more recent effects of globalisation. Nor do apologists for biotechnologies recognise that traditional farming could "feed the projected population without invoking a new Green Revolution, *as long as food, not money*, is the primary goal" (Crouch 2001: 26, my emphasis). In spite of the rhetoric about world hunger, the development of biotechnology has come about not for altruistic reasons, but because it has the potential to earn transnational companies money and to "sustain industrial agriculture" (Schmitz 2001: 45). Profit, not charity, is their goal. One has only to look at the daily stock market, or listen to the latest political statement on innovation, to see the value put on biotechnology stocks and the knowledge economy. New markets, new commodities, new ideas are the newest way of generating capital. Dependence on the exploitation of the poor, however, is not new.

Biotechnology creates an endless spiral of opportunities for research and development, and for capital gain. An example of concern is the standard practice in genetic engineering of crops of inserting "an antibiotic resistance marker, which serves to facilitate detection of the altered gene" (Ferrara and Dorsey 2001: 59). Given the enormous problems of antibiotic resistance, this practice is likely to increase bacterial resistance to antibiotics in the general population,[26] with a particularly strong outcome in poor countries "unable to afford alternative drugs" (Garrett 1994: 414, 438). But for the biotechnology companies, it could be a boon, enabling them to justify genetic engineering of antibiotics to counteract new resistances.

Arpad Pusztai created a scientific and publicity storm when research he carried out on rats fed with GM potatoes showed observable adverse effects. The issue raised by Pusztai's research is the unpredictability that eventuates when a gene ends up in the wrong place because still very little is known about how genes interact (Ferrara and Dorsey 2001: 58–60; Walker 1999: 23).[27] Unpredictability is what the promoters of biotechnology are staking their futures on because it means more and more new

---

26 Laurie Garrett cites Mitchell Cohen, the Centers for Disease Control's director of bacterial research, as stating, "Unless currently effective microbial agents can be successfully preserved and the transmission of drug-resistant organisms curtailed, the post-antimicrobial era may be rapidly approaching in which infectious disease wards housing untreatable patients will again be seen" (1994: 414).

27 For a thorough explanation and critique of how genetic engineering is ideologically constructed, see Ho (1998); see also Perrière and Seuret (2000).

markets. The only predictable thing is that once again the poor are most likely to pay the greatest price.

The use of *Bacillus thuringiensis* (*Bt*) in many genetically engineered plants is another example. This bacterium has been used for many years among organic farmers as a specific natural pesticide (Kneen 1999: 103–117; Lappé and Bailey 1998: 63–72; Steinbrecher 2001: 84–87; McGrath 1995; Woodfin 1997; Pollan 2001: 197–256). Monsanto was one of the earliest players to produce patented plants with the *Bt* toxin inserted.[28] The mechanism for engineering the *Bt* toxin into plants results in a continuous output of *Bt* throughout the entire plant. This again represents a homogenised, decontextualised approach to farming. The entire plant continuously produces the insecticide. The gradual effect on insect pests is increased tolerance of *Bt*, and a side-effect is its reduced usefulness for organic farmers.[29] This also threatens biodiversity and reduces the number of beneficial insects in the environment. *Bt* maize produced by Novartis has been found to kill moths and butterflies who have ingested pollen (Losey 1999: 6733 cited in Steinbrecher 2001: 85).

An indication of the kinds of problems that farmers and consumers are likely to encounter in the future is presaged by what occurred in the first two years of planting *Bt* crops in the USA. In 1996, the first year of mass plantings of Bollgard®, farmers planting *Bt* cotton in Texas and Louisiana "experienced unusually large infestations of cotton bollworm" (Lappé and Bailey 1998: 68). In the same year Monsanto's NUCOTN, another *Bt* cotton, had excessive pest infestations (Steinbrecher 2001: 86). In 1997, prime cotton-growing states – Mississippi, Arkansas, Tennessee and Louisiana – were hit by a major failure in the Roundup Ready™ cotton crops (Lappé and Bailey 1998: 103–105).[30] In the states of Karnataka and Andra Pradesh in India, farmers burnt and destroyed genetically modified

---

28 Monsanto has been granted patents on Bollgard® (cotton), Yieldgard® (corn) and New Leaf® (potatoes).

29 Ferrara and Dorsey point out that the production of Roundup-resistance in plants is one way in which Monsanto is protecting its profit losses on its most profitable product, Roundup, for which the patent has now expired (Ferrara and Dorsey 2001: 61). I would also suggest that it is in the interests of biotechnology companies to reduce the effectiveness of organic pesticides, thereby creating increased reliance on their products. Steinbrecher also points out that the conditions under which *Bt* cotton was grown was ideal for producing *Bt*-resistant insects (Steinbrecher 2001: 86).

30 See Carman (2000) for a discussion of the safety problems of Roundup Ready soybeans.

cotton crops when they found out that they were unknowingly doing trials for Mahyco–Monsanto,[31] the Indian arm of Monsanto (Shiva 2001c: 355).

Uniformity holds a central place in the current ideologies of the owners of agribusinesses which represent the industrialised farming sector. Monoculture cropping was the first stage, followed by the Green Revolution rhetoric of high-yield seeds which displaced landraces and ecologically adapted local seedlines. Genetic engineering of crops – the gene revolution – is just the latest manifestation of uniformity, and it is likely "to be exacerbated by the availability of transgenic seed" (Lappé and Bailey 1998: 101). Timothy Swanson points to the reliance of industrial agriculture on biodiversity, in particular on the "wild stock" (1995: 7) that forms the basis of cultivated crops. He makes two points which suggest that the wild stock will not be able to be sustained over long periods of time. "Plant breeding companies face biological forces that may render their products (cultivated crops) obsolescent within 5–7 years" (1995: 7). And although continuous research is carried out on related species, in order to maintain the vitality of the crop varieties used in agriculture, the cultivated crops must be "continually supplemented with infusions of new, more diverse germplasm". However,

> On average about 7% of the stock of germplasm must be renewed each year at current rates of depreciation. This means that wild varieties and landraces are being accessed at a rate that potentially renews the stock of germplasm every 10–15 years (1995: 7).

If biodiversity is not nurtured *in situ*, the resources for biotechnology will cease to exist. Biodiversity cannot be replicated in laboratories: it requires living ecosystems.[32] The fallacy is that these companies' belief in technology makes them vulnerable to failure. But such potential failure is seen simply as another business opportunity for further research and development.

---

31 Monsanto acquired 26 per cent of Mayhco in 1998. Mayhco was India's largest seed company.

32 The Eden Project in Cornwall, UK, comprising two huge biodomes, is a useful experiment in educating people about the importance of biodiversity, but it goes nowhere near replicating a real ecosystem since it is devoid of birds, animals, insects and micro-organisms which inhabit the plants' home environment. So, it remains a stop on the tourist route which makes much of different exotic world environments, separated only by a short walkway, see Readman *et al.* (2001).

When those in the industrialised countries who are exploiting the resources of the biodiverse-rich countries engage in decontextualised thinking about business opportunities, the consequences are disastrous.

The idea of uniformity and decontextualisation runs so deeply in researchers' beliefs in this area that it has already resulted in significant experimental error when trialing products. *Kelbsiella planticola* SDF20 is "a genetically engineered organism designed to produce ethanol from crop waste" (Burrows 2001b: 70). No one had noticed that it killed not just the intended plants, but all plants growing in the same location. This effect came to life when a PhD student, Michael Holmes, and his supervisor, Elaine Ingram, used an "unusual laboratory technique" (in Burrows 2001b: 71). Instead of using sterile soils, they used real soils, soils which contain micro-organisms essential for uptake of nutrients. *Kelbsiella planticola* SDF20 killed the micro-organisms, but this did not show up in the sterile soils where the micro-organisms were already eliminated. Such experimental design "overlooks the relationship between the components" (Steinbrecher 2001: 77); it ignores the real-life biodiversity of soils, and assumes that plants can be removed from their ecosystems and remain unaffected; it relies on a belief system which valorises fractures, context stripping and a philosophy of sameness. The important issue here is that the production of virus-protected plants threatens the remaining wild plants. The real world is composed of a web of living systems which have developed under very specific local conditions. The latest developments of industrial farming, particularly genetic engineering, represent "a dangerous gamble with the integrity of our natural world" (Steinbrecher 2001: 90). Rupturing the connections between plants, micro-organisms, soils, animals and their ecosystems is a dangerous game. This applies to the kind of research, referred to earlier, into cassava in which the plant's growing environment was context stripped by growing it in a "virus free area" (Iglesias *et al.* 1994: 288).

Terminator technology is centrally placed as a profit-making procedure.[33] Terminator technology enables seed companies to maintain control over the planting of all seeds, making it impossible for farmers to

---

33   In October 1999, Monsanto announced that it would "abandon sterile seed tech-
    nologies" (Romei 1999: 23). Coincidentally, Monsanto shares had dropped in value
    near their 52-week lows (Romei 1999: 23). In spite of this, research into terminator
    technologies in trees does not appear to have slowed.

collect seeds from their harvested crop. If a farmer tries to do so, the seed will simply die during the late-development phase of the plant's growth (Crouch 2001: 32). Like the altruistic rhetoric used for GM crops, this mechanism is defended on environmental grounds. Because of the danger of cross-pollination of GMOs with wild seeds – or with conventional agricultural seeds – biotechnology apologists claim that using terminator seeds will slow down cross-pollination.[34]

Other arguments used to support terminator technologies focus on competition and protection. When US spokespeople for companies and governments use phrases like "making us more competitive", this usually turns out to mean "giving us an advantage no one else has". Brewster Kneen cites Melvin J. Oliver, the primary inventor of terminator technology, who states:

> Our mission is to protect US agriculture, and to make us competitive in the face of foreign competition. Without this, there is no way of protecting the technology (in Kneen 1999: 15).

The interaction between new biotechnologies and marketing exemplified in Golden Rice, which is being touted as the latest "perfect food" (Crouch 2001: 34–35; Shiva 2001a: 40–43). Golden Rice is so-called because it has been engineered to contain carotenoids, high levels of which are present in carrots. Carotenoids are also present in greens, mango, sweet potato and melon, and support Vitamin A production in the body. Vitamin A deficiency is associated with malnutrition, and Golden Rice is being marketed as a panacea for this condition. I had been thinking about this, when I

---

34 Cross-pollination is a serious worry for seed marketers. *Seed World*, a magazine which advertises itself as "Serving the seed marketers of the world", contains an article which suggests possible legal loopholes seed companies could use in the event of being sued by an organic farmer. One of the suggestions is to invoke *force majeure*. John Mandler, a partner in the Minneapolis law firm of Faegre and Benson, writes: "Although it would be difficult to argue that cross-pollination is an unforeseen effect, seed companies may be able to argue that the volume of GMO production, combined with the unpredictability of natural forces, makes it a practical impossibility to produce non-GMO varieties without trace elements of genetic materials" (Mandler 2000: 17). For access to *Seed World* go to www.seedworld.com. Tasmanian organic farmer Greg Whitten wants Tasmania to be completely GM free, as "we're not really safe in Tasmania if there's any (genetically modified crops) here at all" (Darby 2000a: 19, brackets in original).

heard a radio discussion about Vitamin A deficiency and its links to kidney failure, which were particularly evident in the new-born child if the deficiency had been present during pregnancy (Fry 2001). My immediate reaction was to think that all pregnant women should get enough Vitamin A. Only later did it occur to me that this fear reaction is precisely what the biotechnology companies rely upon. I could cite many examples of the trend.

In Australia, deregulation of the dairy industry is resulting in thousands of farmers being pushed to the wall[35] – for a supposed decrease in the price of milk to consumers, which has not eventuated (Dunlop 2001).[36] And in Britain in 2001, the army was called in to kill animals infected by FMD. What all these events have in common is the way in which they persistently feed to the general public the idea of the necessity of technological and economic intervention. *Bt* genes create increased resistance in pests; Golden Rice creates a false market for a supposed nutritional defect which would be better adressed by changing distribution systems and creating new sustainable agricultural practices connected to local conditions; the milk industry in Australia and the cheese industry in France are centralised for the sake of a false economy that is supposedly for consumer benefit, but in the long run is either not worth it, or creates an unwanted homogenisation of a locally based industry. In Britain, FMD highlighted the "appetite for genetic engineering" (Shiva 2001b: 8) and makes us all less resilient and tolerant, at the same time as decreasing diversity. As Sonja Schmitz points out:

> Sustainable agriculture, when defined as regenerative, low-input, diversified, and decentralized, is the antithesis of industrial agriculture. Industrial agriculture depends on obsolescence, high-input, monocultures, and the centralization of power (2001: 49).

An interesting test case for the impact of trade rules and increased liberalisation of the economy is China. Peter Nolan notes that the impact

---

35 In Britain, farmers have suicided and rural businesses have collapsed in reaction to the losses they have incurred from farming crises, particularly FMD: O'Reilly (2001: 8); Daley (2001c: 20); O'Hagan (2001: 24). Similar examples abound everywhere; I personally know of cases of suicide caused by the prospect of financial ruin in the Australian countryside.

36 See www.smh.com.au/news/webdiary/0104/05/A33180-2001Mar30.html.

of new technologies used in farming has caused "immense socioeconomic problems" (2001: 218), including rising unemployment. Complying with the WTO agreements will double the impact of changes in the Chinese farming sector. US policymakers recognise the impact that joining the WTO will have. The US–China Trade Council remarks that

> Decrepit state-owned enterprises need massive overhaul to become internationally competitive. They will be forced to restructure by cutting costs, adopting modern production methods, and eliminating excess employment and overheads (cited in Nolan 2001: 217–218).

To adopt modern production methods is first to industrialise farming, and then to digitise it by introducing GMOs into an economy which has few safeguards for human health.[37] Structural issues already mentioned are the familiar impositions of the World Bank and the IMF, such as reducing overheads, laying off excess labour, and orienting the economy toward export.

In spite of these powerful alliances between corporations and governments (willing or unwilling), there are hopeful signs. There is an increased interest in local initiatives, in sustainable agricultural practices which return energy to the community. Such initiatives are occurring, for instance, in the UK (Norberg-Hodge 2001), Bangladesh (Akhter 2001), Mexico (Esteva 2001), Uganda (Wangoola 2000), and many other places besides. Grassroots activities, local trading areas, farmers' markets, community organisations of many kinds valorise locality and plurality. They put back into the community as much as or more than they take. And their intention goes further than making the financial bottom line work: it is to supply the needs of the community.

The Kyoto Protocol, Plantation Forests and Terminator Trees

The viciousness of the globalisation cycle becomes especially clear when one examines plantations. The proposed Kyoto Protocol on greenhouse

---

37 David Pilling (2000) reports that pharmaceutical giant AstraZeneca is involved in research which uses DNA samples collected from thousands of Chinese schizophrenia patients ostensibly to throw more light on the genetic underpinnings of schizophrenia. One wonders why it is that China has the largest collection of DNA from individuals suffering from schizophrenia.

gas emissions has created a media frenzy around tree planting. But it is not sufficient to plant just any trees, and it matters how many trees are planted, and of what species. In a rush to earn "green points", companies are announcing tree-planting projects (Langelle 2001).

Plantations, like monoculture cropping, produce uniformity. The primary consideration for plantation developers is how quickly will the timber (note timber; not trees) grow, and how uniform it will be when felled. Economic considerations rather than ecological ones are the deciding factors. In Australia, *Pinus radiata* is a favoured species for plantations. *Pinus radiata* is not native, and the experience of walking into a pine plantation is very different from the experience of native bushland. The *Pinus radiata* plantation has a floor covering of needles. No native scrub grows, no wildflowers, not even native grasses. And it is very quiet. The Australian bush is usually full of sounds, particularly bird calls, and it is not unusual to see native wildlife such as lizards, snakes, and at dusk or at night to see or hear nocturnal marsupials.[38]

In contrast to the multiplicity of niches and yields and the interrelationship of species – including human beings – within a wild forest, plantations are constructed by external forces, either large companies or government bodies, and they have a single purpose: the production of timber. The species is usually exotic to the location, having been dislocated from its original environment. Eucalyptus, for example, has developed a bad reputation as an ecosystem destroyer when grown outside Australia. Jaime Aviles, a Mexican journalist, writes, "Eucalyptus is the perfect neoliberal tree. It's fast growing, kills everything near it, and makes a lot of money for a few people" (in Langelle 2001: 116).

All pines are not the same as *Pinus radiata*, and not all eucalyptus trees are the same. Both species, however, are destructive of local conditions when transported and planted in huge grid-like blocks of straight lines in exotic places. Once again the features of globalisation are writ large here: profit motive, appropriation, dislocation, incorporation, commodification, homogenisation, and export.

---

38 This is not intended to romanticise the Australian bush. Of course, areas closer to cities or towns are less likely to have the range and number of fauna. Suburban backyards, however, can host a range of wildlife. What is unusual about the pine plantations is their inhospitability to native fauna.

A recent development in plantations is the creation of a new company, ArborGen, formed specifically to produce genetically engineered "forests". AborGen is a joint venture of International Paper (USA), Fletcher Challenge Forests (NZ), Westvaco Corporation (USA), and Genesis Research and Development, a New Zealand biotechnology company (Langelle 2001: 113–114). Monsanto was originally involved, but pulled out in late 1999 (Rautner and Bond 2001: 2).

The aim of these corporations, in order to please their shareholders, is to maximise profit through exploiting new technologies. Langelle (2001) and Rautner and Bond (2001) outline some of their production strategies.

- produce trees with increased growth rates resulting in faster, more profitable turnover
- achieve insect resistance by inserting the *Bt* gene into the tree's genetic structure
- build resistance to herbicides in order to reduce the amount of herbicide used, and therefore reduce costs to the corporations
- use terminator genes, which provide the corporation with a rhetorical environmental justification that genetically-modified genes will not cross-pollinate to the wild population (not guaranteed, however)
- increase tolerance to salt which allows plantations to be grown in areas where monoculture farming has already destroyed the soil
- reduce lignin content, by which means paper products, including unnecessary packaging materials, can be produced more cheaply and easily (for the corporation).

All of these goals lead to an ever-increasing spiral of homogenisation and commodification. For example, in the Chiapas region of Mexico, the plantation industry is associated with dispossession of indigenous peoples from their land, and from their traditional lifestyles which incorporated a relationship with the forest, its species and its products. Planting huge tracts of land with identical trees destroys the existing ecosystem, but nevertheless earns carbon credits for the corporations. With a genetically engineered increased growth rate, more trees will be planted in quick succession. Corporations – and as a consequence, countries – will receive more carbon credits under the proposed Kyoto treaty,[39] although these

---

39   An earlier version of carbon trading was the Pilot Programme to Protect the Brazilian Amazon (PPB). It was launched at the G-7 meeting in 1990, in time for the

credits will barely cover the increased rate of carbon dioxide emissions from higher rates of long-haul transport for export and industry.[40] Mexico is also the site of a flourishing concentration of export processing zones, the *maquiladoras* (see further discussion in Chapter Six). The increased productivity created by the *maquiladoras* also requires increased production of paper products for packaging. The creation of fast-growing genetically engineered trees, the development of plantations, and the harvesting of trees, is directly related to a shortage of unnecessary packaging materials produced for a variety of industries in the export processing zones. The vicious cycle continues (Langelle 2001: 116).

A further consequence of the dehumanising and decontextualising technologies is that those who work in the industry are trained according to the ideologies of corporate monoculture. Howie Wolke writes of the process of training foresters in the USA. Divergent views are not acceptable, and those with views that could change the policy orientation of the Forest Service are weeded out early in undergraduate courses. Wolke summarises the role of the Forest Service:

> examples of bureaucratic intransigence constitute the daily business of public land management in America. ... two million acres of wilderness devastated each year, hundreds of thousands of more miles of road planned for our National Forests, less solitude, less habitat, fewer wild animals. But more logs, more cows, more mines and oil rigs, and more work for bureaucrats (1999: 89).

Michael Dove makes a similar point in his study of rainforest management in Kalimantan, Indonesia. He argues that whatever of value is found or developed by indigenous forest peoples – particular tree species,

---

UN Conference on Environment and Development (UNCED) in Brazil in 1992. "The economic logic of the PPB was that giving money to reduce carbon dioxide emissions in Brazil would presumably be cheaper than the costs of achieving the same results in European countries themselves. Therefore the PPB could help fulfil the European promise to stabilise emissions at the 1990 level" (Kolk 1996: 294).

40 One could see the entry of Toyota (Langelle 2001: 114) into biotechnology, plantation forest growing, as a cynical exercise designed to offset carbon dioxide produced by cars, in particular the diesel-run engines of four-wheel-drives. If Toyota were genuinely interested in reducing carbon dioxide emissions, their promotion would focus on reduced emissions. Better still, of course, would be reduced dependence on cars.

mineral deposits, butterflies, medicines – will never earn for the forest people what it would earn in the open market. Instead, centralised power appropriates the resource, sometimes for allegedly public interests, and then pockets the profits (1993: 20). A disjunction also occurs between what is known to be valued by indigenous forest peoples and what is valued by government and corporate interests. Dove argues that UN-sponsored development projects define what they will "allow the forest peoples to keep ... butterfly farms, crocodile farms, fish farms and medicinal plant collection"[41] (1993: 21). This list, he suggests, is not for the peoples' empowerment "but for their *impoverishment*" (1993: 21, emphasis in original). For, if empowerment were the goal, the list would include trees for timber, hardwoods, gems and the biodiverse resources which the rainforest holds, and the forest people would be in charge of forest management. His concern is not just for what has been taken away from forests, but for what has been "taken away from forest peoples" (1993: 22).

Michael Dove's research is a refreshing change from much of the disconnected corporate literature which uses words like "sustainability",[42] but cares little for the impact of the research on the local people and their immediate environment. What Dove makes explicitly clear is that "elites do not just control valuable forest resources, they also control the discourse regarding these resources" (1993: 22).

Further research carried out in Kalimantan (Sardjono and Samsoedin 2001; Colfer *et al.* 2001; Salim *et al.* 2001) and other parts of South-East Asia (Cooke 1999) has explored the relationship between traditional values, a conservation ethic and ways of interfacing with forestry and

---

41 The medicinal plant collection will remain in the hands of forest peoples only so long as no cure for cancer, or AIDS, or menopause is found in their region. On 7 June 2001, I visited the World Bank in Washington, DC. In the lobby was a huge display: "Biodiversity in the World Bank's Work". The World Bank is funding indigenous peoples, such as those in Kalimantan, to preserve their heritage because it is worth billions of dollars. It is clear, however, that the forest peoples, the desert peoples, the fisherpeoples are very unlikely to end up billions of dollars richer!

42 A fine example of this is the information about sustainable forestry on the Westvaco website (www.westvaco.com). It appears to have been written for eight- to twelve-year-old readers. I suggest this is not genuine information for concerned consumers, but a campaign of soft advertising. It is in stark contrast to the Greenpeace page on ArborGen (www.greenpeace.org.nz) which provides referenced articles with evidence for its statements. The ArborGen site (www.ArborGen.com) was under construction from 11 July to 31 December 2001.

government officials. As if echoing Dove's plea, Sardjono and Samsoedin recommend that every effort should be made to recognise, strengthen and revitalise traditional approaches, and consciously move away from centralised systems of government control which have led to "the current deplorable situation" (Sardjono and Samsoedin 2001: 133).

Fishing Wild Fish to Feed Domesticated Fish[43]

"FISH AGAINST GLOBALISATION" read one graffitied wall during the S11 protest against the World Economic Forum in Melbourne in 2000 just before the Sydney Olympics. And the fish might well want to protest, since

> industrial fish farming, or aquaculture, is the fastest-growing sector of global fish production ... Globally, more than half the shrimp and salmon consumed in the world is farmed, rather than caught in the wild (Shiva 2000a: 37).

The problems faced by fish farming are remarkably similar to those of agriculture. Industrial aquaculture[44] relies on the production of fishmeal to feed to captive fish. Fishmeal is made up of other fish, caught solely to provide food for farmed fish.[45] This is comparable to the way in which sorghum and other animal feeds are grown solely for cattle feed; or ground-up bone and flesh from other farm animals is mixed into cattle feed. The misuse of resources and the costs to the producer of these additional inputs cannot be justified on economic grounds; rather, it is part of an ideology of control and power. Fishmeal, like wood chips, is profitable. Its profitability is driven by over-capitalised and over-mechanised fleets who overfish depleted stocks, and a significant portion of whose catch is destined to become fishmeal. Fishing with the intention

---

43 Anna-Rosa Martinez i Prat (1995: 7) makes this point writing about the dependence of fish farms on wild fish catches.

44 The term "aquaculture" has a wide range of meanings, from small-scale, context-sensitive aquaculture ponds of traditional farmers to industrialised factory aquaculture utilising intensive systems linked with biotechnological approaches (see Wilks 1995: 121; Halwart, Martinez and Schückler 2000).

45 Fish caught for fishmeal often include "unappetising species", but because they are caught in addition to "appetising" fish, the total stock of fish caught at any one time is even higher than if only appetising fish were caught.

to produce fishmeal is also ecologically destructive. The clear-felling of forests and the destruction of undergrowth and associated trees, discussed earlier, is paralleled by the "pulse fishing" operations, in which an area is fished out to uneconomic levels, and returned to only when fish stocks have recovered (Fairlie, Hagler and O'Riordan 1995: 57). Add to this the trawling of fish with huge nets which destroy local habitats, in particular by killing "the flowers of the land below the water" (Hagler 1995: 75). The industrialised fishing industry is estimated to discard around one-quarter to one-third of all catches (Hagler 1995: 76; Martinez i Prat 1995: 1). Some shrimp fisheries throw back up to fifteen times their catch (Hagler 1995: 76). This has a domino effect on the rest of the marine ecosystem.

As Anna-Rosa Martinez i Prat goes on to argue, the use of drag nets has increased with the development of domesticated fish: "the sea bed is indiscriminately dragged not for shrimps and prawns as it used to be, but for anything that can be turned into fishmeal for shrimp" (1995: 7).

The effects of purse-seine fishing, drag nets, ghost nets and longline fishing are not confined to fish life. These methods also have an impact on other wildlife of the seas, such as dolphins, albatrosses, whales, seals, turtles and dugong, just to name a few species (Miller and Croston 1999).

Intensive aquaculture relies on large injections of capital, and the expropriation of land and water in order to construct ponds, and is based on the pursuit of "profit and export earnings, not hunger" (Wilks 1995: 120). Given that the health of a marine environment can be gauged by the health of its mangroves, the conflict is between those for whom short-term profit is the goal and those for whom maximising biodiversity is the goal. Mangroves both promote marine biodiversity and provide flood protection for coastal peoples, as well as building materials (Wilks 1995: 122). This is the long-term view which sees value in sustaining and maintaining bio-diversity.

The short-term view insists that because the land on which mangroves thrive is ideal for aquaculture (Wilks 1995: 122), it should therefore be used for aquaculture. Such practices, however, lead to the destruction of mangroves (Martinez i Prat 1995: 7) with consequent effects on fish-breeding grounds, seagrass meadows, dugongs and other sea life. Further more, the inputs required in aquaculture include the cost of fishmeal, as well as the usual round of chemicals, pesticides and fertilisers needed to control diseases associated with intensive farming practices. Even with all these intensive inputs, shrimp farms, time after time, have collapsed due to "the uncontrollable spread of pests and diseases" (Martinez i Prat 1995: 7), which decimate the harvest (Shiva 2000a: 42–46). Poisoning of the waters and increased salination of soils are other significant adverse effects of industrial shrimp farming.

It is widely recognised that wild-fish stocks have been severely depleted through over-fishing.[46] Technological developments and export-orientation[47] in an increasingly industrialised approach have hijacked the possibility of survival for many smaller fishing outfits. And, like European farming's production for production's sake, the fishing industry under WTO rules promotes a policy of subsidising "at whatever cost, their national fleets, in a race to continue the depletion of marine biological resources" (Martinez i Prat 1995: 2). The subsidies go not only to fishing companies but to shipbuilders (Fairlie, Hagler and O'Riordan 1995: 56). And as in the case of the farming industry in the European Union, bad investment decisions are "repaid with EC taxpayers' money" (Fairlie, Hagler and O'Riordan 1995: 58).

Efforts to entice fisherpeople into the market economy have had a significant impact on access to fishing grounds, as have attempts to "enclose" fishing grounds (Fairlie, Hagler and O'Riordan 1995: 50). This is similar to the enclosure of the Scottish Highlands and other agricultural lands during the period of European industrialisation and colonisation. The argument used for enclosing fishing grounds is the perennial "tragedy of the commons", a deeply flawed argument that assumes a Darwinian approach as opposed to a respectfully regulated approach of mutual responsibility and respect. As Arthur McEvoy observes, it also assumes a high level of non-communication between people (1990: 226), a feature more consistent with disconnected behaviour in post-modern society than between people in traditional societies.

---

46 Food and Agriculture Organisation 2000; Pollack 1995; Culotta 1994; *Economist* 1994; Kurien 1993. An *Ecologist* editorial notes that "Nine of the world's 17 major fishing grounds are now in precipitous decline, and four are 'fished out' commercially" (1995: 42).

47 Meeting export targets set by the World Bank and the IMF in return for loans has been an important element in the restructuring of the Indian fisheries, and in the granting of deep-sea fishing licences to foreign-owned companies (Kurien 1995: 118). Around one-third of all monies invested in fisheries by the multilateral aid agencies has gone into aquaculture developments (Wilks 1995: 124).

The parallels between fishery-management systems and land-management systems are indicated in a statement made by Sealaska. This organisation for native Alaskan fisherpeople has noticed how control of fishing quotas is shifting from community control to individual transferable quotas,[48] "from rural to urban areas and from residents to non-residents" (McCay and Creed 1994, cited in Fairlie, Hagler and O'Riordan 1995: 62). A western system of distant and disconnected ownership, along with capitalised profit and export-orientation, is being imposed on a system which hitherto has been mainly community-controlled and subsistence-oriented. As with land and forests, such disconnection reduces the level of responsibility felt by the owners for long-term sustainability. Instead, short-term profit, even at the cost of environmental exhaustion, is the favoured approach. Unless investors insist on long-term sustainability, the fishing industry is headed for

[a] technological treadmill, which itself supports powerful political interests, investment in modern fishing is such that the possibility of *not* exploiting an available fishery – let alone disinvesting it – is simply not an option (Fairlie, Hagler and O'Riordan 1995: 55, emphasis in original).

Sustainability problems leave the fishing industry wide open to the appeals of biotechnology.[49] Shrimp which can tolerate high levels of salt or pesticides are considered "ideal", as are fish with a shorter lifespan but increased weight. It is, therefore, not surprising to read of Biogrow, a salmon that allegedly grows to market size in twelve to eighteen months rather than in three years (Shiva 2000a: 51). The company website[50] links

---

48 Leith Duncan (1995) examines the ITQ system in New Zealand, where it has operated longest. He concludes that these quotas "are part of the capitalization of nature and society in the interests of global investors and large corporations" (1995: 102). One of the corporations named in his article as acquiring most of the quotas is Fletcher (see above discussion of Fletcher Challenge's role in bio-engineering of trees in New Zealand). Quotas also require centralised bureaucracies that are "insensitive to local differences" (Fairlie 1995: 109).

49 Biotechnology provides over-capitalised fishing companies with a new product for investors, something which, they claim, will create huge profits in coming years.

50 The interested reader can visit either the A/F Protein company site at www.afprotein. com or its sister company Aqua Bounty at www.aquabounty.com. The company goal is specified as: "to develop fish for aquaculture with improved growth rates and other economically desirable traits as cold tolerance and disease resistance through the use

to a number of research papers which make such claims. They rehearse the same arguments I quoted earlier to justify biotechnology use in agriculture and in forestry.

> Given the rapid decline in world fish stocks, caused mainly by over fishing, it is clear that demand can only be met by aquaculture (Hew and Fletcher 1997: 1).

> The world's fisheries are in danger of commercial extinction due to exploitation and overfishing ... Because fish is an essential protein source for the world population, it is critical that we develop alternative methods to ensure future quantities of fish. Aquaculture appears to be the *only* viable means of meeting the future demands for fish without driving one species after another to the brink of extinction (Fletcher, Goddard and Wu 1999: 24, my emphasis).

Once again, we hear arguments against environmental destruction, without ever examining the reasons for the destruction. These arguments are followed by claims – using scare tactics – that biotechnology (here disguised under the word "aquaculture") is the only avenue open to "save" the fishing industry, and hence avert world hunger.

William Shakespeare in his play *Pericles*, includes the following conversation between two fishermen:

THIRD FISHERMAN: ... Master, I marvel how the fishes live in the sea.

FIRST FISHERMAN: Why, as men do a-land, – the great ones eat up the little ones. (1996: 1040).

This conversation, written during the period when colonisation was expanding into the far reaches of the world, reflects the developing ideology of colonisation. One might hope for a future in which this conversation could be changed to reflect a sea-management system based

---

of gene constructs utilizing antifreeze protein gene promoters" (www. aquabounty. com/company.htm: 15 July 2001: 1). Hedrick *et al.* (2000) argue that one GM salmon escaping from coastal aquaculture pens could threaten wild salmon species, because the first generation has a growth advantage, and therefore mates earlier, but subsequent generations do not survive to sexual maturity.

on common resources and the precautionary principle, which recognises the ongoing importance of the marine environment for the planet's survival. Such a management system involves maintaining fish stocks at levels of abundance, evaluating new techniques before introducing them, and closing some areas for habitat protection (Earle 1995: 70; see also Graham 1943). These principles – which value biodiversity – could then be extended to land. Fisheries could provide a model for imagining ways in which we might plan for the next 40,000 years. Management systems of this kind are still widely in place in indigenous and traditional fishing communities, although they are under threat from the accumulative privatised approach which promotes, instead, Maximum Sustainable Yield (MSY). This is defined by Mike Hagler as "the conjectural highest amount of fish that can be caught in each season without preventing stocks from regenerating" (1995: 74). In other words, a "reasonable" approach is one which takes fisheries to the brink each season by conjecture (see also Smith 1995: 82–83)! The WTO rules favour this unsustainable approach (see Chapter Seven). As Hagler writes:

> Enthusiasts of farming the seas should reflect that upon land, what has grown back after repeated attacks upon the wilderness has not been rich diverse forest, nor even a sustainable monoculture, but degraded woodland, scrub, poor grazing land and ultimately desert (1995: 78).[51]

In sum, I have discussed in this chapter how farming and forestry practices have become further disconnected from communities and commons. With traditional fishing practices as a working model, it might be possible to forge new approaches based on a principle of biodiversity and intergenerational sustainability. This development would, however, rely on stopping the brinkmanship of MSY, and the further capitalisation and privatisation of the fishing industry. It would need to discourage biotechnological research and large-scale, intensive aquaculture that concentrates on a single species (Wilks 1995: 121).

---

51 There have been calls for Australian farming to move in the direction of sustainability rather than intensive farming methods (see Hamilton and Denniss 2001: 17). However, even these calls have been short-sighted, suggesting that horticulture and aquaculture offer an alternative to intensive farming methods.

The Commodification of "Everything"

The purpose of transnational companies is not altruism. It is profit. In order to make profits, companies need to make sales of commodities, goods, services or knowledge. The products developed in the different sectors of industry are those which are easiest to sell, or which are readily commercialised. A system, therefore, which takes account of complexity or of process, a system which considers ethically both means and ends, will not easily sit within the ambit of global corporatisation. Biotechnology prefers the simple answer: one crop grown; one gene shifted; the one-size-fits-all approach to problems.

The increasing role of biotechnologies as a means of implementing globalisation cannot be underestimated. It is not surprising to find transnational corporations focusing on primary industries, as these industries remain the largest untapped resource for profit. For critics of globalisation, primary industries have become the earth's new canary in the mine. Organic and traditional farmers, fisherpeople from around the world, and forest peoples, have become politically active because this is where many of the battles are now being played out (see Luneau 2001 on farmers; Dove 1993 on forests; Fairlie, Hagler and O'Riordan 1995 on fisherpeople). At the forefront of many of these battles are women.

Women as Keepers of Ecosystems

Across the world, women do the vast majority of the maintenance work, as farmers and gardeners, as maintainers of home life and relationship between people and places, both synchronically and diachronically. Indigenous peoples and many Third World peoples, largely women, have managed to maintain the biodiversity of their environments. I suggest that this has a great deal to do with respectful management practices. Where Europeans and European-derived societies have dominated the land, monocultural cropping and harvesting systems have prevailed. By contrast, traditional practices of mixed farming, or harvesting of forests, grasslands, seas, rivers and lakes, which extract sufficient only for sustenance rather than long-term storage, have proven to be economically viable if measured by biodiversity maintenance, not profit. It is not surprising, therefore, that biodiversity is greatest in the colonised areas of the world, because their systems have only recently been subjected to the expansionist, universalist and monocultural systems that dominate the landscapes of the west. As women's role in farming, fishing and forestry within traditional cultures is central, the process of market re-orientation results in the dispossession of women. Women are removed from the centre of these activities to the periphery. They are, once again, invisibilised (they are 0, see Salleh 1997: 36), and women's work is not recognised either as work, or as economically productive. Once again, women's work is regarded as domestic, outside the market economy in which men participate.

My argument is that many women are the wild types. Women have been incredibly resistant to joining the market economy. It has taken over a century, even in the western system, for women to become significant players in the paid workforce.[52] And in many other parts of the world, women remain outsiders. Market economies, whether they be in rural or urban locations, tend to commodify an increasing number of activities. As women vacate the spaces where previously sustaining and caring activities took place, the market rushes in to fill the gap. I am not suggesting that women should remain the unpaid workers, the unrecognised keepers of the natural and social ecosystems. Rather, a wild politics examines the way in which markets function, and asks why is it that they foster men's involvement? Is there another way of organising social systems which is more equitable? Are there other ways of thinking about the interaction between humans and the natural world, particularly in those areas upon which we rely for our food, medicines and shelter?

---

52   The exclusion of women has generally been seen as sexist obstructionism. While I agree, I suggest resistance to dehumanised practices has also played a part.

CHAPTER SIX

PRODUCTION, CONSUMPTION AND WORK: GLOBAL AND LOCAL

> *Biodiversity cannot be conserved until*
> *diversity is made the logic of production*
> – Vandana Shiva (1993a: 146).

Women, although they are not seen to be involved in production, produce a significant amount of food and domestic products for household and local use. Men are pulled into the market economy and the cash economy more quickly than women. This difference is in part due to a perceptual filter fostered by patriarchal and neoliberal ideologies toward seeing what men do as productive. Men, therefore, more readily gain access to the consumer products of western culture and often receive subsidies to help them learn how to drive tractors, use chain saws and motorised boats. Petrol becomes a basic "need", which is purchased so that they can use the new "toys" to which they now have access. This same process is used to pull men into other areas of the cash economy. With access to transport (or it could be access to computers and paper products) men's mobility also increases, providing openings for drawing the cash-earners into the purchasing market, into the world of desire and new "needs" for consumer products. Alcohol, cigarettes, Coca-Cola and the exploitation of women's sexuality are often early take-up "products" for men new to the market economy. Back in the village, women become ever more necessary to the continuation of sustaining work: work which revolves around food production and collection, around the nurturing of children, the ill and the elderly, and includes general maintenance work that keeps domestic and social arenas functioning.

Production and Disparity

As Karl Marx pointed out in *Grundrisse* (1939/1993: 86), production is an abstract concept which encompasses the totality of humanity and has

S11 protestors demonstrating their awareness of the strategies of consumerism.

particular and very specific forms depending on the era and context within which it is situated. The contemporary world is a good example of Marx's range of possibilities, with production spanning the primary (agriculture and mining), secondary (manufacturing and construction), tertiary (services and information), and quaternary – the most immaterial of all – (the virtual) sectors.

The logic of production "creates its own legal relations, form of government etc." (Marx 1939/1993: 88) and is affected by the kind of property relations which exist. In the context of this study, the tensions which exist between private (transnational and individual) property, and communal (public and indigenous) property, are significant, as are the relations of property between dominant and subjugated groups. I am thinking here of men and women, white and black, rich and poor; the matrix of intersections of these threads between oppositions tells us a great deal about how power functions in relation to production.

Two relations stand out as significant in the web of production:

- the transnational sector in relation to indigenous, poor and women's sectors
- the paid sector in relation to the unpaid sector.

The transnational sector is characterised by a cluster of features. The primary feature is its wealth. Because of its wealth, it can trade in completely abstract "products"; it can turn what has been public or communal property for thousands of years into a private and patentable product; it can turn desire into wealth. The transnational sector is highly mobile, and is most likely to draw mobile wealthy white (or other elite) males into its domain. Transnational production is dislocated in space and can locate wherever it is most profitable. At the end of the twentieth century the transnational sector moved very quickly into immaterial production: the NASDAQ index and dot-com industries.

At the other end of this spectrum are women, the poor, and indigenous peoples, as well as large numbers of refugees, exiles and migrants (many of whom fit into the first three categories). The primary feature of the diversity matrix is its poverty. Even if people in this group "own" wealth in the form of land, ecological niches or culture, they can be sure that someone from the transnational sector will eventually appear to appropriate or colonise their wealth, thereby turning it from a free resource to a private product.

The paid and unpaid sectors operate on totally different principles. The paid sector has made a priority of men's work, even though women – particularly poor women – have always been active in paid work. The family wage, the inequitable distribution of wage rates and the incomparable differences in promotion between the sexes are well documented (see, for example, D'Aprano 1995, 2001).

The definition of what is productive has over-determined the way in which productivity is assessed. A Marxist definition of productive labour in a capitalist society is that which creates surplus value (Meulenbelt 1978: 22). Even if one allows for other kinds of labour in non-capitalist societies, housework, altruistic work and subsistence work within the globalised economy all founder on this definition since their purpose is not the creation of surplus, but rather the maintenance of life. The process of globalisation is affecting this "unproductive" sector, because it is co-opting it – or its main players – and turning it into profit.

In the past three decades women have begun to enter the waged labour system in even greater numbers (except in the former Soviet Union and Eastern European states where they have moved in the opposite direction) and a few have moved into high-echelon positions.[1] In spite of these exceptions, high financial reward – and power – is still primarily a domain of men. The continuing difference is commonly called "the gender pay gap".[2] In the paid sector, production is focused on "commodity and surplus value production" (Mies and Bennholdt-Thomsen 1999: 20), the aim of which is the creation of surplus wealth.

The unpaid sector is dominated by women, dispossessed minorities and indigenous peoples. Although they remain unpaid, the work they do is invaluable and contributes significantly to national economies. It is estimated to be worth between one-third and three-fifths of all economic activity (Stretton 2000: 36). Unpaid work, including subsistence, remains largely unrecorded in spite of pressure for the work to be incorporated into the UN System of National Accounts (Waring 1988; Pietila and

---

1 The 2001 figures from the Australian Bureau of Statistics indicate that "Men continue to dominate higher paid professions and at management and board level, while women predominate in low-paid industries such as hospitality, health and community services" (Milburn 2001: 3).

2 Although unemployment is affecting middle-aged and young men significantly, in Australia the "wage gap between men and women widened last year [in 2000] by $7 to reach $166 according to the ABS [Australian Bureau of Statistics]" (Milburn 2001: 3).

Vickers 1991; Henderson 1993; Mies and Bennholdt-Thomsen 1999). The kind of work which tends to cluster in the unpaid sector includes nurturing (children, community relationships, gardens), caring for others (the ill, the elderly, children and sometimes the poor), production of domestic goods for the household (and some small quantities for local trade), growing and harvesting local resources such a forests, gardens, hedgerows, commons and small landholdings, both rural and urban. The focus of production in the unpaid sector is "life" (Mies and Bennholdt-Thomsen 1999: 20), its sustenance and maintenance. As Manfred Max-Neef writes, "nearly half of the world's population and over half the inhabitants of the Third World are statistically invisible in economic terms" (cited in Henderson 1993: 121).

The accumulation of money has become the major rationale for economic policies in the globalised economy. Although a few small nations continue on a trajectory of "maintenance and sustenance of life" (some of the Pacific Island nations, for example), most have been persuaded, induced or coercively pushed toward the accumulation of money through export orientation (Chossudovsky 1998).

The question has to be asked, what is the point of accumulating money if "maintenance and sustenance of life" are not adequately achieved? It is at this juncture that transnational corporations appear, suggesting that they would like to alleviate poverty by introducing cash rewards into the economy. In order to achieve this, land is dug up and destroyed, mixed farms are turned into cash crops, forests are burned and logged, fishing grounds are trawled, rivers are dammed, bridges built, and the search for medicinal compounds is pursued by appropriating the knowledge of the native populations about the wildlife – plants and animals – which inhabit their region. Bioprospecting has been added to the prospecting activities of the colonisers.[3]

Production for money tends to disconnect people from the local. The children of farmers move to the city and lose their connection with their

---

3   The term "prospectors" has some interesting resonances. According to the *Oxford English Dictionary*, prospecting is making a *claim*, and is associated with *drilling* and claiming parcels of land with prospects. A prospectus is an account showing the forthcoming likely profits of a venture *as a means of obtaining support*. As a noun, a prospect is a view of the *landscape* from any position; and when applied to time, it is a view which looks toward the *future*.

roots (I know this from personal experience). Similarly, the transnational company – even in an ostensibly benign form such as the Body Shop[4] – moves in and disconnects local resources, employing the locals, inducing and seducing them into the market economy. So-called oil "production" highlights this. Since the oil was "produced" millennia ago, what is really going on is removal of the oil from its current location to another so it can fuel cars and industry. In the long run, this leads to alienation, not just from local traditions but also in the Marxist sense, from the produce of their labour (how many indigenous people use Body Shop products?).

Consumption and Disparity

Excesses of consumption are not unusual in the twenty-first century. Indeed, the assumption of economic growth is built upon the excessive consumption of the rich sector of the world. I include in the word "rich" those of us who own a computer and/or a car and/or for whom air travel is not a once-in-a-lifetime event. The poor, by contrast, do not have access to a phone (let alone a computer), may ride or drive a collectively owned vehicle, and air travel is well out of their reach.

H. Patricia Hynes (1993/1999a and 1999b), in two groundbreaking essays, examines closely the way in which consumption is structured. She points out that, while efforts are made to reduce population, there is no comparable effort to reduce consumption; indeed, the entire economic system, dependent as it is on "economic growth", presupposes an ever-increasing amount of consumption (1999a: 47). Hynes proposes two separate indicators for consumption analysis. She writes:

> Do men and women consume differently? ... Women as a class are poorer than men worldwide: They eat less, own less, possess less, are invested in less, earn less, spend less. Income is a surrogate for consumption, and we can only conclude that women consume less, proportional to income, than men (1999a: 59–60).

---

4   For a critical view of the Body Shop, see Grossman and Cuthbert (1996) and Teiawa (1997).

Hynes goes on to argue that women and men spend differently. She expresses consumption as an element in an equation in which ^A refers to consumption:[5]

> men [spend] more on luxury items for themselves, such as business junkets, golf courses, gambling, alcohol, tobacco and sex (^ALUXURY), and women more on necessities for their families and households, such as food, clothing, and health care (^ASURVIVAL) (1999a: 60).

Hynes here is pointing to different modes of consumption between women and men. When women consume (and women do most of the daily shopping), they consume for the entire family, including the man if he happens to be a part of the family (^ASURVIVAL). When men consume, they consume primarily for themselves, and they consume products which are not essential for survival (^ALUXURY). Men who were recently pulled into the cash economy tend to spend money on expensive items including cars (and petrol, oil and other maintenance necessities), rifles, motor boats and the like, while women in the same economies will not have access to useful appliances such as washing machines.

The disparity between different worlds of consumption is reflected in the patterns of production and consumption of the global economy. Nike and Gap and a host of other clothing and appliance companies produce nearly all their goods in countries where most of the people are poor, and sell their goods to consumers in countries where most of the people are rich in cash and consumer goods. Indigenous peoples, people living in poor countries, refugees, dispossessed or despised minorities, and children, the elderly and the disabled who lack family support, are more likely to be poor; while within all these groups it is women who are likely to be the poorest.

In all these areas – production, consumption and work – disparity is rife. I suggest that the gulfs between groups can be identified as springing from a western-dominated, global and export-oriented system which is

---

5   The equation has become known as I = PAT. "The impact of humans on the environment (I) is a productof the number of people (P), the amount of goods consumed per person (A), and the pollution generated by technology per good consumed (T)" (Hynes 1999a: 39). Hynes criticises the way in which this equation is structured, and challenges its underlying assumptions, including identifying elements of the "universal P" which are "outside the scope of the formula", such as "the military, trade imbalances and debt and female subordination (1999a: 39).

built upon neoclassical economic systems. In the primary industries discussed in Chapter Five, production for production's sake has become the norm, externalities are ignored, and technological failures provide new business opportunities for biotechnology companies. In the secondary manufacturing industries, production is dislocated, moved into countries where labour, health safety and environmental laws are lax (often at the insistence of companies from rich countries). Production is disconnected from image-making, and more money is spent on marketing than on wages. For example, the US-based organisation Global Exchange "called on Nike to double the wages of its Indonesian workforce, an exercise that would cost it $20 million a year – exactly what Michael Jordan is paid annually to endorse the company" (Klein 2000: 376). Nike raised the wages by a mere 25 per cent. The relationship expressed here is not dissimilar from that highlighted by Michael Dove in his examination of forest peoples. That is, that the dispossessed, the marginal peoples who are exploited can never benefit from any profitable activity as much as do those in control and at the centre.

Among the protests waged against Nike, the one which seems to have had the most significant impact on Nike bosses was the one led by inner-urban young blacks from the Bronx. When they learnt that shoes for which they paid $US100 to $180 were made for around $US5.00, they decided to gather up their old Nikes and dump them in garbage bags outside Nike Town in New York. Mike Gitelson, a social worker at the Edenwald-Gun Hill Neighborhood Center in the Bronx, commented:

> Our kids are exactly who Nike depends upon to set the trends for them so that the rest of the country buys their sneakers. White middle-class adults who are fighting them, well, it's almost okay. But when youth of color start speaking out against Nike, they start getting scared (in Klein 2000: 373).

Because Nike have appropriated black youth culture in their image-making, the executives take notice when it is precisely those groups that rebel. The same response occurs when prostituted women walk out of prostitution and become activists against it (Giobbe 1996: 479–480). These are important lessons in countering global marketing systems. The disparities remain, however. Black youth from the Bronx are still poor, the workers in Indonesia, Vietnam or Cambodia are still poor, Michael Jordan still receives his excessively large payments, and Nike CEO, Phil Knight, still profits from his company's activities. And prostitution increases.

Work and Disparity

"Work" covers a wide range of activities from enforced labour (slavery) to labours of love. The latter is anything you would do willingly, even when other options are open; it may include caring for others or fixing computers, playing music or writing poetry. Between these two extremes sit activities we do on behalf of others, such as nurturing, playing, sustaining, caring, educating, maintaining It also includes work we do in exchange, such as paid work, bartered work – "I'll clean the bathroom, if you'll sweep the verandah", and other work we do for survival, including food preparation, health maintenance, production of clothing or shelter. Work also includes activities we do because the doing of them improves our circumstances or gives us pleasure, growing and maintaining a garden, cleaning our living environments, sustaining friendships and relationships.

The "Protestant work ethic", as originally proposed by Weber (Lessnoff 1994)[6] has been one of the mainstays of capitalist formation. Within a capitalist framework, work as waged labour is essential for creating surpluses of both goods and capital. And within a Marxist framework, it is labour – productive public work – which gives things value. In influential analyses of housework, both these views[7] of work as primarily public, productive and male were challenged by theorists during the 1970s and early 1980s (Mitchell 1971;[8] Oakley 1974; Dalla Costa 1972;[9] Hartmann 1981). From the 1980s onwards, this analysis was extended to recognising the value of subsistence work in Third World

---

6   The original publication was *Protestantische Ethik und der Geist des Kapitalismus*.

7   The liberal view is perhaps best represented by Betty Friedan's *The Feminine Mystique* (1962). But as with most liberal analyses, it describes the situation of housewives but gives women few alternatives, other than aiming to join the system on equal terms with men. See Friedan (1962/1973: 294–331).

8   While not specifically analysing housework, Juliet Mitchell devotes significant space to analysing women's work inside and outside the home. She concludes that in relation to production, it would be technically possible to eliminate the differences between women and men (1971: 144). This is rather like Firestone's view that reproduction could be replaced by artificial means (1971: 193–194). Both theorists suffer the problem of universalising and decontextualising their theory.

9   Christine Delphy and Diana Leonard argue that Dalla Costa "had produced a non-feminist analysis which nevertheless had feminist implications" (1992: 52).

communities, traditional and indigenous societies and other nurturing and maintenance work carried out (largely) by women (Bell 1983; Delphy 1984; Werlhof 1988; Waring 1988). Invisible work has been made visible, and in some instances countable, through these theoretical analyses. An area in which this is most evident is Australia's family law legislation.[10]

Recent analyses of work, while recognising women's contribution, tend to be more concerned with the changing nature of work. Jeremy Rifkin (1995) suggests that the increased digitisation of the globe indicates that we are facing "the end of work". But his use of the word "work" here and his association of it with unemployment and underemployment suggests that he is speaking only about public work and waged work. Viviane Forrester goes further, suggesting that definitions of work relate not just to unemployment, but to unemployability. Globalisation, she argues, has not only taken away millions of jobs; it has "obliterated, erased and blotted out from society" those who can no longer participate in the public workforce (1999: 9). The "excluded" are disappeared not because there is no work, but in order

> to make labour more subject than ever to the whims of speculation and the decision-makers, in a world which must be profitable on *every* level, a world which is reduced to nothing but a vast corporation (1999: 26, emphasis in original).

This process, in turn, as Forrester puts it, leads to the "normalization of social annulment" (1999: 32). Forrester lays the blame for human exclusion on the economic system. She suggests that human beings are no longer a potential source of profit for the market economy and that the globalized system is "fostering an authoritarian economic system indifferent to the inhabitants of this world" (1999: 127, 123). She asks the heretical question "what if growth, far from creating jobs, rather created their elimination from which that growth stemmed?" (1999: 82).

The end of work, in Forrester's view, is problematic because it is disrespectful, creates grief, loss and shame, and annihilates people. This is a step further than the alienation of people through work which Marx

---

10 For a discussion of its impact on farmers, business partners and wives, see Scutt (1997).

pointed to, and indicates a shift from the industrial to the digital world where displacement and emptiness are the norm. The "fictitious and imaginary" market is based on the ability to "speculate on speculation" (1999: 81), and in order to participate in the market, investors "do not even need real estate" (1999: 82) to handle the virtual deals, just a few telephones and computers and a very small staff.

The process here is a familiar one. Dematerialisation of the world, of the economy, of the workplaces – and of people.

André Gorz shifts the debate sideways by suggesting that "*real work is no longer what we do when 'at work'*" (1999: 3, emphasis in original; see also Else 1996: 1).

Solutions to the transformation of the nature of work include revaluing real work, subsistence work, work formerly considered unproductive. Veronika Bennholdt-Thomsen and Maria Mies (1999) suggest that subsistence economies may have an answer, precisely because they do not generate surpluses, and cannot be sold or accumulated in the way in which western capitalist systems can be. Others have proposed a social wage available for everyone that ensures "sufficient social income" (Gorz 1999: 83; Hyman 1999a) to pursue not just work, but also creativity, social networking and socially useful activities.

There is no necessary connection between valuing either paid or unpaid work. The discrepancy in value is ideologically driven. As Prue Hyman (1998) argues, it is neither rational, justifiable nor inevitable that high status and value accrue to those in high-paying work. In a similar vein, Shiva pointed to the "gender dichotomy [that] is created between 'productive' and 'non-productive' work, on the basis of money and price as the only measure of economic worth or wealth" (1989: 220). Hyman, Shiva, Bennholdt-Thomsen, Mies and other critics of globalisation and neoclassical economics are pointing to the political construction of value. On the one hand, the vast majority of poor people do not create surpluses which will gain massively in value as they hold on to them. Instead, their work is used to maintain daily life. On the other hand, the wealthy manage to create more wealth through surpluses compounding, and this can even apply to immaterial wealth.

Workers at the beginning of the twenty-first century experience the best working conditions ever, as well as conditions of slavery. The gap is widening between the "self-possessed" – those working for themselves or in jobs which offer great satisfaction – to the "dispossessed" – those working in inhumane conditions, at decreasing wages, and often for longer hours. There are also the dispensable (Forrester 1999), those who face permanent unemployment, and the disposable (Bales 2000), those pulled into slavery whose lives are deemed worthless. In the global economy, as Christa Wichterich sarcastically points out, women are "cheap, docile and flexible"[11] and "have a competitive advantage over men in meeting the new requirements of the labour market" (2000: ix). Nevertheless, digital enthusiast Sadie Plant goes so far as to suggest that women, because they are "better culturally and psychologically" prepared for the work habits of the new millennium (1997: 42–43), and will outdo their male counterparts in a more highly technologised world. The obvious question is "at what price"?

Global Production

Global production is controlled by the transnational sector. The intention of those in the transnational sector is to accumulate as much wealth as possible. The sector accesses financial support from two sources: previously acquired assets, largely generated by theft of free resources or exploitation of workers, and injection of funds by shareholders. Global production is export-oriented and characteristically dislocated from the source of its primary products. It is disconnected from systems of accountability within the local community, including health and safety of workers, environmental impacts, and social and cultural effects. The goal of global production is short-term profitability.

Swasti Mitter (1986), Althea Cravey (1998) and Miriam Ching Yoon Louie (2001) have looked at the example of the *maquiladoras* of Mexico. The *maquiladoras* are a variation on the export processing zones of other developing countries. Originally restricted to foreign investment in the border region between the USA and Mexico, between 1970 and 1972 the system was opened up to enable foreign investors to establish their businesses anywhere in the country. Investors receive exemption from customs duties and a host of other benefits (see Mitter 1986: 41–43; Tiano 1984). Cravey points out that the Mexican economy has shifted from "a

---

11   This is, of course, a myth which helps to sustain the exploitation of women. See Elson (1983: 5–13); Enloe (1983b: 117).

state-led import substitution emphasis to a neoliberal export-orientation based on transnational investment" (1998: 1). Louie (2001) notes that the move by workers within Mexico to the border regions is often a prelude to migrating across the border into the USA, and in the process becoming pieceworkers within the USA. Saskia Sassen argues that "there is a systemic relation between globalization and feminization of wage labor" (1998: 111). Similar industrial shifts are occurring in many countries and they represent a significant change to the ways in which global economics is conducted. The assumption in much writing on globalisation, even by authors who are critical, is that the shift to export-orientation is a positive one. Export-orientation benefits powerful economies more than it does economies on the margins, many of which are already heavily in debt. The connection between women's poverty and the poverty of nations becomes apparent in pictorial representations. In Joni Seager's *The State of Women in the World Atlas* (1997: 78–79), the map of poverty shows just how widespread is the equation "women equals poverty". The UN estimates that women hold title to about one per cent of all land, and that women "are among the poorest of the poor. Poor men in poor countries have even poorer wives and children" (Seager 1997: 120, 121).[12]

Export is presented as a panacea for economies where deficits are greater than surpluses. Export, it is claimed, will help offset the national debt and will contribute to the country's balance of payments. While all of this might appear to be the case on paper, no consideration is taken of the inputs required to create an export-based economy, nor of the sacrifices expected of the domestic economy in order to sustain export.

The dominating global ideology is one in which the "rights" of capital take precedence over the "rights" of citizens and the nation states that represent their needs. Enterprise bargaining, a system which is modelled on US trade unions,[13] has also been implemented in New Zealand. Prue Hyman argues:

---

12   If one were to define wealth in other ways, either by discounting cash as wealth, or by including women's uncounted work, the figures would change substantially. This would entail changing at least some aspects of the prevailing economic system.

13   It is interesting to note how social institutions are moving more and more toward US models. Compare this with the changes to international patent laws (see Chapter Seven).

The claim of the then National government's Minister of Women's Affairs (Jenny Shipley, later Prime Minister) that the legislation would promote equity for working women was widely challenged. The contention that a deregulated labour market and bargaining at enterprise level benefits women in general is highly dubious (Novitz and Jaber 1990; Hyman 1993). The only women to benefit were those with skills in scarce supply and/or were highly valued, with many women in traditionally female dominated and undervalued work, as well as those pushed into low paid, part time and casualised work, missing out. Inequality among women has thus perhaps become at least as critical as the gap between men and women (2001: 118).

The search for ever-lower wages pits women against one another, both between countries (Enloe 1983b) and within countries (Hyman 2001). Nor is it a simple matter of class and race. Working-class women and women from different ethnic groups (including poor, mostly immigrant, women in rich countries) are competing with one another for jobs. Rural and urban women, young women and older women – wherever they fall in the social and political matrix – cannot assume that there is a paid job for them somewhere. Poor men, and men dispossessed by cultural or geographical factors, also face widespread unemployment.

The fragmentation of those in the diversity matrix can be contrasted with the consolidation and universalisation of those in the transnational sector. The Washington Consensus concentrates the power of corporations of sufficiently significant size to be in it. The impact of the Washington Consensus in lobbying multilateral institutions has achieved benefits for corporations. The universalising principle is well characterised by a 1998 IBM advertisement. As Ian Walker comments:

Great throngs of humanity are shown going nobly about their business, a tiny caption asks "Who is everywhere?" The answer is scrawled on a piece of cardboard and held aloft from the madding crowd. "I am" it reads (2001: 4).

The implication is that IBM is not just everywhere, but also omnipotent and ineffable. It is universal in much the same way as god. Consumers won't need anything else if they have IBM (I AM). The other element of this advertisement is the representations of people from the diversity matrix. Their differences are subsumed under the need for IBM products. They are united – as one – in the ultimate quest for (consumer) satisfaction. Marimba Ani suggests that this connection between god and capitalism is not a new one. Indeed, as she points out:

> One of the most important connections between Christianity and technology since the colonial period is that missionary Christianism paves the way for capitalism and the European-centered market-economy (2000: 185).

Globalisation ensures the entry of western-manufactured commodities – real and virtual – into countries previously colonised by Europeans. The appropriation evident in the advertisements of global corporations is one more variation in the universalising symphony. Coca-Cola[14] has used this approach, as did Benetton in its United Colors of the World advertising campaign. Patricia Williams encountered this when she attempted to publish a critique of her experience as a black woman (albeit a Harvard Professor of Law) who was excluded from a Benetton retail outlet simply on the basis of her skin colour. The article she wrote about this experience was edited to the point where her identity was erased (1991: 48).[15] In a similar vein, when a Nike consumer, Jonah Peretti, wanted his shoes personalised with the word "sweatshop", Nike refused, in spite of its electronic advertising campaign which indicated that consumers' shoes could be personalised on the basis of freedom of choice (Bryden-Brown 2001: 5). Clearly, for corporations there is good freedom of choice and bad freedom of choice. Universal freedom of choice for those in the diversity matrix is still too risky.

Free trade, as structured under WTO rules and under the North American Free Trade Agreement (NAFTA), is having dire implications for women working in factories whose owners benefit from the relaxation of tariffs and trade protection. Elizabeth "Beti" Robles Ortega, who had formerly worked in a *maquiladora* from age fourteen, speaks about the impact of NAFTA on women:

---

14   For a discussion of Coca-Cola's iconic status as the "essence of capitalism", see McQueen (2001).

15   The other important issue raised by Williams in this article is "how the blind application of principles of neutrality" (1991: 48) reinforces the social relations of power.

NAFTA has led to an increase in the workforce, as foreign industry has grown. They are reforming labor laws and our constitution to favor even more foreign investment ... The government is just there with its hands held out ... Ecological problems are increasing. A majority of women are coming down with cancer – skin and breast cancer, leukemia, and lung and heart problems. There are daily deaths of worker women. You can see and feel the contamination of the water and the air. As soon as you arrive and start breathing the air in Acuña and Piedras [border cities between the states of Coahuila and Texas], you sense the heavy air, making you feel like vomiting (in Louie 2001: 70–71).

The work carried out in the export processing zones is for export to rich countries. The electronics industry and the apparel[16] and footwear industries have been two of the major industries in these regions over an extended period of time.[17] Ciudad Juarez, is a Mexican border town where *maquiladoras* service US industries such as electronic and digital equipment assemblage.[18] Work in the electronics industry in Ciudad Juarez includes board level assembly, plastic injection molding, mil spec, avionics, electrostatic powder coating, ionic contamination testing, systems-integration, electromechanics, harness assemblies and cyber optics (Biemann 1999: video). In some instances, several generations of a family have worked in these industries, sometimes in US-based factories. For example, Helen Kim's mother worked as an electronics assembler for Motorola in the late 1970s and 1980s. Her daughter describes the work and its impact on her:

> She complained of headaches and came home with teary eyes from peering through the microscope all day, with her clothes smelling of chemicals, and hair speckled with filament wires and fibers. She sometimes brought work

---

16 The apparel industry has a long history of exploitation of women workers. See Lown and Chenut (1983) for a brief history.

17 A further important manufacturing industry is the toy industry (Matsui 1999: 175). In this way children, too, are pulled into the market economy at an early age, and children become the vectors for drawing parents into the market economy.

18 Ursula Biemann (1999) lists the companies operating in the border region of Ciudad Juarez: General Motors, UTA, Honeywell Bull, RCA, Philips, Chrysler, Stackpole Components, American Safety, General Instruments, Chloride Power Electronics, Nielsen Clearing House, Tyler Science and Technology, Electro Mech Company, Packard Electrics, Siemanns–Albis, Electro Wire Products, Thomson, Potter Blumfield, ACSA, Recon, ITT, Marsh, Edmont Cooper, TED, Ford, and Toshiba.

home, including different log sheets to be completed, as well as the stresses
and tears triggered by competitive relations fostered between women (in
Louie 2001: 182).

Part of the problem is that the work is repetitive, does not build up the
skills of the worker in any way, but does create "major stress and tiredness"
(Biemann 1999). In the same period, but in Korea, Choi Myung Hee
describes the conditions of women in the apparel and footwear industry:

> During the 1970s and 80s companies like Nike, Adidas, Reebok and LA Gear
> flocked to Korea. We worked long hours with toxic glues and chemicals. Now
> 50,000 workers have lost their jobs. Those that can find work, can only do so
> in the service industry, in restaurants and the like (in Louie 2001: 134).

The electronics and apparel industries are perceived as relatively benign,
industries not generally regarded as dangerous. But as can be seen from
these first-hand experiences, when attention is not paid to working
conditions, and health and safety considerations are flouted, they become
dangerous.

The free flow of trillions of dollars daily of digital capital has been
accompanied by a huge increase in international labour migration. The
migration involves "tens of millions of people moving back and forth
across national borders" (Matsui 1999: 176). Some of this movement is of
people from rural communities moving across nearby borders to work in
factories; some is exported domestic labour migrating to Japan (Matsui
1999), Saudi Arabia (Wichterich 2000: 58), France (Bales 1999: 3), or the
USA (Chang 2000). But the largest and most profitable movement is of
women and girls caught up in the sex industry. Prostitution is, as Yayori
Matsui points out, "a product of globalization"; women's bodies reap "the
greatest profit" and it is a "modern form of slavery" (1999: 176) or "the
new slavery" (Bales 1999: 1). Commenting on the structural causes of
migration, Eileen Fernandez from Malaysia says: "We see migration as
the result of structural adjustment programs – we give up our lands, our
products, and finally our people" (cited in Chang 2000: 124).

The Philippines is a case in point. Christa Wichterich cites statistics
which state that "officially 3.5 million Philippine citizens currently work
abroad" (2000: 58). Some unofficial estimates are as high as seven million;

Grace Chang claims that the Philippine government estimates "more than 4 per cent of the country's total population is overseas contract workers" (2000: 129). Domestic workers are subject to intimidation and rape by their employers in some instances. Chang cites the case of Sarah Balabagan, who, when raped by her employer, killed him in self-defence. Eventually sentenced to seven years' imprisonment and a hundred lashes, as well as to a substantial monetary payment to the rapist's family, Sarah Balabagan has become a symbol of the struggle for human rights for overseas domestic workers (2000: 136–137).

The export of domestic labour and the appalling conditions of work in the export processing zones come close to a definition of slavery; but the sexual exploitation of girls and women, and in fewer instances of men and boys, fits the conventional definition of slavery.

Ursula Biemann, in her 1999 video, documents the factors which combine to make the export processing zones sites for "performances of masculinity", that is, of sexual harassment, turning into sexual terror, rape and serial murder. Biemann comments on the disposability of women in a commodity culture.

There is a connection between repetitive sexual violence and the form of production of a high tech culture, between the technologies of identification, reduplication, simulation, and the psychological disposition of the serial killer. In his mind there is a closed circuit between individual desire and collective information, between intimacy and technology. ... Her body is fragmented, dehumanised and turned into a disposable and marketable component.

Biemann's video documents the connection between the violence of the *maquiladoras* of northern Mexico, the commodification of culture, labour and the border, and the violence and commodification of women. The primary commodification in the export processing zones is to satisfy the needs and demands of the transnationals rather than the life requirements of the people who work in the plants. A former worker, Cipriana Jurado Herrera, comments that she had been "head of the line in the first factory that pushed me off. For this kind of work you need to be already very docile" (Biemann 1999). Isabel Velasquez comments that the infra-structure involving digital information and transport networks has been put in place for the companies. She makes the further observation that the Ciudad Juarez does not have a shelter for battered women, in a town where 124 women were registered as having died violent deaths since 1993 (in Biemann 1999).

Slavery[19] is characterised by a system of domination/subordination between two parties. The master–slave relationship is one in which there is no flexibility in the relations of power. It is heavily institutionalised and is usually surrounded by life-threatening sanctions in the event of its breakdown. It is a condition of total disempowerment. All rights are removed. The person of the slave is violated. The slave is accorded no respect, is often isolated and deprived of community and freedom of movement. These features are replicated in the power relationship between nations whose companies manufacture goods in export processing zones, and the countries who host the export processing zones. Biemann (1999) argues that the *maquiladoras* are the materialisation of the power relations between the USA and Mexico.

These days slavery is very commonly spoken of as a practice of the past. Certainly, slavery is rarely officially condoned nowadays, but its practice continues.

Slavery can also characterise the behaviours of groups of people. Just as there could have been no slave trade without people wealthy enough to purchase slaves or brutal enough to capture them, so too colonial nations have held the same relationship over their colonies in many instances, depriving the people of rights and taking from them their wealth. Such a relationship is on the agenda for the relations between transnational corporations and nation states. The former, through the WTO and other international agencies, are attempting to strip sovereignty from people and nations in such a way as to favour only the powerful (whether they be corporations or the wealthiest of nations).

Moving down scale, a replication of these relationships occurs between the cities and the country (Mies and Bennholdt-Thomsen 1999: 125): between the elites, wherever they come from, and the poor (whether the riches consist of money or information); and between men and women.

Our images of slavery remain linked to Hollywood images of slaves of the Roman Empire in movies such as *Ben Hur* or *Spartacus*, or the Black

---

19 Anti-Slavery International estimated that 100 million people worldwide suffer as slaves. This includes child labour (Daly and Goodland 1994: n. 11, 79).

slaves of the television series *Roots*. The commodification of people as tradeable products is at the core of these images. The commodified people of most of these images are male. But the commodification of women is on the increase. The trade in women goes on daily, before our very eyes. Indeed, it contributes hugely to the global economy. As Ninotchka Rosca points out, the trade in women is the third most lucrative criminal activity in the world today, after drugs and narcotics, and the trade in arms and weapons (Rosca 1998: oral presentation).[20]

Not only is the trade in women increasing, but the varieties of commodification are also increasing. Women's and children's bodies are traded in sexual trafficking; images of women and children are presented in all the proliferating forms of media, from print to virtual. Meanwhile, "interactive" sex, using communication tools such as telephone, live video link-up, and the internet, is also on the rise (Hughes 1999).

Under the economistic term "fictitious commodities",[21] body parts are trafficked (Raymond 1993: 154–171) from the South to the North. Raymond's analysis concentrates on the trade between South and North America, but the last decade has seen a considerable expansion of this trade (Chattakar-Aitkins 2001).

Like trafficking, slavery is based upon a view of the world which allows for some individuals or groups to be diminished. It arises from monocultural thinking which posits the other as less than, as "Other". It arises from homogenisation of the "Other", stereotyping, and a diminution of value accorded to anyone living outside the dominant culture. It is no accident that slavery is organised by those who have power, by those whose culture dominates others. Women are not involved in running slavery cartels. Rather, it is generally white and other elite men from rich nations who engage in slave trade practices. These practices range from the importing and exporting of women from "developing" countries, the violation of women through violent practices such as prostitution and pornography (Raymond 1999; Barry 1979, 1995; Biemann 1999; Chattakar-Aitkins 2001), to the purchasing of women as brides over the internet (Hughes 1999). They include many other violations of the psyche, the body and the spirit of women. Frequently they are associated with

---

20 For recent figures on the USA, see Hughes (1999: 176–181).
21 Interestingly, this term was first applied by Polanyi (1944) to describe land and labour.

militarisation and industrialisation. The globalisation of this trade has not been widely challenged, and "there is general acceptance of the use of women for capital accumulation" (Rosca 1998: oral presentation).[22]

Global Consumption

Patterns of consumption follow very closely the patterns determined by production. Those economies whose focus is money spend a great deal of their wealth on the commodities produced for them by the transnational and paid sectors, while the subsistence economies and the unpaid sectors simply do not have the spare cash to consume.

Consumption relies either on need – that is, products or services which cater to the basic needs such as food, shelter, clothing, health services and the passing on of cultural knowledge – or on falsely created wants – consumerism and the purchase of luxury items as status symbols, or simply as a response to market-driven advertising. In the global economy, needs form only the basic stratum of consumption. Beyond their satisfaction is a world of consumption which is determined by the commodification of desire.

Commodification in the first instance created ways of making people aware – through advertising and word of mouth – of the distinctions between products produced by different companies or individuals. Brand names entered the vocabulary. Brand names have now become institutionalised in product branding and are associated with particular kinds of lifestyles and cultural norms.

H. Patricia Hynes dates the origins of consumerism in the USA to the 1920s, with a further resurgence in the 1950s. She writes:

> Consumerism ... picked up enormous momentum in the United States after the war and was rapidly disseminated worldwide, under the gospel of development and the democratization of consumerism, *to gain markets for expanding U.S. industries* (1999b: 192, my emphasis).

In a fascinating history of shopping in the USA, cultural anthropologist Genevieve Bell (2001) cites the following as important landmarks in moving toward consumerism.

---

22 Among those who have challenged is the Coalition Against Trafficking in Women (CATWA) and the associated Network for a New Convention Against Sexual Exploitation. For a broad outline of the policy, see Raymond (nd).

1840s   Advertising and branding logos that stand for something else because newspapers insist that advertisers use 6-point type.

1850s   Department store, Otis, invent the elevator. Also invented in that decade were plate glass windows and rolled steel bars which were turned into girders. These three technologies made department stores possible.

1860s   The development of chain stores. The Atlantic Pacific Tea Company went west.

1880s   Railroads quadruple. In 1883, a railway agent, Mr Roebuck, created the catalogue industry which enabled those in remote areas to participate in capitalism.

1910s   Supermarkets. In the decade of 1910–1920, 60 per cent of car owners were women. Domestic refrigeration began to appear in middle-class homes. Saran wrap was invented. Self-selection became possible for customers, although the first super-markets compelled customers to follow a particular pathway through the store which did not allow them to turn back. The increase in mobility, preservation and individual selection assisted in the development of branding.

1950s   Shopping malls are developed. Huge car parks surrounded shopping malls on the assumption that customers would travel to the malls in individual cars. A concentration of chain and specialty stores provided a very wide selection of goods for shoppers (see Morris 1988; Rifkin 2000: 153–160).

1960s   Credit cards enter the market and AT&T introduces toll-free 1-800 numbers.

1970s   Cable television begins broadcasting.

1980s   Credit cards gain widespread acceptance, and the cashless society becomes a possibility.

1990s   The internet and e-commerce enter the arena of shopping. Branding by high-profile sport stars and brand marketing added to the increasing importance of immaterial elements in global consumerism (see also Rifkin 2000: 102ff; Klein 2000: 369, 3–61).

The beginning of the twenty-first century sees a concertina effect of mass digitisation and immaterialisation of products. Like other aspects of globalisation, it is engaged in a rhetoric of democratisation and accessibility.[23] But this rhetoric ignores the immediate privatisation of immaterial products and services, reinforced by new multilateral trade agreements which move international law into the realm of corporatised US law. Examples of this include the Napster website, which enabled mass downloading of music, before the recording companies stepped in and put a stop to such "free-loading". Knowledge is being privatised through changes to payment conditions placed on the use of scientific and academic journals in libraries. What was once accessible to anyone who walked into a university library must now be paid for through time charges. As a consequence, only registered students and staff – or paid-up library users – can gain access (Correy 2001b). In the area of the life sciences, the first release of the Human Genome Project results (whatever one thinks of the ethics of the project) were made publicly available, but for how long? And in the field of bioprospecting, privatisation through patents is moving at an enormous rate. Novartis in 1997 reported that it owned more than 40,000 patents (Shand 2001: 227). Knowledge and intellectual property have become sought-after commodities, and this immaterial side of a company's assets is becoming more important than the material – land, machinery and labour – in creating corporate value.

The distinction between survival consumption and luxury consumption made by Hynes is reflected in the differences between the patterns of consumption of the poorest groups (the diversity matrix) and the dominant groups (the transnational sector). Using the example of solar cookers, Hynes points to a very simple solution to the overuse of scarce fuel resources (firewood), contaminated water and women's use of time through the widespread use of such technologies (1999b: 189 ff). In 1997 at the VIII Inter-Congress on Science, in Suva, Fiji, on a day devoted to women's perspectives, a solar cooker was demonstrated that uses a very low technology – and an efficient one – to produce food which is nutritious and tasty. The evident question is why such useful technologies are not being made available to refugees, to women in famine- and

---

23 See Hawthorne (2001b: 43) for a brief discussion of this in respect of people with disabilities; for a contrary view, see Komardjaja (2001).

drought-stricken areas, to people in war zones, or simply to poor people wherever they live? An important rider, however, is that even the solar cooker may not be an appropriate technology in every context.

Research on solar cookers is not glamorous, unlike research into wireless internet connections – which the developers imagine they will sell to Africa.[24] These information technology developments are once again disconnected from the real needs of those for whom they are apparently being developed.

The end result might be similar to communities where cash is generated by profit-driven ventures, for example, the relationship between mining companies and indigenous peoples receiving royalties, or between pimps and prostituted women. In cases such as these and export-oriented activities, cash tends to remain in men's hands and be spent on materials to support men's activities such as outboard motors for fishing trawlers, Toyotas and rifles for hunting. In more urbanised settings where poverty is ubiquitous, men also spend money on sex, pornography, sport, cigarettes and gambling. The benefits for women are rarely in proportion to the influx of monetary wealth, and Hynes' equation of men's (^LUXURY) spending – gambling, alcohol, tobacco and sex – tends to prevail over women's (^SURVIVAL) spending on necessities (1999a; see also Matsui 1999).

In the future, such communities may argue about the merits of spending income on wireless technologies or solar cookers. Given the advertising budgets of the companies developing these items, it is not hard to guess the outcome. Yayori Matsui cites sociologist Hew Cheng Sim on the effects of the entry of cash as compensation for dislocation of the Iban peoples of Sarawak when the Batang Ai dam was built:

> Contrary to the legal custom of the Iban people, under which every family has land and property rights, compensation ranging from 10,000 to 40,000 lingits [from $US2500 to $10,000], and a one-acre garden plot, were awarded to the heads of families, most of whom are men. The men, who had rarely seen such

---

24 At an e-commerce seminar run by the Australian Publishers Association on 29 March 2000 in Melbourne, the lack of telecommunications infrastructure in Africa was cited as the reason for significant sales potential on the African continent. An article in the computer section of the *Australian* a few days later suggested that WAP technologies would form the basis of m-commerce, that is, commerce through mobile phones and other WAP appliances (Johnson 2000: 2).

a large amount of cash, spent the money to purchase consumer items such as cars, motorbikes and electric appliances, or to take a *bejarai*, a trip of several months. Consequently, the women's economic power decreased sharply. Furthermore, because they had been robbed of the forest held as common property, the women lost the source of income they received from the forest by foraging for food, fuel and rattan used for weaving (1999: 108).

Such research identifies the complex interweaving of concepts that are fundamental to western property rights against those of a commons approach, and of the ways in which men are seen to be the only ones deserving of compensation, which then draws men into the cash economy and spending on consumer items. As Jeremy Rifkin points out, buying a car signifies an acceptance of our participation in the market economy, and further, that for men the automobile is "an extension of who they are and how they would like others to perceive them" (2000: 73, 74). Sim concludes that women also lost status significantly because they previously had participated in longhouse meetings; "now only men are members of the development committee" (in Matsui 1999: 108). Other consequences for the Iban have been a very high accident rate for men working in the logging industry and, because the wages received are never high enough for survival, people leave their communities and move to urban areas. Some of the women are, by necessity, pulled into the sex industry, while men are drawn into it as consumers of women's bodies. On another continent, the introduction of the open market which followed the fall of the Berlin Wall in 1989 was accompanied by a huge increase in prostitution and pornography, and the same has occurred in Cambodia since 1992 (Matsui 1999: 38).

Hynes also points to the connections between these spending patterns and the sexual exploitation of women and girls. In the case of refugee women's use of solar cookers, Somali women spoke of the fear they have of being raped by bandits while looking for firewood. And how, when there is insufficient fuel, they are "forced to have sex with male camp guards for food and fuel" (1999b: 200).

Global consumption is driven by global production, although in the rhetoric of the transnationals it is usually claimed that consumers "desire" and "demand" certain kinds of products. Consumer demand is said to be behind the aquaculture of nations like the Philippines. Yayori Matsui cites the example of the village of Tamblar in the Philippines. Villagers were forcibly evicted from their community in order to create a new international port. A government official explained it this way:

> This is a development plan of ODAs [Official Development Assistance] from the USA, Japan, Germany and Italy, to promote agricultural- and marine-products processing in this area, improve transportation and promote exportation through the construction of an international airport, a modern port, highways, telephone communication system, and agricultural- and marine-products processing centre and hydraulic power (in Matsui 1999: 83).

The lines are clearly drawn. In Matsui's summary they are between, "on the one hand, American agribusiness and Japanese consumers; on the other hand, local farmers and women workers" (1999: 85). In India, the proposed Narmada Dam is fractured by similar power relations. On the one hand there are "farmers, labourers, *dalits* (untouchables) and adivasis (indigenous peoples)" who sacrifice themselves for India's middle classes, as well as for "politicians, bureaucrats and developers" (Black 2001: 10; see also Roy 1999: 7–101). In Australia, the Ngarrindjeri women who protested the desecration of their sacred sites for the building of an unnecessary bridge have witnessed the sacrifice of the integrity of their culture and spirituality (Bell 1998). And as discussed earlier, power relations between the USA and Mexico are manifested as young women in Mexico produce consumer products for the US market.

What we find in these four locations – the Philippines, India, Australia, Mexico – are the same forces at work, the same kinds of power relations and the same disparities of wealth and poverty. The distinction between the transnational sector and the diversity matrix could not be clearer.

For those of us living in rich countries, there are consequences for consumer choices. When a western consumer buys T-shirts, shoes, electrical appliances and toys, the tag "Made in —" will signify the latest production centre for global capital. The political consumer is faced with one more dilemma: on the one hand, for female consumers there is often the requirement that the purchased item be inexpensive; but then there is also the other side: the poor pay and conditions of the workers. What can make a difference is the recognition that, as Cynthia Enloe points out, there is a relationship between the final purchaser and the maker of, say, the garment (1983b: 119). Recognising this as a relationship, and recognising that both individuals are affected by the decisions of the transnational sector, are important steps in bringing together members of the diversity matrix.

As Michel Chossudovsky states, "those who produce are not those who consume" (1998: 85). This sums up the relationship between the transnational sector and the diversity matrix. The transnational sector has mobility for its funds and its locale. As the Chair of General Electric said, "Ideally every plant you own would be on a barge" (reported by Susan George in Walker 2001: 6). It can disengage from its home base and relocate to another country where labour is cheap, tax holidays are the norm and environmental standards are low. The transnational sector has privileged access to a "diversity" of luxury goods produced in the main from within the cheap-labour nations. Furthermore, the transnational sector has the luxury of mobility through frequent air travel or virtual mobility through telecommunications networks.

People in the diversity matrix, on the other hand, are less mobile and have few resources for consumption. In spite of their engagement in the production of low-cost goods, for many of these producers "basic consumption (for some 85 per cent of the world's population) is confined to a small number of food staples and essential commodities" (Chossudovsky 1998: 84). Dislocation of production from developed countries leads to widespread unemployment in the developed world, with the resulting contraction of consumption in the rich nations for whom goods are being exported from the poorer nations. As a consequence, the latter receive lower prices for their exports and in turn production is increased as a way of maintaining the value of exports. It is a vicious circle of expanded production (through reduced costs on labour via relocation) and contracted consumption.

Cyberconsumption of women provides an interesting parallel to these dynamics of global consumption. Research conducted by Donna Hughes (1999a, 1999b) elucidates the intersection in the global economy between consumption and sexual exploitation, and between the international mobility of elites and the increasing availability of women. The World Sex Guide Home Page has a header: "Where do you want to fuck today?" (Hughes 1999a: 159). Like the colonisers who acquired land so cheaply, and like the bioprospectors, mobile men want to pick up women wherever they are. They can even find out about the local conditions, and, like other prospectors, can report back to their colleagues over the internet.

Via the internet, women's bodies are being globalised, with some women becoming global stars. Donna Hughes describes a woman called "Honey", whom a number of men have returned to visit in a named brothel, and have now begun "keeping a special Web site ... for men to post their experiences of buying this one woman" (1999a: 161). She points out that, "This economic and electronic globalization has meant that women are increasingly 'commodities' to be bought, sold, traded and consumed" (1999a: 158). These transactions occur not only in domestic markets. Women are also export commodities, as trafficked brides (1999a: 168 ff), as a cash crop (1999a: 167), and as a way of potentially generating income to pay foreign debt (Lee 1991, cited in Hughes 1999a: 167) at the recommendation of the UN, the World Bank and even the International Labor Organisation (ILO). All these organisations consider prostitution to be "work", although as Sheila Jeffreys (1997) has pointed out, if it were a job like any other, then vacancies would be listed at unemployment offices. The ILO, in a 1998 report, urged that "the sex sector" be given official recognition for its contribution to gross domestic product in Malaysia, Indonesia, Thailand and the Philippines (Raymond 1999: 1). Raymond argues that making prostitution legal and recognised will justify exploiting women in "sex work" and allow governments to tax "women's earnings to raise desperately needed capital" (1999: 2). Genevieve Bell (2001) notes that, in the development of cyberconsumption, the pornography industry has led the way in introducing credit card sales for e-commerce.

Although it may appear that bodies are very different from farming and factories, many of the same principles are applied to women's bodies, as is shown in Raymond's critique of Belize as an exporter of women for trafficking into prostitution (1999: 2). They provide business opportunities for the transnational sector at the expense of those in the diversity matrix.

Further, the body is subjected to the homogenising influence of globalised fashion (this applies to both men and women). Each season, a new look, appropriated from yet another exotic and marginal culture, is presented as if it had been the fashion designers' original idea, rather than an idea stolen from long-existing cultural traditions. The moo-moo of the 1960s was the first such fashion to have an effect on me; from the 1990s, reflecting perhaps the bioprospectors' interests, one is more likely to find the fashions of indigenous peoples on the racks of fashion boutiques (see Hawthorne 1989).

As Hazel Henderson points out, the "globalization of information" amounts to "spreading wasteful, unsustainable western-style commercial consumerism and its many addictions" (2000: 77). Commodification has moved from a focus on luxury and lifestyle goods to encompass not only the body's needs, but emotional desires, and even our thought processes and experiences.

Like production, consumption has moved into the immaterial domain, a world of *ersatz* experience and virtual sexual gratification, a kind of fantasy place with its roots not in the real world but in a homogenised masculine domain of money, sex and violence. If this analysis appears too stark, I refer the reader to material which shows how these virtual worlds are replicating at an enormous rate on pornographic websites the world over (Hughes 1999a, 1999b). Robert Markley, in his critique of virtual reality, comments that

> the experience of Virtual Reality is intended to send us back to the real reality with a heightened appreciation of the exploitability of our environment. Cyberspace is the ultimate capitalist fantasy (1996: 74).

As I have argued elsewhere (Hawthorne 1999b: 222–235), virtual reality goes as far as commodifying the mind's processes through providing an "experience" that does not have an analogue in the real world. Although film and books and video could be said to provide an "experience" in a similar way, these fantasies and images remain externalised. The viewer or reader can look up, can separate herself from the immersive experience. Virtual reality is more like the experience of hallucinatory drugs than a book or a movie. Moreover, with drugs, the hallucinations are at least the creations of one's own mind, not provided care of Disney or Warner Bros. The virtual, as M. Christine Boyer argues, "represents a complete world: it saturates one's imagination. There is a kind of violence that 'the virtual' exercises on the user's sensibility" (1996: 55).

Commodification in the real world has also been extended. The makers of sex toys, sado-masochistic paraphernalia and the publishers of pornography deem sexual practices unsatisfying if sexual activity occurs without all these extras.

Extreme sports are another variation on commodified experience. In this instance it is the "experience" of fear, and of overcoming that fear, that is sold to the intrepid consumer. Appealing to another market, ecotourism and spiritual tourism (sweatlodges and initiations) sell what is left of wild nature, on the one hand, and of indigenous traditions on the other. In the area of reproduction, designer babies, microinjected sperm, genetic manipulation, IVF – and soon cloned individuals – are all part of the commodification of every aspect of life.

When national currency accounts fall, economists call for more investment, to build industries such as tourism which will draw in foreign currency. Earning foreign currency, however, is a double-edged sword. The resorts and golf clubs built by Japanese developers throughout Asia depend on the dispossession of people as land is turned from a public resource to a private one (and now countable as productive). Ecotourist developments, likewise, have a negative impact, commodifying indigenous and traditional cultures as "exotic" spectacles for the tourist.

The ideology of wealthy western nations masks the existence of these problems of exploitation and dispossession. But globalisation affects each and every citizen. Capital is used to produce ever-increasing profits more and more cheaply, and the products are marketed to fill the gap in increasingly disconnected lives. The internet has become an instant source of global communication located in our workplaces or homes, and increasingly in both. Our bodies have become globalised whether we are impoverished or wealthy.

Global Work

Veronika Bennholdt-Thomsen and Maria Mies provide an insightful critique of wage work. Looking at it "from below", they notice its inherently hierarchical nature (1999: 171), and the ideological dissonance this produces with the idea of democracy. The interests of power – capital, mobility, technology – are to maintain the hierarchies that the powerful literally have invested in through labour and the notion of waged work.

The issue at stake here is the way in which wage work has come to be constituted *as a commodity* rather than as an integrated part of a person's life. This commodity status, in particular, its flexibility, is what makes young male workers and young unmarried women so attractive as wage labourers. Bennholdt-Thomsen and Mies write:

Ageing people who might fall sick are dismissed before they reach pensionable age. Women who might become pregnant are not employed in the first place. Those who come closest to the pure commodity labour power are adult males and young women ... The work situations that come closest to the pure commodity relationship are those in which the employer can hire and fire at will and flexibly define the hours of work and leisure (1999: 174).

Although both men and young women are useful as wage labourers, the kinds of work and the kinds of exploitation are different for women and men. Consider the women working in *maquiladoras* and export processing zones in the Third World; consider the prostitution of women globally, including the new ways in which women are prostituted via the internet; consider the rubbish gatherers in the dumps near Manila. These are all gender-specific forms of exploitation and work.

From Germany (Martin and Schumann 1997) to the USA (Moore 1997), there are cries of "Unfair!" from workers who have lost their jobs through downsizing of multinational corporations – jobs which those workers had reasonably assumed would continue until they were ready to retire. But if workers in the richest nations are hurting, what of those in nations like Mexico, Indonesia, Thailand, the Czech Republic,[25] who are doing the work that, through globalisation and cost-cutting, has shifted to their countries? These people are working under conditions that would not be tolerated in the rich countries. Nike workers in Indonesia work at piece rates of less than $2 a day. In Mexico, the car manufacturers from Flint, Michigan, have moved south of the border where their workers live in cardboard houses (*Foreign Correspondent*, 23 June 1998).

As women are moving into old and newly created types of work, the workplace is said to be becoming feminised. What this means is that work is no longer an activity which is defined by a consistent eight hours a day, five days a week, in a job where employees remain for three to ten years or even a lifetime. Instead, work has become fragmented, short-term, unpredictable, flexible and, above all, changeable and without security. Homogenised large-scale jobs in factories and other industrialised

---

25 Martin and Schumann cite the example of Viessmann boiler makers in Kassell, Germany, with a workforce of 6500. When it was announced that the next gas water-heater models would be made in the Czech Republic, "96 per cent of the workforce" agreed to work an extra three hours of unpaid work a week, rather than have the plant in Germany close down (1997: 130). Such threats work only because similar closures have happened throughout the rich nations.

settings are no longer the norm: except in the developing world. In the rich nations, mass downsizing of huge corporations is taking its toll, forcing large numbers of people, previously continuously employed, into unemployment (Forrester 1999; Gorz 1999; Moore 1997: 12–13; Theobald 1996: 38; Rifkin 1995). The urban sector appears to be "ahead" of the rural sector in so far as agriculture, forestry and fishing are still moving toward – or are still in – an industrialised state. However, primary production is moving inexorably toward digitisation, using biotechnology to replace natural elements, such as seeds, with "software" (Friedland and Kilman 1999: A1) and to eliminate "outdoor agriculture" (Rifkin 1995: 123). Urban work has also been largely restructured, and in some ways mimics the kind of diversity I have argued for in my foregoing chapters. The question is do I endorse this "man-made" diversity?

Global work is disconnected, dislocated and dehumanised. Viviane Forrester documents some of the reasons in her book, *The Economic Horror* (1999). Work, she argues, is on the way out, and the unemployed have become "subject to a world-wide logic which assumes the elimination of … work" (1999: 5). Jeremy Rifkin argues that the global labour force has become "expendable, then irrelevant, and finally invisible in the new high-tech world of global commerce and trade" (1995: 197). Kevin Bales (2000) suggests that the disposability of people, especially of the very poor, is creating a new form of global neo-slavery. André Gorz summarises the reasons for the displacement of people and the mobility of capital.

> With the supra-national state of capital we see for the first time a state free of any territoriality, whose power, though it is imposed from outside on the territorialized states, does not recreate any other political arena outside of them. It is, rather, independent and separated from any society. It is situated in a non-place, when it limits and regulates the power of societies to determine what happens in their place (1999: 15).

The state, separated from its sovereignty, from its territoriality, becomes immaterialised. Colonised peoples recognise this separation, since colonisation created separation of the people from their government through dependence on a colonial power. The separation occurring under globalisation is dependence on corporate power. With only twenty-nine countries in the list of the world's largest 100 economic entities (Appendix, Table 1) it is obvious where the greatest power lies. General Electric is larger than Australia and seventeen other nations which made this list (Sheehan 2001: 32).[26] Five years ago fifty-one of the largest one hundred economic entities were companies (Ho 1997: 10). How long before only eight nations (the G8) remain in the list?[27] The non-place, the atopia which nation states now inhabit, resembles the atopia of cyberspace. It is no accident that digital capital is the most mobile element within the global infrastructure. This atopia, however, like the colonies of the preceding centuries, does resemble the most powerful location of the vast majority of the world's largest economic entities: the USA. And the WTO is implementing and enforcing global trade rules which benefit the biggest player: the USA. The global rules on intellectual property are moving more and more in the direction of US law. The shift in importance is reflected in figures which show that in Australia the export of copyright is worth more than the export of cars (Slattery 2001: 49). Vandana Shiva echoes this writing that "In 1947, intellectual property comprised just under ten per cent of all US exports. In 1986 the figure had grown to thirty-seven per cent and by 1994 it was well over fifty per cent" (2001f: 19).

The status of refugees and immigrant workers, including economic migrants who enter rich countries without the required documentation, provides a key example of globalised work. Yayori Matsui writes of the "feminization of international migration" (1999: 42), with women being defined primarily as domestics (Chang 2000) and prostitutes (Matsui 1999: 46). The result is dislocation from their communities and places of origin which leaves women, especially, vulnerable to violence;[28] they tend to work for much lower wages in worse conditions than the people who live in the rich nations (Chang 2000; Sassen 1998; Bales 2000).

---

26 Of the seventy-one companies listed, many have long histories as "main players" in the world's economy. In 1979, Du Pont, Rhone–Poulenc, Hoechst and Monsanto were four of the top fifteen fibre producers (Gloster, McDevitt and Chhachhi 1983: 16), and Mobil was the largest retailer of apparel and textiles in the USA in 1979 (Chapkis and Enloe 1983b: 127).

27 The G8 countries are: USA, Russia, Japan, Canada, Germany, France, Britain and Italy.

28 Uma Narayan (1997: 83–117) discusses the issue of dowry-murder in the USA and suggests that the distortions that accompany any media coverage are affected by context, including decontextualisation and recontextualisation.

The "free movement" of capital, especially exports from the knowledge economy such as patents, therefore, is not balanced to allow for the "free movement" of labour. Once again the transnational sector has "freedom" at the expense of the basic human freedoms of those in the diversity matrix. The transformation of work relies on a major reassessment of western capitalist ideology. Without such a reassessment of the basics, of how those in western cultures – including those who run the vast corporations and the military and governmental institutions – think about value, about worth, about satisfaction, change will not, and cannot, occur.

Similarly, I believe that in the pursuit of "increased efficiency" it is morally corrupt to downsize corporations while profits are increasing. The market response to downsizing is always an increase in the value of shares. When Australia's biggest company, BHP, closed its steelworks in Newcastle, a town totally dependent on this company, share prices rose. Viviane Forrester points out that this is the usual market response from shareholders (1999: 14, n. 3). Nike, the world's biggest shoe company, had *net* profits of $US400 million, while workers in their Indonesian factories (women and underage girls) were paid a starting rate of $US2.00 per day (Moore 1997: 127–129). Or as André Gorz puts it, "fourteen American board members of Nike have been able to pick up an annual income equal to the wages of 18,000 women workers in the Philippines" (1999: 18).

A process of re-localising work would challenge the global mobility of transnational corporations who are now "difficult to locate" (Forrester 1999: 23) within the global corporate networks they have established.

Among some of the innovations in paid work structures which have arisen in the last couple of decades are family-friendly workplaces which recognise parents' care responsibilities for others, job sharing, teleworking – either from home or in telecottages in suburban, outer urban or rural settings – part-time and casual or on-call work, consultancies or short-term contract work, and portfolio work. The latter involves developing skills in a particular area and then selling these skills to a variety of clients. Writers, artists, musicians, tradespeople, domestic workers, doctors, lawyers, and business people, among others, have been working in this way for a very long time, but it is only relatively recently that office workers, civil servants, carers have done so in significant numbers.

The main manifestation of paid work within the home has been women's participation as "pieceworkers" or "outworkers" (Mitter and

Luijken 1983). Pieceworkers connect to the world outside the home through an entrepreneur or contractor who organises their schedules and deadlines. The dispersed nature of the work, the isolation endured by the women, ensures that wages are kept low, simultaneously reducing overheads and the likelihood of labour disputes (Mitter and Luijken 1983: 63).

In recent years, piecework and contract work have expanded to include a wide range of types of work, including office work. The shift has been made possible by technological changes which make outsourcing – whether to another company or an individual located in a home office – an attractive proposition. As with piecework, overheads are decreased, and the cost to the company is reduced, in part because of the dispersed location of the workers. The most significant change is that there is usually no intermediary, no entrepreneur or "middleman" to hike up the prices with his percentage. The other significant feature of new types of office work is its flexibility. Flexibility is often justified on the grounds that women need it (because of family responsibilities). But flexibility extends not only to the hours of work, but also to types of work, and modes of carrying out work (Eyerman 2000: 70–75). While sounding positive at first, flexibility can become a trap.

The SOHO (small office home office) worker, like the pieceworker, works in isolation, although this may be mediated by an on-line community of other SOHO workers. The SOHO phenomenon has changed the concept of "working from home". I suggest it changed because *men* decided to work from home. For years women have worked in the home, in the garden, on the farm, in the community and the concept of work did not shift. But when, because of technological change, men decide to work from home, suddenly the home office is recognised as a workplace. SOHO work is globalised work in the sense that it is disconnected from place, it is dematerialised work, and it is outsourced to maximise profits.

At the other end of the spectrum from the flexibility of SOHO work is prison work. Coercive institutions as locations for cheap labour are on the increase, and the trend for prisons, around the world, is expansion (Teeple 1995: 117–122). Like export processing zones, prisons provide controlled populations who are distanced and invisible form the public world outside the prison. Gary Teeple argues that the expansion of prisons is directly attributable to the implementation of neoliberal policies and the reduction of the welfare state. With the marketplace having such prominence and the changed definitions of crime having the biggest impact on the poorest members of society, crime rates are rising within the neoliberal definition, in much the same way that unemployment rates are definitional within the neoliberal system. Unemployment can be raised or lowered according to what is defined as work, and how many hours of paid work in a week bar someone from receiving unemployment benefits.

Local Production

Sabine O'Hara redefines "production as a set of interrelated processes" (1997: 145) which, she argues, are embedded in particular, local, concrete contexts. She argues that in order for production to become integrated, "negative externalities need to be internalized into the existing valuation framework" (1997: 145). Unlike global production, which is structured as if it existed in isolation from its context (and if the Chair of General Electric had his way, it would be), O'Hara argues for the view that production "draws upon a web of services provided by invisible and unaccounted for contributions of households and nature", and further that production "is not only inseparably linked to sustaining services but it is dependent on them" (1997: 145, 146).

What becomes mystified in settings of global production is more obviously evident in local production for the purpose of sustenance and life maintenance. This kind of production leads toward connection. It might be connection to the culture, the local produce, the people and land of the community. This is not to imply that community is always unproblematic – theoretically or practically. Dreadful things have happened in the name of community, and this is particularly so in communities with a closed system of belief. A small country town, almost anywhere, is subject to this risk; political or religious groups with closed memberships, or the clubs of the privileged, or monied classes are equally prone to closed belief systems. John Wiseman points to some of the problems of an ethic of localism, and then proposes that the narrowness of localism can be offset if a process of democratisation is put in place at every level (1998: 131).[29]

---

29 For feminist discussions of community, see Young (1995); Weiss and Friedman (1995); for a discussion which emphasises the negative aspect of community, see Sheldrick (1995).

Although connection, as described above, might suggest that only rural communities and people not caught up in consumer culture can really have any hope of "being connected", I would suggest otherwise. There are numerous examples of urban communities shifting their focus away from the homogenised global culture and toward a more integrated and relational approach to living. In such contexts, the interrelated relationships of the production process are much more visible, in much the same way that oral transmission of culture makes visible the relationships and politics within the community.

As H. Patricia Hynes (1996) and others have indicated in their research on city gardens, connection to the land and the locale can be achieved even in densely populated urban settings.

As an example, the city I live in, Melbourne, has two inner-city developments of long standing: the Collingwood Children's Farm and Ceres Community Environment Park in East Brunswick. Both have been developed to create opportunities for urban-dwellers – children and adults – to have access to places where plants are grown and farm animals raised. Ceres also provides local urban people with access to farming techniques including permaculture and bush foods, an organic market with affordable local produce, an example of a lived-in energy-efficient house, and a host of other environmental activities and educational resources.[30]

Not all community developments are focused on farms and nature. There are many other hopeful models for community activities such as arts centres, neighbourhood houses and places that have their origins in a grassroots need for community-based activity.[31] The Footscray Community Arts Centre is an example. Located in Melbourne's inner west, in the heartland of a working-class suburb bordered by some middle-class

---

30   For further information see the Ceres site at www.ceres.org.au and for information on Australian city farms see www.cityfarmer.org/australia97.html, or internationally www.cityfarmer.org.

31   Community centres start for a variety of reasons, often one person has the idea and energy to follow through. However, without local involvement and support, such a "community organisation" will not survive for more than a few years if the initiator monopolises the facilities and organisational structure. Community organisations which have a longstanding history in Melbourne include 3CR – Community Radio, Footscray Community Arts Centre, Ceres, Brunswick Neighbourhood House, Collingwood Community Health Centre, Preston Creative Living Centre, Diamond Valley Learning Centre, just to name a few.

areas, it has developed a rich array of facilities mostly, but not exclusively, for local residents. It hosts organisations such as the Vietnamese Youth Media Group, the Women's Circus,[32] the Performing Older Women's Circus, the Ethiopian Circus, Footscray Fliers, Artlife (a theatre and ceramics program for people with disabilities) and a number of small groups whose focus is music, visual arts, theatre, circus, literature. There are regular exhibitions of local artists' work, and the Footscray Community Arts Centre has become a meeting place for a diverse range of people in the community. There are other centres like this in Australia[33] and elsewhere. It is the community-based focus which makes the difference. Such centres often arise in areas where a mix of ethnic or language groups congregates. I suggest that their basis in diversity is part of their strength as it makes closed belief systems difficult to sustain. Such open organisations do not exist in the dominant culture. Certainly, there are many exclusive clubs to which the wealthy can belong, but they are mostly closed organisations, rarely open to those outside the "money club".[34]

Local Consumption

Just as there are community-based producer groups forming urban farms and gardens and community arts centres, consumer-based groups have also been formed. The Seikatsu Club, a consumer group formed by Japanese housewives affected by their exposure to Minamata disease, was established in the early 1970s. Minamata disease resulted from eating food, especially fish, contaminated by high levels of mercury pollution. These women developed direct relationships with farmers who used ecological principles. But the Seikatsu Club members went further than simply connecting producers and consumers: they began to challenge economic assumptions which dominated international trade (Mies 1993: 260–262). They called for self-reliance and a "self managed lifestyle in order to change the present wasteful lifestyle". As they define their philosophy:

---

32 For a history of this community arts organisation, see Liebmann *et al.* (1997).

33 See also Fisher and Shelton (2002), which documents the arts activities of the Preston Creative Living Centre.

34 A well-known and very exclusive local example is the Melbourne Club, a bastion for rich white men.

We believe that the way to improve the quality of life is to create a simple but meaningful existence, refusing to fall under the having-it-all illusion created by commercial products ... Our visions to rebuild local societies derive from this principle. One of our directions is to create locally based economies (Elkins 1992: 131–132, cited in Mies 1993: 261).

Maria Mies, commenting on the Seikatsu Club, points to the importance of "women's concerns and experiences" in determining the shape of the consumer action (1993: 262). She contrasts the focus on life and community with the atomised self-interest of NIMBYism (not in my back yard). The Seikatsu Club puts great store by the relationship between producer and consumer (Hynes 1999b: 61) which increases trust and ensures quality produce and fair pricing.

Farida Akhter, activist and Executive Director of UBINIG, based in Dhaka, Bangladesh, commented on her visit to Melbourne. She noted that her overwhelming impression was of how few people were in the streets, and how many cars there were (1996: pers. comm.). The car as a lynchpin of consumer society has been recognised before (Henry T. Ford certainly understood its importance) but her comment brought home to me the stark contrast between a society based on atomised self-interested consumers and a people-centred society structured more on notions of community.

Priti Ramamurty suggests evaluating production, consumption and work in a way that is sensitive to both context and process, a methodology which takes account of the everyday realities of women. She suggests the establishment of

[a] feminist commodity chain research that not only locates, and therefore incorporates "women" in empirical analysis but extends the analysis by allowing space for rethinking how women's experiences of globalization are linked, negotiated, contested, resisted, and changed so that the very categories "woman" and "work" are reconstituted (2000: 552).

A feminist methodology of this kind – which allows space for context and connectedness, which respects diversity and location, and which challenges one to rethink basic assumptions about worth and value – would create openings for the kind of society I envision. Taking on board

Summing up the principles of buying local at the S11 protest.

indigenous concerns, using biodiversity as the overall principle alongside the needs of the poorest, such a feminist approach might create the beginnings of a wild politics of work, production and consumption.

Local Work

Discussing the work continuum, there are many positive ideas proposed for making work more satisfying, more oriented toward self-fulfilment for the workers themselves. But if, before this shift can happen, a large number of the dispossessed are sacrificed at the expense of the dominant "self-possessed", what will this mean for society as a whole? Clearly, a different approach needs to be taken, and soon.

Robert Theobald, in a more liberal version of the alternatives proposed by Gorz and Bennholdt-Thomsen (cited above), suggests that a philosophy of "right livelihood" is one way to go. He suggests that such a philosophy would encourage the view that life is a journey of moderation, that while job and work satisfaction are important, not all of life, or all of any work, is constant enjoyment. People learn not to expect utopia, but also understand that no one should have to put up with a life of misery and poverty. Nor should any single group in a society bear the sole burden for doing the shitwork. Such a moderate approach would make multi-billionaires impossible, even unthinkable. That so many people currently die of starvation in a society which has multibillionaires is a sign of moral corruption. A philosophy of right livelihood, or, to use a phrase I prefer from Maria Mies, of a "moral economy" (1995: 13), would make slavery impossible, since it allows for difference, for diversity and for hetero-geneity.

A moral economy would foster a philosophy along the lines of the Ngarrindjeri people with their "moral relationship of people to land" (Bell 1998: 268), and a goal of long-term sustainability. Sustainability also applies to work.

For a job to be sustainable it has to provide sufficient income, or provisions *in lieu* of income, to live without a constant financial struggle; or a *quid pro quo* of good community services which mean that individual or family income does not need to be as high. It should be of few enough hours, or sufficient flexibility of hours, to allow people to have a life outside work. Sustainable work should be sufficiently interesting, challenging or varied; it should foster satisfaction, be stimulating, and extend the depth or range of individuals' skills. It ought to allow workers to take up responsibilities, to be promoted, to work with others or independently according to the needs of the job and the personality of the worker. Stereotyping, and therefore discrimination based on race or sex or any other excuses for prejudice, should not determine a person's work prospects, but nor should anyone be pressured into taking on the white male norm of "all work and no play" in order to get ahead.

The other critical factor, as Veronika Bennholdt-Thomsen and Maria Mies (1999) have indicated, is waste. Gross waste is produced when production is disconnected and large-scale. In a system inspired by bio-diversity, waste would be eliminated altogether through the development of closed systems that resemble biological systems. In transition to a biodiverse system, a job which has the potential to be sustainable, respon-sibility for waste disposal, would lie with the person who produces it. If this principle applied, either men would find themselves doing much more cleaning up, or they would begin to think of ways to produce less waste.

The world is changing at an extraordinary pace. Much of the work done today was unthinkable twenty years ago. What will it be like twenty years from now? What are we doing to take account of all the changes? Sustainable practices will not mean the end of work, but they could lead to very significant changes in prevailing ideas on what constitutes a job. Work, as women well know, goes on long after the job has finished. The likelihood of governments introducing the Universal Basic Income (UBI) is not great (Gorz 1999; Hyman 1999a). The UBI would give many people – the young, the old, the carers, those who work at home or in the community, those studying or retraining, those living a subsistence or semi-subsistence lifestyle – many more options. The armies of people currently engaged in policing social security fraud could be disbanded. Because of the drastic reduction in administrative costs, the UBI would cost little more than current pension and benefit schemes for a comparable number of people (Hyman 1999a). Its introduction would reduce unemployment by reducing the need for what is currently regarded as full-time work. But this idea has received little discussion outside future think-tanks, with the exception of New Zealand.[35] Anne Else summarises sustainable work:

---

35 An explanation for this could be that New Zealand, as an early adopter of the key
    features of globalisation – market deregulation, changes to industrial laws, for
    example – felt the impact of globalisation earlier than other western nations. See

Without families and communities, the economy means nothing. It has no life of its own. Its only purpose is to enable us to live, to care for one another and to raise our children to take our place. If we lose the power to do that, no matter how fast the gross domestic product rises or how much the budget surplus grows, we will have no future worth working for (1996: 159).

Or, as Veronika Bennholdt-Thomsen and Maria Mies suggest, "life", not money, should be at the centre of social and economic structures (1999: 20).

Work which centres on life often involves relationships with others, in communities, families or with nature. And work–life relationships can be unpredictable, slow or simply need to reflect the body's rhythms (Forrester 1999: 19).

Children, for example, are not readily inserted into the demands of the market economy. They get sick at 3 a.m., their needs are unpredictable, and the good times of laughter and play are too important to be hemmed in by rationing "quality time". Neither enjoyment nor misery can be temporally confined. To quote Else again:

family time is doing just the opposite of market time: it's slowing down and lasting longer than it used to. As the demands of adult life grow, children need more time, not less, to prepare for it. But you can't sell children when they don't come up to scratch, any more than they can sell you. You can't restructure them or sack them (1996: 133).

Children require commitment and relationship, but that does not mean that two people – or, frequently one – can provide for all the needs of a child. Smaller communities allow children to grow more independently, to get to know other adults outside their immediate family. Some urban settings also promote this kind of community, but it is relatively rare. Rural communities are more able to offer interconnection, but in many rural areas, isolation can be a problem. Community facilities are centralised – huge shopping centres, sports complexes, entertainment and arts facilities – and because these conglomerates are so heavily capitalised, and therefore

Kelsey (1995); Else (1996); Hyman (1998a, 1999). Political parties in Canada and Ireland have also taken the concept of UBI seriously.

widely dispersed, they are not easily accessible without one's own transport, and they tend to homogenise the goods, the needs and the culture on offer. The latest blockbuster movie, such as *Titanic* or *Lord of the Rings*, is shown in the cinemas of every shopping mall in the same weeks; the fashions on sale have been produced by the same globalised companies, the sporting facilities are dominated by men's global sport culture (especially the football codes and basketball). These globalised artefacts do not satisfy people's need for their own cultural and leisure activities.

Life work would mean slowing down to take account of the seasons' rhythms, to work "in time with human body rhythms" (Forrester 1999: 19), to do things because they maintain and sustain life rather than creating surplus profit.

Housework is very much a matter of maintenance and sustaining life. In looking at housework, one researcher found that "men may create more housework by their presence than they contribute to the household" (Schor 1991). Housework in many households fits Mary Mellor's description of "imposed altruism" (oral presentation, cited by O'Hara 1997: 147). The result of men's presence in a house is reminiscent of the way in which men's fishing activities often increase expenditure and are interrupted completely if there are equipment failures. As it is currently constructed, marriage, for women, tends to increase the number of hours of housework a woman does (Else 1996: 18). Part of the problem here is the need for a deep sense of responsibility, or, as Susanne Kappeler puts it "personal communication behaviour is political" (1995: 52).

In the urban west, and also in many developing countries, women have reduced the number of hours they spend on home production: cooking, sewing, knitting, making household tools, preparing home remedies from plants, or processing food for long-term storage, for example, preserving fruit and vegetables. But for large numbers of women throughout the world, domestic production is still their daily reality.

The gap between the perception of what it is that women and men do in their public and private spaces was brought home to me one day when I was in Adelaide, South Australia: I watch as a man rides a large machine along the edge of the street. It is picking up leaves, dust, small items of paper and rubbish in the same way a vacuum cleaner picks up slightly finer dust and particles in a home. It crosses my mind that this man is being paid to vacuum the streets, while back at home his wife may be expending more energy vacuuming the house without being paid for it, and perhaps doing it after she has completed her day job.

The women whose primary production work I looked at in Chapter Five were faced with the maxim that "women don't work"; and women throughout the world – in rich countries and in poor ones, in rich households and in poor ones – have faced the same maxim.

Until the 1980s, definitions of work also excluded people whose lives are based on subsistence economies. Anderson Mutang Urud, a Kelabit from Sarawak in Malaysia, speaks of the traditions of work in his community:

> My father, my grandfather did not have to ask the government for jobs. They were never unemployed. They lived from the land and from the forest [and] we were never hungry or in need (cited in Sittirak 1998: 5).

Some people living in subsistence economies are now being drawn into the global market economy. As a result, they have become countable. Many are unemployed. While they remained outside the productive zone, they could not be counted – as either employed or unemployed. Such a structure is a double jeopardy. The alternatives are:

- to engage in subsistence work which results in invisibility
- to be engaged in the market economy which results in a sense of material poverty as few of the consumer items available can be afforded; it may also result in dislocation, since in order to obtain work, people travel to cities, to export processing zones, to rural centres of employment, or to another country; it may result in being counted as unemployed.

Globalisation dispossesses people as it brings them into an artificial focus. It removes the ability for self-sustaining living, introduces the market as *sine qua non*, counts the people, and then deems them unemployed, or unproductive. For growth to be factored in, loss and deprivation are a necessity: in the case of Malaysia, growth is leading to deforestation and dispossession of a people who have been sustained by their forest environment for thousands of years.

A number of writers have proposed models for a subsistence existence. Gustavo Esteva draws on the experience of Opciones Conviviales de

Mexico, founded in 1998 in order to reflect on and discuss proposals for social organisation which take account of "diversity and pluralism" (2001: 157). The agenda reflects the desire of its members to respect the ability of Mexicans to find for themselves a place which recognises their own very specific location and needs, including joining forces "with others who are struggling to reclaim and regenerate their commons, the places where they practice subsistence" (Esteva 2001: 157). In Bangladesh, Farida Akhter describes a similar process in the peasant-based movement of Nayakrishi Andolon (New Agricultural Movement). Akhter writes that "the goal of Nayakrishi Andolon is not to produce more food for consumers, but to create life, diversity and '*ananda*' (to live a happy life)" (2001: 168). The strength of Nayakrishi Andolon is due to its grounding in "local and indigenous knowledge systems and then critically integrating the insights of modern science where necessary". Its origins are as a "biodiversity-based production system" (2001: 176; see also Mazhar 2000). A biodiversity-based system leaves room and time for happiness and the rhythms of the body.

Feminists have developed significant critiques of work over the past quarter-century. The discontinuity between paid and unpaid work in women's lives is so obvious on a personal level for most women, that once the parallels between a family budget and economics are drawn, many women are quickly able to see the absurdities of the global capitalist system, its contradictions and inequalities.

In critiques which focus on class, women are frequently left out (still). It took until the 1990s for the union movement at large to recognise the necessity of taking into account the very different needs of women workers, and structuring those needs into working conditions, awards and workplace agreements.[36] Marilyn Waring writes:

> There is no consistency from country to country in the activities that are not
> "economic" [i.e. counted as work]. But there is one unwritten rule: if women
> do it in an unpaid capacity in their homes, in their garden plots, or in the
> community, it is housework (1988: 28).

---

36 The work of Zelda D'Aprano (1995, 2001), as a first-hand observer and activist, is important in the Australian context.

Women's work is still invisible. Just as, "women don't fish" and "women don't farm", the refrain "women don't work" can still be heard echoing in from the past.

On the farm where I grew up, only one person – my father – "worked". None of what the rest of us did was considered work. It included droving sheep, collecting eggs, feeding the chooks, milking the cow, classing wool, housework, maintaining the house by painting, changing globes, fixing washers on taps, gardening, sewing, cooking. In that district, almost no one was unemployed. Some were poor. Some were better off. Those who could afford it, employed others. It might be only during the busiest times, but almost everyone worked some of the time. The women, of course, worked all the time. But few of them called it work.

As Waring points out, the satisfaction of human needs – food, shelter, love, clothing, the production of household goods, medicinal substances – none of these needs are considered economically "productive". Production, in the neoclassical system, exists only outside the domestic sphere. Women who make clothes for their children to wear to school do not contribute economically. And yet, as common sense tells us, these clothes makes it possible for children to go to school and focus on things other than survival. In our consumerist age, homemade clothes may not assuage the desire for branded products, but at least they are comfortable or warm.

Within the neoclassical economic world of globalisation – and with such a definition of work – the majority of the world's women do not work. But from research done on how women use their time, it is clear that women work. The delayed entry of women into the official market economy does give women some advantage when it comes to challenging the dominant culture. Because many women are not caught up in the web of markets, they can go on even when the cash dries up, since they are less dependent on producer and consumer systems. The women in Turner and Brownhill's (2001) study were able to resist the process of globalisation because they remembered the collective work groups they had used to produce food in one another's gardens (see Chapter Four). Elisabeth Meyer-Renschhausen (2001) depicts a similar independence from global markets on three organic farms in East Germany, all of whose inhabitants live at a subsistence level, selling produce to Berlin when surpluses occur. Veronika Bennholdt-Thomsen also calls for the "resuscitation of urban subsistence technologies" (2001: 230) and a greater connection between the cities and their surrounding countryside. If this aim were combined with town planning and an architecture which prioritises sustainability, community, connection, and diversity (Mollison 1978; Mobbs 1998; Rogers 1997), along with changes to the concept of work (Gorz 1999), it might be possible to begin in earnest the process of shifting toward a culture inspired by biodiversity.

The Military as Gross Producer and Consumer

It is not my intention to analyse in depth the role of the military in the process of globalisation and in the increasing dislocation of resources. But the military cannot be ignored for its role as both wasteful producer and consumer. The military, as an arm of colonising nations, has always had a role in the dispossession of the colonised. Played out in different ways in different nations, the outcome has usually been the same. Indigenous communities worldwide are the main sites of nuclear testing, with devastating results for the people and with long-term effects on the environment (dé Ishtar 1994, 1998; LaDuke 1999; Kuletz 1998).

The military, through dictatorships, has become a way for elites in poor countries to accumulate vast assets, maintain secret bank accounts, and retain temporal power as has been the case, for example, in Indonesia, the Republic of Congo, and Angola in recent years.

The internet is a military invention. The internet can and has been used for beneficial purposes for activism (the demolition of the MAI agreement, and the networking of grassroots organisations are two examples) and for creativity, but the logic of the internet draws it in the direction of the dominating culture. Increased privatisation – payment for time use such as in accessing scientific information (Correy 2001b), the increased mobility of digital capital, and the exploitation of the diversity matrix (prostitution, cultural appropriation, molecular and bioprospecting) – is creating a network that works for the elites of the world. Like the infrastructure of the export processing zones, the infrastructure of the internet is intended for the owners of capital, not for those who labour to produce it.

Conclusion

The globalisation of production, of work and of consumption is resulting in large displacements of people – the poor and women – in both the rich and the poor countries. The process can be summarised as follows.

Transnational companies, through increased disconnection from the place of origin, begin to focus more on profit than on responsibility to their community. They realise that greater profits are to be made by shifting their centres of production from countries where wages are relatively high to countries where wages are barely high enough to live on. They close their factories and move off-shore. In the process, thousands of people become unemployed, and eventually invisible. In the poor country, the cheapest workers are drawn into the economy; in the main these are indigenous peoples, rural people and young women. Prior to working in transnational companies, they have lived outside the market economy and contributed to local and domestic economies, often with very little need for cash. Within the transnational company structure, they are exploited, given the most meaningless tasks, sometimes enslaved or criminalised. They cannot move to other countries unless they do so as sex workers or as donors of body parts, as illegal immigrants, refugees, or temporary guest workers with few legal rights. They become dependent on the cash economy through debt, and because they no longer have access to common resources such as forests, coastal or estuarine fishing grounds, or land which allows them to grow their own food, they are further impoverished.

Dislocation of production creates dislocation in work. The person evicted from the wage-work system finds her- or himself in a system predicated on jobs, but which has no jobs to offer. The jobless are incessantly forced to look for non-existent jobs, jobs which have been exported to a country with low wages. In the poor country, health and safety regulations are compromised, environmental safeguards are rare, and tax is minimised. In addition, the infrastructure is geared toward the needs of the transnationals, not of the workers. In many instances, it is paid for in loans from the Official Development Assistance coffers of Japan, or the World Bank, or similar regional organisations such as the Asian Development Bank. The person in the poor country can sometimes find employment, but in jobs which have high accident rates, jobs which further dispossess them and their communities through environmental degradation, or jobs which do not offer any future, or any skill development which could be used to improve their situation.

Dislocation of consumption is the next occurrence. Coca-Cola is available everywhere, as are McDonald's and a host of other junk foods, and branded consumer products. In every city, in every airport, one sees the same retail outlets offering the same goods or slight variations on them. As consumers, it is almost impossible to know how and where and by whom a particular product is made. If it is made in Saipan, in the Northern Marianas, it is labelled "Made in the USA". Gap and Nike have had bad press for the poor conditions of their workers, but how many consumers translate this into action? And if not Gap or Nike, does the consumer know whether Reebok or Adidas has any better a track record? With diversification within companies, can the consumer know in what other areas their favourite brand name is operating? Orin Langelle identifies Toyota's role in the emerging biotechnology business (2001: 114). Bioengineered trees – so they claim – will grow quickly and create carbon credits, excusing Toyota from reducing carbon dioxide emissions from the cars it produces. Corporations are also coming up with the means for disguising a brand which has had bad publicity. Many Nike products include the "swoosh" but not the word "Nike". Interlocking ownership of numerous brand names means that even those who want to boycott certain products or companies need to keep a constant track of transnational mergers and buy-outs. Simply remembering the long lists of brands can be a daunting task. In the area of drug companies and biotechnology, there has been an extraordinary number of mergers and renamings of companies, so that companies with compromised track record can start again. Table 2 in the Appendix summarises some of the name changes in companies discussed in this book.

André Gorz lays the blame for the way in which globalisation has developed on "the pre-eminence of the criteria of financial profitability" (1999: 5). To put it in terms of Marimba Ani's (2000) analysis, the inspiration for corporate globalisation is the accumulation of money. A different inspiration, such as biodiversity, would enable the development of very different systems, closer to the one suggested by the concept of wild politics.

I suggest, therefore, that western culture is standing at a crossroads: it can move forward toward a society defined by accumulation and dislocation, or toward one in which location, self-organisation and diversity determine social relations.

CHAPTER SEVEN

MONOCULTURES AND
MULTILATERAL TRADE RULES

> *Biodiversity cannot be saved with biotechnology.*
> *Only a commitment to diversity at all levels*
> *can nurture other species; monocultures*
> *are the problem, not the solution*
> – Martha L. Crouch (2001: 36).

Two background systems – patents law and multilateral trade agreements – are central to the operation of new global rules. In turn, these systems are underpinned by concepts of equality built upon European liberal philosophy, systems of knowledge which valorise universalism and objectivity, power relations which enable the powerful to increase their power at the expense of the powerless, and western property ownership rules which are built upon disconnection from place. These systems have all been challenged in the last three decades by radical thinkers from the diversity matrix.

Although all of these groups have offered interesting challenges, those which I have found most useful in developing a critique of global corporatisation are feminist and indigenous theories, with some additional input from class and environmental perspectives. Feminism as "a thorough-going critique of male domination wherever it is found and however it is manifested" (Thompson 2001: 21) is critical to all of my theoretical analyses, and I suggest that corporate globalisation is an extreme form of masculinist domination. It allies itself with other dominations of wealth and cultural elitism and with a displaced sensibility based on universalism, objectivity, disconnection from nature and neoliberal utilitarianism.

Opposite: Street theatre during Melbourne's S11 protest in 2000.

Patents

The history of patents mirrors important shifts in western systems of law, in concepts of property rights, and in what counts as "property". Patents are the product of a western, European-American legal system, a concept which emerged gradually through a combination of royal or elite privilege combined with laws on mining. Erich Kaufer describes the process by which common law on mining rights was gradually developed to include the concept of invention. During the medieval period, the European Alps were an important centre for mining, in particular for silver ore. A common-law tradition existed in the Alps which concerned the how "mining, timber use, and water use property rights" were obtained (Kaufer 1989: 2).[1] This is the point – the late medieval era – which represents in the European development of ideas the critical intersection between intellectual property rights and property rights represented by real property, land, including the overlapping concept of exclusive access. New locations for ore sites were accidentally discovered, or, in the language of the period, "invented" (Latin *invenire*, meaning accidental discovery). As ore bodies became increasingly difficult to access, they required increased capital investment in order to drain water out of the ore site. The financiers of these developments were granted special privileges enabling them to recoup their investment through the ore dug from the mine.

Alongside these changes in the notion of "invention" came developments in the Italian city states, and Venice, for instance, was in need of specialists in drainage. In 1323, the Venetians extended privileges to Johannes Teuthonicus, a German master of the "water arts" developed in the mines. The Venetians asked him to invent grain mills which would satisfy the various needs of a growing population, as well as draining the lagoons and dredging the canals. They asked that he build a model, and if it proved useful he would receive a grant and privileges. The first patent code was developed in March 1474, and provided rewards for inventiveness among its citizens (Kaufer 1989: 5; Shiva 2001f: 14).

In the northern European states, notions of property were shifting. Private ownership of land is relatively recent, and it was only in the sixteenth century that the English Enclosure Acts shifted the idea of ownership

---

1   As Vandana Shiva would say, this is a local system which has become universalised through colonisation.

from "ownership in common" to "private property". The Enclosure Acts assigned exclusive rights to the natural world, including land, waterways, mineral deposits, crops and animal herds, and resulted in the mass dispossession of poor people. This was an early move in the direction of privatisation. At this time the laws applied in England only. When colonisation by European monarchs began, the monarchs sent out "letters patent" with the captains of their ships. The "letters patent" enabled European monarchs to claim ownership rights to "newly discovered lands" through the granting of certain exclusive and open privileges to the carriers of "letters patent".[2] This development represented the beginning of the process of colonisation, and indicated a shift toward disconnection from the place of residence. Although other empires throughout history had expanded their lands to cover territories distinct from their homelands, this was the first move to expand that imperial intent to a truly global extent, and incorporate lands from many continents, including lands the very existence of which had been deemed questionable in the preceding centuries.

Notions of privatisation, disconnection and universalism are critical to the shifting conceptions of ownership in the early stages of capitalism. They are accompanied by a massive grab for land wherever it might be, resulting in the concentration of ownership in the hands of a very small elite, primarily European monarchs. The lands acquired by the European monarchs led to an enormous growth in European economies, founded on the resources, the goods and the labour of the lands and their peoples in the colonies. European monarchies were – and remain – pre-eminently masculine structures, massively favouring the fathers and the sons of the aristocracy. As Maria Mies argues, the sexual division of labour reflects the international division of labour between the rich and poor countries of the world (1986/1999: 74–144). These developments also led to significant waves of migration, the first of which was the migration of Europeans, and the forced migration of Africans, to the Americas. The central features of globalisation are, therefore, already visible by the sixteenth century.

---

2   "In medieval Europe, royal letters closed by a seal were called 'litterae clausae;' those that were sealed but open were 'litterae patentes.' Litterae patentes thus were open documents granting the holder certain rights, privileges, titles or offices" (Kaufer 1989: 1).

In 1623, during the reign of James I of England, the English parliament passed the *Statute of Monopolies* (Kaufer 1989: 6), which prevented the Crown from capriciously giving monopolies to favourites or selling the monopolies to raise money. An inventor, therefore, was granted a limited monopoly on his or her invention. Exempted from its ban was:

> any grant of a "patent of monopoly" to the "first inventor" of any new manufacture which applied to industry, process or piece of equipment *already known abroad* or something newly "invented" in the modern meaning of the word (Heaton 1964: 482, my emphasis).

Structured into the patent law, therefore, is the right to appropriate (steal) from abroad. England was encouraging her citizens to copy the inventions of others and claim them as her own, encouraging what would be called "capitalist enterprise", or "initiative". This idea has a contemporary equivalent in the bioprospecting industry.

In 1641, in the colony of New England, the General Court of Massachusetts also outlawed monopolies, following the model of the earlier English law. Similar laws were passed in Connecticut (1672) and South Carolina (1691). The laws allowed public ownership for the common good, but the implications were different since the colony was not an independent monarchy, and the South Carolina law makers spoke of "patents not as sovereign grants, but as a fulfillment of the rights of the inventor" (Kaufer 1989: 7). Today, the anti-monopoly laws in the USA remain a potent force, as can be seen in the US government's case against Microsoft in 2000. Such a law might have resulted in a very different history of patents, had public ownership become the direction of future shifts in law. That, however, was not to be so. Instead, in 1770, the US Constitution, Article 1, Section 8, secured exclusive rights for authors and inventors, and in 1793, the first federal patent law came into force in the USA.

The institutionalisation of patents came about when Richard Arkwright invented a new kind of spinning machine – the water-powered spinning frame – which enabled the process of spinning to be industrialised, changing it from a cottage industry to a factory-based industry. It gave the English spinners a competitive advantage which they were keen to maintain. The British parliament "enacted a series of restrictive measures, including the prohibition of the export of Arkwright machinery or the emigration of any workers who had been employed in factories using the Arkwright invention" (Burrows 2001a: 239). Fines and jail sentences backed up the patent provisions.

In 1790, Samuel Slater, who had previously worked in the Arkwright mills, migrated to the USA where, from memory, and with financial backing, he created an "entire Arkwright factory and all its equipment" (Burrows 2001a: 239). The result was that the North Americans were able to build their own machines and develop industry in their own way, thereby becoming independent of European monopolies over power and invention, and showing just how profitable theft could be. The *US Patent Act* followed in 1793, and defined the inventions which could be eligible for patent protection. It did not include organic or naturally occurring substances for patent protection. In the meantime, in England, Arkwright's patent was challenged, and in 1785 was annulled (Heaton 1964: 553).

In examining the most important international agreements on intellectual-property rights, it emerges that a significant number of them have not been agreed to by the USA. The USA has not entered into the following agreements (Benko 1987: 51–55):

- Berne Convention (1886): provides protection for copyright on literary and artistic works (the US is a party to the 1952 Universal Copyright Convention)
- Madrid Agreement (1891): regulates the source of goods and the registration of marks
- Hague Agreement (1925): provides for international deposit of industrial designs
- Lisbon Agreement (1958): provides for protection of appellations of origin
- Locarno Agreement (1968): seeks to establish international uniformity in registration of industrial designs
- Trademark Registration Treaty (1973): intends to facilitate international uniformity in trademarks
- Budapest Treaty (1977): covers the patenting of micro-organisms and moves in the direction of globalisation with a single "international depository authority" whereby a culture sample is deposited

It is significant that the USA has been very reluctant to join international agreements in the past. I suggest it is because this "omission" allowed for copying of inventions developed outside the USA, and was intended to reduce the likelihood of litigation. In the light of recent global developments and occurrences – such as the patent granted on basmati rice in 1997 to Texas-based RiceTec and the subsequent protests by Indian farmers against the patent (Shiva 2001c: 357–358; Dutfield 2000: 87–88) – the decision of the USA not to ratify the Lisbon Agreement proved to be significant. The USA has not signed the Convention on Biological Diversity, and President George W. Bush has continued to resist all arguments in favour of ratifying the Kyoto Protocol.

The Lisbon Agreement was followed by the Paris Convention (1967), which covered the protection of industrial property including "patents, utility models, industrial designs, trademarks, service marks, trade names and indications of source or appellations of origin" (Lal Das 1999: 361).

Until 1931, patents were limited to an industry, a process or a piece of equipment, and, with the Berne Convention (1886), to copyrights on products of the imagination as they had been in the eighteenth-century patent laws. In 1931, a significant change occurred when Henry F. Bosenberg was granted a patent for "Climbing or Trailing Rose". His was the first patent on a plant. The ruling covers plants which reproduce asexually – not tubers, but does include "cultivated sports, mutants, hybrids, newly found seedlings or a plant found in an uncultivated state" (35 USC Sec 161 Patents for Plants cited in Wilson 2001: 292). In 1939, Title 35 of the *US Patent Act* allowed for patents on new and useful information, not just finished products. By the end of World War II, when the Bretton Woods institutions were being established, these two significant changes had occurred. Their significance lies in the widening of opportunities for acquiring patents. They make it possible to gain profits from research and development and/or from observing what others do and lodging a patent in one's own home territory. The *Plant Variety Protection Act, 1970* (USA) expanded the 1931 ruling to include protection of certain sexually reproduced plants which, in turn, has led to the current extreme consolidation of the seed industry.

In 1961, the International Convention for the Protection of New Varieties of Plants (UPOV)[3] was ratified, including by the USA.

---

3   UPOV stands for Union Internationale pour la Protection des Obtentions Végétales: International Convention for the Protection of New Varieties of Plants.

Protection is afforded through special titles or patents; it covers the use of plant varieties for commercial use, and the plant has to be clearly distinguishable (Benko 1987: 52).

The objective of the UPOV agreement and its amendments (1961, 1978, 1991) was to "grant certain exclusive rights to plant breeders who develop new varieties of plants" (Lal Das 1999: 365). Over time, the agreement has come to favour plant breeders more heavily than it does farmers. And it is the extension of these rights which has made it possible to prohibit farmers from saving patented seed and replanting it in the following season.

In 1985, "an arbitrary decision of the US Patent and Trade Mark Office in the Hibberd case ... redefined plants as machines" (Shiva 2001f: 98). The "*Ex parte Kenneth Hibberd*" decision resulted in the granting of patents on "the tissue culture, seed, and whole plant of a corn line selected from tissue culture" (Shiva 2001f: 77; *Ex Parte Hibberd 227 USPQ (BNA) 443*, at 444). More than 260 claims were approved, concentrating intellectual ownership of plants. The UPOV agreement, especially the 1991 amendments, tends to protect the rights of industry rather than the rights of farmers (Shiva 2001c: 357). Interestingly, by 1996 the USA was the only country to have signed the UPOV 1991 agreement, which reduced the ability of plant-variety breeders to re-use a protected variety as a source of a new variety, and made the farmers' privilege of re-selling harvested seed optional. This amendment is significant because it fosters the intensification of the power of seed companies over individuals such as gardeners and farmers.

The problem with UPOV 1991 as it stands is that it is "as monopolistic as patent regimes" (Shiva 2001f: 101). Like patents, the legislation introduces standardisation which, when translated into plants in a field, results in vulnerability to pests and diseases. And because it makes the continuation of farmers' varieties impossible, it destroys biodiversity (Shiva 2001f: 100).

In 2001, the *Plant Variety Protection Act, 1970* was being tested again in the US courts, in the case of *Pioneer v. JEM Ag Supply*, which focuses on the purchase of bags of patented (non-GMO) seed. The case is about utility patents which restrict the re-use of seed, and selling of seed by farmers and independent seed companies. The result, if Pioneer wins the case, will be increased concentration of the seed market, homogenisation of seed because of restricted utility, and prevention of public access to patented seed (Dechant 2001: 6).

All these changes initiated in the 1960s constituted thoroughgoing shifts in the way in which originality was perceived and rewarded. But the following decade was to see even more radical change to the structures of patents law.

The first event occurred in 1972 when Ananda Mohan Chakrabarty applied for a patent on micro-organisms which can increase the oil-degrading properties of certain bacteria. Chakrabarty licensed the patent to his employer, General Electric. The patent was subsequently granted on the genetic engineering process, but was denied on the bacteria itself which, as a living organism, was considered unpatentable subject matter under title 35, US Code 101. But General Electric and Chakrabarty appealed the 1972 decision arising from the Court of Customs and Patent Appeals; this time, the court ruled in their favour, and General Electric was issued with Patent No. 4,259,444. The ruling was challenged in 1978 when the Commissioner of Trademarks sought *certiorari*[4] for the *Diamond v. Chakrabarty* case because it contradicted the existing law in Title 35. In 1980, the Supreme Court, in a close five-to-four decision, upheld the ruling in *Diamond v. Chakrabarty*. At the time there was no legislation in Congress to uphold the contradiction, but the Supreme Court judgment effectively led the way in shifting the law on patents (Wilson 2001: 292–295). Beth Burrows, in an interview conducted in 1994 with an anonymous industry analyst, asked why *Diamond v. Chakrabarty* seemed to have been uncontroversial at the time. The analyst replied:

When we went for life patents, they were kept quiet by the fact that the first patent applied for was for a microorganism that could eat oil. You think that was an accident? What environmentalist was going to get in the way of something that might clean up oil spills? (in Burrows 2001a: 248).[5]

---

4   This refers to issuing a writ to procure records from a lower court for review in a higher court.

5   But I remember a reaction from concerned academics. I was a student in the Philosophy Department at the University of Melbourne in 1980, and I recall seeing on a notice board in the corridor a call for help to protest against the shift in patent laws. I noticed first the reference to seeds, a familiar item for a farm-bred student, then I read the document, and although I did nothing about it, it had an enduring impact on me.

The Chakrabarty decision opened the way for biotechnology, and in 1986 the biotechnology regulatory framework was codified. It regarded genetic engineering as simply an extension of traditional plant and animal breeding. In 1987, the US Patent Office used the Chakrabarty decision to expand the legal definition of "man-made", with the result that multi-cellular organisms – including animals – became eligible for patent protection. With an approach not dissimilar to the oil-eating micro-organisms, but this time focusing on cancer research, the Oncomouse became the first animal patent. The patent covered all non-human "onco-animals". This means that DuPont owns the patent for any species which are bio-engineered to contain a wide variety of genes which cause cancer. An attempt was made to have a two-year moratorium on animal patenting, but the 1988 *Transgenic Animal Patent Reform Act* was defeated in Congress.

The European Patent Office decided that the Oncomouse (application No. 85 304 490.7) was not patentable, as a mouse, but that the process was (Bercovitz 1991: 152). This debate in Germany, no doubt, was influenced by a mass protest involving over 200 organisations including feminists, environmentalists and church bodies, which led the European parliament to pass a resolution in February 1993 in which it communicated its "decisive resistance against the granting of this patent" (GID 1993: 7).[6]

In Europe and Japan (and many other countries) plants and animals remain ineligible for patent protection, although "microbiological processes or the products thereof" can be patented (Benko 1987: 44; Bercovitz 1991). This difference in approach has created conflict, and is generally phrased as "uncertainties" (Benko 1987: 44) created by these laws. But it is not a matter of uncertainty, it is a matter of a difference of law. Such re-phrasings are found frequently in the literature on patents and copyright;[7] they are particularly evident in differences in approach between developed and Third World nations or between indigenous knowledge and corporate knowledge. For example, although the wealth of developed western nations has been made possible through the colonisation of land, of

---

6   This information was drawn to my attention by Renate Klein, who also provided the translation.

7   For a discussion on copyright with particular reference to developments in software see Woo (2000).

resources, and, more recently, of knowledge about medicinal uses of plants, the wealthy countries now complain that the less developed countries are "stealing Western technologies" (Benko 1987: 29).

Vandana Shiva makes an interesting observation about the connections between the origins of capitalism and the development of western systems of property rights. She refers to the work of John Locke (1632–1704), and her description of his writings about property and the process of stealing that capitalism legitimises is instructive. As Shiva interprets him:

> Only capital can add value to appropriated nature, and hence only those who own capital have the natural right to own natural resources; a right that supersedes the common rights of others with prior claims. Capital is thus defined as a source of freedom, but this freedom is based on the denial of freedom to the land, forests, rivers and biodiversity that capital claims as its own. Because property obtained through privatization of the commons is equated with freedom, those commoners laying claim to it are perceived to be depriving the owners of capital of their freedom (2001f: 43).

Vandana Shiva succinctly summarises the connection between bio-prospecting, globalisation, and the transnational sector's view of claims by indigenous peoples about ownership of their knowledge of natural resources. It is not surprising, therefore, to find these views enshrined in multilateral agreements on Intellectual Property Rights (IPRs) which have their origins in western systems of property law.

Multilateral Trade Agreements and the Shape of International Law

In 1947, the General Agreement on Tariffs and Trade (GATT) was signed in Geneva by twenty-three countries. GATT was developed as part of the 1944 Bretton Woods institutions, which include the World Bank and the IMF. Over the last fifty-five years the world has changed considerably, and some of the principles on which GATT is based no longer hold. Environmental issues, for example, are not written into the agreement, and "GATT has consistently failed to keep up with the global environ-mental crisis" (Daly and Goodland 1994: 77).

What has changed little, however, is the shape of power in its insti-tutionalised forms. The multilateralisation of the world economy has

developed in tandem with globalising institutions, which have sewn up the rules that govern behaviour of states and corporations in such a way as to benefit those who hold power. The constitutional frameworks which have been developed – the Bretton Woods institutions, the WTO, NAFTA – work to the advantage of transnational capital (Gill 1997: 11). To approach these frameworks from below disadvantages those in the diversity matrix – whether they are constituted as individuals or as a group or community, or whether the frameworks are applied in the larger context of nations, cultures and even cross-cultural marginality. Power imbalances show most starkly in situations of sudden change, such as those that have occurred with the demise of communism in Eastern Europe, in the Asian financial crash of 1997, in the continuing crisis afflicting African nations, and in the ability of the USA to maintain its market buoyancy reasonably well in the face of the collapse of the twin towers of the World Trade Center on 11 September 2001.[8] Fantu Cheru and Stephen Gill argue that crises of this nature are the result of "a global system of political economy that is profoundly unequal in terms of power and distributional consequences" (1997: 162). Power and its consequences are central to the mechanisms of multilateral trade agreements, which have been gradually increasing in importance since the 1970s, to the extent that in the twenty-first century, multilateralism has become the major shaper of international relations. Multilateralism in a context of very small differences in power could operate equitably if it worked on principles such as those which have been elaborated here: if biodiversity rather than profit were the inspiration; if diversity rather than "monocultures of the mind" (Shiva 1993a) were a guiding principle; if outcomes and consequences were measured by their benefit to the poorest rather than to the elites – then the rules governing multilateral agreements would be very different from what they are now.

The view that free trade, bolstered by multilateral agreements, is beneficial to everyone, is specifically articulated in the GATT (1992). The GATT document specifies that the only tension between trade and

---

8   Market values did drop significantly, particularly in areas directly affected by the attack, such as insurance and airlines, but it did not lead to mass collapses of companies. It is also likely that the war will bring economic relief in some sectors of the economy (see Waring 1988 for a discussion on how war bolsters the economy). For a discussion of the impact of 11 September on business, see Randall (2001: 188–202).

its impact on the environment lies in the correct assigning of value to environmental resources, and that at least as much environmental and man-made capital should be passed on to the next generation as was received. Sustainable development, in this view, will be a realistic goal, and as much trade as possible can then flow from it (GATT 1992: 20). The argument I am pursuing here, however, is more like that of Inge Røpke (1994), who puts forward a case for less trade. The context of trade, its environmental impacts through appropriation and privatisation of knowledge, as well as the sheer amount of energy expended in moving goods around the world, are all crucial considerations in discussions of the benefits or losses of free trade.

Multilateral Trade Negotiations and the Convention on Biological Diversity

Between 1973 and 1979, the Tokyo Round of Multilateral Trade Negotiations took place. Tariff reduction was its main focus. This Round strengthened disciplines on non-tariff measures, unfair trade and obstructions to trade. Agreement covered areas of subsidy, dumping, government procurement, technical barriers to trade, customs valuation, import licensing, civil aircraft, dairy products and bovine meat (Lal Das 1999: 5).

The Uruguay Round of Multilateral Trade Negotiations, which followed between 1986 and 1994, dealt with new areas of trade that were of interest to developed countries, including services, intellectual property rights and investments. High-technology, knowledge-intensive industries and increased flexibility in investment opportunities became more important than commodities and manufactured goods. The results of this round of negotiations can be seen in debates about copyright, patents and intellectual property, as well as in issues focusing on health and service provisions through local and regional authorities. During the Uruguay Round of negotiations, the Convention on Biological Diversity (CBD) was introduced at the 1992 Earth Summit in Rio de Janeiro. The CBD at first appeared to have the potential to protect biodiverse countries from exploitation of their resources in the event of discoveries of new plants. Two obstacles, however, are in the way of its effectiveness: firstly, the USA, where most large bioprospecting corporations are based, has not signed it; and secondly, the convention contains a loophole, which is that transnational corporations and bioprospectors can still source colonial collections gathered prior to 1992.[9] That there is, at least, some protection afforded to biodiversity is due in large part to solidarity among delegates from the South in maintaining "sovereignty over natural resources" (Law 1997: 182). Article 8(j) of the convention states:

> Subject to national legislation, respect, preserve and maintain knowledge innovations and practices of indigenous and local communities embodying traditional lifestyles relevant for the conservation and sustainable use of biological diversity and promote their wider application with the approval and involvement of the holders of such knowledge, innovations and practices and encourage the equitable sharing of the benefits arising from the utilization of such knowledge, innovations and practices (in Shiva 1993a: 166).

There are, however, some problems with the measured neutrality of this article (as is frequently the case with language in much official documentation).

First of all there is the problem of national legislation, and the question of whether such legislation is well thought out and provides adequately for the poorest groups, or even for the profitability of small companies based inside the country; or whether it has been put together under pressure from transnational companies, or for the profit of the state and corporate magnates. Implementation, therefore, can become a major hurdle, although efforts have been made to suggest model laws to assist in the implementation of the CBD (Posey and Dutfield 1996: 147–153; Shiva 2001c: 356–357). Among the suggestions are to maintain the right for communities "to veto commercial exploitation" (Posey and Dutfield 1996: 147) or, conversely, to share profits if the community agrees to commercialisation.

How "indigenous and local communities" will be able to maintain their "knowledge innovations" is also important. It is possible for these

---

9   The Royal Botanic Gardens at Kew, London, has agreements to return some benefits of research or collection to its partners. Such partnerships are entered into with other institutions (never individuals), usually botanic or scientific institutions (Posey and Dutfield 1996: 72). Indigenous peoples rarely have institutional status. There is a Catch-22 for indigenous peoples: for an institution to have standing in international fora it has to accept the basic worldview of neoliberalism; if it were organised with the aim to maintain the integrity of indigenous systems, it would likely be discounted and not recognised.

communities to maintain their culture but be simultaneously dispossessed of it and remain extremely poor (Dove 1993).

The CBD also asks that indigenous and local communities "promote the wider application" of traditional knowledge, but the text does not indicate any means by which "wider application" should be promoted. As Darrell Posey points out, "Biodiversity prospectors assume that organisms and ecosystems are wild and therefore part of the public domain" (1996: 8). Like so many before them, the prospectors enclose, appropriate and commodify the public domain, turning it into a private resource. What happens in the majority of cases is that bioprospectors enter a community, talk with the people and find out which plants have commercial potential. These plants, which may already be held in colonial collections outside the community, are then commodified, patented and made profitable – not for the community, but for the transnational company. The only plants still protected are those which were never collected and deposited in a scientific, national or private collection prior to 1992. Appropriation is not limited to plants. It can also take the shape of cultural appropriation of religious rituals or images, or of community events or artwork or music through photography, filming or sound recording (Posey and Dutfield 1996: 116). Stephen Gray, in discussing Australian Aboriginal art, refers to art as a "'nature or incident' of land ownership: the two in fact are quite inseparable if not actually the same" (1993: 11). Art, as much as land, cannot be appropriated without disrupting communal systems of reciprocity and responsibility.

In such circumstances, the "wild" is being appropriated because it is perceived to be separate from the human world. But, as I have argued throughout this book, the "wild" is not uninhabited or unclaimed. It is not a *terra nullius*. Rather, the wild is and should be a continuous part of our life, and of the lives of those who will live with the earth we leave behind. Intergenerational issues, and the possibility of collective owner-ship in the present and the future, are areas which need to be explored urgently.

Faced with these problems, national laws need to put the require-ments and wishes of communities at the centre of legislation, rather than the pursuit of individual or corporate profit. For instance, collectors could be required to abide by conditions, such as meeting ethical-conduct requirements, signing legal documents, detailing plans for collection and later storage, and crucially returning of the new (and old) knowledge to the community. Such agreements could limit the possibility of patent applications made from within or outside the country of collection (Posey and Dutfield 1996: 149). Maintaining control of the resources by the local communities is similar to Tuhiwai Smith's (1999) suggestion that indigenous peoples should control research undertaken of their cultures by outsiders.

The CBD does argue for "the equitable sharing of the benefits" of knowledge innovation. But again, the text fails to specify who should share and who should benefit. With overwhelming appropriation of indigenous and traditional knowledge, it is the powerless who are asked to share, and the powerful who for the most part get to benefit. The court battles over neem and basmati rice are good examples of the tensions between traditional knowledge beneficiaries and transnational beneficiaries (Dutfield 2000: 66, 87–88, 132–134; Shiva 2001f: 56–61). Posey and Dutfield suggest that it is not sufficient to share profits with the community, but that "IPR protection for the knowledge" should be put in place (1996: 148). The Brazilian *Indigenous Societies Act* goes further, insisting on "The provision that IPR of indigenous communities are perpetual" (Posey and Dutfield 1996: 152).

The CBD is phrased in language that echoes my earlier discussion of "not seeing", as it ignores differences in power and resources, and disregards several facts: for instance, that for some indigenous peoples benefits would need to be restricted to the local community and that universalising benefits can result in biodiversity loss, as occurred with the Ethiopian plant endod[10] (Posey and Dutfield 1996: 81). Local knowledge is "fragile because it is local" (Hunn 1999: 24). And the value of traditional environmental knowledge is cross-culturally cumulative. By contrast, western science strives for universal relevance and global scope. It also privileges the standardisation of knowledge through valorising the written over the oral, the abstract over the real. The Ngarrindjeri women of South Australia confronted the contradictions of the universal/local, and written/oral, as well as the specialised knowledge of women and men (or of some women who have more specialised knowledge than do some other women) in their battle against the development of the bridge linking Hindmarsh

---

10 See the discussion under the sub-heading, TRIPs later in this chapter.

Island to the mainland (Bell 1998; von Doussa 2001). These are issues of the intricate connection between cultural and intellectual property and the protection of basic human rights (Stephenson 1999: 235).

Equity of outcome is not related in any way to equity of inputs. This recalls the generalised failure of the "tragedy of the commons" argument because it ignores social and physical context, and takes for granted that private benefit – either for a corporation or for an individual, as in "economic man's" maximising utility – is always more important than public benefit, whether collective or individual. As Fairlie, Hafler and O'Riordan make quite plain, "many apparent Tragedies of the Commons are, upon investigation, revealed instead to be Tragedies of Enclosure" (1995: 61).

Although, as Darrell Posey and Graham Dutfield highlight (1996: 104), the CBD at least specifically mentions indigenous and local communities, the vagueness of the language means that the implementation of the CBD will be determined by the political and cultural will of the people in power. If profit, corporatisation, continued biopiracy and appropriation remain the norm, little will change. If, however, the direction of global culture were to shift and issues such as biodiversity became central, and importantly, the poorest and most vulnerable citizens moved to the centre of decision-making structures, then the CBD could become a powerful force in guiding change and priorities.

Such a shift is not yet apparent among most politicians, and is certainly not on the agenda of the transnational corporations. And for all the goodwill toward indigenous and traditional knowledges expressed in the CBD – in particular mechanisms spelt out in articles 16 and 18.4 – it needs to be actively implemented through an appropriate vision for its workability. For example, Article 16.1 includes biotechnology and the issue of "sustainable use of biological diversity" (Shiva 1993a: 169). When there is a conflict over resources – such as in the fishing or forestry industries – the benefits rarely point in the direction of the indigenous or traditional owners. Further, research programs mentioned in Article 18.5 are most likely to be useful to local communities if projects are framed according to the needs of the community, not the needs of outsiders (Tuhiwai Smith 1999: 123–141; Posey and Dutfield 1996: 156ff). A project funded by a transnational company with the aim of determining the active ingredients of a range of plants or naturally occurring substances which then went on to patent the active ingredient – even if it proved universally beneficial to people's health and paid some royalties to the local community – would not, in my view, be a positive outcome. In order to abide by the spirit of the CBD, such research programs should be devised by local communities themselves, using their priorities as central to the framing of the research and the accountability of those engaged in the research.

The CBD also deals with protocols. Posey and Dutfield argue that biosafety protocols should "cover the impact of biotechnology and its risks on local communities" (1996: 110). With the increasingly blemished record of companies such as Monsanto, Aventis/AgrEvo, A/F Protein/ AquaBounty, Fletcher Challenge (aka Rubicon) and numerous others engaged in biotechnology, Article 18.5 sounds unrealistic. The companies have all been the subject of protests from farmers, from indigenous fishing peoples, from people concerned about the long-term well-being of forests. Yet, their only response has been to change their names,[11] to create nice-sounding propaganda uploaded on to accessible websites[12] (or to have the website endlessly "under construction"), and do nothing other than con-tinue on the same research road without acknowledging the wishes and needs of local people.

The real outcome of the Uruguay Round of GATT is that it "obligates all signatory states, including over 80 developing nations to implement intellectual property provisions for plant varieties and microorganisms" (Shand 1998: 2). Through such multilateral pressure, obligations based on appropriative western systems of law are creating moral and legal contradictions for developing nations. If nations sign up, they effectively give transnational companies *carte blanche* access to intellectual knowledge from traditional resources developed over centuries (or millennia) by their people. If they decide not to sign up, they remain outside the club of nations with whom the rich countries will willingly trade. The latter is a difficult decision for countries whose economies have already been made dependent on global trade systems by developing export-oriented industries in order to earn hard currency.

---

11 See Appendix, Table 2. It is also possible that, by changing their names and thereby their legal identities, they are protecting themselves from litigation.

12 See, for example the Westvaco website (www.westvaco.com).

Darrell Posey and Graham Dutfield pose the question: "Are legally binding international agreements useful?" (1996: 101). After considering the points raised above, I suggest they are not very likely to be, since the international agreements are phrased in the language of the powerful, and the careful neutrality disguises an unequal playing field – on which, if no changes occur, it is rich countries and their transnational companies who score. For social change to move in the direction of indigenous and traditional peoples (or farmers who want to farm sustainably and organically), a great deal has to happen by way of national legislation. Similarly and crucially, significant attitudinal changes have to take place even to begin the process. One hopeful sign is a change in Costa Rican law.

In April 1998, Costa Rica passed the *Ley de Biodiversidad* (Biodiversity Law), an ambitious law which attempts to implement the CBD. Its general principles include in summary:

- respect for all forms of life
- the elements of biodiversity are meritorious
- respect for cultural diversity
- intra- and inter-generational equity (Dutfield 2000: 111).

It remains to be seen whether the principles will be upheld or subverted through the multilateral structures. What follows is a discussion of the other important multilateral instruments.

The World Trade Organisation (WTO)

The World Trade Organisation came into existence in 1995 in Marrakesh. Its foundation followed the ratification of GATT, and it now has responsibility for regulating world trade. Although there has been a name-change and an extension of responsibilities, the foundations of the WTO are those built up during the GATT period (1948–95). The aim of the establishment of the WTO was to "harmonise" legal trade arrangements for member countries. Among the "harmonisations" which have been sought over many decades are those relating to patents.

> We favour harmonization of national patent laws, and we look to the ultimate goal of a true universal or multinational patent (Trowbridge 1967, cited in Schäfers 1991: 57).

The implicit and explicit aim is the worldwide spread of western systems of law to satisfy the "needs of industrialized countries" (Pretnar 1990: 249; see also Posey and Dutfield 1996: 94). The regulation of trade does not focus on the people who produce goods; rather, it focuses on those who benefit most from globalisation, namely, transnational corporations, international banks and national elites. As Michel Chossudovsky points out, the GATT agreement "violates fundamental peoples' rights, particularly in the areas of foreign investment, biodiversity and intellectual property rights" (1998: 35). One principle that has not changed since 1948 is the push by the USA to open up world markets for its own goods. GATT has been successful in making world markets more susceptible to US goods, or to goods produced by US companies in other cheap-labour markets.

The founding of the WTO was accompanied by Trade Related Intellectual Property rights (TRIPs). Intellectual Property Rights (IPRs) cover promotion of technological innovation; technology transfer; provisions for patents, copyright, trademarks, geographical indications (basmati rice, champagne), industrial designs, layout designs of integrated circuits, undisclosed information (trade secrets) (Lal Das 1999: 355–393). The General Agreement on Trade in Services (GATS) is also part of the WTO provisional[13] intentions. The GATS includes provisions for supply of services from one country to another. When complete liberalisation has occurred, free trade in services is potentially possible without any restrictions. This favours rich countries, and corporations specialising in service provision. Free trade in services makes it difficult to create locally oriented and responsive services, whether through community action, local government or private business initiatives.[14]

---

13 Unlike TRIPs, GATS has not yet been implemented.
14 Although space prevents me from discussing the impact of GATS in detail, the WTO provision for compulsory twenty-year Exclusive Marketing Rights (EMRs) on patent drugs is having a negative impact on poor people in the poorer nations of the world. The arguments rehearsed here for patents on seeds and the effect of WTO provisions are much the same as the effects of patents on drugs and the impact of GATS (see Shiva 2001f: 86–93 and Oxfam 2001 for a discussion of the issues; for a fictional treatment, see Le Carré 2001). The privatisation of knowledge and the increased privatisation of educational facilities will also be affected by GATS. In each case, the gap between rich and poor widens. That this should be the case in areas which have a fundamental impact on the quality of peoples' lives – food security, health and education – I consider a travesty of social justice.

The WTO initiatives were a rehearsal for what was intended to be the ultimate provision for multilateral trade agreements, namely the Multilateral Agreement on Investment (MAI), which was developed by rich countries in the OECD, and intended to be ratified on 21 October 1998. Due to a worldwide internet campaign, the MAI failed to be ratified. The campaign was spearheaded from Canada, initially with Tony Clarke and Maude Barlow playing a critical role in its defeat (see Clarke and Barlow 1997). The MAI would have flattened the system of multilateral investment, and harmonised investment rules in member countries, thereby opening worldwide competition to local community-based and corporate projects. An example is health care (also covered by GATS): community health centres could be taken over by large US-based health maintenance organisations (HMOs) without any recourse from the local community. A multinational HMO could sue a local council if the HMO believed it had been "discriminated" against.

Likewise, educational services could be offered worldwide by large, asset-rich US institutions, thereby simultaneously widening the gap between educational institutions in the rich countries as well as promulgating a US-centred educational system even more widely than it is at present. Cultural colonisation, as Ama Ata Aidoo has pointed out, has long been a part of the colonisation process (1977: 86). The multilateral agreements have the potential to further institutionalise the colonisation process and make it ever more difficult for the colonised to resist the process, since it is supported by international law.

The MAI would also have limited the application of environmental regulations, and health and safety practices, as well as the return of benefits to local communities. The implications of the MAI were far-reaching and would have resulted in the further separation and depletion of local resources and local control of all resources.

Another example which shares many of the features of the multilateral agreements discussed above is the failed attempt within the UN to ratify the Small Arms Trade Agreement. The agreement was an attempt to curb illegal trade in small arms (AK-47), but the US Under-Secretary of State, John Bolton, argued that it "contains measures contrary to our [US citizens'] right to keep and bear arms" (in Romei 2001:13). The implication of the Small Arms Trade Agreement would have been that US arms manufacturers and dealers stood to lose a great deal of trade. As a result, this UN initiative, which could also have curbed the activities of warlords, criminals, "terrorists" and violent men, failed to be passed.[15]

Trade Related Intellectual Property rights (TRIPs)

Trade Related Intellectual Property Rights and Trade Related Investment Measures (TRIMs) began as important instruments of GATT (and were later picked up by the WTO). TRIPs means that US patent laws are internationalised so that the laws apply worldwide. And since US patent laws are much broader (than, for instance, European laws) and allow for the patenting of life forms (as discussed above) they open the way to greater exploitation of the bio-resources of poorer nations. This is effectively an infringement of national sovereignty, and protects not the labour and knowledge of ordinary people, but the property of trans-national corporations. Institutionally, the US patent system is supported by TRIPs. It is not surprising to learn that the TRIPs clauses had their genesis among corporations headquartered in the US. "Pfizer and IBM co-founded the Intellectual Property Committee" (Burrows 2001a: 250, n. 7). Pfizer and IBM are listed as numbers seventeen and thirty-one of the world's largest economic entities (Sheehan 2001: 32). Also on the Intellectual Property Committee were eleven other major corporations: Bristol–Myers Squibb, Hewlett Packard, DuPont, General Electric, Time–Warner, Rockwell, Monsanto, Johnson and Johnson, Proctor and Gamble, the FMC Corporation, and Merck (Awang 2000: 134).[16]

Trade Related Investment Measures (TRIMs), on the other hand, originally tended to bolster the independence of a nation, allowing it to insist that the investing party return something to the country where the business is located. Support of local businesses, the composition of boards of directors, balancing import and export are all part of the *quid pro quo* of TRIMs. But these measures have already been severely restricted, and the implementation depends on the level of global power in specific countries. The USA, Europe and Japan insisted on restrictions to TRIMs measures, and have "identified TRIMs as a violation of the spirit of GATT" (Clarke

---

15 It is an interesting, if tragic, irony that the USA was refusing to support a multilateral agreement on small arms trade fewer than three months before 11 September 2001, on the assumption that those using small arms within the borders of the USA would not be engaged in terrorist activity.

16 Shiva 2001f: 96 also includes General Motors.

and Barlow, 1997: 22). Not surprisingly, these are the investment-rich areas of the world. Countries outside these blocs who pushed for TRIMs have limited means for protecting their particular "investment", whether it be old-growth forest as in the case of Canada, fish populations in island nations of the Pacific, particular indigenous industries, such as kelp harvesting in the Scottish Isles, or living beings (see discussion of HGDP below). The powerful, the "old" colonisers of the nineteenth century, and the industrial rich of the twentieth and twenty-first centuries are, once again, the winners, while the powerless, the colonised countries, the countries rich in natural resources and relatively poor in investment and industrial clout, are the losers (see Appendix, Table 3). As Mahadev G. Bhat points out:

> Genetic resources that are found to have commercial prospects are commonly found in the wildlands of developing countries whereas commercial manu-facturers claiming intellectual property rights to those genetic resources are commonly multinational companies (1996: 207).

The asymmetry between resources and capital is a long-standing one, and its origins go back to the earliest days of capitalism. As with earlier colonial relationships, the push is toward homogenisation across cultures, and "penetration" of the new environment by dominant cultural values. Corporate penetration is threatening biocultural diversity, and it is not unusual to find conflicts over intellectual property rights arising in the countries listed above.

The move in all these agreements is toward a false universalisation[17] of laws applying to trade. It means that corporations have only one set of laws to negotiate. The laws are internationally consistent, and they will not change according to the vagaries of internal political shifts in govern-ment policy. This intention would be laudable if the context were fair and equitable, but given the inequalities of power, the policy is, effectively, the imposition of a trade monoculture. As I argue elsewhere (Hawthorne

---

17 It is false universalisation in Fukuyama's sense, in that corporate freedom "to pursue their selfish private interest is absolute" (1992: 203) and it is a perversion of the concept of freedom. The universalisation of trade rights does not increase the freedom of the poorest individual, therefore, it is not universal even in theory.

1999: 123), monocultures invariably benefit the powerful. TRIPs and TRIMs are no exception. As Bhat points out:

> the unimproved genetic material or genetic materials that have been partially developed by farmers through field trials and common-sense knowledge are treated as open-access resources (1996: 210).

What TRIPs means in this context is that public resources can be used by private companies as the starting point for their research. When the companies finally isolate a component of the genetic resource, they then privatise it and sell it to, among others, the same communities who developed the original stock. Local access to the stock is lost, and further, the multinational companies are usually reluctant to pay royalties to the people who originally developed the resource.[18]

The neem tree, *Azadirichta indica*, grows in Asia and Africa. In India, it has been used for millennia as an insect repellent, spermicide, natural medicine for skin diseases, sores and rheumatism. It is an ingredient in toothpaste and soaps, and can be used to prevent fungal growth such as rust and mildew (Becker 1994: 20). Known in India as the "blessed tree", the "free tree" (Shiva 2000b: 40) and the "curer of all ailments" (Lemonick 1995: 51), the neem tree was not perceived by the west as anything other than a "lowly tree" (Stone 1992: 1070; Shiva 2000b: 40) until the 1970s. Nor did western commentators put much store by challenges to the biopiracy accusation raised by Indian critics such as Vandana Shiva or activists such as Jeremy Rifkin (in Lemonick 1995: 51). With the potential for being the best natural pesticide available (Stone 1992: 1072), such a product has a huge projected income. Dutfield notes that there have been forty applications for patents on neem in the USA, and 153 worldwide (Dutfield 2000: 66, 132), including some from India. In 1992, industrial seed developers were paying a mere $US300 per ton for the seeds, the raw material. With research and development value added, the current income amounts to hundreds of millions of dollars. In 1992, sales of natural neem pesticides stood at $US450 million (Stone 1992: 1072). The potential turnover is therefore 1.5 million times greater than what was received by

---

18 Shaman Pharmaceuticals, a company which claims to pride itself on its equitable arrangements with indigenous communities, "has yet to make a firm commitment regarding the payment of royalties" (Posey and Dutfield 1996: 39).

the growers of the raw material! The gap is so great that it is almost incomprehensible, and I would say it amounts to theft. In 1994, a group comprising the Research Foundation for Science, Technology and Ecology based in India, the International Federation of Organic Agriculture Movements and the European Greens challenged one of the neem patents, held by W. R. Grace, in the European Patent Office. On 10 May 2000, Patent No. 0,436,257 on neem was revoked. It was revoked on the grounds that it constituted "piracy of existing knowledge systems and lacked novelty and inventiveness" (Shiva 2000b: 42; Shiva 2000c: 5). Shiva and Holla-Bhar (1993) also cite the African soapberry, the endod, *Phytolacca dodecoandra*, a plant cultivated by Ethiopian women for centuries as a detergent, fish intoxicant, and a spermicidal contraceptive (Burrows 2001a: 243; Dorsey 2001: 276; Shiva and Holla-Bhar 1993). The endod was found to be effective in controlling zebra mussels which have clogged the pipes in the Great Lakes. The potential profit on the molluscicide runs to many millions of dollars. With projected commercial uses in the North American fishing industry, the endod could turn out to be a valuable piece of intellectual property, something which African nations, if they were able – or indeed willing – to commercialise it, could turn endod into a tradeable commodity of their own. But the University of Toledo, Ohio, which undertook the research on endod, "refuses to donate their process patent on endod to non-profit organisations in Ethiopia" (Dorsey 2001: 276; Posey and Dutfield 1996: 81).

Finding ways to protect wild resources is urgent. In Kenya in the 1980s when an unprotected species, *Maytenus buchananni*, was discovered to have potential as an anti-cancer drug, the entire adult population of the plant was harvested under the auspices of the US National Cancer Institute (Oldfield 1984; Bhat 1996: 212; Dorsey 2001: 276): not only was the future existence of the species threatened, but also future research on extracts of the plant. When foreign companies or government institutes move into areas stricken by poverty, the local people will often do whatever they can to maximise their livelihood. If there is no future benefit[19] in maintaining healthy wild stock, why would anyone think of conservation when the hunger and poverty is now?

---

19 The future benefit would be denied if transnational companies could come in, harvest the resources, separate the active chemical agent, patent and sell that agent back to the country of origin without any payment of royalty to the originating nation.

Another anti-cancer drug developed from plants is the Western Australia smokebush (genus *Conospermum*), which was collected by the US National Cancer Institute between in the 1960s and 1981. When the smokebush was first collected and screened, no useful active ingredients were found. In the late 1980s it was screened again; a compound, conocurvane, was extracted and tested for its effect on HIV. "Even in low concentrations, it was found to 'inactivate' the virus" (Christie 2001: 181).

In January 1993 the US Department of Health and Human Services applied for a US patent (No. 5,672,607, granted in September 1997) and a year later it applied for an Australian patent (No. 680,872, granted in August 1997). As Jean Christie points out, this "gave its US owner exclusive monopoly rights to use the compounds from the WA plant, to decide who would be licensed to use them, and at what cost." (2001: 181). The issue here is not only the violation of indigenous rights (the smokebush has been recorded for its use in traditional medicine, see Fourmile 1996: 36–41) but also the blurring of sovereign rights to territory including land, plants, and resources. Although an Australian company[20] was later granted an exclusive worldwide licence by the National Institute of Health, Christie shows that it is not clear whether Aboriginal usage led the US National Cancer Institute to the plant, or whether the local indigenous peoples will have their intellectual property protected in any way.

A further problem is that local communities might not realise that they have a "product" with commercial value. Part of the reason might be that commercialisation of life is not integral to indigenous ontology, as it is in US and western cultures. An example cited by David Stephenson is that of "Hopi blue". Blue corn was traditionally valuable as a staple food crop, as well as for its role in ceremonial purposes. With increased commercialisation of blue corn (for corn chips and other "Mexican" food products), there is global potential for profit-making. Hopi blue is now a registered trademark which poses "a potential legal threat to any Hopi who begins to market products under the name Hopi" (Stephenson 1999:

---

20 The agreement was between the US National Cancer Institute, the Western Australian government and the Australian Medical and Research Development Corporation (AMRAD). AMRAD is in the process of screening a wide range of other native plants, and has entered into contracts with Merck Sharpe and Dohme (USA), Kanegafuchi Chemical Industry Company (Japan), Sandoz (now Novartis, Switzerland), Rhône-Poulenc (now Aventis, France) (in Christie 2001: 183). Over 750,000 extracts had been tested by 1997.

244). In commercialising blue corn, even if the traditional farmers agree
to grow the crops for profit, their methods of growing are likely to be
progressively turned toward monoculture farming. The increased assimilation into commercial production would have the effect of gradually
eroding Hopi culture. Given the documented erosion of British and French
styles of farming through globalisation and increased industrialisation of
farming, there can be no doubt of the negative impact of corporate needs
on farmers, whether in Britain, France, North and Central America (corn),
Africa (the endod), Asia (neem), South America (quinoa), the Pacific
(kava), or Australia (Western Australia smokebush).[21]

It is not only blue corn whose traditional uses are threatened by
increased commercialisation, but also corn as a central symbolic crop to
indigenous peoples throughout the Americas. Corn or maize, like the
neem tree in India, plays a central role in the indigenous culture of the
Americas.[22] Rigoberta Menchú, writing of the indigenous culture of
Guatemala, says that "Maize is the center of everything for us. It is our
culture." And, upon marriage, the following prayer is uttered: "Mother
earth may you feed us. We are made of maize, of yellow maize and white
maize" (1989: 55, 67).

The development of corn parallels the neem tree experience. Corn
has two ways of reproducing: self-pollination and cross-pollination. Traits
can be easily selected by inbreeding through self-pollination over several
generations, but the yield of such a line is poor. However, if two such
inbred lines are crossed, there is increased vigour in the resulting hybrid.
By double-crossing two strands, a commercial hybrid has been produced.
But at a cost. Seeds from corn raised from hybrid seeds cannot be saved
and used for future planting because their yields are erratic and poor.

21 For further reading on how these crops have been appropriated and commodified by
    pharmaceutical companies, see Shand (1998). On corn, see Correy (2001); Ament
    (2001). On the endod, see Shiva and Holla-Bhar (1993); Dorsey (2001); Posey and
    Dutfield (1996). On neem, see Shiva (2001f: 57–61). On quinoa, see Shand (1998),
    Christie (2001). On kava, see Shand (1998). On Western Australia smokebush, see
    Christie (2001).
22 Not only were there many different species of corn available and adapted to different
    regions in which they grew, but also many hundreds of different ways of preparing
    corn for consumption. Kuhnlein and Receveur examine the different ways in which
    indigenous diets have changed with the widespread introduction of industrialised
    food (1996: 426ff).

This means that farmers have to purchase seed from seed companies every year (Yapa 1993: 262). Furthermore, corn is a relatively easy plant to modify genetically. By 1999, twelve different varieties had been genetically engineered and deemed safe for field use. Just one of these, produced by Hi-Bred (a subsidiary of DuPont), "requires access to thirty-eight different patents controlled by sixteen separate patent holders" (Shand 2001: 227). Where, in this equation, are the indigenous peoples who developed corn in the first place?

My father, a farmer for seventy years (from 1913 to 1983), has told me that on the farm we had,[23] there was an average yield of thirty bushels of wheat per acre, and that most years, approximately one bushel per acre of seed would be saved for replanting the following year. His comment on this was that "you knew the quality of the seed you were planting, and could therefore predict more accurately the outcome for the year". Only in the event of a year with poor-quality seed would he go out and buy seed; when he did so, it could be from a neighbour or a local stock and station retailer whose seed reflected the needs of the local environment. Under TRIPs, the exchange of seed between farmers has become illegal, unless that seed can be shown to be covered by a patent or a *sui generis* – a one-of-a-kind – system. The seed cost to my father in an average year was approximately 3.3 per cent of the net yearly income. Bhat indicates that seed costs from 1993 to 1994 in the state of Karnataka, India, constituted 7.18 per cent of variable paid-out costs for irrigated corn. Even taking into account the variables of country, location, climate, and time, given that net income is likely to be higher than variable costs (unless the farm is being run at a loss in average years), the cost involved in buying seed is considerable, and the smaller the farmer, the higher the cost will be per acre (1996: 210).

Numerous food crops are being modified by biotechnology; and corn, soya beans, tomatoes and potatoes are among those most heavily researched. Aventis StarLink corn became well-known in 2000 when millions of bushels of unapproved corn were sent to hundreds of grain elevators around the USA, leading to contamination of the food supply

---

23   The farm was located on the southwest slopes of New South Wales, an area with approximately forty-five millimetres of rain annually. The soil, like most Australian soils, is not high in organic matter, but is rich in iron, which gives it about the same colour as fired terracotta (and makes it almost as hard).

(Eichenwald 2000: 13). In October 2000, Kellogg closed one of its production plants because it "could not find corn guaranteed to be free of genetically modified grain" (*International Herald Tribune* 2000: 11).

A host of other potential biological resources is currently being screened. If they turn out to be commercially viable, the systems in place under multilateral agreements will not protect the intellectual property rights of the communities from which the resources originally came. The informal systems, including the pressures of globalisation, tend to encourage biopiracy. Even in the event that some aspects of the CBD are respected, this might encourage local farmers to move toward mono-culture cropping and export of the plant resource themselves. Neither of these courses of action is likely to be of long-term value. An example from the Philippines of the crossover between patent ownership and export dependency is cited by Father Brian Gore.

> Yves St Laurent ... have bought one of the most aromatic flowers in Negros, they have the patent for it. Now they're going to put up farms growing this flower. Meanwhile we're not growing food for the people (2001: 3).

The companies have the resources to do whatever development they want. Patenting the lily from Negros is piracy. Piracy is an unlawful activity. However, piracy by multinational companies is not only allowed, it is enshrined in, and protected by, international trade agreements policed by the WTO. Growing export produce such as flowers, sugar, coffee, cotton, tobacco, pulls small producers into the global capital system, and as a result they grow less food to eat. This will be as true of the biotechno-logically engineered plants as it is of non-GMO plants. Trading systems will continue to be dominated by the seed companies and corporate giants. They will not create new ways of "feeding the hungry", simply modified ways of exploiting the poor.

Food Security

Food security is a central concern for all people, and of daily concern to poor people throughout the world. Only those with decent incomes and resources do not think about this issue constantly. And it is a problem which has persisted throughout human existence (George 1991).[24] It is

---

24   Susan George's classic critique of world hunger, *How the Other Half Dies*, was first published in 1976.

easy for the well-off to forget just how fundamental an issue food security is, particularly for women and children. Women and children make up the poorest of the world's poor and, even in the well-fed nations, women and children starve. Women are responsible for feeding those around them who depend on their work, and in this struggle for existence, women often eat less than those who depend on them.

Hazel Henderson (2000: 73) argues that "economics is still about scarcity", while Jeffner Allen points to the concept of scarcity as central to patriarchal ideology.

Scarcity, the patriarchal construct that makes it appear necessary to choose who is to be secure and who underfed, selects and justifies that women are the undernourished, the exhausted, the untimely dead. Scarcity spirals (1996: 46).

The scarcity argument is used as a big stick to beat women when poor women have children. "Overpopulation!" cry the Malthusian descendants, the well-fed men of the world. But scarcity is an integral part of the capitalist equation of supply and demand. On the other side is the concept of unlimited growth. This notion is challenged by members of the diversity matrix.

We challenge the whole growth-oriented development paradigm dictated by the logic of greed and profit. The models, views and practices generated out of this paradigm invariably ignore farmers, fishing communities, indigenous people, women and other marginalized groups. It widens inequality and injustice. Violence, militarization, social and political instability are intricate components of this mode of development (South Asian Workshop on Food Security 1996: 4).

A look at the composition of the organisation which controls world food security makes it clear that neither women nor the people who produce food – farmers, fishers, and forest peoples – are part of the equation.

The UN Food and Agricultural Organisation, Codex Alimentarus – the agency responsible for setting standards for food production – is dominated by multinational junk food producers. Among them are Nestlé, General Mills, Kraft, Purina, PepsiCo, Coca-Cola.

At Codex, Nestlé is said to have more personnel on different government delegations than there are on any one government delegation (Clarke and Barlow 1997: 119).

It is a sad irony that women produce, collect, prepare and cook most of the world's food, and get to eat so little of it. Women's bodies produce food for infants, but even when breastfeeding (Smith 1997; Draper 1996), women rarely eat more than at other times. Without sufficient nourishment, breastfeeding women themselves become malnourished. Women, in their small-scale efficient domestic food production and collection, tend to produce a greater quantity of food than do men in high-speed boats or with high-powered rifles. In a similar way, traditional relationships between nomadic pastoralists and settled agriculturalists are easily destroyed when western capitalist, export-oriented economics takes hold of a developing economy. Michel Chossudovsky argues that the combination of resettlement programs with the influx of imported cereals such as rice and wheat in the form of food aid actually worsened the situation in Somalia (1998: 101–102). Continued destruction of the exchange economy of nomadic pastoralists, combined with the dumping of subsidised US grains, effectively destroyed the Somali economy, making it dependent instead of self-sufficient, as it had been in the early 1970s. As Chossudovsky concludes:

> famines in the age of globalisation are man-made. … They are not the consequence of "a scarcity of food" but of a structure of global oversupply which undermines food security and destroys national food agriculture (1998: 107).

Resisting the shift toward globalised poverty and destruction of economies, a statement on food security by the Bangladeshi organisation UBINIG suggests the following move:

> Food production and command over the market must remain in the hands of small farmers. It is crucial that we demand prohibition of large agribusinesses from entering food production and processing as well as food trade. The localisation and regionalisation of food production is absolutely a necessity to ensure food security (South Asian Workshop on Food Security 1996: 7–8).

One of the problems of existing food distribution is that food flows often out of countries where it is most needed. In Nigeria in 1967, rice is exported and the Biafran people starve; in Zimbabwe in 1992, tobacco is exported in a year of bumper crops, and "the famine forces the population to eat termites" (Chossudovsky 1998: 106). Dependency on food aid should not be the norm. Food aid is too easily misused as a political football. I suggest that the entire system of export needs serious scrutiny. But with neoclassical economic systems determining the international agenda for trade, the demand of the Global Politic is that where a surplus exists, the product should be moved to an area where there is demand. And because the poor have no money, they do not constitute a demand.

> Armed with MAI restrictions on performance requirements, these corpo-
> rations would be in a position to ensure that no national government could
> demand food quality standards that are higher than the international standards
> they themselves had set as part of Codex (Clarke and Barlow 1997: 119–120).

This restriction could be used to prevent organic and biodynamic farmers from being supported by governments, or it could also be used to put brakes on farmers who resist planting GM seed. Clarke and Barlow note that management of agricultural supply could be affected. The deregulation of the dairy industry (Dunlop 2001) and of the poultry industry are examples of the way in which the MAI, or a similar multilateral agreement, could be used against primary producers, which will have direct impacts on consumers.

Although the MAI was not passed, NAFTA now exists, the WTO is moving in the same direction, and further free-trade agreements – the Free Trade Areas of America (FTAA) and the Asia Pacific Economic Cooperation forum (APEC), for example – are being considered or put in place.

In 1996, Susan George suggested that the food security of South-East Asia was in great danger, and that the forces of free trade should be reined in (1996: 4). Her prescience, however, had no effect on the subsequent crisis in Asia. What questions should we now be asking about the economy, the environment, methods and patterns of production and consumption? The situation of export-oriented developing economies is not improving; instead, their domestic infrastructures are being eroded and their environments suffer pollution. Farming, forests and fisheries industries are staggering. And what of the farmers who grow rice, cassava, njahe beans, or who harvest shellfish, hunt small animals, gather forest root vegetables and herbs? What of the people in Manhattan and Göttingen and Melbourne who have started communal gardens where fruits and vegetables and herbs and flowers are grown? Will they want to drink only Coca-Cola and eat only Nestlé chocolates? Or are they wanting something more? Something better?

Preserving biodiversity is a priority which must concern all critics of globalisation. It is not about individuals or the profit of companies, biodiversity is a collective good for all – humanity and the planet – and legislation should be moving in the direction of preservation, not exploitation. The 1992 Convention on Biological Diversity, Article 8(j), suggests that innovations developed by particular communities or by indigenous peoples should be given protection. Such protection could ensure open access to seed lines and other resources, as well as payment of royalties for wild stock removed from a region. Wild stock and genetic resources are equivalent to ore bodies, which are indeed subject to leases and payments to local, state or national governments.[25] However, while commercial exploitation might return income to communities, it must not be at the risk of extinction, or economic dependency on export. Just as forests and fishing grounds can be harvested to exhaustion, the over-harvesting of wild species should be prohibited with enforceable safe-guards.

Industrial diversity and inventiveness are at risk. The products of indigenous plant varieties are at risk. Cultural diversity is at risk. And even the existing legal frameworks which have an impact on environmental codes, labour rights and social-justice programs – imperfect as they may be – are at risk. In the not too distant future in developing countries and former colonies, states will have a significantly reduced role in their own economies.

Conventional economics does not sit easily with ecological concerns, since the dominant economic theory assumes biophysical constancy. Neoclassical economics puts little store by context-sensitivity, and tends

---

25 Whether such leases are fair, and whether payments are made to the most appropriate group (for example, to indigenous peoples) is a matter of the particular circumstances. The principle of payment, however, remains the same.

to posit a homogeneity that simply does not exist. Since biodiversity is the touchstone of the biophysical sphere, and local knowledge the most important feature in its management, an economics which takes no notice of – cannot see – these things can never adequately describe environmental systems. Further, the continuing universalising of economic strategies for globalised markets threatens precisely the elements that most need protection from exploitation on a global scale.

The Multilateral Agreement on Investment (MAI)

The MAI, if it had been ratified, would have removed many more boundaries for capital and transnational trade and intensified the increasing global monoculture. It might be argued that because the MAI was not ratified, it is no longer of any concern.

However, the agenda of transnational capital has not changed. The MAI is an important case study for anyone concerned with global social and economic justice. For these reasons, I discuss some of the salient features of the MAI which are being recycled in other regional trade agreements including NAFTA, the FTAA, and APEC. It is not unlikely that the main elements of the MAI will eventually return in a revised form as a global trade agreement.

The MAI (or an agreement modelled on it) is, quite simply put, a way of ensuring that powerful nations and powerful corporations do not face any restrictions on their activities in the global market. In other words, the MAI model allows transnational corporations to pursue business ventures anywhere, without any domestic regulations or restrictions.[26]

The MAI is phrased in the language of "rights", co-opting hard-fought-for ideas and concepts in ways which favour the powerful. The recurring phrases are "treatment no less favourable" (Clause on National Treatment and Most Favoured Nation Treatment, 1.) and "fair and equitable treatment" (Clause on Investment Protection, 1.1). One must immediately ask, from whose standpoint is the treatment fair and equitable? The difference between "equal" and "same" is a seasoned debate in ethics, feminism and political philosophy. If there are to be fair outcomes, two parties starting from unequal positions require unequal

---

26 An interesting intersection exists, in the global economy, between the international mobility of elites and their capital and the increasing availability of women through cyberprostitution, see Hughes (1999a, 1999b).

treatment in order to achieve a just outcome. Equality of treatment, when access to resources and power are unequal, simply results in preserving the status quo or accentuating the relations of power.

Because equal treatment must be applied, no distinction can be made between products that are the same. So fish caught using drift nets could not be excluded from the market because that would be "discrimination"; likewise, timber produced by clear-cutting of old-growth forest could not be banned.

The effect of "integrationalist language" (Posey and Dutfield 1996: 117) in the multilateral agreements is much the same as the effect of assimilationist policies within social and cultural settings. That is, it tends to flatten differences in a misguided attempt to universalise their applicability. All it succeeds in doing is to make it easier for the bigger players to get their own way under the guise of "fairness" and "equality".

Globally, the world has moved into an era in which the "rights" of (big) capital take precedence over the "rights" of (small) citizens and the nation states which represent their needs. The MAI model protects transnational company investments in sectors such as biological prospecting and drug development by offering compensation for any "expropriated investment" or "any other measure having similar effect". This includes any government action that would "have the effect of depriving an investor of its investment" (Clarke and Barlow 1997: 46).

Conserving biodiversity in a particular region could result in having to compensate mining companies for, say, Native Title claims on land for which the mining company holds a prospecting lease – and not just for current income losses, but also for future income losses. Multilateral agreements modelled on the MAI have the potential to bankrupt national, state and local governments.

Public enterprises which are supported through subsidies or incentives from governments could also be open to litigation on the basis that they "cause injury" to foreign corporations. This would clearly hamper the ability of governments to raise revenues via taxes and put them back into social or environmental projects. Also, governments could not insist that foreign companies maximise the domestic benefit by value-adding prior to export, and thereby retain more wealth inside the borders of the nation. The possible outcome is that resources may be depleted and sold at a lower level of return, while the transnational company adds value –

and therefore makes its profits – in another country. The country from which the raw resources came is therefore denied the revenue when the raw materials are turned into manufactured goods. This is a replica of the old model of colonisation.

In respect of taxation, although the framers of the MAI considered other "measures to curb the taxing powers of governments" (Clarke and Barlow 1997: 49), in the final document, taxation is excluded. The intent of the proposal, nevertheless, was to reduce the taxation "burden" of foreign investors, that is, transnational corporations. The big winner in such a taxation regime would be the USA, Japan and some European countries, where most transnational corporations have their head offices.

The MAI model is not about social responsibility or a better deal for the powerless. It is instead a further instrument for moving resources out of the public sphere, away from the commons, and into the hands of the private sector. In the last decade many businesses have been restructured. Next it is the turn of governments, whose focus will no longer be the well-being of their citizens, but rather the welfare of big business. This is justified – and indeed necessitated – on the grounds that if business is growing, then the economy is in good shape. But anyone with a foot in the real world knows that economic growth does not always mean benefits for people; that quality is just as important as quantity, and that context is what determines judgement on whether a particular action has a positive or negative outcome. The ideology of homogeneity is rampant in the model of the MAI.[27]

> The essence of independence is the reconstruction of the local economy, development of local enterprises, and retaining as much of the income and value-added in the domestic economy. The MAI is designed to erode significantly this right of national governments (Martin Khor cited in Clarke and Barlow 1997: 55).

The MAI is ideologically connected to the Human Genome Project (HGP) and to free access to indigenous knowledge and to genetic resources – "without discrimination". The flow of genetic knowledge is

---

27 See Michael Moore (1997: 50–63) for a humorous approach to corporate welfare cheats.

from the "underdeveloped" countries to the overdeveloped. Australia, New Zealand and South Africa[28] are in a middle position, being "developed" in their acceptance of western legal frameworks. They are also important resources of biological diversity. This is especially true of Australia where there are many unique species, both plants and animals. It is to be expected that the knowledge built up over millennia by Aboriginal people will be harvested over the next century. How much of these unique resources will remain in Australia at the end of that period will depend on what measures the Australian government takes to protect them. But with developments looming in patent legislation and multilateral agreements modelled on the MAI, some safeguards in place are urgently required. As Tony Clarke and Maude Barlow point out:

> International state-sanctioned bans to protect endangered species might not be permitted by the MAI if the bans interfered with the trade and investment interests of a member country or corporation (1997: 95).

This means that if, for instance, a small nocturnal marsupial were discovered in the vicinity of a proposed uranium mine (which is not beyond possibility), under MAI rules, the marsupial would be sacrificed. Similarly, cultural repositories, such as cave paintings, could only be saved if governments were to pay sufficient compensation for loss of company profits, that is, if governments have sufficient resources to do so. In this cash-strapped era when capital is readily shifted, tax is avoided, and profits are shipped off-shore, governments may not have the ability to make payments over and over again. In the Philippines, Clarke and Barlow estimate that:

> Roughly 40 percent of the country's entire land area has been set aside for lease to foreign mining corporations like Placer Dome. They would have exclusive rights to explore and mine this land for twenty-five years, renewable

---

28 In South Africa, the trade in *muti*, indigenous medicines, is valued at $A500 million. But as in other regions "development" and "progress" are having the biggest impact on women because common lands are being fenced (Rangan 2002: 16–25). The San people of the Kalahari desert have entered an agreement with Pfizer to share future royalties on the hoodia plant which Pfizer plans to market and sell as a drug to counter obesity (Barnett 2002: 3).

for a further twenty-five, and they would be granted 100 percent control of equity. They would receive a five-year tax holiday, renewable every five years, 100 percent repatriation of profits, attendant water and timber rights, easement rights to evict communities, and the right to settle their own labour disputes without government interference (1997: 100–101).

In sum, the MAI model has the potential to threaten social rights, including social services such as health delivery systems; not only public hospitals, but also community and women's health services in the not-for-profit sector. There is the potential for carefully constructed mixes of private and public organisations to be completely dismantled. The MAI model could readily foster an increased disparity of available services to the "deserving" and "undeserving" poor. What will be the consequences for community and social development? Does the future hold foreign-owned companies with an emphasis on the bottom line coming in and providing – for a fee, of course – services which a community can easily supply for itself? While the local community can stimulate the development of relationship and connection, the multinational agenda is to standardise all procedures and treatments regardless of context. It is clear that a multinational health company's only response to the needs of local communities is to homogenise. How can they know enough about a community's distinct history and mix of peoples? And will they care?

Traditional Resource Rights (TRRs) and Community Intellectual Rights (CIRs)

Darrell Posey and Graham Dutfield suggest that international trade relations should go beyond intellectual property rights, and instead focus on Traditional Resource Rights (TRRs). The concept of Traditional Resource Rights builds upon the convention of Intellectual Property Rights (IPRs) but takes more account of tangible and intangible resources which are held collectively by indigenous peoples and communities with a strong traditional heritage. As Posey and Dutfield point out: "Privatization or commoditization of their resources is not only foreign but incomprehensible or even unthinkable" (1996: 95). TRRs cover a range of rights, integrating cultural and biological diversity.

In India, traditional and tribal peoples are forcefully agitating for Community Intellectual Rights (CIRs). These rights are intended to protect knowledge held within a community for which no one person has the final say. CIRs would recognise the communal ownership of knowledge, and also allow for the protection of knowledge or resources which remain undisclosed. Such recognition extends to the acknowledgement of traditional or indigenous peoples as "innovators" (Posey 1996: 15).

Some have argued that indigenous peoples' IPRs should not be treated any differently from those of others (Stenson and Gray 1997), but as Dutfield (2000: 62) makes clear, this equation is based on the liberal misconception of how traditional knowledge systems work, including assuming that all knowledge of indigenous or traditional peoples is in the public domain. The assumption of complete transparency of knowledge mirrors the legal fiction perpetrated in the Hindmarsh Island case over women's business and sacred sites, in which it was assumed that all women of the community had access to the same knowledge. In fact, such knowledge systems are nuanced in complex ways (Bell 1998), which take account of the particular social, and even personal, context – in other words, what it is that makes one person a "knower" while another is not. It cannot be assumed, therefore, that knowledge of plants deemed "sacred" in traditional societies was widely and publicly available throughout the community. Just as western systems of land tenure have been used to dispossess peoples all around the world, and, in the case of Australia under *terra nullius*, invisibilised Native Title altogether, so too the imposition of western IPRs on traditional and indigenous knowledge communities threatens further dispossession. As Graham Dutfield summarises the problem:

> It is perhaps this point, that one IPR system is being universalized and prioritized to the exclusion of all others, that causes the most legitimate disquiet among those peoples and communities that are least able to benefit from what is to them an imposed system (2000: 63–64).

In legislation which is implicitly racist, US and Japanese patent systems do not recognise "undocumented traditional knowledge" (Dutfield 2000: 64). Documentation under this legislation involves being "reported (and thereby validated) by scientists and published in learned journals or otherwise made available to the public" (Dutfield 2000: 65; see also Shiva 2001f: 18). Such legislation institutionalises and legitimises intellectual property theft, through not recognising that access to knowledge in many indigenous communities is earned, nor that it is reliably passed on through oral traditions. Indigenous communities wanting to protect their knowledge face a Catch-22. In order for it to be protected under the western IPR system, it must be told to a representative of western culture (a researcher, for example) and be written up in a reputable scientific journal.[29] But, in order to achieve this "protection", the rules of the community will be broken, and cultural disintegration is a possible outcome.

A further hurdle faced by indigenous communities lies in tracing the originator of the knowledge which may have been passed on through individuals related by kinship, by gender (see Mogina 1996; Bell 1983/ 2002; 1998), or through some other system of honour within a community. Patents tend toward universalisation, private ownership, and disconnection from place. They are, therefore, unlikely to be able to "accommodate the subtleties and complexities of many non-western proprietary systems" (Dutfield 2000: 69). Western systems also tend to assume that there is a single opposing system in operation, whereas there is considerable inventiveness and diversity of systems in existence among indigenous and other traditional non-western systems. There is no single rule which will work for everyone. Even the concept of ownership is problematic. As indicated in the earlier discussion on indigenous conceptions of land, ownership is more appropriately conceptualised as a responsibility for sustaining relationship *with* the land, rather than ownership or propriety *over* the land. Knowledge may be shared with others at particular times, or in association with certain events. Similarly, seeds might also be freely shared rather than traded.

If the IPR system being developed under the multilateral trade regimes is really intended to benefit the holders of knowledge, rather than benefit those who can profit most, significant changes will need to be made to the rules. It seems likely, however, given the way the rules are currently phrased and being implemented, that the intent is not to benefit all holders of knowledge, but rather to create further opportunities for profit on the part of the elites and the dominant players in world trade.

---

29 CIRs have not been enacted, although they are under consideration in India (Posey 1996: 15).

TRRs, or some other system which is developed to benefit those most likely to be dispossessed by western IPRs, could create the conditions for a fair way of proceeding with the protection of indigenous and traditional knowledge. The biggest hurdle to grassroots protection is the irresponsibility of the dominant culture (Kappeler 1995). Part of the difficulty is why should systems be developed in the first place? Simply to protect the western-desired products and knowledge from exploitation? Women face similar dilemmas in the construction of laws intended to protect them from violence. In the instance of TRRs, the goal is protection from intellectual violence and cultural colonisation and appropriation.

The Human Genome Project (HGP) and the Human Genome Diversity Project (HGDP)

> *We value the efforts of protection of the Biodiversity but we reject being included as part of an inert diversity which pretends to be maintained for scientific and folkloric purposes*
> – Paragraph 59, Kari-Oca Declaration and the Indigenous Peoples' Earth Charter in Darrell Posey and Graham Dutfield (1996: 194).

Two projects, the Human Genome Project (HGP)[30] and the Human Genome Diversity Project (HGDP), nicknamed the vampire project by some indigenous groups (Horvitz 1996; Posey 1996: 8; Rifkin 1998: 57), were initiated during the 1990s. Trillions of dollars have already been expended on the HGP alone, but the cost is justified on the grounds of finding cures for both rare and common diseases, or at the very least of increasing our understanding of human genetics. Laudable as these goals may seem, both projects have been plagued by criticism, in particular with regard to the patenting of human genetic material without the permission from the (supposed) donor.

The theft of land and knowledge on the material and cultural levels is now being paralleled by the theft of body parts and genetic material. Through the collection of individuals' cells (via blood samples, cheek scrapings and specimens taken during surgery), pharmaceutical companies

---

30 I find it strange that in 2001, Oxfam appears to support the HGP. Its Briefing Paper on the World Trade Organisation is prefaced by Sir John Sulston, co-founder of the HGP (Oxfam 2001: 2).

are creating cell lines and then patenting them as products. In 1993, when the first draft of the proposal for the HGDP appeared, the response of indigenous peoples was "silence and sadness" (Burrows 2001a: 244).

John Moore, an oil worker on an Alaskan pipeline, became an early unwilling participant in the HGP. He was treated for hairy-celled leukemia in 1976 and his enlarged spleen was "harvested" for white blood cells. His doctor then cultivated these cells into a continuing cell line and found that it was capable of producing blood proteins which could be used to treat immuno-suppressive diseases (Vidal and Carvel 1994: 13). Moore later discovered that his doctor and the University of California had obtained a US patent on this "invention", US Patent No. 4,438,032, and then sold the cell line to pharmaceutical company, Sandoz, in 1984 (Shiva 2001f: 8). At no time was Moore asked for permission to remove sample cells from his spleen, nor was he informed that these cells were being developed into a cell line. It was not until 1991 that he became aware that a patent had been granted on his own cells. Moore asked some pertinent questions, such as: "How has life become a commodity?" and stated "I believe that all genetic material extracted from human beings should belong to society as a whole, and not be patentable" (in Vidal and Carvel 1994: 13). By 1994, Moore's cell line had earned around $US3 billion for its owners. Moore received nothing but a small damages settlement out of court. More importantly, the court ruled that Moore did not own the cells which were taken from his body (*Moore v. Regents of the University of California: 1990*). Nor did the court recognise the emotional pain caused to Moore by the experience, his sense of "the dehumanisation of having one's cells conveyed to places and for purposes one does not know of" (in Burrows 2001a: 246).[31]

The HGDP, which aims to collect material from isolated populations (for example, the Basque people) and indigenous peoples, is facing similar problems. In 1995 the US government "issued itself a patent on a foreign citizen" (Horvitz 1996: 34). The foreign citizen in this case was a Hagahai man from Papua New Guinea whose blood was being used without consent to develop new drugs. The patent – US Patent No. 5,397,696 –

---

31   There is perhaps an interesting parallel here between the person whose cells are removed without his or her knowledge, and without his or her consent, and the rape of a woman who is unconscious at the time of rape. In each case there is no conscious knowledge, but what remains is a sense of utter betrayal and violation.

was withdrawn after massive protests by indigenous peoples in December 1996 (Shand 1998). Similar cases have been reported concerning cell lines from Solomon Islanders. A twenty-six-year-old Guaymi Indian woman from Panama had her T-cells appropriated, and an application was made: patent claim number WO9,208,784 (Awang 2000: 131). Debra Harry, an advocate for the Nevada-based Indigenous People's Coalition on Biodiversity, says, "Now it's colonialism on a molecular level ... For us, genes are our ancestry, our heredity and our future generations. They are not to be tampered with" (in Horvitz 1996: 34). Under international pressure from non-government organisations and indigenous peoples' organisations, the applications for patents on the samples taken from the Hagahai and the Guaymi peoples were withdrawn (Tauli-Corpuz 2001: 264) in November 1993, but the cell line has neither been destroyed nor returned to its rightful owner (Awang 2000: 131).

At issue, among other things, are two competing worldviews. The Guaymi of Panama view such commodification as violating "the integrity of life itself, and our deepest sense of morality" (Shand 1994: 11). Like Ani (2000), the Guaymi see themselves as connected to the whole, not separable into parts, cells, or genes. There is no remedy for the degree of violation they experienced through these western techniques. On the other hand, the US patent laws specify precisely how life can be owned, patented, and "invented" by scientists and corporations.

Like the concept of *terra nullius* enshrined in Australian law until 1992, "The vacancy of targeted lands has been replaced by the vacancy of targeted life forms and species manipulated by the new technologies" (Shiva 1997: 2). And as Victoria Tauli-Corpuz (2001: 263) argues, the HGDP perpetuates an outmoded view of race, and is likely to have racist outcomes. Jeanette Armstrong, an indigenous woman from Canada, on first hearing of the HGDP, said:

> You people. We thought you folks had taken everything you could. You took our land, you took our homes. You stole our pottery and our songs and our blankets and our designs. You took our language and in some places you even took our children. You snatched at our religion and at our women. You destroyed our history and now, now it seems you come to suck the marrow from our bones (in Burrows 2001a: 244).

When John Moore made a legal challenge to the use of his cell line, he was branded as a man "against the progress of science" (in Burrows 2001a: 247). Organic farmers protesting against the use of GMOs in agriculture are pejoratively labelled in exactly the same way. They are called "anti-science spoilers, people who are against any technology or science" (Correy 2001a: Transcript 2).

Darrell Posey points to the inherent conflict between indigenous and western systems of knowledge within the structure of international multilateral agreements. He provides a warning on what are perceived by some as very positive and generous agreements, among them the Rio Declaration, the Convention on Biological Diversity, Agenda 21 and Forest Principles:

> Despite what are generous words, indigenous and traditional peoples are faced with a difficult conundrum. On the one hand, their contribution of a central role in sustainable development and conservation and rights as decision-makers and beneficiaries are recognised far beyond any previous international binding conventions. On the other hand, by accepting the terms of these agreements, indigenous peoples must accept that ultimate control over resources lies with nation states (Posey 1997: 228).

Sandra Awang (2000) also points out (like Shiva 1993a) that IPRs are promoted as new ways of looking at knowledge, whereas in fact they represent the "institutionalisation of *Western orientation toward information as a world system of thinking*" (Awang 2000: 125, emphasis in original). The pretence that enclosing knowledge systems through patents is going to benefit indigenous and traditional peoples is as morally corrupt as is the pretence that colonisation makes underdeveloped countries rich through catch-up development (Mies 1986, 1994).

Companies such as Monsanto are very clear about what they want in terms of IPRs. Richard Shear declares Monsanto's view:

> Monsanto, like many companies, looks forward to investing in the development of agriculture throughout the world. When intellectual property laws are improved, like those in Brazil, companies such as Monsanto will invest in biotech, manufacturing and technology transfer (2000: 37).

What Richard Shear means here by "improved" is that indigenous and traditional peoples will allow the corporations to use their knowledge base in any way the companies like, and without any reciprocation to the community. Monsanto, like other companies of its ilk in the transnational sector, neither sees that there is a competing knowledge system in place, nor acknowledges the need to take seriously the claims of indigenous ownership, in much the same way that liberal, utilitarian economics does not see the need to take seriously the claims of women, children or poor people (Plumwood 1996: 157; Kappeler 1995: 5).

One of the key flaws in the HGDP is the area of "informed consent" and the ability of the parties to "negotiate". Consent is problematic between two parties with unequal access to power. But it is typically in circumstances where there are power differentials that consent is insisted upon. Consent is also used by the state and the powerful to make the powerless feel as though they have some control over their lives. I suggest it is a false sense of control, and one that fools the powerless into colluding with those in power.[32] Janice Raymond points out that the word "compliance" is more useful than "consent" because "compliance is required by the very fact of having to adapt to conditions of inequality" (nd: 7).

In the examples discussed above of the Hagahai man and of John Moore, "consent" is a ludicrous term to use, whereas "compliance" does convey the situation of inequality. The Hagahai man is more likely to have been tricked, to have been ill-informed before complying; his understanding of what was asked for was in a cultural context so alien to him that it is unlikely it was in any way equivalent to the English-language meaning of the agreement. Such language advantage is usually held by the person or group in power wanting the informed consent of another. How many of us fully understand the contractual language of lawyers, of airlines, of car salespeople, of doctors? How much greater is the chance of misunderstanding, not just across language barriers, but across huge cultural gulfs also, when the conceptual worlds are very different? Negotiation is problematic in similar ways to those discussed under

---

32 For further discussion of consent in relation to the HGDP see Posey and Dutfield (1996: 166–168). They also highlight illegal efforts by Hoffman–La Roche in conjunction with the NIH at obtaining samples from the indigenous Aeta people of the Philippines.

"consent". Negotiation, like consent, gives the powerless a sense of having control. But it is illusory control. Indeed, I contend that negotiation is at best a cover-up for failure of communication, but a more likely interpretation is that pseudo-communication is the intention.

However, negotiation has not even been attempted in the commodification of life, currently under way for human and other life forms. For example, in the case of the cell line from the Guaymi woman from Panama, the interest was profit. The Guaymi carry a virus which, because it stimulates the production of antibodies, could prove commercially profitable in treating leukemia and AIDS patients.

Both Jeremy Rifkin and Vandana Shiva use the metaphor of "enclosures" in discussing the series of shifts which have occurred over the last 500 years of western culture in relation to land, and to the privatisation of other areas of public activity. Since the enclosures in Europe it has not taken long for other parts of the earth's surface to be made commercially tradeable: the air, the seas, the electromagnetic spectrum, and most recently, the genetic spectrum.[33]

Enclosing the land in the sixteenth and seventeenth centuries meant privatising it, making it commercially valuable and transferable. The outcome for the poor was dispossession, since they no longer had access to common publicly held land, the commons. The enclosure of land transformed the lives of peasants and villagers, whose reciprocal obligations were suddenly severed. No longer was there any cause for the woman to agist her neighbour's cow for free, no longer would anyone plough the fields of other villagers in neighbourly reciprocity, and a whole swathe of communal village activities which traditionally took place on the village green ceased to be possible (unless a rental fee was paid to the "owner"). Land became a possession, something to be traded commercially. Like today's indigenous communities, European peasants had been possessed

---

33 For an extensive discussion on global commons, see Susan Buck (1998). She argues that although developing countries have put the brakes on the first-come-first-served principle for resources that can be considered common heritage, and in spite of attempts to foil the developed nations, in practice, international law continues to favour the powerful. For example, as she comments: "The seabed mineral regime was modified in 1994 to satisfy the developed nations before the Law of the Sea Treaty entered into force" (1998: 29). The result was that the Law of the Sea Treaty, with the exception of provisions for deep-sea mining, became a "classic case of enclosure" (1998: 84).

by the land, as was it passed down through the generations and between the people of one community. The enclosure movement brought fragmentation, a parcelling up of the land into plots, valued according to its productivity. People began asking for wages when they worked on their neighbour's land. Time was divided into working hours and non-working hours. But, as already discussed in the previous chapter, women continued to work without a break through the non-working hours as well as the times when (mostly) men went out to work for wages. The poor, too, could not easily fragment their time, especially as many had become landless with the introduction of fences. Similarly, the indigenous owners of colonised lands were dispossessed, their land being settled by the colonising farmers, miners, and townsfolk. And when some land remained for them to use, it was claimed by governments, and its use could easily be revoked in the event of a lucrative mineral discovery.

With enclosure of cell lines, and the subsequent patenting of their products, the body is fragmented; money is paid not to the original self from whom the cell came, but to the new "owners" of the patent. Bodies, and parts of bodies, become saleable items.[34] With cell lines removed from individuals, as in the case of John Moore, and individuals as representatives of a group or population, as in the cases of the Hagahai and Guaymi, the trade in life has entered a new era. As indicated above, the impact on the people affected by the theft is deep, and threatens their personal and communal integrity. The "enclosure" of people's bodies – which I perceive as the fragmentation[35] of self – is a new form of dispossession and colonisation. Patenting of cell lines is effectively an enslavement, for profit, of the bodies of people who have already suffered massive dispossession. The Mataatua Declaration on Cultural and Intellectual Property Rights of Indigenous Peoples calls for a "moratorium on any further commercialization of indigenous medicinal plants and human genetic materials ... until indigenous communities have developed appropriate protection mechanisms" (Posey and Dutfield 1996: 207, Paragraph 2.8).

---

34 The sale of body parts is not new. For a discussion, see Raymond (1995); Chattakar-Aitkins (2001).

35 For informative critiques of theoretical and bodily fragmentation, see Klein (1996, 1999, 2001a).

The new possessors are the already rich and powerful, the elites of nations, and predominantly the elites of the capitalist developed world, the transnationals. By contrast, the dispossessed are mostly the colonised, sometimes the landless; they are poor, they are most often Black, they do not have access to transnational power, their only power is local. Just as colonisers of previous centuries sent their missionaries, their entrepreneurs, their farmers, their military to take possession of the "uncivilised" lands, so now the transnationals and governments of powerful nations send their scientists into the field to reap the harvest of bio-colonialism. And like the pirates of previous centuries, they rarely ask permission, or pay for their contraband. The history books tell us that Columbus "discovered" the Americas, that Cook "discovered" Australia, when, in reality, indigenous cultures had already long thrived in these lands. The corporate scientists, like the colonisers of an earlier era, are removing cell lines in ways similar to those used to remove from the hands of the colonised the most productive and fertile lands. And through bio-prospecting, the bio-colonisers are appropriating and enclosing the knowledge of peoples who have long used certain plants and animals for ritual and medicinal purposes. How seriously, then, can we take the claims of "discovery" by corporate scientists of new drugs, of methods of isolating certain compounds and active ingredients?

The Amazon, Africa, Australasia and India have all been explored by corporations in their search for the new "gold":[36] new compounds and active ingredients. This knowledge is not just stumbled on. Discussion with local peoples with knowledge of the area is a critical part of the process. Ironically, under the pretence of "fairness", this "discovery" is then followed by the application of homogenised intellectual property rights (GATT and TRIPs). Trade regulations, of course, prevent so-called discrimination against foreign-owned companies, as it is modelled in the MAI. Theft and travesty are words that better describe such bio-colonialism.

---

36 Australian Aboriginal people refer to gold as "white man's dreaming" (Joy Smith 1986: pers. comm.).

Conclusion

Globalisation has changed the world. This change has occurred on a number of levels simultaneously. In this chapter I have highlighted the impact of globalisation, through patents and the WTO trade structures, on disenfranchised and poor peoples, in particular indigenous and rural peoples. I have given examples of how bioprospecting is threatening the knowledge base of peoples who have managed to sustain the earth, in some cases for many millennia. The WTO rules are undermining the sovereign status of nations so much that domestic industries cannot survive the onslaught of heavily weighted competition by transnational corporations who use right as might. As Tony Clarke and Maude Barlow so cogently point out:

> Wherever they go – Citizen Exxon or Citizen Ford, Citizen Mitsubishi or Citizen Shell, Citizen Sony or Citizen GE, Citizen IBM or Citizen Microsoft, Citizen Pepsi or Citizen McDonald's – their political rights as investors are constitutionally guaranteed and protected (1997: 163).

A global economy built in the image of stateless, contextless capital is a system created by those who have a great deal to gain from it. In Beth Burrows' words:

> Whether the booty was neem from India, or endod from Ethiopia, or the cells of a man from Seattle, or the cheek-scrapings of indigenous peoples, or the biodiversity of an entire Costa Rican rainforest, or one important microorganism from the hot springs of Yellowstone National Park, the value of biodiversity is difficult to exaggerate (2001a: 243).

Just as privatisation, disconnection and universalism were important in the early stages of capitalism, they remain important in the increasing concentration of ownership in the global economy. This economy of the powerful – primarily a knowledge-based economy, immaterialised through information and biotechnologies – is recolonising members of the diversity matrix. The increasingly intensive knowledge and services sector is where the new profits are to be made. And patents are crucial to this growth. In the USA, patent applications went up by an incredible 38 per cent in the six months from October 2000. By February 2001, there were more than 175,000 patent applications on human gene sequences (Bunting 2001). With patents so important to profit, transnational legal structures have been put in place, or are being proposed, in order to protect the new (old) knowledge economy. As I have argued in this chapter, IPRs are not intended to protect the rights of indigenous peoples or others from the diversity matrix. They are intended to increase the protection around bundled property rights for the transnational sector. The continuing appropriation and privatisation of the poor – whether it be land, labour, knowledge, plant and animal life or body parts – is leading to more and more social and personal disconnection, a disconnection promoted under the banner of universal liberalism and neoliberal economic globalisation.

CHAPTER EIGHT

WILD POLITICS

In thinking through the issues raised in this book, I have many times encountered obstacles, and on each occasion I wondered whether it would be the undoing of my research. But on each occasion, I have come out the other side more convinced than ever that people, collectively, need a new way of living with the planet. I am not the first, and hopefully not the last, to have these insights. More work is urgently needed to analyse all the local and global permutations of globalisation and their effects on individuals and communities.

My analysis has highlighted a series of patterns that emerge when looking deeply into processes involved in the spread of globalisation. Globalisation is not a development that could easily have arisen from within societies with different features. It is a distinct outgrowth of western capitalist and patriarchal systems that is manifested in the salient features which characterise the global economic system. Challenges to globalisation have come from many quarters. The ones I have focused on are feminism, ecology and the insights of indigenous peoples. The attribute of connection is what distinguishes – and unites – these three movements for me and makes them powerful challengers of the dominant culture. Following from Robin Morgan (1990: 51), it is disconnection that characterises globalisation.

Power, in its strongest forms, tends toward disconnection. It does this through different means, according to the type of power wielded and the degrees of difference between those wielding and those affected by it. Power is often indirect. Authority is dependent on disconnection, and the disconnection is respected by both the powerful and the powerless. Violence, that is, coercive power, may be very direct in its use, but it also tends to leave the individuals involved – both perpetrators and victims – dissociated. An internal disconnection occurs as a way of coming to terms, cutting off from the pain of violence. As one moves along the spectrum of powers toward more stable, but conventionally less strong forms, as discussed in Chapter Two, connection becomes more important. Attitudinal change occurs not because of coercion or violence, but because a person has been convinced – whether rationally or irrationally – by a particular argument or way of looking at the world. It is this kind of power which will be required to shift the inspiration of western culture from profit motive to biodiversity.

Knowledge, too, has different structures according to the culture from which it has developed. Indigenous knowledges are local and connected. There is a direct relationship between people and the subject of their knowledge. Western knowledge, on the other hand, has become increasingly disconnected from reality. This can best be seen in the way in which economics is structured around assumptions which have almost nothing to do with real life; or in the way in which the international economy rests on immaterial transactions which are pure abstraction of numbers through the trading of futures, derivatives or put and call options. Or it can be seen in the increasingly important emphasis on

Banner from S11 protest, Melbourne, 2000.

immateriality[1] through computer networks, biotechnological advances, and shifts in farming methods that pay little or no attention to the ecology of place. Feminists have challenged some of these abstractions, and have highlighted the importance of concrete knowledge, of contextualisation, of the particularities of individual location. In a similar way, ecology has pointed to the importance of place, and the local.

Western culture has tended toward what Marimba Ani calls "abstractification" (2000: 107). In so doing, western knowledge has dislocated itself in an erroneous attempt to rise above the particular and the local. Dislocation has been a useful intellectual strategy for the colonising cultures, enabling them to send representatives out into the world with the feeling that if only everyone could be as "civilised" as they were, the world would be a better place.

The problem with this one-size-fits-all approach is that it benefits only those at the top, or those whose conditions are similar enough to squeeze into the appropriate mould. Women, as a social group, have rarely fitted easily. Likewise, the poor of many countries, especially groups marginalised within broad geographic or cultural regions, generally cannot or do not abide by the rules of the dominant culture and simultaneously maintain their integrity. And the indigenous peoples of nearly all nations have not fitted the mould. If we are to move toward a world in which people are genuinely respected for their local, particular selves, we will need a system of knowledge that is generated from local cultural systems in much the same way as biodiversity flourishes when the ecological systems are intact. Every reduction in biodiversity reduces its overall health; every move toward homogenisation reduces its resilience. So too with human society.

As noted in Chapter Three, the process of orienting an economy toward export is one of disengagement, dislocation and displacement. Neoclassical economics moves in this direction, creating disconnection from the real world. The way in which externalities are calculated is a symptom of disconnection from the situated position of a person living in a particular community. Simply going shopping these days in a suburban shopping centre in Australia is an exercise in disconnection. The baby

---

1   Western culture has literally deified immateriality, and the transcendent God of Christianity is perhaps its most intrinsic immaterial formulation.

corn comes from Thailand, the cashew nuts from Vietnam, the lemons from California. The distances traversed by these commodities for the simple purpose of supplying a consumer in Australia is wasteful in the extreme, especially since Australia itself produces all these foods. It involves cartage over enormous distances by road, rail and air, with the concomitant expenditure of fuel, the uncounted externalities of pollution and global warming, and the cost of maintaining the infrastructure of these transport systems. Added to this cost of externalities are the packaging materials used to protect the food on its travels, as well as the pesticides and possible biotechnological interventions used to increase shelf life. Exports of cut flowers to Europe have also become a dollar earner in Australia, as they have in the Philippines.

Disconnection is structured into the system of neoclassical economics. Not only is it disconnected from the real biophysical world, it also pays little attention to the relationships between economic players, most of whom do not fit the model of "rational economic man" pursuing "his" own selfish interests. Many unacknowledged players are women, trying to maintain the lives of people around them, including children and dependent men. But the homogenised philosophy is portrayed as the only model for living in a modern world (Fukuyama 2001: 15), a restatement of Margaret Thatcher's dictum "There is no alternative".[2]

Attitudes to land ownership or relationship to land are central in defining how a culture perceives itself. Western culture is increasingly disconnected from a relationship to land. Land sales are made in the absence of both the vendor or the buyer. This is in stark contrast to the relationship between people and land which exists in many traditional and indigenous societies, where land is a relationship for which one is responsible, and, which involves one in practices of sustenance and maintenance. Patrick Dodson refers to the concept of "land literacy", that is, the ability to read the landscape. In speaking of his relationship to the land, he says:

---

2   Francis Fukuyama states that "We remain at the end of history because there is only one system that will continue to dominate world politics – that of the liberal democratic West" (2001: 15). For a very different perspective, in which many alternatives are discussed, see Bennholdt-Thomsen, Faraclas and von Werlhof (2001).

Many Australians don't know how to think themselves into the country, the land. They find it hard to think with the land. We Aboriginal people find it hard to think without the land. My grandfather taught me how to think about relationships by showing me places. He showed me where the creeks and rivers swirl into the sea, the fresh water meets the salt, the different worlds of ocean and river are mixing together (in Kauffman 1998: 169).

And Doreen Kartinyeri, an elder of the Ngarrindjeri, says:

Looking at the Ngarrindjeri nation, the sites, the burial grounds, the middens, and the people, it's all one, it's connected together. It goes in a circle and that circle should not be broken, not with sites, not with people, not with land, skies, and waters (in Bell 1998: 249).

One finds similar feelings articulated by those who do have an intimate relationship with land. Their beliefs arise from indigenous cultures (Langton 1998; Gunn Allen 1998; Tuhiwai Smith 1999) or they are feminists (Daly 1978; Griffin 1978; Somerville 1999), ecologists (Salleh 1997; Plumwood 1993), town planners (Rogers 1997), farmers (Hawthorne 1991, 1995; Pretty and Shah 1997: 48 ff), fisherfolk (Smith 1995: 85), or some other group whose lives bring them into close connection with the natural environment.

Disconnection from the biophysical world and from the land characterises contemporary industrial farming. Crops are grown as monocultures in exotic locations, further disconnected from their local environment through the application of fertilisers, pesticides, herbicides and a host of new technologies that come under the rubric of biotechnology, including terminator seeds, patented and genetically modified plants, and fast-growing trees with a high lignin content (see Chapter Five). In animal husbandry, disconnection allows a cow to be perceived simply as a milk producer, an udder disconnected from the rest of her body,[3] and makes it possible to feed herbivores a carnivorous diet because it increases production.[4] Disconnection is also fostered through the dislocation of

---

3   This is not dissimilar from the way in which pornography depicts a woman solely as breasts or a hole available to satisfy the sexual pleasure of men. Such a view supports the flourishing practice of prostitution.

4   In fact, if one counts the cost of externalities, such as the slaughter of many thousands of animals because of BSE, it is not an economically viable or productive approach.

trees, and the growing of exotic species in plantations far from the original native environment. The shift to biotechnological solutions is increasing disconnection from the environment, creating ever more distance between the plant and its ecological niche. It is leading to a reduction in biodiversity, since standardisation and homogenisation are the intention of the corporations whose finances control these industries. Each failure of the technology becomes another business opportunity, and removes itself further from the real world. Disconnection fuels irresponsibility. It contributes to maintaining the profit motive without regard for human or planetary consequences.

In the increasingly urban environment, disconnection is structured into the architecture and transport systems of most cities. In cities where the car is important, work, entertainment, shopping and sporting venues are widely separated from one another.[5] In a global economy, production and consumption are more and more separated and thus disconnected. A T-shirt is made in India from cotton imported from the USA (Ramamurthy 2000), and sold by global stores in Hong Kong, London and Frankfurt; a T-shirt with "Made in America" on the label is produced in Saipan with Indian cotton (see Chapter Six). Like primary production, goods produced in this system are disconnected from systems of accountability. Because corporations are able to hide lines of responsibility, when things go wrong, most of the culprits go free.

In the global economy, work is disconnected, dislocated and dehumanised. Most work in its current form disconnects people from themselves and their communities. Unemployment is no alternative in this context since it tends to disconnect people socially, making it impossible for them to play a participatory role in the community. Over-employment disconnects people through decreased time for relationships with partners, families, friends and social networks. And yet neither of these is an extreme manifestation of work, unlike slavery, or work within prisons or export processing zones. Even further disconnected are those disposed of by the global economic system, who have no hope of getting work of any kind, who, as Viviane Forrester (1999) argues, are discarded from the social fabric.

---

5   During visits to Los Angeles, I am always struck by the utter structural "necessity" of a car. I have found it almost impossible to walk to shops, confronted by freeways to somehow go under, over, or around. This is a symptom of disconnection in city planning.

The pattern of disconnection is found in the forms of international agreements and trade rules which are being institutionalised through the World Trade Organisation and through intellectual property rights which valorise disconnection (see Chapter Seven). Knowledge, in the form of intellectual property rights, is being displaced from its origins, and through a process akin to theft, the originators of the knowledge are dispossessed of their rights to use their knowledge in ways which accord with their cultural priorities. Further dispossession occurs as the corporations make profits without any accountability or return to the original community. The issue here is not simply a matter of royalties, but also of cultural respect and integrity. Patents privatise, commodify and universalise what were often free, common resources. They disconnect knowledge from place, and turn it into profit. The World Trade Organisation and its associated institutions, agreements, protocols and instruments seeks to further universalise western property systems; the result is the progressive intensification of poverty among the world's poorest peoples. Under the rubric of equality of treatment, greater inequality is put in place.

All the above systems rely on a disconnected neoliberal utilitarian philosophy which is grounded in an ethic developed throughout the period of European colonisation, itself an inherently disconnecting process. Utilitarianism depends on a separation of means and ends, of the personal from the political. The natural world, animals, plants, human beings are simply cogs whose purpose is to serve corporate profit and those who control the corporations.

Universalism based on sameness produced a reaction that brought state communism to its knees. Universalism based on homogenised commodification is in the process of bringing capitalism to its knees, because it fails to take account of ecological limits. The global system is using people for profit, making them a part of a utilitarian scheme of efficiency where difference is flattened and profit comes at the cost of human dignity.

I propose, instead, a system that depends on connection, on sustainability over a very long period of time, and one that recognises that each person, just like each plant or animal or micro-organism in an ecosystem, is an integral part of a web of relationships. I propose a system that has biodiversity at the centre; one in which epistemological multiversity recognises the specialness of everyone wherever they come from; one which encourages the wild types to thrive, the wild child to laugh.

Wild Politics: A vision for the next 40,000 years

I have in mind a wild politics, a vision which I hope could be sustained for at least 40,000 years. As I mentioned in Chapter Four, this idea comes from a talk originally given in Australia by Lilla Watson in 1984 on "Aboriginal Women and Feminism". Watson commented that to Aboriginal people in Australia, the future extends as far forward as the past. In that case, she said, we have a 40,000-year plan. In a similar vein the Kari-Oca Declaration and the Indigenous Peoples' Earth Charter begins with the following statement in its preamble: "We, the Indigenous Peoples, walk to the future in the footprints of our ancestors" (in Posey and Dutfield 1996: 189).[6] Wild politics is the view that diversity is central to the existence of life, to the sustenance of the planet, and to the health of human society. I attempt to outline some principles which will assist humanity to continue to live. Some cultures around the world already live by these principles; some individuals are fighting to make people more aware of the possibilities; and some groups are beginning to move in the direction of wild politics (Bennholdt-Thomsen *et al.* 2001). Where we are now is at the other end of the continuum, dominated by technoglobal corporatisation.

Central to this book is the concept and practice of biodiversity. Marimba Ani (2000) in her discussion of western culture undertakes to expose its inspiration, which she names as domination. I extend her analysis to name profit as the inspiration for globalisation. My proposal is to signal a culture whose inspiration is biodiversity. I choose biodiversity over diversity because diversity, as we have seen in Chapter Three, can easily be appropriated. It has already been appropriated by global companies as part of advertising programs appealing to young people in a global market. Biodiversity as inspiration, however, is not easily appropriated.[7] It "just is".

---

6 In eleven appendices to their book, Posey and Dutfield (1966) reproduce important charters and declarations from UN and indigenous organisations regarding rights of indigenous peoples.

7 I note with sadness, however, that the World Bank is making appropriative moves on biodiversity. In 2001, I visited the World Bank headquarters in Washington. At the time of my visit, there was a huge display entitled "Biodiversity in the World Bank's Work". The display told of the many projects the World Bank is associated with in countries around the world. It stated that 226 projects had received $US1 billion in the past ten years, as well as $US1.2 billion in co-funding. Another interesting convergence was occurring in the foyer where four women were putting up a display of indigenous

When I say that biodiversity "just is", what I mean is that an appreciation of biodiversity is part of its philosophy; that is, it does not exist (unlike shopping malls) for anyone's profit. Biodiversity is an integral part of the existence of life on Earth. It is people as much as anything else. We live in the midst of biodiversity, and if it goes, so will we. Certainly, under the current transnational profit regime, biodiversity is being appropriated through corporate biopiracy.

An appeal to biodiversity implies activity and participation as opposed to disconnected domination. I am thinking here of something like the difference between the wild in the sense of wild type on the one hand, and on the other of wild as in National Park wilderness separated out from the real world because it might prove useful at a later time, or because it is nice to have a place to go to relax for those with the time and the means to get there (see Chapter Four). The wild type cannot be genetically modified, since at the moment when this happens it is no longer a wild type. Resistance to appropriation is important in developing a wild politics.

Below, I sketch out some of the ways in which the central themes of this book might be transformed were we to live in a culture driven not by profit, universalisation, homogenisation, disconnection and utilitarianism, but by the wild, biodiversity, locatedness and knowledge of local conditions, epistemological multiversity, connection, and relationship.

Power, in a system for which biodiversity is central, would be dispersed rather than concentrated. In order to recognise biodiversity, one must recognise the importance of each player, no matter how small. The microorganisms in the soil have an enduring effect on the way in which plants grow. In a cultural setting, the consequences of decisions and actions on the powerless are the test of whether they are worth pursuing. A dynamic stability in power relations can be reached, given time, and given the willingness to genuinely see the world through the eyes of others. Violence breeds violence, but understanding opens the world to creativity, new ideas, and to revisiting practices that work. Participation and responsible decision-making are important in gaining stability, without losing the

---

artefacts from around the world, entitled "Biodiversity and its Products". These are just the latest means of drawing traditional and indigenous communities into the homogenising ambit of the World Bank and global capital. Note that women are used as the World Bank's "messengers".

dynamism of a living system. To make an analogy with ecosystems, the existing system rewards only the peak predators.

Knowledge is an ever-changing and developing system which encapsulates the experiences of generation after generation of people living in communities. Relationship is essential to the development of knowledge. Knowledge also arises in response to the environment. Indigenous peoples' knowledge is a distillation of a history of local conditions, careful observation framed, as with all knowledge, within a particular cultural tradition. And as the Mataatua Declaration on Cultural and Intellectual Property Rights of Indigenous Peoples makes clear, "Indigenous flora and fauna are inextricably bound to the territories of indigenous communities and any property right claims must recognize their traditional guardianship" (in Posey and Dutfield 1996: 207, Paragraph 2.6). Overriding such knowledge with an imposed, disconnected, and displaced system means losing valuable insights into how a particular place and space can best be sustained over millennia. Women's insights into how their bodies work have been displaced through so-called objective science and disconnected medicalisation. Feminists have challenged this view in recent decades (as in past eras), and a more complex understanding of women's bodies is now emerging. The corporatisation of knowledge is a relatively recent development. In a system where biodiversity is central, and an epistemological multiversity is respected, the integrity of knowledge systems will also be respected.[8]

Economic interconnectedness is central to a system based on biodiversity. Such an economics, as I have discussed in Chapter Three, is being developed (O'Hara 1995; Gowdy and McDaniel 1995; McMahon 1997). It recognises that no part of the whole can be changed without affecting every other part. Biodiversity loss cannot easily be reversed, and the ramifications of lost biodiversity will affect humanity forever – in human time spans – since genetic diversity can recover only over many millions of years. This new approach recognises that economics is

---

8   This does assume that a knowledge system which promotes profit and violence would not easily arise, and that if it were to arise at all, its people through discussion and developing understanding would see that such a path would result in their own deprivation. Put differently, its people would change their minds. I realise that this is a rather optimistic view of human society, but for the purpose of this thought experiment, I will run with it.

grounded in the real lives of people, whose lives in turn are affected by where and how they live. Unlike neoclassical economics, wild politics economics is based not on decontextualisation and profit, but on embeddedness and sustaining of life. Under such a regime, export-driven economies with uncounted externalities would not exist. This does not mean that trade would cease, but the profit of shareholders and companies in far-away countries would not be its main purpose. Trade may well cross international boundaries, ply the seas, and be airborne, but its purpose would be the sustenance of life, developing creativity and innovative systems for survival of communities, cities and geographic regions. In addition, the cost of externalities such as habitat loss and pollution caused by transport would be factored into the cost of goods.

A system based on biodiversity is not simply a return to a rural paradise. Rather, it involves thinking creatively about the most productive (in a genuine sense) ways of giving everyone a chance at a fulfilling, but not wastefully excessive, life. Creativity and happiness may be dependent on a full stomach – of nourishing food – but they are not dependent upon profit.

Reconceptualising relationship with land is going to take a lot of deep thinking and reorganising. Land reform has been a slogan in many revolutionary movements for change, and land dispossession has accompanied colonisation and industrialisation in nearly all parts of the world. Land, as well as the water courses,[9] the seas and the air, are the basis of our existence. They are not commodities to be owned. Access to land, to the produce and resources of land, is a common wealth of all of humanity, and of other living beings on the planet. The integrity of a rock's existence should also be taken into account. Biodiversity suggests that the rock is integral to the existence of the lichen, or the ant, or the lizard, or the woman sunning herself in the morning's warmth. Ownership of the enduring common heritage such as land and water is an act of decontextualised imagination and hubris. Our relationship to urban land is just as important as the ways in which we live in cities (Hynes 1996; Bennholdt-Thomsen 2001).

Work is an activity carried out initially to increase our chances of survival. The worm could be seen to be working as it aerates the soil through which it passes. Human work could have the same result, which

---

9 For a critique of water ownership, and an optimistic proposal for the future, see Petrella (2001).

is to leave the world a richer place, a world with the possibility of sustaining itself for many tens of thousands of years. Indeed, if we can make it through the next 40,000 years, the earth will be well placed to survive much longer. Cosmic accidents might occur, of course, but a profit-driven world would not fare any better. Some theorists of work (Gorz 1999; Hyman 1993, 1999, 2001; Else 1996) have suggested that work could not only sustain itself over thousands of years, but could also leave the world a richer place if every person received an income. This income would not be dependent on any activity, but would be more than sufficient to maintain good health, and enable the person to participate in the society as equitably as anyone else. The gain to the world would be immense if the billion or so people who currently devote all their efforts to physical survival were able to devote their time to creativity and inventiveness.[10] Such systems of trust, because they generate goodwill, tend toward reciprocated trust and are less likely to be abused than systems that impose conditions.[11]

Production is an outcome of work. If work were fulfilling and socially responsible, production too would follow in its wake. Making "biodiversity the logic of production" (Shiva 1993a: 146) changes the nature of production. Export processing zones would be unthinkable. Inhuman wages and working conditions would be counterproductive. A multiversity of approaches to production would draw out all the creativity and inventiveness of people. It would allow for growing food, trees, flowers and medicinal plants in ways that best suit their growth rather than in existing ways that best suit the markets or distribution systems without recourse to the consequences of these actions. Biotechnology would not fill the spaces of previous technological failures; instead, self-sustaining systems could be developed, systems which contribute to the community rather than leading to poverty and starvation.

Consumption would be reduced. Not because consumption in and of itself is bad, but because its current level in the rich countries is not sustainable. Consumption could cease to be a need, cease to fill the gap displaced through a lack of meaning in a society driven by profit. Consumption would be transformed into a reciprocal process that allows

---

10   I am grateful to Janet Mackenzie for mentioning this point.
11   In Australia, welfare under the conservative Howard government (1996–) has moved toward a philosophy of pseudo-equality called "mutual obligation". Such a system engenders mistrust.

individuals to grow physically or intellectually; it could assist in sustaining relationships between people. Goods produced purely for profit would not survive in this environment, although goods which enhance beauty, well-being and health might.

As mentioned above, trade would not cease, just as economics would continue. Its purpose, however, would be to move goods produced in one area, because of particular environmental, social or cultural conditions, to another, at a price that accurately reflects the inputs and incorporates any external costs as a part of the price. Trading accounts would continue to be kept, between nations, or communities or regions, but determined and conscious efforts would be made to keep deficits and surpluses to a minimum. Also, the system of accounts would include work currently rendered invisible (subsistence, domestic, unpaid, caring work). Maintaining the health of the whole is as important at the international level as it is at the local level. Rules of trade, as they stand, would need to be overhauled and the language of equal access changed to reflect equitable outcomes. Global interdependence would grow, and social and cultural interaction could flourish with increased cross-cultural understanding.

These ideas for a wild politics are not a blueprint.[12] They form the beginnings of an outline. The drawing will need to be developed and given colour by many people from diverse places and with a wonderful array of approaches. The drawing might never be finished; it is how we get on to the road there that counts.

If the wild were the driving force of the culture, the *asili* (Ani 2000), the seed (Shiva 1993a), life (Bennholdt-Thomsen and Mies 1999), *jukurrpa* (as the Warlpiri of Central Australia would say, see Bell 1983/ 2002), the world would function in very different ways. In this new world, biodiversity would become the inspiration for the culture, the defining spirit, or what Ani calls *utamaroho*. This spirit would result in very different behaviours and institutions, at both local and global levels, and the creation of a particular kind of thought, or *utamawazo*. It would result in a very different relationship with the biophysical world, one that would make it difficult to destroy land by mining, bombing, industrial farming or commercial development, all of which are predicated on profit and

---

12 There are already many good ideas being proposed by a wide range of people, including the Tobin Tax and the ideas put forward by David Suzuki and Holly Dressel (2002).

disrespect. With a relationship of connection between people and the land, there would be great reluctance to do things solely for short-term profit, when the long-term consequences are destructive. In a world of wild politics, it would be impossible to imagine terminator seeds, GMOs, molecular colonisation, biotechnologies and reproductive technologies which violate women's bodies, since these would be perceived as deeply destructive. The vicious cycle of technological failure followed by business opportunity followed by yet another technological failure would be broken. These and other cycles of violence could be replaced by a system which focuses instead on life-oriented outcomes, on systems which are premissed on a germinating matrix, *asili*, seed, wild type. Within such a system, it would not be possible to separate out the wild as a place far removed from human life, and the eradication of cultural diversity would be unimaginable. Educational, health, commercial and artistic endeavours would flourish in an environment enriched by epistemological multiversity. In a world enlivened by wild politics, members of the diversity matrix are the hope for the future. Within wild politics are new ways of thinking, and in this quest for new behaviours and institutions are also the seeds of a future which will hold dear to the driving force of wildness, and a politics which grows out of this longing.

What I hope for is a world filled with richness, texture, depth and meaning. I want diversity with all its surprises and variety. I want an epistemological multiversity which values the context and real-life experiences of people. I want a world in which relationship is important, and reciprocity is central to social interaction. I want a world which can survive sustainably for at least 40,000 years. I want a wild politics.

APPENDIX

Table 1: The world's 100 largest economic entities

The world's 100 largest economic entities as of 28 February 2001. The figures represent total market capitalisation of stock markets (domestic equities only) expressed in billions of US dollars, and the world's biggest companies, ranked by market capitalisation as of the final week of March 2001. Adapted from Sheehan (2001: 32).

	Countries	Companies
1	USA	
2	Japan	
3	UK	
4	France	
5	Germany	
6	Switzerland	
7	Canada	
8	Italy	
9	Hong Kong	
10	Holland	
11	Spain	
12		General Electric (USA)
13	Australia	
14	Sweden	
15	Taiwan	
16		Microsoft (USA)
17		Exxon Mobil (USA)
18		Pfizer (USA)
19		CitiGroup (USA)
20	South Africa	
21		Wal-Mart (USA)
22		Royal Dutch (EUR)
23		WorldCom (USA)
24	Brazil	
25		BP Amoco (EUR)

	Countries	Companies
26		Vodafone (EUR)
27		Intel (USA)
28	Finland	
29	South Korea	
30		AIG (USA)
31		IBM (USA)
32		Merck (USA)
33		AOL–TimeWarner (USA)
34		GlaxoSmithKline (EUR)
35	Singapore	
36		SBC Comm (USA)
37	Belgium	
38		Cisco (USA)
39		Verizon (USA)
40		Toyota (JAP)
41	Mexico	
42		Johnson & Johnson (USA)
43		Nokia (EUR)
44		Coca-Cola (USA)
45	Malaysia	
46		Bristol–Meyers (USA)
47	Denmark	
48		Philip Morris (USA)
49		Novartis (EUR)
50		HSBC (HK)
51	Greece	
52		Home Depot (USA)
53		Nippon T&T (JAP)
54		Roche–Genen (EUR)
55		Total–Fina–Elf (EUR)
56		Chevron–Texaco (USA)
57		Morgan Chase (USA)
58		AT&T (USA)
59		Berkshire Hathaway (USA)
60		Oracle (USA)
61		Bank America (USA)
62		Eli Lilly (USA)
63		Proctor and Gamble (USA)
64		Tyco–Mattel (USA)
65	Ireland	
66		AstraZeneca (EUR)

	Countries	Companies
67		Wells Fargo (USA)
68		China Mobile (HK)
69		EMC (USA)
70		Fannie Mae (USA)
71		Nestlé (EUR)
72		BellSouth (USA)
73		American Home (USA)
74		AT&T Wireless (USA)
75		Allianz (EUR)
76		Deutsche Tel (EUR)
77		Abbott Labs (USA)
78		Pharmacia–Monsanto (USA)
79		Morgan Stanley (USA)
80		Telefonica (EUR)
81		Amgen (USA)
82	Norway	
83		UBS (EUR)
84		Dell Computer (USA)
85	Israel	
86		Sun Microsystems (USA)
87		PepsiCo (USA)
88		Sony (JAP)
89	Portugal	
90		Vivendi–Univ (EUR)
91		Texas Instruments (USA)
92	Chile	
93		ING (EUR)
94		Nortel (CAN)
95		Amgen (USA)
96		France Telecom (EUR)
97		Viacom–CBS (USA)
98		Qwest Comm (USA)
99		Aventis (EUR)
100		Hewlett Packard (USA)

Table 2: Companies, countries and name changes

Novartis	Switzerland	Formed in 1996 from Ciba–Geigy and Sandoz.
Aventis	Germany/France	A merger between Germany's Hoechst, France's Rhone–Poulenc and AgrEvo, a joint subsidiary of Hoechst and Schering (Perrière and Seuret 2000: 11); AgrEvo a subsidiary of Aventis, formed from Hoechst and Rhone–Poulenc.
Astra–Zeneca	UK/Sweden	Formed from a merger between Zeneca and Astra.
DuPont–Pioneer	USA	DuPont owns Pioneer HiBred (world's largest seed company); Hy-line International – world's oldest laying-hen breeding company since 1936 (Kneen 1999: 60).
Monsanto	USA	Owns DeKalb Genetics, Asgrow and Holden – USA; Sementes Agroceres – Brazil; Unilever's Plant Breeding International. Monsanto tried to acquire Delta and Pine Land Company, which developed the terminator technology (Tokar 2001: 9); Monsanto (USA) merged with Pharmacia and UpJohn – 1999 (Tokar 2001: 9); Monsanto today wants to be known as Pharmacia (O'Hagan 2001).
Fletcher Challenge	NZ	Rubicon and ArborGen.
ArborGen		International Paper (USA), Fletcher Challenge Forests (NZ), Westvaco Corporation (USA), and Genesis Research and Development, a New Zealand biotechnology company.

Table 3: Areas of highest cultural and biological diversity

Areas of highest cultural diversity		Areas of highest biological diversity
	Indonesia	Colombia
Nigeria	Australia	China
Cameroon	India	Peru
Papua New Guinea	Mexico	Malaysia
	Zaire	Ecuador
	Brazil	Madagascar

The countries in the left column of Table 3 represent countries in which more than 200 languages are spoken. Those on the right are considered "megadiverse" for the number of unique species. The middle column represents countries which display characteristics of both cultural and biological diversity (adapted from Durning, Worldwatch Institute, 1992; reproduced in 1999: 250; see also Posey 1996).

GLOSSARY

Appropriation

Appropriation is the mechanism by which one culture or community takes from another without permission. Appropriation occurs in areas as diverse as knowledge, land, resources, culture, spirituality, bodies and parts of bodies. Biopiracy, molecular colonisation, and spiritual appropriation are three recent forms, and what they have in common is the use of systems of the powerless group within the diversity matrix, by a group with more power.

Asili

A Kiswahili word, *asili* is the logos of a culture (Ani 2000: xxv). It is the seed at the centre of a culture, its driving force, or the "germinating matrix" (Ani 2000: 498). It is the ideological stance which makes sense of the behaviours of the people in the culture, and of its major institutions and creations, and the kind of cultural ethic supported by various rewards and sanctions. Law, religion and worldview emerge from the chrysalis of the *asili*. In western culture the *asili* is characterised by separation and universalism. This book proposes that if the *asili* of western culture could shift, it would involve "fundamental changes in conception of the 'other' and of behavior towards others" (Ani 2000: 517). If the *asili* were to shift to the idea of the "wild" as a central metaphor for thought and ideology, a whole raft of cultural forms would have to change. The "wild" is comparable to the seed (as described by Shiva), to life (as described by Mies), to *jukurrpa* (as described by Bell 1983/2002).

Atopia

From Greek τοποσ (topos) meaning place, and the prefix "a-" meaning not. A non-existent place. As William Gibson famously said in *Neuromancer* (1984), "There's no there, there." Cyberspace is the ideal atopia, and the transnational sector would like to find a way to do this in the real world. Ironically, Gertrude Stein apparently said of the USA, "There's no there there".

381

Betroffenheit

A German word used by Maria Mies (1999: xi) to express participatory engagement with research, one which impels the researcher not only to reflect but also to act.

Biodiversity

Biodiversity is the complex self-sustaining system of an ecological niche in a very particular locale. It includes diversity in genetics, within species and within ecosystems. It includes plants, animals and micro-organisms. It "encompasses all of the species that currently exist on Earth, the variations that exist within species, and the interactions that exist among all organisms and their biotic and abiotic environments as well as the integrity of these interactions" (Gowdy and McDaniel 1995: 182). I expand the notion of biodiversity to take in cultural diversity, and I explore the idea that bio-diversity could be the inspiration for culture.

Consent

Consent is a method by which one party is granted permission to carry out particular actions that have an impact on the other party. Consent can be asked for in circumstances of equal power relations, but in such circumstances it is rarely formalised, and might more correctly be called consensus. For example, consent is not typically asked for when giving another person a gift; decisions often emerge without formal assent after a conversation between two or more individuals.

Consent is what a person in power expects from another person who is putting herself in their hands – who is powerless or has reduced power – when there is a possibility that the one without power will change her mind. Consent is a ploy that the powerful use to legitimate whatever they do. Legally speaking, it changes the act from one of violation to one that is acceptable. Consent is only required when people are vulnerable in some way: legally, medically, emotionally, sexually, as research objects. Consent is used by the state and the powerful to make the powerless feel as though they have some control over their lives. It is not real control, but a pseudo-control, which fools us into colluding with those in power. Written consent is usually only requested when there is some danger of things going wrong, or one party is much more likely to benefit from the transaction. Doctors insist on written consent when a risky medical treatment is offered. Doctors, lawyers, accountants, banks, sporting organisations all ask for my consent;

children, hairdressers, relatives, friends never do. Janice Raymond suggests that compliance is a more useful term to use (nd: 7).

Context

Context involves particular, local and situated conditions and circumstances in which an event occurs. Context means recognising uniqueness, and not attempting to make blanket rules which universalise inappropriately from one local context or one situation to all others. Context takes account of meaning, of circumstances, of location in time and place, and of consequences.

Diversity

Diversity is a feature of healthy, resilient systems: from the biodiversity of the natural world to the cultural diversity of the human world. The more diverse a system is, the more likely it is to adapt successfully to shocks and changed conditions. I regard diversity as a core principle of an envisioned culture of wild politics (monoculture and homogeneity are the predominant forces in technoglobal culture).

Diversity matrix

The diversity matrix comprises the group of people who are most vulnerable to encroaching globalised systems. They are poor, often women, mostly black; they include indigenous peoples, the so-called "underclasses" and slaves, gypsies, nomads, refugees, political exiles; and then there are those who do not meet the expectations of the dominant culture: the disabled or the ill, lesbians, eco-activists and some radicals. The primary feature of the diversity matrix is its poverty.

Domestication

Domestication is the process by which wild-stock organisms are genetically modified over generations in order to create particular breeding stock.

Ecosystem

An ecosystem is an interrelated system of plants and animals associated with micro-organisms and non-living components in an environment. Examples of ecosystems include rainforests, grasslands, marine environments, urban environments.

Exclusive Marketing Rights

A provision in the WTO agreements which ensures that patents apply for a compulsory twenty-year period. During this time, for countries that are members of the WTO, it is illegal to manufacture generic drugs. The effect is to increase the cost of drugs in member countries.

Globalisation

Globalisation is a universalised system of monetary and cultural trade which benefits the rich sectors of the world, including the transnational sector. It is built upon western knowledge and property systems, and assumes that these are regarded as universally good regimes.

Incorporation

Incorporation is the process by which the transnational sector appropriates the diversity matrix (e.g. the term "diversity" is used to market products such as clothes, department stores, body products, see Klein 2000: 110–118). The transnational sector incorporates the diversity matrix through commodification, and distorts the products at the other end (another version of Mary Daly's [1978] reversals).

Intellectual Property Rights

First developed under European and North American law as a mechanism to protect individual and industrial inventions (Posey and Dutfield 1996: 1).

Jukurrpa

Jukurrpa is a concept which is usually translated as "dreaming" and is widely used by the Warlpiri of the Central Australian desert. The jukurrpa is not only time past, but also the present, and the framework of knowledge provided by the ancestral beings is "a force in the lives of the living" and "a moral code" (ibid). The jukurrpa is not a fixed law/lore, but rather a fulcrum from which change within the culture can occur. It provides "the structural potential for change" (Bell 1983/2001: 90, 91) within a particular framework of social and cultural forms and is a part of the overall interfunctioning system. Plants, animals, rocks, the nature of the landscape and soil, its water courses, places and the people all play a part in the interfunctioning system of the jukurrpa.

Landrace

Landraces are varieties of wild stock which have been developed by farmers over many, sometimes thousands, of seed generations selected to suit very particular local environments. Landraces tend to be more diverse than other domesticated breeding stock conventionally used in modern agriculture. Landraces maintain their connection with the specific local conditions under which they were developed. They are considered valuable because of their genetic traits. They are sometimes called "folk varieties" or "peasant varieties".

Local

The local is a specific place for which a community of people has particular feelings, about its culture, its environment and its people. Local knowledge is developed within the context of local conditions.

Maquiladoras

Foreign-owned assembly plants of northern Mexico, which emphasise transnational investment in export-oriented commodities. They are Mexico's version of the export processing zones found in many developing economies.

Miwi

Miwi is a Ngarrindjeri word meaning a knowledge feeling, located in the stomach. It is a feeling which indicates the truth of knowledge claims, and it is felt. It is often related to places, so that a place can create a feeling of peace or of feeling ill-at-ease. *Miwi* allows for a direct emotional engagement with the environment, and the wisdom gained from *miwi* connects to the physical environment.

Mpambo

Mpambo is a word from the Lusoga language of Uganda which means "the best of the seeds that are kept for propagation". Paul Wangoola uses this as a metaphor in his development of the concept of multiversity as a resistance to modernisation and colonisation of knowledges (Wangoola 2000).

Multiversity

Multiversity is an epistemological approach that takes account of the location and context of the knower. It values local knowledge. It does not attempt to straitjacket those in what I call the diversity matrix.

Negotiation

The term "negotiation" has similar problems to those discussed under "consent". Negotiation is about doing deals: "I'll give you this, if you give me that." Power relations are important in negotiation. Negotiation is used by the powerful as a way of pretending to give the powerless more say. The employer agrees that the employee will get more money, but other aspects of the job may be changed so that the employee works longer hours. Negotiation, like consent, gives the powerless a sense of having control. But it is illusory control. Indeed, negotiation can be a cover-up for an intended failure of communication.

Power

I define power as various forms of behaviour which characterise relationships between people. The stronger forms of power (violence and authority) tend toward disconnection, while the softer, but more stable, forms of power (attitudinal and attractional) foster connection and engagement.

Prakriti

A primordial energy which encompasses both stillness and dynamism. The Sanskrit word *Prakriti* is associated with abundance, and offers the idea of relationship between humanity and nature. Vandana Shiva (1989: 39) describes the nature of *Prakriti* as "activity and diversity". *Prakriti* is associated with women, and the female principle in Indian Hindu thought.

Precautionary principle

In 1992, at the UN Conference on Environment and Development, the precautionary principle was written into the Rio Declaration on Environment and Development, and signed by the participating Heads of States. It is one of the guiding principles for a number of international treaties, including the biodiversity convention and the global climate change treaty. The focus of the precautionary principle is that where serious or irreversible damage is a threat, lack of scientific certainty should not be used to postpone or prevent cost-effective measures to protect the environment. Member countries are responsible for applying the precautionary principle according to their capabilities (Palmlu 1998).

Sustainability

Sustainability requires a very long-term commitment to survival, and its true worth is realised when actions by humans enable an ecosystem to maintain or enhance its biodiversity over many thousands of years. Gradual changes in ecosystems might take place in response to changing climate patterns, but the use made of the ecosystem is responsive rather than causative.

Terminator technology

A biotechnology which causes proprietary seeds to self-destruct. The term was first used by the Rural Advancement Foundation International (RAFI) in March 1998 when a patent was awarded to the Delta and Pine Land Company along with the US Department of Agriculture. It is Patent No. 5,723,765: Control of Plant Gene Expression. Biotechnology companies use the term "technology protection system". The result of using terminator technology (also called suicide seeds) is that the seeds of the plant do not grow in the second generation. The consequence is that farmers can no longer grow their own seeds collected during harvest. In order to grow another crop they have to buy more seed from the corporation (Crouch 2001: 31–32).

Traditional Resource Rights

Developed to protect inalienable rights of indigenous peoples, including intangibles such as spiritual manifestations. Resource refers to all "knowledge and technology, esthetic and spiritual qualities, tangible and intangible sources that together are deemed by local communities necessary to ensure healthy and fulfilling lifestyles for present and future generations" (Posey and Dutfield 1996: 3).

Transnational sector

The transnational sector is currently in the process of globalising the diversity matrix. It is taming it, removing the features of diversity from it, homogenising it, eliminating its uncontrollable "wild types". The transnational sector is characterised by a cluster of features. The primary feature is its wealth. Because of its wealth (an attribute of power) it can force changes in the structures of global trade and politics. The transnational sector can be summarised by listing a host of brand names: GeneralElectric, Microsoft, GlaxoSmithKline, Exxon–Mobil, Pfizer, Wal–Mart, Novartis, Aventis, Pharmacia–Monsanto, AOL–TimeWarner, are just some of the world's largest hundred economic entities.

UBINIG

The Policy Research for Development Alternative is a policy research foundation founded in 1984 in Bangladesh. UBINIG is a grassroots organisation which works directly with the people, promoting research, supporting campaigns on social issues, and organising workshops and international conferences on women's health, reproductive technologies, genetic engineering and population control. UBINIG's executive director is Farida Akhter.

Utamaroho

A neologism created by Marimba Ani from the Kiswahili word, *utamaduni* "civilisation" and *roho* "spirit life". *Utamaroho* is what she characterises as the inspiration of a culture, its ethos, its emotional responses. *Utamaroho* can be thought of as the spirit of the culture. Ani argues that the *utamaroho*, or inspiration, of European culture is domination: domination is carved into all of its structures. It is present in every institution and every sanctioned behaviour, especially those which dispossess "the other" or which offer a means of control over nature, land and resources. Ani critiques the way in which western culture has been imposed on peoples all around the world and made out to be a higher and more evolved form of "civilisation", thereby justifying the wholesale destruction or appropriation of languages and other aspects of culture (2000: 15–17). In the world of wild politics proposed in this book, biodiversity would become the inspiration for the culture, its defining spirit, or its *utamaroho*.

Utamawazo

A neologism created by Marimba Ani from the Kiswahili word, *utamaduni* "civilisation" and *wazo* "thought". *Utamawazo* describes "culturally structured thought" (2000: xxv). *Utamawazo* "is structured by ideology and bio-cultural experience" (2000: 15). It creates cultural authority and explains the ways in which different cultural perspectives develop. This book proposes that diversity could become the *utamawazo* of the culture. Diversity would become the organising principle of institutions and behaviours, and in this setting, each cultural practice could be tested against the diversity principle.

Walu

Used by the Ngiyambaa people of western New South Wales, *walu* describes the interaction between different elements of the Australian bush: the hanging strips of bark, the scattered leaves, the "disordered" look.

Wild

Wild, as in unconstrained, is a key political concept in my work. Wild allows for the unpredictable, for life's surprises. It keeps us in touch with the biophysical world, an especially important factor in a heavily urbanised society. In the natural world, wild stock is the generative aspect of biodiversity. In the human sphere, the wild can be regarded as the generative force of creativity, cultural diversity and epistemological multiversity.

Wild politics

A politics grounded in the local. A philosophy of wild politics puts relationships, life and connection first. Wild politics is inspired by biodiversity, and attempts to bring that inspiration to play into human and social contexts.

Wild type

The wild type in genetics is the unregulated, undomesticated genotype that ensures genetic vitality and biodiversity. A wild type cannot be modified, since if it were, it would no longer be a wild type. In a metaphorical sense, then, it has an in-built resistance to appropriation.

Wilderness

A wilderness is an area in which biodiversity is promoted, either because there is no prior human habitation (Antarctica is one of the few places which fits this definition) or because it is maintained sustainably over many generations through interaction with human inhabitants.

World Intellectual Property Organisation

WIPO is an intergovernmental organisation created by a legal instrument under public international law, the Convention on the Establishment of the World Intellectual Property Organisation, signed at Stockholm on 14 July, 1967, which came into force in 1970 (Schäfers 1991: 49).

Wurruwarrin

Wurruwarrin is a word used by the Ngarrindjeri people of southeast Australia. "Knowing and believing in *wurruwarrin* is the answer to understanding it" (Tom Trevorrow in Bell 1998: iii).

Zenana

Women's apartments, a Bengali term.

ABBREVIATIONS

ABC	Australian Broadcasting Corporation
AMRAD	Australian Medical and Research Development Corporation
APEC	Asia Pacific Economic Cooperation forum
BSE	bovine spongiform encephalopathy (mad cow disease)
CBD	Convention on Biological Diversity
CJD	Creuzfeldt-Jacob disease
COICA	Coordinador de Organizaciones de los Pueblos Indigenas de la Cuenca Amazona (Coordinating Body of Indigenous Organisations of the Amazon Basin)
DCS	Dominant Culture Stupidity
EMR	Exclusive Marketing Rights
EU	European Union
FAO	Food and Agriculture Organisation of the United Nations
FGM	female genital mutilation
FMD	foot-and-mouth disease
FTAA	Free Trade Areas of America (to come into force in 2005)
GATS	General Agreement on Trade in Services (an instrument of the WTO)
GATT	General Agreement on Tariffs and Trade
GIS	Geographic Information Systems
GM	genetically modified
GMO	genetically modified organisms
HDGP	Human Genome Diversity Project
HGP	Human Genome Project
HMO	Health Maintenance Organisation
HYV	high-yielding varieties (seeds)
ILO	International Labour Organisation
IMF	International Monetary Fund
IPC	Intellectual Property Committee

IPR	Intellectual Property Rights
ITQ	Individual Transferable Quotas
IVF	in-vitro fertilisation
MAFF	Ministry of Agriculture, Fisheries and Food, UK
MSY	Maximum Sustainable Yield
NAFTA	North American Free Trade Agreement (came into force 1 January 1994)
NCI	National Cancer Institute (USA, part of NIH)
NIH	National Institutes of Health (USA)
NIMBY	not in my back yard
ODA	Official Development Assistance
OECD	Organisation for Economic Cooperation and Development
RAFI	Rural Advancement Foundation International
rBGH	recombinant Bovine Growth Hormone
SOHO	small office, home office
TCS	true cassava seeds
TRIMs	Trade Related Investment Measures
TRIPs	Trade Related Intellectual Property rights
TRRs	Traditional Resource Rights
UBI	Universal Basic Income
UBINIG	The Policy Research for Development Alternatives, Bangladesh
UNCED	UN Conference on Environment and Development, 1992
UNDP	United Nations Development Project
UNSCEAR	United Nations Scientific Committee on the Effects of Atomic Radiation
UNSNA	United Nations System of Accounts
UPOV	Union Internationale pour la Protection des Obtentions Végétales (International Convention for the Protection of New Varieties of Plants)
WEF	World Economic Forum
WIPO	World Intellectual Property Organisation
WTO	World Trade Organisation

BIBLIOGRAPHY

ABC TV News. (1998). Sydney. Australian Broadcasting Corporation. 28 April.

Acker, Joan, Kate Barry and Johanna Esseveld. (1991). "Objectivity and Truth: Problems in Doing Feminist Research." Fonow, Mary Margaret and Judith A. Cook, Eds. *Beyond Methodology: Feminist Scholarship as Lived Research.* Bloomington and Indianapolis: Indiana University Press: 133–153.

Adams, Carol. (1990). *The Sexual Politics of Meat.* Cambridge: Polity/Blackwell.

Adams, Patricia. (1991). *Odious Debts: Loose Lending, Corruption and the Third World's Environmental Legacy.* London and Toronto: Earthscan.

Agarwal, Bina. (1994). *A Field of One's Own: Gender and Land Rights in South Asia.* Cambridge: Cambridge University Press.

Aidoo, Ama Ata. (1977). *Sister Killjoy, or the Reflections of a Black-eyed Squint.* London: Virago.

Aiken, Kirsten. (2000). "Qld Zinc Mine Opens." ABC News Online. 29 December. 2001. www.abc.net.au/pm/s116029.htm

Akhter, Farida. (1990). *Women and Trees: Trees in the Life of Women in Kaijuri Village.* Dhaka: Narigrantha Prabartana.

—— (1992). *Depopulating Bangladesh: Essays on the Politics of Fertility.* Dhaka: Narigrantha Prabartana.

—— (1995). *Resisting Norplant: Women's Struggle in Bangladesh Against Coercion and Violence.* Dhaka: Narigrantha Prabartana.

—— (1996). "Cars and People." Personal communication. Melbourne. April.

—— (2001). "Resisting 'Technology' and Defending Subsistence in Bangladesh: Nayakrishi Andolon and the Movement for a Happy Life." Bennholdt-Thomsen, Veronika, Nicholas G. Faraclas and Claudia von Werlof, Eds. *There is an Alternative: Subsistence and Worldwide Resistance to Corporate Globalization.* London: Zed Books; Melbourne: Spinifex Press: 167–177.

Allen, Jeffner. (1996). *Sinuosities: Lesbian Poetic Politics.* Bloomington and Indianapolis: Indiana University Press.

Allen, Paula Gunn. (1986). *The Sacred Hoop: Recovering the Feminine in American Indian Traditions.* Boston, MA: Beacon Press.

—— (1998). *Off the Reservation: Reflections on Boundary-Busting, Border Crossing, Loose Canons.* Boston: Beacon Press.

Ament, Lucy. (2001). "Managing Liability for GM Crops a Major Concern." GeneEthics Network. www.geneethics.org

Amsden, Alice H., Ed. (1980). *The Economics of Women and Work*. Harmondsworth, UK: Penguin.

ANAWA, Anti-Nuclear Alliance of Western Australia. (2001). "The Pangea Proposal for an International Nuclear Waste Dump in Outback Western Australia." 7 December. 2001. www.anawa.org.au/waste/pangea.html

Anderson, Luke. (2000). *Genetic Engineering, Food and Our Environment: A Brief Guide*. Melbourne: Scribe.

Anderson, Sarah, John Cavanagh, with Thea Lee and and the Institute for Policy Studies. (2000). *Field Guide to the Global Economy*. New York: The New Press.

Andrews, Lynn V. (1987). *Crystal Woman: The Sisters of the Dreamtime*. New York: Warner Books.

Ani, Marimba. (2000). *Yurugu: An African-Centered Critique of European Cultural Thought and Behavior*. Trenton, NJ, and Asmara, Eritrea: Africa World Press.

"Ants Show Way on Biodiversity." (1998). Melbourne: *Age*. 1 October: 29.

Anzaldúa, Gloria. (1987). *Borderlands/La Frontera: The New Mestiza*. San Francisco: Spinsters/Aunt Lute.

Archibald, Linda and Mary Crnkovich. (1995). "Intimate Outsiders: Feminist Research in a Cross-Cultural Environment." Burt, Sandra and Lorraine Code, Eds. *Changing Methods: Feminists Transforming Practice*. Peterborough, Ont.: Broadview Press: 105–125.

Arditti, Rita, Renate Duelli Klein and Shelley Minden, Eds. (1984). *Test-tube Women: What Future for Motherhood?* London: Pandora.

Asante, Molefi Kete. (1999). *The Painful Demise of Eurocentrism: An Afrocentric Response to Critics*. Trenton, NJ, and Asmara, Eritrea: Africa World Press.

Atkinson, Judy. (1997). "Indigenous Therapies: An Indigenous Therapy Approach to Transgenerational Trauma." Paper presented at Trauma, Grief and Growth: Finding a Path to Healing. University of Sydney. 7–10 May.

—— (2002). *Trauma Trails, Recreating Song Lines: The Transgenerational Effects of Trauma in Indigenous Australia*. Melbourne: Spinifex Press.

Awang, Sandra S. (2000). "Indigenous Nations and the Human Genome Diversity Project." Dei, George J. Sefa, Budd L. Hall and Dorothy Goldin Rosenberg, Eds. *Indigenous Knowledges in Global Contexts: Multiple Readings of Our World*. Toronto: OISE/UT published in Association with University of Toronto Press: 120–136.

Baer, Lars Anders. (1998). "Initiatives for Protection of Rights of Holders of Traditional Knowledge, Indigenous Peoples and Local Communities."

Paper presented at Roundtable on Intellectual Property and Indigenous Peoples. Geneva: World Intellectual Property Organization: 1–6.

Baker, Richard. (2001). "Slaughter Economic: Scientist." Melbourne: *Age*. 6 March: 6.

Bakker, Isabella. (1997). "Identity, Interests and Ideology: The gendered terrain of global restructuring." Gill, Stephen, Ed. *Globalization, Democratization and Multilateralism*. Basingstoke: Macmillan in association with United Nations University Press: 127–139.

Bales, Kevin. (2000). *Disposable People: New Slavery in the Global Economy*. Berkeley: University of California Press.

Bandler, Faith. (1994). "Slavery and Resistance in Australia." Hawthorne, Susan and Renate Klein, Eds. *Australia for Women: Travel and Culture*. Melbourne: Spinifex Press: 11–15.

Bar On, Bat-Ami and Ann Ferguson, Eds. (1998). *Daring To Be Good: Essays in Feminist Ethico Politics*. New York and London: Routledge.

Barbier, Edward B. and Michael Rauscher. (1995). "Policies to Control Tropical Deforestation: Trade Intervention Versus Transfers." Perrings, Charles, Karl-Göran Mäler, Carl Folke *et al.*, Eds. *Biodiversity Loss: Economic and Ecological Issues*. Cambridge, UK: Cambridge University Press: 260–282.

Barnett, Antony. (2002). "Bushmen Win Royalties on 'miracle' pill." London: *Guardian Weekly*. 4–10 April: 3.

Barry, Kathleen. (1979). *Female Sexual Slavery*. New York: New York University Press.

—— (1995). *The Prostitution of Sexuality: The Global Exploitation of Women*. New York and London: New York University Press.

Bartky, Sandra Lee. (1978). "Toward a Phenomenology of Feminist Consciousness." Vetterling-Braggin, Mary, Frederick A. Elliston and Jane English, Eds. *Feminism and Philosophy*. Totowa, NJ: Littlefield, Adams and Co.: 22–34.

Bartlett, Richard H. (1993). *The Mabo Decision. Commentary by Richard H. Bartlett and the full text of the decision in Mabo and others v. State of Queensland*. Sydney: Butterworths.

Bartolo, Renee E. and Greg J. E. Hill. (2001). "Remote Sensing and GIS Technologies as a Decision-making Tool for Indigenous Land Management." *Indigenous Knowledge and Development Monitor 9* (1): 8–11.

Baskin, Yvonne. (1998). *The Work of Nature: How the Diversity of Life Sustains Us*. Washington, DC: Island Press.

Bates, Daisy. (1938). *The Passing of the Aborigines: A Lifetime Spent Among the Natives of Australia*. London: John Murray.

Beauvoir, Simone de. (1949/1972). *The Second Sex*. (H. M. Parshley, Trans.) Harmondsworth, UK: Penguin Books.

Becker, Gary. (1995). "Nobel Lecture: The Economic Way of Looking at Behaviour". Febrero, Ramón and Pedro S. Schwartz, Eds. *The Essence of Becker*. Stanford, CA: Hoover Institution Press: 663–658.

Becker, Hank. (1994). "Neem Oil Locks Out Spores." *Agricultural Research 42* (6): 20–21.

Beckett, Andy. (1994). "The Safe Way to Shop." Melbourne: *Age*. 7 May: 34–39.

Bell, Diane. (1981). "Women's Business is Hard Work: Central Australian Aboriginal Women's Love Rituals." Charlesworth, Max, Howard Morphy, Diane Bell and Kenneth Maddock, Eds. *Religion in Aboriginal Australia*. St Lucia: University of Queensland Press: 344–369.

—— (1983/2002). *Daughters of the Dreaming*. Sydney: Allen and Unwin/ Melbourne: Spinifex Press.

—— (1987). *Generations: Grandmothers, Mothers and Daughters*. Melbourne: McPheeGribble/Penguin Books.

—— (1997). "Desperately Seeking Redemption." *Natural History 106* (2): 52–3.

—— (1998). *Ngarrindjeri Wurruwarrin: The World That Is, Was, and Will Be*. Melbourne: Spinifex Press.

Bell, Diane and Renate Klein, Eds. (1996). *Radically Speaking: Feminism Reclaimed*. Melbourne: Spinifex Press.

Bell, Genevieve. (2001). "A Theory of Shopping: A Feminist Reading of eCommerce." Washington, DC: George Washington University. 7 June.

Bellos, Alex. (2000). "Brazil's 50-year 'Invasion'." Sydney: *Weekend Australian*. 22–23 April: 12.

Beneria, Lourdes and Savitri Bisnath. (2000). "Gender and Poverty: An Analysis for Action." Lechner, Frank J. and John Boli, Eds. *The Globalization Reader*. Malden, MA: Blackwell Publishers: 172–176.

Benko, Robert. (1987). *Protecting Intellectual Property Rights: Issues and Controversies*. Washington, DC: American Enterprise Institute for Public Policy Research.

Bennholdt-Thomsen, Veronika. (2001). "What Really Keeps Our Cities Alive, Money or Subsistence?" Bennholdt-Thomsen, Veronika, Nicholas G. Faraclas and Claudia von Werlof, Eds. *There is an Alternative: Subsistence and Worldwide Resistance to Corporate Globalization*. London: Zed Books; Melbourne: Spinifex Press: 217–231.

Bennholdt-Thomsen, Veronika, Nicholas G. Faraclas and Claudia von Werlof. (2001). *There is an Alternative: Subsistence and Worldwide Resistance to Corporate Globalization*. London: Zed Books; Melbourne: Spinifex Press.

Bennholdt-Thomsen, Veronika and Maria Mies. (1999). *The Subsistence Perspective: Beyond the Globalised Economy*. London: Zed Books; Melbourne: Spinifex Press.

Bercovitz, Alberto. (1990). "The Challenge of Protecting Biotechnology, Software and Other New Technologies." *Patinova '90: Strategies for the Protection of Innovation. Proceedings of the First European Congress on Industrial Property Rights and Innovation.* Madrid: Kluwer Academic Publishers and Deutscher Wirtschaftsdienst: 149–158.

Bergmann, Barbara. (1986). *The Economic Emergence of Women.* New York: Basic Books.

Bernal, Martin. (1987). *Black Athena: The Afroasiatic Roots of Classical Civilization.* London: Free Association Books.

Bertell, Rosalie. (1985). *No Immediate Danger: Prognosis for a Radioactive Earth.* London: The Women's Press.

—— (2000). *Planet Earth: The Latest Weapon of War: A Critical Study into the Military and the Environment.* London: The Women's Press.

Bhat, Mahadev G. (1996). "Trade-related Intellectual Property Rights to Biological Resources: Socioeconomic Implications for Developing Countries." *Ecological Economics 19*: 205–217.

Bhatt, Sujata. (1988). *Brunizem.* Manchester: Carcanet.

Bidesi, Vina R. (1994). "How 'the Other Half' Fishes: Accounting for Women in Fisheries in the Pacific." Emberson-Bain, 'Atu, Ed. *Sustainable Development or Malignant Growth? Perspectives on Pacific Island Women.* Suva, Fiji: Marama Publications: 123–130.

Biehl, Janet. (1991). *Rethinking Ecofeminist Politics.* Boston: Southend Press.

Biemann, Ursula. (1999). *Performing the Border.* (Video.) Switzerland.

Bird, Carmel, Ed. (1998). *The Stolen Children: Their Stories.* Sydney: Random House.

Black, Maggie. (2001). "The Day of Judgement." *New Internationalist* (336): 9–11.

Bly, Robert. (1992). *Iron John: A Book About Men.* Shaftsbury, Dorset, and Rockport, MA: Element.

Booth, William. (2001). "The Right to Walk on the Beach Runs into the NIMBY Complex." Melbourne: *Age.* 31 December: 11.

Boric, Rada and Mica Mladineo Desnica. (1996). "Croatia: Three Years After." Corrin, Chris, Ed. *Women in a Violent World: Feminist Analyses and Resistance Across "Europe".* Edinburgh: Edinburgh University Press: 133–150.

Boyer, M. Christine. (1996). *CyberCities.* New York: Princeton Architectural Press.

Brain, Peter. (1999). *Beyond Meltdown: The Global Battle for Sustained Growth.* Melbourne: Scribe Publications.

Brodribb, Somer. (1992). *Nothing Mat(t)ers: A Feminist Critique of Postmodernism.* Melbourne: Spinifex Press.

Brøsted, Jens, Jens Dahl, Andrew Gray, Hans Christian Gulløv, *et al.*, Eds.

(1985). *Native Power: The Quest for Autonomy and Nationhood of Indigenous Peoples.* Bergen, Norway: Universitetsforlaget AS.

Brown, Katrina. (1994). "Approaches to Valuing Plant Medicines: The Economics of Culture or the Culture of Economics?" *Biodiversity and Conservation 3* (8): 734–750.

Brown, Paul. (1999). "Monsanto Withdraws Sterile Gene." Melbourne: *Age.* 6 October: 15.

Brown, Rita Mae. (1974). "The Last Straw." Bunch, Charlotte and Nancy Myron, Eds. *Class and Feminism.* Baltimore: Diana Press: 13–23.

Brownmiller, Susan. (1976). *Against Our Will: Men, Women and Rape.* Harmondsworth, UK: Penguin.

Bryden-Brown, Sarah. (2001). "No Sweat: Why Nike Wouldn't Just Do It." Sydney: *Weekend Australian.* 24–25 February 2001: 5.

Buck, Susan. (1998). *The Global Commons.* London: Earthscan.

Bunting, Madeleine. (2001). "Intellectual Property Agreements are Making Too Much Money for the West." London: *Guardian.* 12 February.

Burrows, Beth. (2001a). "Patents. Ethics and Spin." Tokar, Brian, Ed. *Redesigning Life: The Worldwide Challenge to Genetic Engineering.* Melbourne: Scribe Publications; London and New York: Zed Books; Montreal: McGill-Queen's University Press; Johannesburg: Witwatersrand University Press: 238–251.

—— (2001b). "Safety First." Tokar, Brian, Ed. *Redesigning Life: The Worldwide Challenge to Genetic Engineering.* Melbourne: Scribe Publications; London and New York: Zed Books; Montreal: McGill-Queen's University Press; Johannesburg: Witwatersrand University Press: 67–74.

Butler, Susan. (2001). "Koori." Melbourne: *Age.* 22 September: 9.

Buzan, Tony. (1990). *The Mind Map Book.* London: BBC Books.

Çagatay, Nilüfer and Günseli Berik. (1994). "What has Export-oriented Manufacturing Meant for Turkish Women?" Sparr, Pamela, Ed. *Mortgaging Women's Lives: Feminist Critiques of Structural Adjustment.* London: Zed: 78–95.

Caputi, Jane. (1987). *The Age of Sex Crime.* London: The Women's Press.

Carman, Judy. (2000). "The Problem with the Safety of Roundup Ready Soybeans." *Synthesis/Regeneration* (Winter): 34–36.

Carson, Rachel. (1962/1986). *Silent Spring.* Harmondsworth, UK: Penguin.

Carvel, John. (1994). "He Lost his Spleen to Science; Now He Vents It." Melbourne: *Age.* 10 November: 15.

Chang, Grace. (2000). *Disposable Domestics: Immigrant Women Workers in the Global Economy.* Boston: South End Press.

Chapkis, Wendy and Cynthia Enloe, Eds. (1983). *Of Common Cloth: Women in the Global Textile Industry.* Amsterdam: Transnational Institute.

Chapman, Chapman and Binalong v. Luminis, Fergie, Saunders, Tickner and Commonwealth of Australia (No. 5). (2001). FAC 1106. 21 August.

Chattakar-Aitkins, Arlene. (2001). "Trapped in the White Space: The Allegations and Denials of Organ Trafficking." Women's Studies, School of Social Inquiry. Melbourne: Deakin University. PhD.

Cheru, Fantu. (2000). "The Local Dimensions of Global Reform." Pieterse, Jan Nederveen, Ed. *Global Futures: Shaping Globalization.* London: Zed Books: 119–132.

Cheru, Fantu and Stephen Gill. (1997). "Structural Adjustment and the G7: Limits and Contradictions." Gill, Stephen, Ed. *Globalization, Democratization and Multilateralism.* Basingstoke: Macmillan in association with United Nations University Press: 141–169.

Chossudovsky, Michel. (1998). *The Globalisation of Poverty: Impacts of IMF on World Bank Reforms.* London: Zed Books.

Christie, Jean. (2001). "Enclosing the Biodiversity Commons: Bioprospecting or Biopiracy." Hindmarsh, Richard and Geoffrey Lawrence, Eds. *Altered Genes II: The Future.* Melbourne: Scribe: 173–186.

Clark, Marc. (1989). "Gambling and Guns: Casinos and Bingo Divide Indian Bands." *Maclean's 102* (38): 21–22.

Clarke, Tony. (1996). "Mechanisms of Corporate Rule." Mander, Jerry and Edward Goldsmith, Eds. *The Case Against the Global Economy and For a Turn Toward the Local.* San Francisco: Sierra Club Books: 297–308.

Clarke, Tony and Maude Barlow. (1997). *The Multilateral Agreement on Investment and the Threat to Canadian Sovereignty.* Toronto: Stoddart Publishing Co.

Coburn, Justin. (2000). "A Deadly Struggle for People's Right to be Different." Melbourne: *Age.* 28 February: 13.

Cohen, Mitchel. (2001). "Biotechnology and the New World Order." Tokar, Brian, Ed. *Redesigning Life: The Worldwide Challenge to Genetic Engineering.* Melbourne: Scribe Publications; London and New York: Zed Books; Montreal: McGill-Queen's University Press; Johannesburg: Witwatersrand University Press: 306–313.

COICA/UNDP. (1994). *Statement: Basic Points of Agreement from the COICA/UNDP Regional Meeting on Intellectual Property Rights and Biodiversity.* Santa Cruz de la Sierra, Bolivia: Coordinating Body of Indigenous Peoples of the Amazon Basin (COICA)/ United Nations Development Programme (UNDP). 28–30 September.

Colfer, Carol J. Pierce, Joseph Woelfel, Reed L. Wadley and Emily Harwell. (2001). "Assessing People's Perceptions of Forests: Research in West

Kalimantan, Indonesia." Colfer, Carol J. Pierce and Yvonne Byron, Eds. *People Managing Forests: The Links between Human Well-being and Sustainability.* Washington, DC: Resources for the Future; Bogor, Indonesia: Center for International Forestry Research: 135–154.

Collard, Andrée with Joyce Contrucci. (1988). *Rape of the Wild.* London: The Women's Press.

Cook, Alistair. (2000). "Letter from America." Sydney: ABC Radio National. 12 April.

Cooke, Fadzilah Majid. (1999). *The Challenge of Sustainable Forests: Forest Resource Policy in Malaysia, 1970–1995.* Sydney and Honolulu: Asian Studies Association of Australia in association with Allen and Unwin and University of Hawai'i Press.

Coombs, Herbert Cole. (1996). *Shame on Us.* Canberra: Centre for Resource and Environmental Studies.

Copelan, Rhonda. (1994). "Surfacing Gender: Reconceptualizing Crimes Against Women in Time of War." Stiglmayer, Alexandra, Ed. *Mass Rape: The War against Women in Bosnia-Herzogovina.* Lincoln and London: University of Nebraska Press: 197–218.

Corea, Gena. (1985). *The Mother Machine: Reproductive Technologies from Artificial Insemination to Artificial Wombs.* New York: Harper and Row.

Correa, Carlos. (2000). *Intellectual Property Rights, the WTO and Developing Countries: The TRIPs Agreement and Policy Option.* Penang: Third World Network; London: Zed Books.

Correy, Stan. (2001a). "GM Crops 2000: The Unmaking of a Genetically Modified PR Campaign." *Background Briefing.* Sydney: ABC Radio National (Australia). 21 January. www.abc.net.au/m/talks/bbing/stories/s231839.htm

—— (2001b). "Knowledge Indignation: Road Rage on the Information Highway." *Background Briefing.* Sydney: ABC Radio National. 12 August.

Costanza, Robert, Ed. (1991). *Ecological Economics: The Science and Management of Sustainability.* New York: Columbia University Press.

Couch, Jen. (2001). "So the Party is Over? The Global Justice Movement, Post 11 September 2001." Melbourne: Friends of the Earth Bookshop. 15 November.

—— Jen. (in progress). "This is What Democracy Looks Like: Capturing the Culture of Anti-globalisation Resistance." Social Inquiry and Community Studies Department. Melbourne: Victoria University. PhD.

Coulloupas, Andrew. (1998). "The Green Blues." *Background Briefing.* Sydney: ABC Radio National. 26 April. www.abc.net.au/rn/talks/bbing/stories/s10825.htm

Counsel, Jane. (2001). "PNG Names Date for BHP's Ok Tedi Exit." Melbourne: *Age.* 9 August: 5.

Cozart, Bernadette. (1999). "The Greening of Harlem." Wilson, Peter Lamborn and Bill Weinberg, Eds. *Avant Gardening: Ecological Struggle in the City and the World.* Brooklyn, NY: Autonomedia: 35–37.

Cravey, Altha J. (1998). *Women and Work in Mexico's Maquiladoras.* Lanham, MD: Rowman and Littlefield Publishers, Inc.

Crespigny, Anthony de. (1970). "Power and Its Forms." Crespigny, Anthony de and Alan Wertheimer, Eds. *Contemporary Political Philosophy.* London: Nelson: 39–53.

Crouch, Martha L. (2001). "From Golden Rice to Terminator Technology: Agricultural Biotechnology Will Not Feed the World or Save the Environment." Tokar, Brian, Ed. *Redesigning Life: The Worldwide Challenge to Genetic Engineering.* Melbourne: Scribe Publications; London and New York: Zed Books; Montreal: McGill-Queen's University Press; Johannesburg: Witwatersrand University Press: 22–39.

Culotta, Elizabeth. (1994). "Is Marine Biodiversity at Risk?" *Science 263* (5149): 918–920.

Cuomo, Christine J. (1994). "Ecofeminism, Deep Ecology, and Human Population." Warren, Karen J., Ed. *Ecological Feminism.* London and New York: Routledge: 88–105.

Cutting Edge. (2001). Sydney. SBS TV. 6 March.

D'Aprano, Zelda. (1995). *Zelda.* Melbourne: Spinifex Press.

—— (2001). *Kath Williams: The Unions and the Fight for Equal Pay.* Melbourne: Spinifex Press.

Daley, Paul. (2001a). "Meat Crisis Forces UK to Look Before it Eats." Melbourne: *Age.* 10 March: 22.

—— (2001b). "Vet Suffers as He Shares UK's Farm Ordeal." Melbourne: *Age.* 21 April: 27.

—— (2001c). "Livelihoods Drift Away in a Smoke of Burning Animals." Sydney: *Sydney Morning Herald.* 24 March: 20.

Dalla Costa, Mariarosa. (1972). *The Power of Women and the Subversion of the Economy.* Bristol.

Dalla Costa, Mariarosa and Giovanna F. Dalla Costa, Eds. (1995). *Paying the Price: Women and the Politics of International Economic Strategy.* London: Zed Books.

Daly, Herman E. (1999b). "Globalization versus Internationalization: Some Implications." *Ecological Economics 31* (1): 31–37.

—— (1999a). "Sustainable Growth: An Impossibility Theorem." Dryzek, John S. and David Schlosberg, Eds. *Debating the Earth: The Environmental Politics Reader.* Oxford: Oxford University Press: 285–289.

Daly, Herman E. and Robert Goodland. (1994). "An Ecological-economic Assessment of Deregulation of International Commerce under GATT." *Ecological Economics* 9: 73–92.

Daly, Mary. (1978). *Gyn/Ecology: The Metaethics of Radical Feminism.* Boston: Beacon Press.

—— (1984). *Pure Lust: Elemental Feminist Philosophy.* Boston: Beacon Press.

Daly, Mary with Jane Caputi. (1987). *Websters' First Intergalactic Wickedary of the English Language.* Boston: Beacon Press.

Darby, Andrew. (2000a). "Farmer Fears Pollution from Modified Crops." Melbourne: *Age.* 26 August: 19.

—— (2000b). "GM Firm Says it can Beat Tasmanian Ban." Melbourne: *Age.* 24 August: 9.

—— (2001). "Crop Companies Flouted GM Controls, Says Minister." Sydney: *Sydney Morning Herald.* 7 April: 11.

Davis, Lennard J. (1995). *Enforcing Normalcy: Disability, Deafness and the Body.* London: Verso.

Davis, Tom Pa Tuterangi Ariki. (1992). *Vaka Saga of a Polynesian Canoe.* Auckland; Raratong and Suva: Polynesian Press; Institute of Pacific Studies, University of the South Pacific.

dé Ishtar, Zohl. (1994). *Daughters of the Pacific.* Melbourne: Spinifex Press.

—— Ed. (1998). *Pacific Women Speak Out for Independence and Denuclearisation.* Christchurch: The Raven Press.

—— (2001). "Recollections of 1995 Moruroa Atoll Protests." Personal communication. Melbourne, July.

De Soto, Hernando. (2001). *The Mystery of Capital: Why Capitalism Triumphs in the West and Fails Everywhere Else.* London: Black Swan.

Dechant, David. (2001). "Pioneer v. JEM AgSupply May Sprout Rude Awakening." GeneEthicsNetwork. www.geneethics.org

Delphy, Christine. (1984). *Close to Home: A Materialist Analysis of Women's Oppression.* (Diana Leonard, Trans.) London: Hutchinson.

Delphy, Christine and Diana Leonard. (1992). *Familiar Exploitation: A New Analysis of Marriage in Contemporary Western Societies.* London: Polity Press.

Deutsche Bank, ad. (2000). "Local Knowledge and Global Expertise." *Australian Financial Review.* Monday 29 May: 11.

Diamond, Irene. (1994). *Fertile Ground: Women, Earth and the Limits of Control.* Boston: Beacon Press.

Diamond, Jared. (1991). *The Rise and Fall of the Third Chimpanzee.* London: Vintage.

Diamond v. Chakrabarty. (1980). 447 US 303.

Dingle, Tony. (1988). *Aboriginal Economy: Patterns of Experience*. Melbourne: McPhee Gribble.

Diop, Cheikh Anta. (1974). *The African Origin of Civilization: Myth or Reality*. (M. Cook, Trans.) Westport, CT: Lawrence Hill.

Dirie, Waris. (1998). *Desert Flower: The Extraordinary Life of a Desert Nomad*. London: Virago.

Dodds, Felix, Ed. (2000). *Earth Summit 2002: A New Deal*. London: Earthscan.

Dodds, Susan. (1994). "Property Rights and the Environment." Cosgrove, Laurie, David G. Evans and David Yenken, Eds. *Restoring the Land: Environmental Values, Knowledge and Action*. Melbourne: Melbourne University Press: 47–58.

Dodson, Patrick. (1998). "Afterword 1: Thinking with the Land." Kauffman, Paul, Ed. *Wik, Mining and Aborigines*. Sydney: Allen and Unwin: 169–170.

Donath, Susan. (2000). "The Other Economy: A Suggestion for a Distinctively Feminist Economics." *Feminist Economics 6* (1): 115–123.

Dorkenoo, Efua. (1994). *Cutting the Rose: Female Genital Mutilation – The Practice and its Prevention*. London: Minority Rights Publication.

Douez, Sophie. (2001). "Eating GM Food is Safe: Expert." Melbourne: *Age*. 4 July: 9.

Dove, Michael R. (1993). "A Revisionist View of Tropical Deforestation and Development." *Environmental Conservation 20* (1): 17–24.

Doyal, L. and I. Gough. (1991). *A Theory of Human Need*. New York: Guildford.

Draper, Susan. (1996). "Breast-Feeding as a Sustainable Resource System." *American Anthropologist 98* (2): 258–265.

Drew, Wayland. (1999). "Killing Wilderness." Willers, Bill, Ed. *Unmanaged Landscapes: Voices for Untamed Nature*. Washington, DC, and Covelo, CA: Island Press: 73–81.

Du Bois, Barbara. (1983). "Passionate Scholarship: Notes on Values, Knowing, and Method in Feminist Social Science." Bowles, Gloria and Renate Duelli-Klein, Eds. *Theories of Women's Studies*. London: Routledge and Kegan Paul: 105–116.

Du Plessis, Rosemary. (1995). "Of Wild Women and Hairy Men: Reflections on Mytho-poetic Constructions of Fe/male Archetypes." *Broadsheet* (205): 27–30.

Duncan, Leith. (1995). "Closed Competition: Fish Quotas in New Zealand." *Ecologist 25* (2/3): 97–104.

Dunlevy, Maurice. (2001). "All's Well on Home Front for Expats." Sydney: *Australian*. 17 April: 2.

Dunlop, Ian. (2001). "Milk Deregulation is Good for You: Pull the Udder One." *Margo Kingston's Webdiary*. 30 March. 2001. www.smh.com.au/news/webdiary/0104/05/A33180-2001Mar30.html

Durning, A. (1992). *Guardians of the Forest*. Washington D.C.: Worldwatch.

Dutfield, Graham. (2000). *Intellectual Property Rights, Trade and Biodiversity*. London: Earthscan Publications.

Dworkin, Andrea. (1981). *Pornography: Men Possessing Women*. London: The Women's Press.

—— (1983). *Right-wing Women: The Politics of Domesticated Females*. London: The Women's Press.

Earle, Michael. (1995). "The Precautionary Approach to Fisheries." *Ecologist 25* (2/3): 70.

Economist. (1994). "The Tragedy of the Oceans." *The Economist 330* (7855): 21–24.

Ehrenreich, Barbara. (2001). "The Fundamental Mystery of Repressing Women." Melbourne: *Age*. 23 November: 15.

Eichenwald, Kurt. (2000). "Hunt Widens for Traces of Gene Corn." *Herald Tribune International*. 16 October: 13.

Elabor-Idemudia, Patience. (1994). "Nigeria: Agricultural Exports and Compensatory Schemes – Rural Women's Production Resources and Quality of Life." Sparr, Pamela, Ed. *Mortgaging Women's Lives: Feminist Crtitiques of Structural Adjustment*. London: Zed Books: 134–164.

Elkins, Paul. (1992). *A New World Order: Grassroots Movements for Global Change, Seikatsu Club Consumers Cooperative*. London: Routledge.

Else, Anne. (1996). *False Economy: New Zealanders Face the Conflict between Paid and Unpaid Work*. Auckland: Tandem Press.

Elson, Diane. (1983). "Nimble Fingers and Other Fables." Chapkis, Wendy and Cynthia Enloe, Eds. *Of Common Cloth: Women in the Global Textile Industry*. Amsterdam: Transnational Institute: 5–13.

Emberson-Bain, 'Atu, Ed. (1994). *Sustainable Development or Malignant Growth? Perspectives of Pacific Island Women*. Suva, Fiji: Marama Publications.

Emmerij, Louis. (2000). "World Economic Changes at the Threshold of the Twenty-first Century." Pieterse, Jan Nederveen, Ed. *Global Futures: Shaping Globalization*. London: Zed Books: 53–62.

Emmott, Steve. (2001). "No Patents on Life: The Incredible Ten-year Campaign against the European Patent Directive." Tokar, Brian, Ed. *Redesigning Life: The Worldwide Challenge to Genetic Engineering*. Melbourne: Scribe Publications; London and New York: Zed Books; Montreal: McGill-Queen's University Press; Johannesburg: Witwatersrand University Press: 373–384.

Enloe, Cynthia. (1983a). *Does Khaki Become You? The Militarisation of Women's Lives*. London: Pluto Press.

——— (1983b). "We Are What We Wear – The Dilemma of the Feminist Consumer." Chapkis, Wendy and Cynthia Enloe, Eds. *Of Common Cloth: Women in the Global Textile Industry*. Amsterdam: Transnational Institute: 115–119.

——— (1989). *Bananas, Beaches and Bases: Making Feminist Sense of International Politics*. London: Pandora.

Essays on the Mabo Decision. (1993). Sydney: The Law Book Company Limited.

Estes, Clarissa Pinkola. (1992). *Women Who Run with Wolves: Contacting the Power of the Wild Woman*. London: Rider.

Esteva, Gustavo. (2001). "Mexico: Creating Your Own Path at the Grassroots." Bennholdt-Thomsen, Veronika, Nicholas G. Faraclas and Claudia von Werlof, Eds. *There is an Alternative: Subsistence and Worldwide Resistance to Corporate Globalization*. London: Zed Books; Melbourne: Spinifex Press: 155–166.

Etienne, Marie and Eleanor Leacock. (1980). *Women and Colonization*. New York: Praeger.

Eyerman, Ann. (2000). *Women in the Office: Transitions in a Global Economy*. Toronto: Sumach Press.

Fairlie, Simon. (1995). "Who is Weeping Crocodile Tears? Britain's Fishing Industry and the EU Commons Fisheries Policy." *Ecologist* 25 (2/3): 105–114.

Fairlie, Simon, Mike Hagler and Brian O'Riordan. (1995). "The Politics of Overfishing." *Ecologist* 25 (2/3): 46–73.

Falk, Richard. (1999). *Predatory Globalization: A Critique*. Cambridge: Polity.

Fanon, Frantz. (1973). *The Wretched of the Earth*. (Constance Farrington, Trans.) Harmondsworth, UK: Penguin Books.

FAO. (2000). *FAO Yearbook Fishery Statistics: Capture Production 1998. FAO Yearbook Fishery Statistics. Vol. 86/1*. Rome. 703.

Faraclas, Nicholas G. (2001). "Melanesia, The Banks and the BINGOs: Real Alternatives are Everywhere Except in the Consultants' Briefcases)." Bennholdt-Thomsen, Veronika, Nicholas G. Faraclas and Claudia von Werlof, Eds. *There is an Alternative: Subsistence and Worlwide Resistance to Corporate Globalization*. London; Melbourne: Zed Books; Spinifex Press: 67–76.

Ferber, Marianne. (1982). "Women and Work: Issues of the 1980s: A Review Article." *Signs* 8 (2): 273–295.

Ferrara, Jennifer. (2001). "Paving the Way for Biotechnology: Federal Regulations and Industry PR." Tokar, Brian, Ed. *Redesigning Life: The Worldwide Challenge to Genetic Engineering*. Melbourne: Scribe Publications;

London and New York: Zed Books; Montreal: McGill-Queen's University Press; Johannesburg: Witwatersrand University Press: 297–305.

Ferrara, Jennifer and Michael K. Dorsey. (2001). "Genetically Engineered Foods: A Minefield of Safety Hazards." Tokar, Brian, Ed. *Redesigning Life: The Worldwide Challenge to Genetic Engineering*. Melbourne: Scribe Publications; London and New York: Zed Books; Montreal: McGill-Queen's University Press; Johannesburg: Witwatersrand University Press: 51–66.

Firestone, Shulamith. (1971). *The Dialectic of Sex: The Case for Feminist Revolution*. London: Paladin.

Fisher, Judi and Beth Shelton. (2002). *Face to Face: Making Dance and Theatre in Community*. Melbourne: Spinifex Press.

Flannery, Tim. (1994). *The Future Eaters*. Sydney: Reed.

Fletcher, Garth L., R. Alderson, E. A. Chin-Dixon, M. A. Shears, *et al.* (1997). "Sustainable Aquaculture". *2nd International Symposium on Sustainable Agriculture*. Oslo, Norway. 2–5 Nov.

Fletcher, Garth L., Sally V. Goddard and Yaling Wu. (1999). "Antifreeze Proteins and Their Genes: From Basic Research to Business Opportunity." *Chemtech 30* (6): 17–28.

Floro, Maria Segrario. (1994). "The Dynamics of Economic Change and Gender Roles: Export Cropping in the Philippines." Sparr, Pamela, Ed. *Mortgaging Women's Lives: Feminist Crtitiques of Structural Adjustment*. London: Zed Books: 116–133.

Folbre, Nancy. (1994). *Who Pays for the Kids? Gender and the Structures of Constraint*. New York: Routledge.

"Foot-and-mouth Fears Escalate." (2001). Melbourne: *Melbourne Express*. 15 March: 2.

Ford, Carole. (2001). "Still Invisible: The Myth of the Woman-friendly State." Faculty of Arts. Melbourne: Deakin University. PhD.

Foreman, Dave. (1998). "Putting Earth First." Dryzek, John S. and David Schlosberg, Eds. *Debating the Earth: The Environmental Politics Reader*. Oxford: Oxford University Press: 358–364.

Forrester, Viviane. (1999). *The Economic Horror*. London: Polity Press.

Fourmile, H. (1996). "Protecting Indigenous Property Rights in Biodiversity." *Current Affairs Bulletin*: 36–41.

Fowler, Cary, Pat Mooney, Eva Lachkvics and Hope Shand. (1988). "The Lords of Life: Corporate Control of the New Biosciences." *The Laws of Life: Another Development and the New Biotechnologies, Development Dialogue 1–2*. Uppsala: Dag Hammarskjöld Foundation.

Fox, Matthew. (1985). *Illuminations of Hildegard of Bingen*. Santa Fe, NM: Bear and Company.

Franklin, Roger. (1998). "Fence Me In." Melbourne: *Age*. 10 March: 13.

Fraser, Andrew. (2001). "Spilt Milk." Sydney: *Australian*. 13 March: 30.

Freire, Paulo. (1971). *Cultural Action for Freedom*. Harmondsworth, UK: Penguin Books.

—— (1972). *Pedagogy of the Oppressed*. Harmondsworth, UK: Penguin Books.

French, Marilyn. (1992). *The War Against Women*. Melbourne: Penguin Books.

Friedan, Betty. (1962/1973). *The Feminine Mystique*. Harmondsworth, UK: Penguin Books.

Friedland, Jonathan and Scott Kilman. (1999). "As Geneticists Develop an Appetite for Greens, Mr. Romo Flourishes." New York: *Wall Street Journal*. 28 January: A1.

Fry, Rae. (2001). "Vitamin A in Pregnancy." *The Health Report*. Sydney: ABC Radio National. 9 July.
www.abc.net.au/rn/talks/8.30/helthrpt/stories/s326333.htm

Frye, Marilyn. (1983). "To See and Be Seen: The Politics of Reality." Frye, Marilyn, Ed. *The Politics of Reality*. Trumansburg, NY: The Crossing Press.

Fuentes, Annette and Barbara Ehrenreich. (1983). *Women in the Global Factory*. Boston: South End Press.

Fukuyama, Francis. (1992). *The End of History and the Last Man*. London: Penguin Books.

—— (2001). "History Beyond the End." Sydney: *Australian*. 9 October: 15.

Gale, Jason. (2000). "No Plan to Close Ok Tedi." Melbourne: *Age*. 21 July 2000: 2.

Garrett, Kirsten. (2001). "Drop the Debt." *Background Briefing*. Sydney. ABC Radio National (Australia). 9 September.

Garrett, Laurie. (1994). *The Coming Plague: Newly Emerging Diseases in a World Out of Balance*. London: Virago.

GATT. (1992). *International Trade 90–91, Vol. 1 including Special Topic: Trade and the Environment*. Geneva.

Gbadegesin, Adeniyi. (1996). "Management of Forest Resources by Women: A Case Study from the Olokemeji Forest Reserve Area Southwestern Nigeria." *Environmental Conservation 23* (2): 115–119.

George, Susan. (1991). *How the Other Half Dies: The Real Reasons for World Hunger*. London: Penguin Books.

—— (1996). *Questionable Compatibility: Trade Liberalization and Food Security*. Manila: Isis International.

GHFB, Ghana Free Zones Board. (2000). "The New Free-Zone Gateway to West Africa." *International Herald Tribune*. 28 June: 12.

Gibson, William. (1984). *Neuromancer.* New York: Ace Books.

GID. (1993). "Masseneinspruch gegen Krebsmaus." *Gen-Ethischer Informations Dienst* (84): 7.

Gill, Stephen. (1997). "Global Structural Change and Multilateralism." Gill, Stephen, Ed. *Globalization, Democratization and Multilateralism.* Basingstoke: Macmillan in association with United Nations University Press: 1–17.

Gilligan, Carol. (1982). *In a Different Voice: Psychological Theory and Women's Development.* Cambridge, MA: Harvard University Press.

Gilpin, Alan. (2000). *Environmental Economics: A Critical Overview.* Chichester: John Wiley and Sons.

Gimbutas, Marija. (1989). *The Language of the Goddess.* New York: Harper and Row.

—— (1991). *The Civilization of the Goddess: The World of Old Europe.* San Francisco: HarperSanFrancisco.

Gina-Whewell, Lamour. (1995). "Roviana Women in Traditional Fishing." Matthews, Elizabeth, Ed. *Fishing for Answers: Women and Fisheries in the Pacific Islands.* Suva, Fiji: Women and Fisheries Network: 19–27.

Giobbe, Evelina. (1996). "The Market Place of Ideas." Bell, Diane and Renate Klein, Eds. *Radically Speaking: Feminism Reclaimed.* Melbourne: Spinifex Press: 479–480.

Global Witness. (1998). *A Rough Trade: The Role of Companies and Governments in the Angolan Conflict.* Global Witness. December. www.oneworld.org/globalwitness/reports/Angola/title.htm

Gloster, Margherita, Martha McDevitt and Amrita Chhachhi. (1983). "Restructuring: The Cutting Edge." Chapkis, Wendy and Cynthia Enloe, Eds. *Of Common Cloth: Women in the Global Textile Industry.* Amsterdam: Transnational Institute: 15–23.

Goodland, Robert. (1996). "Growth has Reached its Limit." Mander, Jerry and Edward Goldsmith, Eds. *The Case Against the Global Economy and For a Turn Toward the Local.* San Francisco: Sierra Club Books: 207–217.

Goodland, Robert and Herman E. Daly. (1993). "Why Northern Income Growth is Not the Solution to Southern Poverty." *Ecological Economics 8* (2): 85–101.

—— (1996). "If Tropical Export Bans are So Perverse, Why are There So Many?" *Ecological Economics 18* (3): 189–196.

Goodland, Robert, Herman E. Daly and El Serafy, Eds. (1991). *Environmentally Sustainable Economic Development: Building on Brundtland.* Environment Department Paper 46. Washington DC: World Bank.

Gorz, André. (1999). *Reclaiming Work: Beyond the Wage-based Society.* London: Polity Press.

Gowdy, John and Carl N. McDaniel. (1995). "One World, One Experiment: Addressing the Biodiversity-Economics Conflict." *Ecological Economics 15* (3): 181–192.

Gowdy, John and Sabine O'Hara. (1995). *Economic Theory for Environmentalists.* Delray Beach, FL: St Lucie Press.

Grace, Patricia. (1994). "Ngati Kanguru." *The Sky People and Other Stories.* Auckland: Penguin. 25–43.

Gray, Stephen. (1993). "Wheeling, Dealing and Deconstruction: Aboriginal Art and the Land Post-Mabo." *Aboriginal Law Journal 3* (63): 10–12.

Green, Caroline. (2000). "Where Now for the Victims of Ok Tedi?" *Horizons 8* (4): 12–13.

Greer, Germaine. (1971). *The Female Eunuch.* London: Paladin.

Griffin, Susan. (1978). *Woman and Nature: The Roaring Inside Her.* New York: Harper and Row.

Grossman, Michele and Denise Cuthbert. (1996). "Bodyshopping: Maternity and Alterity in *Mamatoto*." *Cultural Studies 10* (3): 430–448.

Guajardo, Guadalupe. (2001). "Leadership at the Margins of Society: Recognizing, Honoring, Celebrating and Employing the Wisdom in Subcultural Leaders." School of Consciousness and Transformation. San Francisco: California Institute of Integral Studies.

Guha, Ramachandra. (1989). "Radical American Environmentalism and Wilderness Preservation: A Third World Critique." *Environmental Ethics 11*: 71–81.

Guillaumin, Colette. (1995). *Racism, Sexism, Power and Ideology.* London and New York: Routledge.

Guinier, Lani. (1997). "Afterword." Guinier, Lani, Michelle Fine and Jane Balin, Eds. *Becoming Gentlemen: Women, Law School and Institutional Change.* Boston: Beacon Press: 98–101.

Guinier, Lani, Michelle Fine, Jane Balin, Ann Bartow, *et al.* (1997). "Becoming Gentlemen: Women's Experiences at One Ivy League Law School." Guinier, Lani, Michelle Fine and Jane Balin, Eds. *Becoming Gentlemen: Women, Law School and Institutional Change.* Boston: Beacon Press: 27–84.

Hacker, Sally L. (1990). "Technological Change and Women's Role in Agribusiness: Methods of Research and Social Action." Smith, Dorothy E. and Susan M. Turner, Eds. *Doing It the Hard Way: Investigations of Gender and Technology.* Boston: Unwin Hyman: 89–102.

Haebich, Anna. (2000). *Broken Circles.* Fremantle: Fremantle Arts Centre Press.

Hagler, Mike. (1995). "Deforestation of the Deep: Fishing and the State of the Oceans." *Ecologist 25* (2/3): 74–79.

Halwart, Matthias, Manuel Martinez and Angelika Schückler. (2000). *Small Ponds Make a Big Difference: Integrating Fish with Crop and Livestock Farming*. Rome: Food and Agriculture Organization in conjunction with Farm Management and Production Economics Service, and Inland Water Resources and Aquaculture Service. www.fao.org/docrep/003/x7156e/x7156e00.htm

Hamilton, Clive and Richard Denniss. (2001). "Farming the Future." Melbourne: *Sunday Age*. 11 March: 17.

Hand, Guy. (1999). "The Forest of Forgetting." Willers, Bill, Ed. *Unmanaged Landscapes: Voices for Untamed Nature*. Washington, DC, and Covelo, CA: Island Press: 135–143.

Hardin, Garret. (1968/1999). "The Tragedy of the Commons." Dryzek, John S. and David Schlosberg, Eds. *Debating the Earth: The Environmental Politics Reader*. Oxford: Oxford University Press: 23–34.

Harding, Sandra. (1991). *Whose Science? Whose Knowledge? Thinking from Women's Lives*. Ithaca, NY: Cornell University Press.

Hardt, Michael and Antonio Negri. (2000). *Empire*. Cambridge, MA: Harvard University Press.

Hartmann, Betsy. (1994). "Consensus and Contradiction on the Road to Cairo." de Olivera, Rosiska Darcy and Thais Corral, Eds. *Terra Femina 3: Population: The Human Factor. On Life, Love, Death and Exile*. Rio de Janeiro: IDAC – Institute of Cultural Action: 15–24.

Hartmann, Heidi. (1981). "The Family as the Locus of Gender, Class and Political Struggle: The Example of Housework." *Signs 6* (3): 366–94.

Hawken, Paul, Amory Lovins and L. Hunter Lovins. (1999). *Natural Capitalism: Creating the Next Industrial Revolution*. Boston: Little, Brown and Company.

Hawthorne, Hugh. (1998). Recollections. Wagga Wagga, New South Wales. 17 March.

Hawthorne, Susan. (1976). "In Defence of Separatism." Philosophy Department. Melbourne: La Trobe University. BA (Honours). Unpublished.

—— Ed. (1985). *Difference: Writings by Women*. Sydney: Brooks Waterloo.

—— (1987). *Interview with Flora Nwapa*. Jerusalem. Israel Radio. April.

—— (1989a). "The Politics of the Exotic: The Paradox of Cultural Voyeurism." *Meanjin 48* (2): 259–268.

—— (1989b). "Writing Women's Lives: International Political Fictions." *Coming Out Show*. Sydney, National: ABC Radio National. 9 September.

—— (1990a). "Die Politik des Exotischen: Das Paradoxen des kulturellen Voyeurismus." *Beiträge: Geteilter Feminismus 27*: 109–119.

—— (1990b). "In Defense of Separatism." Gunew, Sneja, Ed. *Feminist Knowledge: A Reader*. London and New York: Routledge: 312–318.

—— (1991a). "What Do Lesbians Want?" *Journal of Australian Lesbian Feminism* *1* (2): 22–34.

—— (1991b). "Mother Tongues and Memory." Paper presented at the Association for the Study of Australian Literature Conference. Charles Sturt University, Wagga Wagga. 1 July.

—— (1993). "Wild Politics: A Manifesto." *People's Perspectives* (4 and 5): 26–27.

—— (1994). "A Case of Spiritual Voyeurism. Review of Mutant Message Down Under by Marlo Morgan." *Feminist Bookstore News 17* (4): 31–33.

—— (1995a). "Plotting Circles in the Mind." Scutt, Jocelynne A., Ed. *City Women, Country Women: Crossing Boundaries.* Melbourne: Artemis Publishing: 107–116.

—— (1995b). "Spirutueller Voyeurismus. Review of *Traumfänger* by Marlo Morgan." *Virginia* (Nr. 18, March).

—— (1996a). "From Theories of Indifference to a Wild Politics." Bell, Diane and Renate Klein, Eds. *Radically Speaking: Feminism Reclaimed.* Melbourne: Spinifex Press: 483–501.

—— (1996b). "Real Worlds and Virtual Worlds." *Metro* (108): 31–36.

—— (1997). "Theories of Power and the Culture of the Powerful." Klein, Renate, Ed. *Feminist Theory Knowledge and Power: Study Guide and Reader.* Geelong: Deakin University Press.

—— (1998). "New Information Technologies and the Problem of Cultural Transparency and Appropriation". *Communities Networking/Networking Communities.* Victoria University, St Albans Campus, Melbourne: Community Information Victoria: 65–70. 27 and 28 February.

—— (1999a). "Connectivity: Cultural Practice of the Powerful or Subversion from the Margins?" Hawthorne, Susan and Renate Klein, Eds. *Cyber-Feminism: Connectivity, Critique and Creativity.* Melbourne: Spinifex Press.

—— (1999b). "Cyborgs, Virtual Bodies and Organic Bodies: Theoretical Feminist Responses." Hawthorne, Susan and Renate Klein, Eds. *CyberFeminism: Connectivity, Critique and Creativity.* Melbourne: Spinifex Press.

—— (2000). "Women's Bodies and Cyberfeminism." *Ockam's Razor.* Sydney: ABC Radio National, Australia. 30 April. www.abc/rn.net.au

—— (2001a). "The Clash of Knowledge Systems: Local Diversity in the Wild versus Global Homogeneity in the Marketplace." Bennholdt-Thomsen, Veronika, Nicholas G. Faraclas and Claudia von Werlof, Eds. *There is an Alternative: Subsistence and Worlwide Resistance to Corporate Globalization.* London: Zed Books; Melbourne: Spinifex Press: 77–90.

—— (2001b). "Disability and Diversity: Challenges to Normalisation and Sameness." *Women in Action* (2): 40–44.

—— (2001c). "Wild Bodies/Technobodies." *Women's Studies Quarterly* *Fall/Winter.* 54–69.

Hawthorne, Susan and Renate Klein, Eds. (1999). *CyberFeminism: Connectivity, Critique and Creativity.* Melbourne: Spinifex Press.

Heaton, Herbert. (1964). *Economic History of Europe.* New York: Harper & Row.

Hedrick, Philip W., Vanessa K. Rashbrook and Dennis Hedgecock. (2000). "Effective Population Size of Winter-run Chinook Salmon Based on Microsatellite Analysis of Returning Spawners." *Canadian Journal of Fish and Aquatic Science* 57: 2368–2373.

Henderson, Hazel. (1993). *Paradigms in Progress: Life Beyond Economics.* London: Adamantine Press Limited.

—— (1999). *Beyond Globalization: Shaping a Sustainable Global Economy.* West Hartford, CT: Kumarian Press.

—— (2000). "Life Beyond Global Economic Warfare." Pieterse, Jan Nederveen, Ed. *Global Futures: Shaping Globalization.* London: Zed Books: 63–82.

Hew, Choy L. and Garth Fletcher. (1997). "Transgenic Fish for Aquaculture." *Chemistry and Industry:* 1–8.

Hewlett, Sylvia Ann. (1986). *A Lesser Life: The Myth of Women's Liberation in America.* New York: Warner Books.

Hill Collins, Patricia. (1991). "Learning from the Outsider Within: The Social Significance of Black Feminist Thought." Fonow, Mary Margaret and Judith A. Cook, Eds. *Beyond Methodology: Feminist Scholarship as Lived Research.* Bloomington and Indianapolis: Indiana University Press: 35–59.

Ho, Mae-Wan. (1998). *Genetic Engineering – Dream or Nightmare? The Brave New World of Bad Science and Big Business.* Penang: Third World Network; Bath: Gateway Books.

Hoagland, Sarah Lucia. (1988). *Lesbian Ethics: Toward New Value.* Palto, CA: Institute of Lesbian Studies.

Hocking, Barbara. (1993). "Reflections on the Mabo Case: From *Cooper v Stuart* through *Milirrpum* to *Mabo.*" *Essays on the Mabo Decision.* Sydney: The Law Book Company Limited: 69–85.

Hodge, Amanda. (2001). "Organic Produce Gene Alert." Sydney: *Australian.* 1 May: 4.

Holcombe, Susan. (1995). *Managing to Empower: The Grameen Bank's Experience of Poverty Alleviation.* London: Zed Books; Dhaka: University Press Limited.

Holtzman, Steven R. (1994). *Digital Mantras: The Languages of Abstract and Virtual Worlds.* Cambridge, MA: MIT Press.

Honadle, George. (1999). *How Context Matters: Linking Environmental Policy to People and Place.* West Hartford, CT: Kumarian Press.

Horvitz, Leslie Alan. (1996). "'Vampire Project' Raises Issue of Patents for Humans." *Insight on the News 12* (27).

Hossain, Rokeya Sakhawat. (1988). *Sultana's Dream and Selections from The Secluded Ones*. New York: The Feminist Press.

Hotaling, Norma. (1996). "Prostitution: Getting Women Out." Paper presented at Violence, Abuse and Women's Citizenship. Brighton, UK. 10–15 November 1996.

Hughes, Donna. (1999a). "The Internet and the Global Prostitution Industry." Hawthorne, Susan and Renate Klein, Eds. *CyberFeminism: Connectivity, Critique and Creativity*. Melbourne: Spinifex Press: 157–184.

—— (1999b). *Pimps and Predators on the Internet: Globalizing the Sexual Exploitation of Women and Children*. Kingston, RI: Coalition Against Trafficking in Women.

Hunn, Eugene S. (1999). "The Value of Subsistence for the Future of the World." Nazarea, Virginia D., Ed. *Ethnoecology: Situated Knowledge/Located Lives*. Tucson: University of Arizona Press: 23–36.

Hyman, Prue. (1993). "Equal Pay for Women after the Employment Contracts Act: Legislation and Practice – the Emperor with No Clothes?" *New Zealand Journal of Industrial Relations 18* (1): 44–57.

—— (1994). *Women and Economics*. Wellington: Bridget Williams Books.

—— (1998). "Are Widening Labour Market Earnings Differentials Entirely/Partly/Not At All Economically Rational/Justified/Inevitable?" *Proceedings of the Eighth Conference on Labour, Employment and Work, November 1998*: Institute of Geography, Victoria University of Wellington: 110–116. June.

—— (1999a). "Universal Basic Income: A Useful Proposal for Feminists". *Proceedings of 1998 Women's Studies Association Conference, Women's Studies Association*. New Zealand: 112–117.

—— (1999b). "Widening Earnings Differentials in the 1980s/1990s: A Feminist Critique". *International Association for Feminist Economics*. Ottawa, Canada.

—— (2001). "Lesbians and Economic/Social Change: Impacts of Globalisation on Our Community(ies) and Politics." *Journal of Lesbian Studies 5* (1–2): 115–132.

Hynes, H. Patricia. (1993). *Taking Population out of the Equation: Reformulating I = PAT*. North Amherst, MA: Institute on Women and Technology.

—— (1996). *A Patch of Eden: America's Inner City Gardeners*. White River Junction, VT: Chelsea Green Publishing Company.

—— (1999a). "Taking Population out of the Equation: Reformulating I = PAT." Silliman, Jael and Ynestra King, Eds. *Dangerous Intersections: Feminist Perspectives on Population, Environment, and Development*. Cambridge, MA: South End Press: 39–73.

——— (1999b). "Consumption: North American Perspectives." Silliman, Jael and Ynestra King, Eds. *Dangerous Intersections: Feminist Perspectives on Population, Environment, and Development.* Cambridge, MA: South End Press: 189–201.

Iglesias, Carlos, Clair Hershey, Fernando Calle and Ana Bolaños. (1994). "Propagating Cassava (*Manihot esculenta*) by Sexual Seed." *Experimental Agriculture 30* (3): 283–290.

The Indigenous World, 1998–99. (1999). Copenhagen: International Work Group for Indigenous Affairs (IWGIA).

Jacobs, Jane. (1961). *The Death and Life of Great American Cities: The Future of Town Planning.* Harmondsworth: Penguin.

——— (1984). *Cities and the Wealth of Nations.* New York: Pelican.

Janeway, Elizabeth. (1980). *Powers of the Weak.* New York: Alfred A. Knopf.

Jayaweera, Swarna. (1994). "Structural Adjustment Policies, Industrial Development and Women in Sri Lanka." Sparr, Pamela, Ed. *Mortgaging Women's Lives: Feminist Critiques of Structural Adjustment.* London: Zed Books: 96–115.

Jeffreys, Sheila. (1997). *The Idea of Prostitution.* Melbourne: Spinifex Press.

Jeffs, Sandy. (2000). *Poems from the Madhouse.* Melbourne: Spinifex Press.

jen jen, jenjen@vampirehunter.com. (2001). "don't worry, be happy." 26 March.

Jennings, Norman S. (1999). *Child Labour in Small-scale Mining: Examples from Niger, Peru and Philippines.* Geneva: ILO. Sectoral Activities Programme, Industrial Activites Branch, Working Paper. 1999. www.ilo.org/public/english/dialogue/sector/papers/childmin/

Johnson, Eva. (1985). "A Letter to my Mother." Hawthorne, Susan, Ed. *Difference: Writings by Women.* Sydney: Waterloo Press (available from Spinifex Press): 35.

Johnson, Geoff. (2000). "Preparing a Strategy for m-commerce." Sydney: *Australian IT.* 4 April: 2.

Jomo, K. S. (Kwame Sundaram) and Shymala Nagaraj. (2001). *Globalization versus Development.* Basingstoke, Hampshire, and New York: Palgrave.

Jopson, Debra, Mark Metherell and Darrin Farrant. (2000). "We'll Fight On, Vow Stolen Children." Sydney: *Sydney Morning Herald.* 12–13 August: 1.

Kappeler, Susanne. (1995). *The Will to Violence: The Politics of Personal Behaviour.* London: Polity Press; New York: Teachers College Press; Melbourne: Spinifex Press.

"Kari-Oca Declaration and the Indigenous Peoples' Earth Charter." (1996). Posey, Darrell A. and Graham Dutfield, Eds. *Beyond Intellectual Property: Toward Traditional Resource Rights for Indigenous Peoples and Local Communities.* Ottawa: International Development Research Centre: 189–198.

Karl, Marilee. (1996). *Inseparable: The Crucial Role of Women in Food Security*. Manila: Isis International.

Kartinyeri, Doris. (2000). *Kick the Tin*. Melbourne: Spinifex Press.

Katona, Jacqui. (1997). "Uranium Mining and the Mirrar People of Kakadu." *Visions and Actions for Peace: Conference Proceedings International Physicians for the Prevention of Nuclear War*. Canberra: Medical Association for Prevention of War.

Kaufer, Erich. (1989). *The Economics of the Patent System*. Chur: Harwood Academic Publishers.

Kauffman, Paul. (1998). *Wik, Mining and Aborigines*. Sydney: Allen and Unwin.

Kelsey, Jane. (1995). *Economic Fundamentalism*. London: Pluto Press.

Khor, Martin. (1996). "Global Economy and the Third World." Mander, Jerry and Edward Goldsmith, Eds. *The Case Against the Global Economy and For a Turn Toward the Local*. San Francisco: Sierra Club Books: 47–59.

Kimmel, Michael S. and Michael Kaufman. (1993). "The New Men's Movement: Retreat and Regression with America's Weekend Warriors." *Feminist Issues 13* (2): 3–22.

King, Ynestra. (1981a). "Feminism and the Revolt of Nature." *Heresies 4* (1): 12–16.

—— (1981b). "The Eco-feminist Imperative." Caldicott, Leonie and Stephanie Leland, Eds. *Reclaim the Earth: Women Speak Out for Life on Earth*. London: Women's Press: 9–14.

Klein, Naomi. (2000). *No Logo*. London: Flamingo: HarperCollins.

—— (2001). "More Powerful than a Logo Motive." Sydney: *Sydney Morning Herald*. 8–9 December: 4–5.

Klein, Renate. (1983). "How to Do What We Want to Do: Thoughts About Feminist Methodology." Bowles, Gloria and Renate Duelli Klein, Eds. *Theories of Women's Studies*. London: Routledge and Kegan Paul: 88–104.

—— (1989a). *The Exploitation of a Desire: Women's Experiences with In Vitro Fertilisation*. Geelong: Women's Studies Summer Institute.

—— (1989b). *Infertility: Women Speak Out About Their Experiences of Reproductive Medicine*. London: Pandora.

—— (1996). "(Dead) Bodies Floating in Cyberspace: Post-modernism and the Dismemberment of Women." Bell, Diane and Renate Klein, Eds. *Radically Speaking: Feminism Reclaimed*. Melbourne: Spinifex Press; London: Zed Books: 346–358.

—— (1999). "The Politics of CyberFeminism: If I'm a Cyborg Rather than a Goddess will Patriarchy Go Away?" Hawthorne, Susan and Renate Klein, Eds. *CyberFeminism: Connectivity, Critique and Creativity*. Melbourne: Spinifex Press: 185–212.

—— (2001a). "Globalized Bodies in the 21st Century: The Final Patriarchal Takeover?" Bennholdt-Thomsen, Veronika, Nicholas G. Faraclas and Claudia von Werlof, Eds. *There is an Alternative: Subsistence and Worldwide Resistance to Corporate Globalization*. London: Zed Books; Melbourne: Spinifex Press: 91–105.

—— (2001b). "Eugenics." Personal communication. December.

Kloppenburg, Jack J. R. and Beth Burrows. (2001). "Biotechnology to the Rescue? Ten Reasons Why Biotechnology is Incompatible with Sustainable Agriculture." Tokar, Brian, Ed. *Redesigning Life: The Worldwide Challenge to Genetic Engineering*. Melbourne: Scribe Publications; London and New York: Zed Books; Montreal: McGill-Queen's University Press; Johannesburg: Witwatersrand University Press: 103–110.

Kneen, Brewster. (1999). *Farmageddon: Food and the Culture of Biotechnology*. Gabriola Island, BC: New Society Publishers.

Kolk, Ans. (1996). *Forests in International Environmental Politics: International Organisations, NGOs and the Brazilian Amazon*. Utrecht: International Books.

Komardjaja, Inge. (2001). "The Internet Empowers Women with Disabilities." *Women in Action* (2): 45–48.

Korzeniewicz, Miguel. (2000). "Commodity Chains and Marketing Strategies: Nike and the Global Athletic Footwear Industry." Lechner, Frank J. and John Boli, Eds. *The Globalization Reader*. Malden, MA: Blackwell Publishers: 155–166.

Kosko, Bart. (1993). *Fuzzy Thinking*. London: Flamingo.

Krieger, Susan. (1983). *The Mirror Dance: Identity in a Women's Community*. Philadelphia: Temple University Press.

Kuhn, Thomas S. (1976). *The Structure of Scientific Revolutions*. Chicago: University of Chicago Press.

Kuhnlein, Harriet V. and Olivier Receveur. (1996). "Dietary Change and Traditional Food Systems of Indigenous Peoples." *Annual Review of Nutrition 16*: 417–442.

Kuletz, Valerie. (1998). *The Tainted Desert: Environmental and Social Ruin in the American West*. New York and London: Routledge.

Kurien, John. (1993). "Ruining the Commons: Coastal Overfishing and Fishworkers' Actions in South India." *Ecologist 23* (1): 5–12.

—— (1995). "Joint Action Against Joint Ventures: Resistance to Multinationals in Indian Waters." *Ecologist 25* (2/3): 115–119.

LaDuke, Winona. (1999). *All Our Relations: Native Struggles for Land and Life*. Cambridge, MA: South End Press.

Lal Das, Bhagirath. (2000). *The World Trade Organisation: A Guide to the*

Framework for International Trade. Penang: Third World Network; London: Zed Books.

Langelle, Orin. (2001). "From Native Forest to Frankenforest." Tokar, Brian, Ed. *Redesigning Life: The Worldwide Challenge to Genetic Engineering.* Melbourne: Scribe Publications; London and New York: Zed Books; Montreal: McGill-Queen's University Press; Johannesburg: Witwatersrand University Press: 111–125.

Langton, Marcia. (1998). *Burning Questions: Emerging Environmental Issues for Indigenous Peoples in Northern Australia.* Darwin, NT: Centre for Indigenous and Cultural Resource Management, Northern Territory University.

Lappé, Mark and Britt Bailey. (1998). *Against the Grain: Biotechnology and the Corporate Takeover of Your Food.* Monroe, MN: Common Courage Press.

Law, David. (1997). "Global Environmental Issues and the World Bank." Gill, Stephen, Ed. *Globalization, Democratization and Multilateralism.* Basingstoke: Macmillan in association with United Nations University Press: 171–193.

Le Carré, John. (2001). *The Constant Gardener.* Sydney: Hodder Headline.

Le Guin, Ursula. (1980). *The Lathe of Heaven.* London: Granada Publishing.

Lechner, Frank J. and John Boli, Eds. (2000). *The Globalization Reader.* Malden, MA: Blackwell Publishers.

Lee, R. B. and I. de Vore, Eds. (1968). *Man the Hunter.* Chicago: Aldini.

Lele, Uma, Willam Lesser, Gesa Horst Kotte-Wesseler and Derek Byerlee. (2000). "Intellectual Property Rights, Agriculture and the World Bank." Lele, Uma, Willam Lesser and Gesa Horst Kotte-Wesseler, Eds. *Intellectual Property Rights in Agriculture: The World Bank's Role in Assisting Borrower and Member Countries.* Washington, DC: Rural Development: Environmentally and Socially Sustainable Development, World Bank: 1–21.

Lemonick, Michael D. (1995). "Seeds of Conflict: Critics say a U.S. Company's Patent on a Pesticde from an Indian tree is 'Genetic Colonialism'." *Time* *146* (13): 50–51.

Lentin, Ronit, Ed. (1997). *Gender and Catastrophe.* London and New York: Zed Books.

Leopold, Aldo. (1970). *A Sand Country Almanac: With Essays on Conservation from Round River.* New York: Random House.

Lessnoff, Michael H. (1994). *The Spirit of Capitalism and the Protestant Ethic: An Enquiry into the Weber Thesis.* Aldershot, Hants; Brookfield, VT: Edward Elgar.

Leunig, Michael. (1996). "How Do I Get Real?" Melbourne: *Age.* 20 April: 16.

Liddell and Scott, Eds. (1986). *Greek-English Lexicon.* Oxford: Oxford University Press.

Liebmann, Adrienne, Jen Jordan, Deb Lewis, Patricia Sykes, *et al.*, Eds. (1997). *Women's Circus: Leaping Off the Edge*. Melbourne: Spinifex Press.

Lim, Shirley Geok-lin. (1994). *Monsoon History*. London: Skoob Books.

Loomis, Ruth with Merv Wilkinson. (1995). *Wildwood: A Forest for the Future*. Gabriola, BC: Reflections.

Lopez, Atencio. (1998). "Initiatives for the Protection of Holders of Traditional Knowledge, Indigenous Peoples and Local Communities." Paper presented at Roundtable on Intellectual Property and Indigenous Peoples. Geneva: World Intellectual Property Organization: 1–5. 15 September 2000.

Lorde, Audre. (1984). "The Master's Tools Will Never Dismantle the Master's House." *Sister Outsider*. Trumansburg, NY: The Crossing Press: 110–113.

Lori, Wolfgang. (1995). "Patents on Native Technology Challenged." *Science* 269 (5230): 1506.

Louie, Miriam Ching Yoon. (2001). *Sweatshop Warriors: Immigrant Women Workers Take on the Global Factory*. Boston: South End Press.

Lown, Judy and Helen Chenut. (1983). "The Patriarchal Thread: A History of Exploitation." Chapkis, Wendy and Cynthia Enloe, Eds. *Of Common Cloth: Women in the Global Textile Industry*. Amsterdam: Transnational Institute: 25–37.

Luneau, Gilles. (2001). *The World is Not for Sale: Farmers Against Junk Food: José Bové and François Dufour Interviewed by Gilles Luneau*. (Casparis, Anna de) London: Verso.

Mabo v. the State of Queensland (No. 2). (1992). *Mabo* (No. 2). 3 June 1992.

MacGregor, David. (1998). *Hegel and Marx After the Fall of Communism*. Cardiff: University of Wales Press.

Mackenzie, Janet. (2002). "Exchange relationship". Personal communication.

MacKinnon, Catharine A. (1983). "Feminism, Marxism, Method and the State: An Agenda for Theory." Abel, Elizabeth and Emily K. Abel, Eds. *The Signs Reader*. Chicago: University of Chicago Press.

——— (1987). "Whose Culture? A Case Note on *Martinez v. Santa Clara Pueblo*." *Feminism Unmodified: Discourses on Life and Law*. Cambridge and London: Harvard University Press: 63–69.

Mahony, Pat and Christine Zmroczek. (1996). "Working-class Radical Feminism: Lives Beyond the Text." Bell, Diane and Renate Klein, Eds. *Radically Speaking: Feminism Reclaimed*. Melbourne: Spinifex Press: 67–76.

——— Eds. (1997). *Class Matters: 'Working-class' Women's Perspectives on Social Class*. London: Taylor and Francis.

——— (1999). *International Perspectives on Women and Social Class*. London: Taylor and Francis.

Mairs, Nancy. (1992). "On Being a Cripple." *Plaintext*. Tucson and London: University of Arizona Press: 9–20.

Majeke, Moyisi. (2001). "Primageniture? A New Guise for Globalisation." *Agenda* (49): 89–91.

Mamidipudi, Annapurna. (2000). "'Analoging' the Digital: Can Pre-colonial Modes of Production, Community and Commerce Appropriate e-commerce?" Paper presented at Third International Crossroads in Cultural Studies Conference. Birmingham, UK.

Mander, Jerry and Edward Goldsmith, Eds. (1996). *The Case Against the Global Economy and For a Turn Toward the Local*. San Francisco: Sierra Club Books.

Mandler, John. (2000). "Blowing in the Wind: Will GMO Pollen Drifts Create New Legal Hassles for Seed Companies?" *Seed World* (June): 15–17.

Mansell, Michael. (1993). "Australians and Aborigines and the Mabo Decision: Just Who Needs Whom the Most?" *Essays on the Mabo Decision*. Sydney: The Law Book Company Limited: 48–57.

Mantilla, Karla. (2000). "Banking on Women: Structural Adjustment 101. An Interview with Pamela Sparr." Washington, DC: *Off Our Backs*. July: 8–11.

Manuh, Takyiwaa. (1994). "Ghana: Women in the Public and Informal Sectors under The Economic Recovery Plan." Sparr, Pamela, Ed. *Mortgaging Women's Lives: Feminist Crtitiques of Structural Adjustment*. London: Zed Books: 61–77.

Mares, Peter. (2001). *Borderline: Australia's Treatment of Refugees and Asylum Seekers*. Sydney: University of New South Wales Press.

Markley, Robert. (1996). "Boundaries: Mathematics, Alienation, and the Metaphysics of Cyberspace." Markley, Robert, Ed. *Virtual Realities and their Discontents*. Baltimore: The Johns Hopkins University Press: 55–79.

Marshall, Paul, Ed. (1988). *Raparapa Kularr Martuwarra: Fitzroy River Drovers' Stories*. Broome: Magabala Books.

Martin, Hans-Peter and Harald Schumann. (1997). *The Global Trap: Globalization and the Assault on Democracy and Prosperity*. (Patrick Camiller, Trans.) London and New York: Zed Books; Bangkok: White Lotus; Sydney: Pluto Press; Pretoria: Human Sciences Research Council; Montréal: Black Rose Books.

Martinez i Prat, Anna-Rosa. (1995). "Fishing Out Aquatic Diversity." 15 July. 2001. www.grain.org/publications/jul95/jul951.htm

Martinez-Alier, Joan. (2000). "Environmental Justice as a Force for Sustainability." Pieterse, Jan Nederveen, Ed. *Global Futures: Shaping Globalization*. London: Zed Books: 148–174.

Martinez-Alier, Joan with Klaus Schlupmann. (1987). *Ecological Economics*. Oxford: Basil Blackwell.

Marx, Karl. (1939/1993). *Grundrisse: Foundations of the Critique of Political Economy*. (Martin Nicolaus, Trans.) London: Penguin in association with *New Left Review*.

—— (1972). "Economic and Philosophic Manuscripts of 1844." Tucker, Robert C., Ed. *The Marx Engels Reader*. New York: W. W. Norton and Company: 54–103.

"Mataatua Declaration on Cultural and Intellectual Property Rights of Indigenous Peoples." (1996). Posey, Darrell A. and Graham Dutfield, Eds. *Beyond Intellectual Property: Toward Traditional Resource Rights for Indigenous Peoples and Local Communities*. Ottawa: International Development Research Centre: 205–208.

Mathews, Freya. (1994). "*Terra Incognita*: Carnal Legacies." Cosgrove, Laurie, David G. Evans and David Yenken, Eds. *Restoring the Land: Environmental Values, Knowledge and Action*. Melbourne: Melbourne University Press: 37–46.

Matsui, Yayori. (1999). *Women in the New Asia*. London: Zed Books; Melbourne: Spinifex Press; Bangkok: White Lotus.

Matthews, Elizabeth, Ed. (1995). *Fishing for Answers: Women and Fisheries in the Pacific Islands*. Suva, Fiji: Women and Fisheries Network.

Mayhew, Anne. (1999). "Value." Peterson, Janice and Margaret Lewis, Eds. *The Elgar Companion to Feminist Economics*. Cheltenham, UK: Edward Elgar: 732–737.

Mazhar, Farhad. (2000). "Biodiversity-based Rural Strategy for 'Poverty Alleviation'. Insights from the Experience of Nayakrishi Andolon (New Agricultural Movement) of Bangladesh." Paper presented at the 15th Session of the Global Biodiversity Forum. UNEP, Gigiri, Nairobi, Kenya. 12–14 May.

McCoy, Alfred W. (1991). *The Politics of Heroin: CIA Complicity in the Global Drug Trade*. Chicago, IL: Lawrence Hill Books.

McEvoy, Arthur. (1990). "Toward an Interactive Theory of Nature and Culture." Worster, D., Ed. *The Ends of the Earth: Perspectives on Modern Environmental History*: Cambridge.

McGrath, Mike. (1995). "Save Bt!: Genetically Engineered Potato Threatens Effectiveness of *Bacillus thuringiensis* as an Organic Pesticide." *Organic Gardening 42* (7): 7.

McGuire, Michael. (2000). "Rich Males Hog Net Aisles." Sydney: *Australian*. 19 January: 3.

McLaren, Deborah. (1998). *Rethinking Tourism and Ecotravel: The Paving of Paradise and What You Can Do to Stop It*. West Hartford, CT: Kumarian Press.

McLeod, Ramon G. (1994). "Fierce Debate Expected in Cairo." San Francisco: *San Francisco Chronicle*. 2 September: 1.

McMahon, Martha. (1997). "From the Ground Up: Ecofeminism and Ecological Economics." *Ecological Economics 20*: 163–173.

McMichael, Tony. (2001). *Human Frontiers, Environments and Disease: Past Patterns, Uncertain Futures*. Melbourne: Cambridge University Press.

McNeely, Jeffrey A. (1997). "Interaction between Biological Diversity and Cultural Diversity." Paper presented at Indigenous Peoples, Environment and Development Conference. Zürich: International Work Group for Indigenous Affairs (IWGIA) and Department of Social Anthropology, University of Zürich: 173–196. 15–18 May 1995.

McQueen, Humphrey. (2001). *The Essence of Capitalism: The Origins of Our Future*. Sydney: Sceptre.

Mead, Aroha. (1997). "How Are the Values of Maori Going to Be Considered and Integrated in the Use of Plant Biotechnology in New Zealand?" *Pacific World 46* (March): 10–11.

Meadows, Donella H., Dennis L. Meadows and Jørgen Randers. (1992). *Beyond the Limits*. Post Mills, VT: Chelsea Green.

Meadows, Donella H., Dennis L. Meadows, Jørgen Randers and William H. Behrens III. (1972). *The Limits to Growth*. New York: Universe Books.

Melbourne, Hineani. (1995). *Maori Sovereignty: The Maori Perspective*. Auckland: Hodder Moa Beckett.

Menchú, Rigoberta. (1989). *I, Rigoberta Menchú: An Indian Woman in Guatemala*. (Ann Wright, Trans.) London and New York: Verso.

Merchant, Carolyn. (1980). *The Death of Nature: Women, Nature and the Scientific Revolution*. San Francisco: Harper and Row.

—— (1999). "From: Ecological Revolutions: Nature, Gender, and Science in New England." Willers, Bill, Ed. *Unmanaged Landscapes: Voices for Untamed Nature*. Washington, DC, and Covelo, CA: Island Press: 164–170.

Merrifield, John. (1996). "A Market Approach to Conserving Biodiversity." *Ecological Economics 16* (3): 217–226.

Meulenbelt, Anja. (1978). "On the Political Economy of Domestic Labour." *Quest IV* (2): 18–31.

Mies, Maria. (1983). "Towards a Methodology for Feminist Research." Bowles, Gloria and Renate Duelli Klein, Eds. *Theories of Women's Studies*. London: Routledge and Kegan Paul: 117–139.

—— (1986/1999). *Patriarchy and Accumulation on a World Scale: Women in the International Division of Labour*. London: Zed Books; Melbourne: Spinifex Press.

—— (1991). "Women's Research or Feminist Research? The Debate Surrounding Feminist Science and Methodology." Fonow, Mary Margaret and Judith A. Cook, Eds. *Beyond Methodology: Feminist Scholarship as Lived Research*. Bloomington and Indianapolis: Indiana University Press: 60–84.

—— (1993). "Liberating the Consumer." Mies, Maria and Vandana Shiva, Eds. *Ecofeminism*. New Delhi: Kali for Women; London: Zed Books; Melbourne: Spinifex Press: 251–263.

—— (1994). "People or Population." de Olivera, Rosiska Darcy and Thais Corral, Eds. *Terra Femina 3: Population: The Human Factor. On Life, Love, Death and Exile*. Rio de Janeiro: IDAC – Institute of Cultural Action: 41–63.

—— (1999). "Preface to the New Edition." *Patriarchy and Accumulation on a World Scale: Women in the International Division of Labour*. London: Zed Books; Melbourne: Spinifex Press: vii–xix.

Mies, Maria and Veronika Bennholdt-Thomsen. (1995). "Some Theoretical Aspects of New Commons in Industrialized Countries." Paper presented at Reinventing the Commons. Bonn, Germany. 4–5 November.

Mies, Maria, Veronika Bennholdt-Thomsen and Claudia von Werlof. (1988). *Women: The Last Colony*. New Delhi: Kali for Women.

Mies, Maria and Vandana Shiva. (1993). *Ecofeminism*. Melbourne: Spinifex Press.

Milburn, Caroline. (2001). "The Changing Workplace: Men Need not Apply." Melbourne: *Age*. 22 December: 3.

Miles, Angela. (1996). *Integrative Feminisms: Building Global Visions, 1960s–1990s*. New York: Routledge.

Millar, Melanie Stewart. (1998). *Cracking the Code: Who Rules the Wired World?* Toronto: Second Story Press.

Miller, Carol J. and Jennifer L. Croston. (1999). "WTO Scrutiny v. Environmental Objectives: Assessment of the International Dolphin Conservation Program Act. (World Trade Organization)." *American Business Law Journal* 37 (1): 73–127.

Millett, Kate. (1972). *Sexual Politics*. London: Abacus.

Minh-ha, Trinh T. (1989). *Woman Native Other: Writing, Postcoloniality and Feminism*. Bloomington and Indianapolis: Indiana University Press.

Mitchell, Jean. (1973). *Woman's Estate*. Harmondsworth: Penguin Books.

Mitchell, William J. (1995). *City of Bits: Space, Place, and the Infobahn*. London and Cambridge, MA: The MIT Press.

Mitter, Swasti. (1986). *Common Fate, Common Bond: Women in the Global Economy*. London: Pluto Press.

Mitter, Swasti and Anneke van Luijken. (1983). "A Woman's Home is Her Factory." Chapkis, Wendy and Cynthia Enloe, Eds. *Of Common Cloth:*

Women in the Global Textile Industry. Amsterdam: Transnational Institute: 61–67.

Mladjenovic, Lepa and Divna Matijasevic. (1996). "SOS Belgrade July 1993–1993: Dirty Streets." Corrin, Chris, Ed. *Women in a Violent World: Feminist Analyses and Resistance Across "Europe".* Edinburgh: Edinburgh University Press: 118–132.

Mobbs, Michael. (1998). *Sustainable House.* Sydney: Choice Books.

Mogina, Jane. (1996). "Sustainable Development." Paper presented at the 6th International Interdisciplinary Congress on Women. University of Adelaide, Australia, 21–26 April. Tape available from Instant Conference Taping, PO Box 62, Daw Park, SA 5041 Australia.

Mohanram, Radhika. (1999). *Black Body: Women, Colonialsism, and Space.* Minneapolis and London: University of Minnesota Press.

Mohanty, Chandra Talpade. (1997). "Under Western Eyes: Feminist Scholarship and Colonial Discourses." Visvanathan, Nalini, Lynn Duggan, Laurie Nisonoff and Nan Wiegersma, Eds. *The Women, Gender and Development Reader.* London: Zed Books: 79–86.

Mollison, Bill and David Holmgren. (1978). *Permaculture I: A Perennial Agricultural System for Human Settlements.* Melbourne: Transworld.

Moore, Michael. (1997). *Downsize This.* New York: Harper Collins.

Moore v. Regents of the University of California. (1990). 793P.2d 479, 271, *California Reporter* 146.

Moran, Katy. (1999). "Toward Compensation: Returning Benefits from Ethnobotanical Drug Discovery to Native Peoples." Nazarea, Virginia D., Ed. *Ethnoecology: Situated Knowledge/Located Lives.* Tucson: University of Arizona Press: 249–262.

Moravec, Hans. (1988). *Mind Children: The Future of Robot and Human Intelligence.* Cambridge, MA, and London: Harvard University Press.

Morgan, Marlo. (1994). *Mutant Message Down Under.* New York: Harper-Collins.

Morgan, Robin. (1970). "Introduction: The Women's Revolution." Morgan, Robin, Ed. *Sisterhood is Powerful: An Anthology of Writings from the Women's Liberation Movement.* New York: Vintage: xiii–xl.

—— Ed. (1970). *Sisterhood is Powerful: An Anthology of Writings from the Women's Liberation Movement.* New York: Vintage.

—— (1977). *Going Too Far: The Personal Chronicle of a Feminist.* New York: Random House.

—— (1982). *The Anatomy of Freedom: Feminism, Physics and Global Politics.* Garden City, NY: Anchor Press/Doubleday.

—— Ed. (1984). *Sisterhood is Global.* London.

—— (1990). *The Demon Lover: On the Sexuality of Terrorism*. London: Mandarin.

—— (2002). *The Demon Lover: The Roots of Terrorism*. London: Piatkus.

—— (1992). "The Word of a Woman." *The Word of a Woman: Selected Prose, 1968–1992*. New York: W. W. Norton; London: Virago. 275–293.

Morris, Meaghan. (1988). "Things to Do in Shopping Centres." *Grafts: Feminist Cultural Criticism*: 193–225.

Morrison, Toni. (1993). *Playing in the Dark: Whiteness and the Literary Imagination*. New York: Random House.

Moulton, Janice. (1989). "A Paradigm of Philosophy: The Adversary Method." Garry, Ann and Marilyn Pearsall, Eds. *Women, Knowledge and Reality: Explorations in Feminist Philosophy*. Winchester, MA: Unwin Hyman: 5–20.

Mowaljarlai and Jutta Malinic. (2001). *Yorro Yorro, Everything Standing Up Alive: Rock Art and Stories from the Australian Kimberley*. Broome, WA: Magabala Books.

Müller, Christa. (2001). "Women in the International Gardens: How Subsistence Production Leads to New Forms of Intercultural Communication." Bennholdt-Thomsen, Veronika, Nicholas G. Faraclas and Claudia von Werlof, Eds. *There is an Alternative: Subsistence and Worldwide Resistance to Corporate Globalization*. London: Zed Books; Melbourne: Spinifex Press: 189–202.

Murray, Pat and Paul Willis. (2001). "How Well are Publically Funded Tree Planting Schemes, Serving Us?" *Earthbeat*. ABC Radio National. 1 December. www.abc.net.au/rn/science/earth/stories/s434241.htm

Myron, Nancy and Charlotte Bunch, Eds. (1975). *Lesbianism and the Women's Movement*. Baltimore: Diana Press.

Naess, Arne. (1998). "The Shallow and the Deep, Long-Range Ecology Movement: A Summary." Dryzek, John S. and David Schlosberg, Eds. *Debating the Earth: The Environmental Politics Reader*. Oxford: Oxford University Press: 353–357.

Namjoshi, Suniti. (1993). *St Suniti and the Dragon*. Melbourne: Spinifex Press.

—— (1996). "Introduction 2. An Invitation: The Web as a Medium for Poetry and Dense Text?" *Building Babel*. Melbourne: Spinifex Press: xvii–xxix.

Namjoshi, Suniti and Gillian Hanscombe. (1986). *Flesh and Paper*. Seaton, England: Jezebel Books and Tapes.

Narayan, Uma. (1997). *Dislocating Cultures: Identities, Traditions, and Third World Feminism*. New York and London: Routledge.

Nazarea, Virginia D. (1998). *Cultural Memory and Biodiversity*. Tucson: University of Arizona Press.

—— (1999). "Lenses and Latitudes in Landscapes and Lifescapes." Nazarea,

Virginia D., Ed. *Ethnoecology: Situated Knowledge/Located Lives.* Tucson: University of Arizona Press: 91–106.

Nelson, Julie A. (1996). *Feminism, Objectivity and Economics.* London and New York: Routledge.

—— (1997). "Feminism, Ecology and the Philosophy of Economics." *Ecological Economics 20*: 155–162.

Newell, Patrice. (2000). *The Olive Grove.* Penguin Books: Melbourne.

Nganampa Health Council and the Nyaayatjarra, Pitjantjatjara and Yungkunyatjatjara Women's Council Women's Health Project. (1996). "Our Health Project." Bell, Diane and Renate Klein, Eds. *Radically Speaking: Feminism Reclaimed.* Melbourne: Spinifex Press: 516–518.

Niesche, Christopher. (2001). "Low Phosphate, But What a Laundering!" Sydney: *Australian.* 11–12 August: 28.

Nolan, Peter. (2001). *China and the Global Economy: National Champions, Industrial Policy and the Big Business Revolution.* New York: Palgrave.

Norberg-Hodge, Helena. (1991). *Ancient Futures: Learning from Ladakh.* San Francisco: Sierra Club Books.

—— (1996a). "The Pressure to Modernize and Globalize." Mander, Jerry and Edward Goldsmith, Eds. *The Case Against the Global Economy and For a Turn toward the Local.* San Francisco: Sierra Club Books: 33–46.

—— (1996b). "Shifting Direction: From Global Dependence to Local Inter-dependence." Mander, Jerry and Edward Goldsmith, Eds. *The Case Against the Global Economy and For a Turn Toward the Local.* San Francisco: Sierra Club Books: 393–406.

—— (1996c). "Break up the Monoculture: Why the Drive to Create a Homogenized World Must Inevitably Fail." *Nation.* 15 July: 200–204.

—— (2001). "Local Lifeline: Rejecting Globalization – Embracing Localization." Bennholdt-Thomsen, Veronika, Nicholas G. Faraclas and Claudia von Werlof, Eds. *There is an Alternative: Subsistence and Worldwide Resistance to Corporate Globalization.* London: Zed Books; Melbourne: Spinifex Press: 178–188.

Novitz, Rosemary du Plessis and Nabila Jaber. (1990). "Pay Equity, the 'Free' Market and State Intervention." *New Zealand Journal of Industrial Relations 15* (3): 251–262.

Nwapa, Flora. (1986). *Cassava Song and Rice Song.* Lagos: Tana Press.

O'Brien, Anthony. (2001). *Against Normalisation: Writing Radical Democracy in South Africa.* Durham and London: Duke University Press.

O'Hagan, Andrew. (2001). *The End of British Farming.* London: Profile Books and the London Review of Books.

O'Hara, Sabine U. (1995a). "Sustainability: Social and Ecological Dimensions." *Review of Social Economy* 53 (4): 529–551.

—— (1995b). "Valuing Socio-diversity." *International Journal of Social Economics* 22 (5): 31–49.

—— (1996). "Discursive Ethics in Ecosystems Valuation and Environmental Policy." *Ecological Economics* 16 (2): 95–107.

O'Neill, Graeme. (2001). "Ironing Out Fears." Melbourne: *Sunday Herald*. 13 May: 52.

O'Reilly, David. (2001). "A Battered Nation Calls on Bulldog Spirit as Crisis Bites Deeper." Melbourne: *Age*. 18 March: 8.

Oakley, Ann. (1974). *The Sociology of Housework*. London: Robertson.

Oelschlaeger, Max. (1991). *The Idea of Wilderness: From Prehistory to the Age of Ecology*. New Haven and London: Yale University Press.

"Off the Street …" (1994). *Vogue* (April): 337.

Oldfield, M. L. (1984). *The Value of Conserving Genetic Resources*. Washington, DC: US Department of Interior, National Park Service.

Ortiz, Teresa. (2001). *Never Again a World Without Us: Voices of Mayan Women in Chiapas, Mexico*. Washington, DC: The Ecumenical Program on Central America and the Caribbean (EPICA).

Orwell, George. (1973). *1984*. Harmondsworth, UK: Penguin Books.

Oxfam. (2001). *Patient Injustice: How World Trade Rules Threaten the Health of Poor People*. London: Oxfam. Briefing Paper: 1–37. February. www.oxfam.org.uk/cutthecost

Palmlu, Ingar. (1998). "Editorial." *Human Environment V* (3).

Park, Geoff. (1994). "The Polynesian Forest: Customs and Conservation of Biological Diversity." Morrison, John, Paul Geraghty and Linda Crowl, Eds. *Science of Pacific Island Peoples: Land Use and Agriculture*. Suva, Fiji: Institute of Pacific Studies, University of the South Pacific. 2: 131–154.

Parry, J. T. (1994). "Aerial Photography in Pre-European Agriculture and Fishing in Fiji." Morrison, John, Paul Geraghty and Linda Crowl, Eds. *Science of Pacific Island Peoples: Land Use and Agriculture*. Suva, Fiji: Institute of Pacific Studies, University of the South Pacific. 2: 155–180.

Pateman, Carole. (1988). *The Sexual Contract*. Cambridge, UK: Polity Press.

Patterson, Orlando. (1982). *Slavery and Social Death: A Comparative Study*. Cambridge, MA, and London: Harvard University Press.

Perrière, Robert Ali Brac de la and Franck Seuret. (2000). *Brave New Seeds: The Threat of GM Crops to Farmers*. London: Zed Books.

Peterson, V. Spike. (1996). "The Politics of Identification in the Context of Globalization." *Women's Studies International Forum 19* (1/2): 5–15.

Petrella, Riccardo. (2001). *The Water Manifesto: Arguments for a World Water Contract.* (Patrick Camiller, Trans.) London: Zed Books; Dhaka: University Press Ltd; Bangkok: White Lotus; Halifax, NS: Fernwood Publishing; Cape Town: David Philip; Bangalor: Books for Change.

Phelps, Bob. (2000). "Gene Tech for Dinner – No Thanks!" *Habitat 28* (3): 22–23.

—— (2001). "Starlink Corn Creates a Stink." *GeneEthics.* 21 September. www.geneethics.org.au

Phillips, Susan Burton. (1993). "Reconstructing the Rules for the Land Rights Contest." *Essays on the Mabo Decision.* Sydney: The Law Book Company Ltd: 1–22.

Pieterse, Jan Nederveen, Ed. (2000). *Global Futures: Shaping Globalization.* London: Zed Books.

Pietila, Hilkka and Jeanne Vickers. (1991). *Making Women Matter: The Role of the United Nations.* London: Zed Books.

Pilling, David. (2000). "Study Probes Mental Illness." *Financial Times.* 11 April.

Plahe, Jagjit Kaur and Pieter van de Gaage. (2000). "The Titanic Transnationals: Corporate Accountability and Responsibility." Dodds, Felix, Ed. *Earth Summit 2002: A New Deal.* London: Earthscan: 229–243.

Plant, Sadie. (1997). *Zeros + Ones: Digital Women + the New Technologies.* London: Fourth Estate.

Plumwood, Val. (1993). *Feminism and the Mastery of Nature.* London: Routledge.

—— (1994). "The Ecopolitics Debate and the Politics of Nature." Warren, Karen J., Ed. *Ecological Feminism.* London and New York: Routledge: 64–87.

—— (1996). "Nature, Self, and Gender: Feminism, Environmental Philosophy, and the Critique of Rationalism." Warren, Karen J., Ed. *Ecological Feminist Philosophies.* Bloomington and Indianapolis: Indian University Press: 155–180.

Polanyi, Karl. (1944). *The Great Transformation.* Boston, MA: Beacon Press.

Pollack, Susan. (1995). "The Last Fish." *Sierra 80* (4): 48–55.

Pollan, Michael. (1998). "Playing God in the Garden." *New York Times Magazine* (October 25): 44ff.

—— (2001). *The Botany of Desire: A Plant's-eye View of the World.* London: Bloomsbury.

Posey, Darrell A. (1996). "Protecting Indigenous Peoples' Rights to Biodiversity." *Environment 38* (8): 6–19.

Posey, Darrell A. (1997). "Biodiversity Conservation, Traditional Resource Rights and Indigenous Peoples." Paper presented at Indigenous Peoples, Environment and Development. Zürich: International Work Group for

Indigenous Affairs (IWGIA) and Department of Social Anthropology, University of Zürich: 219–240. 15–18 May 1995.

Posey, Darrell A. and Graham Dutfield. (1996). *Beyond Intellectual Property: Toward Traditional Resource Rights for Indigenous Peoples and Local Communities*. Ottawa: International Development Research Centre.

Pretnar, Bojan. (1990). "The European Communities and the Meaning of Patents and Trademarks for Developing Countries." *Patinova '90: Strategies for the Protection of Innovation. Proceedings of the First European Congress on Industrial Property Rights and Innovation*. Madrid: Kluwer Academic Publishers and Deutscher Wirtschaftsdienst: 249–253.

Pretty, Jules N. and P. Shah. (1997). "Making Soil and Water Conservation Sustainable: From Coercion and Control to Partnerships and Participation." *Land Degradation and Development 8*: 39–58.

Pronk, Jan. (2000). "Globalization: A Developmental Approach." Pieterse, Jan Nederveen, Ed. *Global Futures: Shaping Globalization*. London: Zed Books: 40–52.

Pryor, Cathy. (2000). "New Struggle Looms after Wik People Win Six-year Land Battle." Sydney: *Australian*. 4 October: 5.

Purple September Staff. (1975). "The Normative Status of Heterosexuality." Myron, Nancy and Charlotte Bunch, Eds. *Lesbianism and the Women's Movement*. Baltimore, MD: Diana Press: 79–83.

Quinby, Lee. (1994). *Anti-Apocalypse: Exercises in Genealogical Criticism*. Minneapolis: University of Minnesota Press.

Rajaee, Farhang. (2000). *Globalization on Trial: The Human Condition and the Information Civilization*. Ottawa: Kumarian Press.

Rakova, Ursula. (2000). "Fighting for Land." *Horizon 8* (4): 8–9.

Ram-Bidesi, Vina. (1995). "Changes to Women's Roles in Fisheries." Matthews, Elizabeth, Ed. *Fishing for Answers: Women and Fisheries in the Pacific Islands*. Suva, Fiji: Women and Fisheries Network: 71–90.

Ramachandra, Guha. (1989). "Radical American Environmentalism and Wilderness Preservation: A Third World Critique." *Environmental Ethics 11* (Spring): 71–83.

Ramamurthy, Priti. (2000). "The Cotton Commodity Chain, Women, Work and Agency in India and Japan: The Case for Feminist Agro-Food Systems Research." *World Development 28* (3): 551–578.

Randall, Jeff. (2001). "Earthquake in the Global Economy". Baxter, Jenny and Malcolm Downing, Eds. *The Day That Shook the World: Understanding September 11th*. London: BBC Worldwide; Sydney: ABC Books. 188–202.

Rangan, Haripriya. (2002). "The Muti Trade: South Africa's Indigenous Medicines." *Diversity 2* (6): 16–25.

Rautner, Mario and Benjamin D. Bond. (2001). *Genetically Engineered Trees in New Zealand.* Auckland: Greenpeace. A Greenpeace Background Briefing: 1–4. 11 July. www.greenpeace.org.nz

Rawick, George P. (1972). *From Sundown to Sunup: The Making of Black Community.* Westport, CT: Greenwood Publishing Co.

Raymond, Janice G. (1986/2001). *A Passion for Friends: Toward a Philosophy of Female Affection.* London: The Women's Press; Melbourne: Spinifex Press.

—— (1979/1994). *The Transsexual Empire: The Making of the She-Male.* New York: Teachers College Press.

—— (1995). *Women as Wombs: Reproductive Technologies and the Battle over Women's Freedom.* Melbourne: Spinifex Press.

—— (1999). *Legitimating Prostitution as Sex Work: UN Labor Organization (ILO) Calls for Recognition of the Sex Industry.* Amherst, MA: Coalition Against Trafficking in Women.

—— (nd). *Report to the Special Rapporteur on Violence Against Women.* Geneva: United Nations. 1–20.

Readman, Jo, Annamaria Murphy, Mike Andrews, Tony Kendle, *et al.* (2001). *Eden Project: The Guide.* London: Transworld Publishers.

Reedy, Riripeti and Jean Mitaera. (1997). "Walking the Vision: A Model of Strategic Development for Pacific Peoples in Aotearoa New Zealand." Paper presented at VIII Inter-Science Congress. University of the South Pacific, Suva, Fiji. July 13.

Reich, Michael R. (1991). *Toxic Politics: Responding to Chemical Disasters.* Ithaca, NY: Cornell University Press.

Reinharz, Shulamit. (1983). "Experiential Analysis: A Contribution to Feminist Research." Bowles, Gloria and Renate Klein, Eds. *Theories of Women's Studies.* London: Routledge and Kegan Paul: 162–191.

—— (1992). *Feminist Methods in Social Research.* New York: Oxford.

Reynolds, Henry. (1990). *The Other Side of the Frontier.* Melbourne: Penguin Books.

Rich, Adrienne. (1976). *Of Woman Born: Motherhood as an Institution.* Boston: Beacon Press; London: Virago.

—— (1979). "Disloyal to Civilization: Feminism, Racism and Gynephobia." *On Lies, Secrets and Silence: Selected Prose, 1966–1978.* New York and London: W. W. Norton: 276–310.

—— (1980). "Compulsory Heterosexuality and Lesbian Existence." *Signs* 5 (4): 631–660.

Richardson, Peter and Jean Jacques Van-Helten. (1982). "Labour in the South African Gold Mining Industry, 1886–1914." Marks, Shula and Richard

Rathbone, Eds. *Industrialisation and Social Change in South Africa: African Class Formation, Culture, and Consciousness, 1870–1930*. London: Longman. 77–98.

Richburg, Keith. (1998). "Profit and Loss in Irian Jaya." Melbourne: *Age*. 5 December: 25.

Richer, David L. and Elke Simon. (2000). "Perspectives from Industry: AgrEvo." Lele, Uma, Willam Lesser and Gesa Horst Kotte-Wesseler, Eds. *Intellectual Property Rights in Agriculture: The World Bank's Role in Assisting Borrower and Member Countries*. Washington, DC: Rural Development: Environmentally and Socially Sustainable Development, World Bank: 38–41.

Rifkin, Jeremy. (1995). *The End of Work: The Decline of the Global Labor Force and the Dawn of the Post-Market Era*. New York: Tarcher/Putnam.

—— (1998). *The Biotech Century: Harnessing the Gene and Remaking the World*. New York: Tarcher/Putnam.

—— (2000). *The Age of Access: How the Shift from Ownership to Access is Transforming Modern Life*. London: Penguin Books.

Rioja, Isabel Ramos and Kim Manresa. (1999). *The Day Kadi Lost Part of Her Life*. (Nikki Anderson, Trans.) Melbourne: Spinifex Press.

Risler, Jane. (1999). *Lateline*. Sydney. ABC Television.

Robertson, Claire C. (1997). "Black, White, and Red All Over: Beans, Women, and Agricultural Imperialism in Twentieth Century Kenya." *Agricultural History* 71 (3): 259–299.

Roddick, Anita, Ed. (2001). *Take It Personally: How Globalization Affects You and Powerful Ways to Challenge It*. London: Thorsons.

Rogers, Richard. (1997). *Cities for a Small Planet*. London: Faber and Faber.

—— (1998). "City Limits." *Australian Magazine*. 7–8 February: 22–26.

Romei, Stephen. (1999). "Terminator May be a Dead Loss." Sydney: *Weekend Australian*. 9–10 October: 23.

—— (2001). "World Bears Burden of America's Right to Arms." Sydney: *Weekend Australian*. 14–15 July: 13.

Roodman, David. (1996). "More Indigenous Lands Condemned." *World Watch* 9 (4): 7–8.

Røpke, Inge. (1994). "Trade, Development and Sustainability – A Critical Assessment of the 'Free Trade Dogma'." *Ecological Economics 9*: 13–22.

Rorty, Richard. (1979). *Philosophy and the Mirror of Nature*. Princeton, NJ: Princeton University Press.

Rosca, Ninotchka. (1998). "Beyond the Sex Wars: Feminism, Sexuality and Power in a Commodity Culture." Paper presented at National Women's Studies Association Conference. SUNY, Oswego, NY. 14 June.

Rose, Deborah Bird. (2000). *Dingo Makes Us Human: Life and Land in an Australian Aboriginal Culture.* Cambridge: Cambridge University Press.

Rosser, Bill. (1987). *Dreamtime Nightmares.* Melbourne: Penguin Books.

Rovira, Guiomar. (2000). *Women of the Maize: Indigenous Women and the Zapatista Rebellion.* London: Latin American Bureau.

Rowland, Robyn. (1993). *Living Laboratories: Women in Reproductive Technologies.* Sydney: Pan Macmillan.

Roy, Arundhati. (1999). *The Cost of Living.* London: Flamingo.

Roy, Ash Narain. (1999). *The Third World in the Age of Globalisation: Requiem or New Agenda?* Delhi: Madhyam Books; London: Zed Books.

"Rural Reporter." (2000). Sydney: ABC Radio National. 19 July.

Sachs, Carolyn. (1996). *Gendered Fields: Rural Women, Agriculture and Environment.* Boulder: Westview Press.

Said, Edward W. (1995). *Orientalism: Western Conceptions of the Orient.* London: Penguin.

Salim, Agus, Mary Ann Brocklesby, Anne Marie Tiani, Bertin Tchikangwa, *et al.* (2001). "In Search of a Conservation Ethic." Colfer, Carol J. Pierce and Yvonne Byron, Eds. *People Managing Forests: The Links between Human Well-Being and Sustainability.* Washington DC: Resources for the Future; Bogor, Indonesia: Center for International Forestry Research: 155–166.

Salleh, Ariel. (1984). "Deeper than Deep Ecology: The Eco-feminist Connection." *Environmental Ethics 6* (4): 339–345.

—— (1992). "The Ecofeminism/Deep Ecology Debate." *Environmental Ethics 14* (3): 195–216.

—— (1997). *Ecofeminism as Politics: Nature, Marx and the Postmodern.* London: Zed Books.

Sandilands, Catriona. (1997). "Wild Democracy: Ecofeminism, Politics and Desire Beyond." *Frontiers 18* (2): 135–147.

—— (1999). *The Good-natured Feminist: Ecofeminism and the Quest for Democracy.* Minneapolis: University of Minnesota Press.

Sardjono, Mustofa Agung and Ismayadi Samsoedin. (2001). "Traditional Knowledge and Biodiversity Conservation: The Benuaq Dayak Community of East Kalimantan, Indonesia." Colfer, Carol J. Pierce and Yvonne Byron, Eds. *People Managing Forests: The Links between Human Well-being and Sustainability.* Washington, DC: Resources for the Future; Bogor, Indonesia: Center for International Forestry Research: 116–134.

Sassen, Saskia. (1998). *Globalization and Its Discontents: Essays on the New Mobility of People and Money.* New York: The New Press.

Schäfers, Alfons. (1990). "Aspects of the Worldwide Activities of WIPO (World

Intellectual Property Organization)." *Patinova '90: Strategies for the Protection of Innovation. Proceedings of the First European Congress on Industrial Property Rights and Innovation.* Madrid: Kluwer Academic Publishers and Deutscher Wirtschaftsdienst: 49–64.

Schama, Simon. (1996). *Landscape and Memory.* London: Fontana.

Schmitz, Sonja A. (2001). "Cloning Profits: The Revolution in Agricultural Biotechnology." Tokar, Brian, Ed. *Redesigning Life: The Worldwide Challenge to Genetic Engineering.* Melbourne: Scribe Publications; London and New York: Zed Books; Montreal: McGill-Queen's University Press; Johannesburg: Witwatersrand University Press: 44–50.

Schoeffel, Penelope. (1995). "Women in Fisheries in the Pacific Islands: A Retrospective Analysis." Matthews, Elizabeth, Ed. *Fishing for Answers: Women and Fisheries in the Pacific Islands.* Suva, Fiji: Women and Fisheries Network: 7–18.

Schor, Juliet. (1991). *The Overworked American.* New York: Basic Books.

Schumacher, E. Fritz. (1973). *Small is Beautiful: The Study of Economics as if People Mattered.* London: Abacus.

Scrinis, Gyorgy. (1995). *Colonizing the Seed: Genetic Engineering and Techno-Industrial Agriculture.* Melbourne: Friends of the Earth.

—— (1999). "Sowing the Demon Seed." Melbourne: *Age.* 7 June: 13.

Scutt, Jocelynne A. (1992). "Women, Paidwork and the National Wage, or When is a Bargain Not a Bargain? When Enterprise Bargaining Replaces Centralised Wage Fixing." Council, National Women's Consultative, Ed. *Pay Equity and Enterprise Bargaining.* Canberra: Australian Government Publishing Service.

—— (1997). "'Married to the Job' versus 'Doing the Job': Paidwork, Unpaidwork and the Role of Women as Farmers, Business Partners and Business Wives." *The Incredible Woman: Power and Sexual Politics, Vol. 2.* Melbourne: Artemis Publishing: 109–121.

Seager, Joni. (1993). *Earth Follies: Feminism, Politics and the Environment.* London: Earthscan.

—— (1997). *The State of Women in the World.* Harmondsworth: Penguin Books.

Seccombe, Mike. (2000). "GM Seeds May be in Food Chain: Monsanto." Sydney: *Sydney Morning Herald.* 26 August: 3.

Security, South Asian Workshop on Food. (1996). *South Asian Statement of Concern to the World Food Summit.* Dhaka: UBINIG.

Serote, Morgane Wally. (1998). "Initiatives for Protection of Rights of Holders of Traditional Knowledge, Indigenous Peoples and Local Communities." Roundtable on Intellectual Property and Indigenous Peoples. Geneva: World Intellectual Property Organization: 1–10. 23–24 June.

Shand, Hope J. (1994). "Extracting Human Resources." *Multinational Monitor June*: 11.

—— (2001). "Gene Giants: Understanding the 'Life Industry'." Tokar, Brian, Ed. *Redesigning Life: The Worldwide Challenge to Genetic Engineering*. Melbourne: Scribe Publications; London and New York: Zed Books; Montreal: McGill-Queen's University Press; Johannesburg: Witwatersrand University Press: 222–237.

—— (1998). "Biopiracy, Biodiversity and People: The Right to Say 'No' to Monopoly Patents that Are Predatory on the South's Resources and Knowledge." *Human Environment V* (1).

Shear, Richard H. (2000). "Perspectives from Industry: Monsanto." Lele, Uma, Willam Lesser and Gesa Horst Kotte-Wesseler, Eds. *Intellectual Property Rights in Agriculture: The World Bank's Role in Assisting Borrower and Member Countries*. Washington, DC: Rural Development: Environmentally and Socially Sustainable Development, World Bank: 34–37.

Sheehan, Paul. (2001). "Global Warning." Sydney: *Sydney Morning Herald*. Saturday, 31 March: 32.

Shelley, Mary. (1987). *Frankenstein*. London: Penguin.

Shiel, Fergus. (2001). "Five Things You Didn't Know About: Foot-and-Mouth Disease." Melbourne: *Age*. 5 March: 2.

Shildrick, Margrit. (1995). "Against Sisterhood: Ethics and Others." Paper presented at Women's Studies Network Conference, Stirling, Scotland. June 1995.

Shiva, Vandana. (1989). *Staying Alive: Women, Ecology and Development*. New Delhi: Kali for Women; London: Zed Books.

—— (1991). *The Violence of the Green Revolution: Third World Agriculture, Ecology and Politics*. Penang: Third World Network; London: Zed Books.

—— (1993a). *Monocultures of the Mind: Perspectives on Biodiversity and Biotechnology*. Penang: Third World Network.

—— (1993b). "The Chipko Women's Concept of Freedom." Mies, Maria and Vandana Shiva, Eds. *Ecofeminism*. London: Zed Books; Melbourne: Spinifex Press; Halifax, NS: Fernwood Publishing; New Delhi: Kali for Women: 246–250.

—— (1994). "The Seed and the Earth: Biotechnology and the Colonisation of Regeneration." Shiva, Vandana, Ed. *Close to Home: Women Reconnect Ecology, Health and Development*. London: Earthscan; New Delhi: Kali for Women: 128–143.

—— (1995). "Epilogue: Beyond Reductionism." Shiva, Vandana and Ingunn Moser, Eds. *Biopolitics: A Feminist and Ecological Reader on Biotechnology*. London: Zed Books; Penang: Third World Network: 267–284.

—— (1996a). *Caliber of Destruction: Globalization, Food Security and Women's Livelihoods.* Manila: Isis International.

—— (1996b). "Subversions." Subversions Conference, University of Melbourne. Notes taken by Susan Hawthorne. 27 April.

—— (1997). *Biopiracy: The Plunder of Nature and Knowledge.* Boston, MA: South End Press.

—— (2000a). *Stolen Harvest: The Hijacking of the Global Food Supply.* Cambridge, MA: South End Press.

—— (2000b). *Tomorrow's Biodiversity.* London: Thames and Hudson.

—— (2000c). "Global Capital, Local Resources." 27 October. www.abc.net.au/specials/shiva.htm

—— (2001a). "Genetically Engineered 'Vitamin A Rice': A Blind Approach to Blindness Prevention." Tokar, Brian, Ed. *Redesigning Life: The Worldwide Challenge to Genetic Engineering.* Melbourne: Scribe Publications; London and New York: Zed Books; Montreal: McGill-Queen's University Press; Johannesburg: Witwatersrand University Press: 41–43.

—— (2001b). "Nurturing a Sense of the Sacred." *Maple Street Co-op News*: 1, 8.

—— (2001c). "Seed Satyagraha: A Movement for Farmers' Rights and Freedoms in a World of Intellectual Property Rights, Globalized Agriculture and Biotechnology." Tokar, Brian, Ed. *Redesigning Life: The Worldwide Challenge to Genetic Engineering.* Melbourne: Scribe Publications; London and New York: Zed Books; Montreal: McGill-Queen's University Press; Johannesburg: Witwatersrand University Press: 351–360.

—— (2001d). "Globalization and Poverty." Bennholdt-Thomsen, Veronika, Nicholas G. Faraclas and Claudia von Werlof, Eds. *There is an Alternative: Subsistence and Worlwide Resistance to Corporate Globalization.* London: Zed Books; Melbourne: Spinifex Press: 57–66.

—— (2001e). "Golden Rice and Neem: Biopatents and the Appropriation of Women's Environmental Knowledge." *Women's Studies Quarterly* 29 (1 and 2): 12–23.

—— (2001f). *Protect or Plunder? Understanding Intellectual Property Rights.* London: Zed Books.

Shiva, Vandana and R. Holla-Bhar. (1993). "Intellectual Piracy and the Neem Tree." *Ecologist 23*: 223–227.

Siebenhüner, Bernd. (2000). "Homo Sustiens: Towards a New Conception of Humans for the Science of Sustainability." *Ecological Economics 32* (1): 15–25.

Silber, Cathy. (1995). "Women's Writing from Hunan." Gerstlacher, Anna and Margit Miosga, Eds. *China for Women: Travel and Culture.* Melbourne: Spinifex Press: 13–20.

Silko, Leslie Marmon. (1996). *Yellow Woman and a Beauty of the Spirit: Essays on Native American Life Today*. New York and London: Simon and Schuster.

—— (1999). *Gardens in the Dunes*. New York: Simon and Schuster.

Simon, Michael. (2000). "Fishing for the Future." *Horizons 8* (3): 8–9.

Sipolo, Jully. (1994). "Solomon Blue." Emberson-Bain, 'Atu, Ed. *Sustainable Development or Malignant Growth? Perspectives of Pacific Island Women*. Suva, Fiji: Marama Publications: 134.

Sittirak, Sinith. (2000). *The Daughters of Development: Women in a Changing Environment*. London: Zed Books; Melbourne: Spinifex Press.

Siu, Choong Tet. (1997). "Scorched Earth." *Asiaweek 23* (40): 36–42.

Slatter, Claire. (1994a). "For Food or Foreign Exchange? Regional Interests versus Global Imperatives in Pacific Fisheries Development." Emberson-Bain, 'Atu, Ed. *Sustainable Development or Malignant Growth? Perspectives on Pacific Island Women*. Suva, Fiji: Marama Publications: 131–148.

—— (1994b). "Banking on the Growth Model? The World Bank and Market Policies in the Pacific." Emberson-Bain, 'Atu, Ed. *Sustainable Development or Malignant Growth? Perspectives on Pacific Island Women*. Suva, Fiji: Marama Publications: 17–36.

—— (1995). "For Food or Foreign Exchange? Subsistence Fisheries and the Commercial Harvesting of Marine Resources in the Pacific." Matthews, Elizabeth, Ed. *Fishing for Answers: Women and Fisheries in the Pacific Islands*. Suva, Fiji: Women and Fisheries Network: 137–147.

Slattery, Luke. (2001). "The Value of a Bright Idea." *Weekend Australian Magazine* (11–12 August): 49–51.

Slind-Flor, Victoria. (1996). "High Court Gambling Case May Give States Big Payoff; The Supreme Court Ruled Out Indian Tribes' Suits against States. Did It Also Immunize States from All IP Claims?" *The National Law Journal 18* (45): B1.

Smith, Dorothy E. (1978/1989). "A Peculiar Eclipsing: Women's Exclusion from Man's Culture." Klein, Renate and Deborah Lynne Steinberg, Eds. *Radical Voices: A Decade of Feminist Resistance from Women's Studies International Forum*. Oxford: Pergamon Press: 3–21.

—— (1987). *The Everyday World as Problematic: A Feminist Sociology*. Milton Keynes: Open University Press.

—— (1990). *The Conceptual Practices of Power: A Feminist Sociology of Knowledge*. Toronto: University of Toronto Press.

—— (1992). "Feminist Reflections on Political Economy." Connelly, M. Patricia and Pat Armstrong, Eds. *Feminism in Action*. Toronto: Canadian Scholars' Press: 1–21.

—— (1993). *Texts, Facts, and Femininity: Exploring the Relations of Ruling.* London and New York: Routledge.

—— (1999). *Writing the Social: Critique, Theory and Investigations.* Toronto: University of Toronto Press.

Smith, Joy. (1986). "White Man's Dreaming." Personal communication.

Smith, Julie P. (1999). "Human Milk Supply in Australia." *Food Policy 24*: 71–91.

Smith, M. Estellie. (1995). "Chaos, Consensus and Common Sense." *Ecologist 25* (2/3): 80–85.

Söderbaum, Peter. (1992). "Neoclassical and Institutional Approaches to Development and the Environment." *Ecological Economics 5* (2): 127–144.

—— (2000). *Ecological Economics.* London: Earthscan.

Somerville, Margaret. (1999). *body/landscape journals.* Melbourne: Spinifex Press.

Sonntag, Viki. (2000). "Sustainability: In Light of Competitiveness." *Ecological Economics 34* (1): 101–113.

Sparr, Pamela. (1994). "Feminist Critiques of Structural Adjustment." Sparr, Pamela, Ed. *Mortgaging Women's Lives: Feminist Critiques of Structural Adjustment.* London: Zed Books: 13–39.

Spretnak, Charlene. (1991). *States of Grace: The Recovery of Meaning in the Postmodern Age.* San Francisco: HarperSanFrancisco.

Stähler, Frank. (1994). "Biological Diversity: The International Management of Genetic Resources and Its Impact on Biotechnology." *Ecological Economics 11* (3): 227–236.

Stanley, Alessandra. (1998). "A Disaster that Had to Happen." Melbourne: *Age.* 12 May: 9.

Stanley, Liz and Sue Wise. (1983). "'Back into the Personal' or: Our Attempt to Construct 'Feminist Research'." Bowles, Gloria and Renate Duelli Klein, Eds. *Theories of Women's Studies.* London: Routledge and Kegan Paul: 192–209.

—— (1991). "Feminist Research, Feminist Consciousness, and Experiences of Sexism." Fonow, Mary Margaret and Judith A. Cook, Eds. *Beyond Methodology: Feminist Scholarship as Lived Research.* Bloomington and Indianapolis: Indiana University Press.

Steinbrecher, Ricarda A. (2001). "Ecological Consequences of Genetic Engineering." Tokar, Brian, Ed. *Redesigning Life: The Worldwide Challenge to Genetic Engineering.* Melbourne: Scribe Publications; London and New York: Zed Books; Montreal: McGill-Queen's University Press; Johannesburg: Witwatersrand University Press: 75–102.

Steingraber, Sandra. (1999). *Living Downstream: An Ecologist Looks at Cancer and the Environment.* London: Virago.

Stenson, Anthony and Tim Gray. (1997). "Cultural Communities and Intellectual Property Rights in Plant Genetic Resources." Hayward, T. and J. O'Neill, Eds. *Justice, Property and Environment: Social and Legal Perspectives.* Aldershot and Brookfield, VT: Ashgate Publishing. 178–193.

Stephenson, David J., Jr. (1999). "A Practical Primer on Intellectual Property Rights in a Contemporary Ethnoecological Context." Nazarea, Virginia D., Ed. *Ethnoecology: Situated Knowledge/Located Lives.* Tucson: University of Arizona Press: 230–248.

Stephenson, June. (1991). *Men Are Not Cost-Effective: Male Crime in America.* Ventura, CA: Diemer, Smith Publishing Company, Inc.

Stiglmayer, Alexandra, Ed. (1994). *Mass Rape: The War Against Women in Bosnia-Herzegovina.* Lincoln and London: University of Nebraska Press.

Stoltenberg, John. (1990). *Refusing to be a Man.* London: Fontana Collins.

Stone, Richard. (1992). "A Biopesticidal Tree Begins to Blossom: Neem Seed Oil has Insect Toxicologists Buzzing about its Potential as a Source of Natural Insecticides." *Science 255* (5048): 1070–1072.

Stretton, Hugh. (2000). *Economics: A New Introduction.* Sydney: University of New South Wales Press.

Strong, Geoff. (2000). "GM Crop Dumped at Tip." Melbourne: *Age.* 25 March: 1, 8.

Suter, Keith. (2000). *In Defence of Globalisation.* Sydney: University of New South Wales Press.

Suzuki, David and Holly Dressel. (2002). *Good News for a Change: Hope for a Troubled Planet.* Sydney: Allen and Unwin.

Swanson, Timothy. (1995). "The International Regulation of Biodiversity Decline: Optimal Policy and Evolutionary Product." Perrings, Charles, Karl-Göran Mäler, Carl Folke *et al.*, Eds. *Biodiversity Loss: Economic and Ecological Issues.* Cambridge: Cambridge University Press: 225–259.

—— (1996). "The Reliance of Northern Economies on Southern Biodiversity: Biodiversity as Information." *Ecological Economics 17* (1): 1–8.

Swanson, Timothy and Timo Göschl. (2000). "Property Rights Issues Involving Plant Genetic Resources: Implications of Ownership for Economic Efficiency." *Ecological Economics 32* (1): 75–92.

Sylvester, Christine. (1995). "African and Western Feminisms: World-Traveling, the Tendencies and Possibilities." *Signs 20* (4): 941–969.

Tacconi, Luca. (2000). *Biodiversity and Ecological Economics: Participation, Values and Resource Management.* London: Earthscan.

Taniera, Temawa and Jean Mitchell. (1995). "Notes from Kiribate (August 1992)." Matthews, Elizabeth, Ed. *Fishing for Answers: Women and Fisheries in the Pacific Islands.* Suva, Fiji: Women and Fisheries Network: 29–32.

Tapsubei Creider, Jane. (1992). *The Shrunken Dream*. Toronto: Women's Press.

Tauli-Corpuz, Victoria. (2001). "Biotechnology and Indigenous Peoples." Tokar, Brian, Ed. *Redesigning Life: The Worldwide Challenge to Genetic Engineering*. Melbourne: Scribe Publications; London and New York: Zed Books; Montreal: McGill-Queen's University Press; Johannesburg: Witwatersrand University Press: 252–270.

Te Awekotuku, Ngahuia. (1991). *Mana Wahine Maori: Selected Writings on Maori Women's Art, Culture and Politics*. Auckland: New Women's Press.

Teaiwa, Keterina Martina. (1997). "Body Shop Banabans and Skin Deep Samaritans." Paper presented at VIII Pacific Science Inter-Congress. University of the South Pacific, Suva, Fiji. 17 July.

Teeple, Gary. (1995). *Globalization and the Decline of Social Reform*. Toronto: Garamond Press; Atlantic Highlands, NJ: Humanities Press.

Thaman, Konai Helu. (1994). "Environment-friendly or the New Sell? One Woman's View of Ecotourism in Pacific Island Countries." Emberson-Bain, 'Atu, Ed. *Sustainable Development or Malignant Growth: Perspectives of Pacific Island Women*. Suva, Fiji: Marama Publications: 183–191.

Thaman, Randolph R. (1994). "Pacific Island Agroforestry: An Endangered Science." Morrison, John, Paul Geraghty and Linda Crowl, Eds. *Science of Pacific Island Peoples: Land Use and Agriculture*. Suva, Fiji: Institute of Pacific Studies, University of the South Pacific. 2: 191–221.

Theobald, Robert. (1997). *Reworking Success: New Communities at the Millennium*. Gabriola Island, BC: New Society Publishers.

Thompson, Denise. (2001). *Radical Feminism Today*. London: Sage Publications.

Thoreau, Henry David. (1862/1994). *Walking*. San Francisco: HarperSan-Francisco.

Tiano, Susan. (1984). *Maquiladoras, Women's Work and Unemployment in Northern Mexico*. Chicago: University of Chicago.

Tidwell, Mike. (1996). *Amazon Stranger: A Rainforest Chief Battles Big Oil*. New York: Lyons and Burford.

Tipler, Frank J. (1994). *The Physics of Immortality: Modern Cosmology, God and the Resurrection of the Dead*. New York: Anchor Books/Doubleday.

Tokar, Brian, Ed. (2001). *Redesigning Life: The Worldwide Challenge to Genetic Engineering*. Melbourne: Scribe Publications; London and New York: Zed Books; Montreal: McGill-Queen's University Press; Johannesburg: Witwatersrand University Press.

Tolova'a, A. (1994). "Past and Present Practices in Agriculture and Fisheries in Samoa." Morrison, John, Paul Geraghty and Linda Crowl, Eds. *Science of Pacific Island Peoples: Land Use and Agriculture*. Suva, Fiji: Institute of Pacific Studies, University of the South Pacific. 2: 223–230.

Tomlinson, John. (1999). *Globalization and Culture*. Chicago: University of Chicago Press.

Torres Souder, Laura M. (1994). "Psyche Under Seige: Uncle Sam Look What You've Done to Us." Emberson-Bain, 'Atu, Ed. *Sustainable Development or Malignant Growth: Perspectives of Pacific Island Women*. Suva, Fiji: Marama Publications: 193–198.

Toyne, Phillip. (2001). "Ingredient's GM Status: Certification Issues for Manufacturing Quality Assurance." Paper presented at Strategic Food Industry Conference 2001. Sydney: *GeneEthics*. 5 June.

Trakansuphakon, Prasert. (1997). "The Wisdom of the Karen in Natural Resource Conservation." Paper presented at the Indigenous Peoples, Environment and Development Conference. Zürich: International Work Group for Indigenous Affairs (IWGIA) and Department of Social Anthropology, University of Zürich: 157–171. 15–18 May 1995.

Trask, Haunani-Kay. (1986). *Eros and Power: The Promise of Feminist Theory*. Philadephia, PA: University of Pennsylvania Press.

Tribune, International Herald. (2000). "Kellogg Closes Plant over Corn Concerns." *International Herald Tribune*. 23 October: 11.

Trinca, Helen and Anne Davies. (2000). *Waterfront: The Battle that Changed Australia*. Sydney: Doubleday.

Tucker, Michael. (1999). "Can Solar Cooking Save the Forests?" *Ecological Economics 31* (1): 77–89.

Tucker, Robert C., Ed. (1972). *The Marx Engels Reader*. New York: W. W. Norton and Company.

Tuhiwai Smith, Linda. (1999). *Decolonising Methodologies: Research and Indigenous Peoples*. London: Zed Books; Otago: University of Otago Press.

Turbayne, Colin. (1971). *The Myth of Metaphor*. Columbia, SC: University of South Carolina Press.

Turnbull, David. (1997). "Reframing Science and Other Local Knowledge Traditions." *Futures 29* (6): 551–562.

Turner, Jack. (1999). "Economic Nature." Willers, Bill, Ed. *Unmanaged Landscapes: Voices for Untamed Nature*. Washington, DC: Island Press: 113–130.

Turner, Terisa T. and Leigh S. Brownhill. (2001). "'Women Never Surrendered' The Mau Mau and Globalization from Below in Kenya 1980–2000." Bennholdt-Thomsen, Veronika, Nicholas G. Faraclas and Claudia von Werlof, Eds. *There is an Alternative: Subsistence and Worlwide Resistance to Corporate Globalization*. London: Zed Books; Melbourne: Spinifex Press.: 106–132.

UBINIG. (1996). "Declaration of People's Perspectives on 'Population'

Symposium." Bell, Diane and Renate Klein, Eds. *Radically Speaking: Feminism Reclaimed*. Melbourne: Spinifex Press: 519–524.

UN. (1992). "Convention on Biological Diversity." *Monocultures of the Mind: Perspectives on Biodiversity and Biotechnology*. London: Zed Books; Penang: Third World Network: 161–184.

UNDP. (1993). *Human Development Report*. New York: Oxford University Press.

—— (2001). *Human Development Report*. New York: United Nations Development Programme.

UNEP. (1992). *Convention on Biological Diversity*. New York: United Nations.

UNIFEM. (2001). "Strengthening Women's Economic Capacity." 28 November. www.undp.org/unifem/economic.htm

—— (2001). "Strengthening Women's Economic Capacity: Eradicating Feminized Poverty." 28 November. www.undp.org/unifem/ec_pov.htm

United Nations, Report of the Secretary-General. (1995). *From Nairobi to Beijing: Second Review and Appraisal of the Implementation of the Nairobi Forward-looking Strategies for the Advancement of Women*. New York: United Nations.

UNSCEAR. (2000). *2000 Report to the UN General Assembly: Annex J: Exposures and Effects of the Chernobyl Accident*: United Nations. 491ff. www.iaea.org/worldatom/Press/Focus/Chernobyl-15/unscear_report.pdf

Van Sertima, Ivan, Ed. (1989). *Black Women in Antiquity*. London: Transaction Books.

Vanclay, Frank and Geoffrey Lawrence. (1996). "Farmer Rationality and the Adoption of Environmentally Sound Practices; A Critique of the Assumptions of Traditional Agricultural Extension." *Journal of Agricultural Education and Extension 1* (1).

Vickers, Jeanne. (1991). *Women and the World Economic Crisis*. London: Zed Books.

Vickers, Jill McCalla. (1982). "Memoirs of an Ontological Exile: The Methodological Rebellions of Feminist Research." Finn, Geraldine and Angela Miles, Eds. *Feminism in Canada*. Montreal: Black Rose Books: 27–46.

Vidal, John and John Carvel. (1994). "Genetic Harvest." Melbourne: *Age*. 24 November: 13.

Walker, Ian. (2001). "Global Resistance." *Background Briefing*. Sydney: ABC Radio National (Australia). 18 February. www.abc.net.au/m/talks/bbing/stories/s247509.htm

Walker, Jamie. (1999). "Science's Hot Potato." Sydney: *Weekend Australian*. 9–10 October: 23.

Wane, Njoki Nathani. (2000). "Indigenous Knowledge: Lessons from the Elders – A Kenyan Case Study." Dei, George J. Sefa, Budd L. Hall and Dorothy

Goldin Rosenberg, Eds. *Indigenous Knowledges in Global Contexts: Multiple Readings of Our World.* Toronto: OISE/UT published in Association with University of Toronto Press: 54–69.

Wangoola, Paul. (2000). "Mpambo, the African Multiversity: A Philosophy to Rekindle the African Spirit." Dei, George J. Sefa, Budd L. Hall and Dorothy Goldin Rosenberg, Eds. *Indigenous Knowledges in Global Contexts: Multiple Readings of Our World.* Toronto: OISE/UT published in Association with University of Toronto Press: 265–277.

Waring, Marilyn. (1988). *Counting for Nothing: What Men Value and What Women are Worth.* Sydney: Allen and Unwin.

—— (1994). "Ecological Economics." Shiva, Vandana, Ed. *Close to Home: Women Reconnect Ecology, Health and Development.* London: Earthscan; New Delhi: Kali for Women: 155–161.

Waters, Malcolm. (1995). *Globalization.* London and New York: Routledge.

Watson, Lilla. (1984). "Aboriginal Women and Feminism". Keynote Speech Presented at Fourth Women and Labour Conference. Brisbane. July.

Watts, Michael. (2000). "Poverty and the Politics of Alternatives at the End of the Millennium." Pieterse, Jan Nederveen, Ed. *Global Futures: Shaping Globalization.* London: Zed Books: 133–147.

Weber, Max. (1970). "The Types of Authority and Imperative Co-ordination." Olsen, Marvin E., Ed. *Power in Societies.* London: Collier Macmillan: 35–39.

Weiss, Penny A. and Marilyn Friedman, Eds. (1995). *Feminism and Community.* Philadelphia: Temple University Press.

Werlof, Claudia von. (1988). "Women's Work: The Blind Spot in the Critique of Political Economy." Mies, Maria, Veronika Bennholdt-Thomsen and Claudia von Werlof, Eds. *Women: The Last Colony.* New Delhi: Kali for Women: 13–26.

Wertheim, Margaret. (1995). *Pythagoras' Trousers: God, Physics and the Gender Wars.* Sydney: Random House.

—— (1999). *The Pearly Gates of Cyberspace: A History of Space from Danye to the Internet.* Sydney: Doubleday.

Whitt, Laurie Ann. (1998). "Resisting Value-Bifurcation: Indigenist Critiques of the Human Genome Diversity Project." Bar-On, Bat-Ami and Ann Ferguson, Eds. *Daring to be Good: Essays in Feminist Ethico-Politics.* London and New York: Routledge.

"Why Ecowoman?" (1997). *Ecowoman 1* (1): 1.

"Why the Mirrar Oppose the Jabiluka Uranium Mine." (2000). Mirrar community. 16 August. 2000. www.mirrar.net/indexer.htm

Wichterich, Christa. (2000). *The Globalized Woman: Reports from a Future of Inequality*. London: Zed Books; Melbourne: Spinifex Press.

Wickramasinghe, Anoja. (1994). *Deforestation, Women and Forestry: The Case of Sri Lanka*. Utrecht: Institute for Development Research Amsterdam.

Wilks, Alex. (1995). "Prawns, Profit and Protein: Aquaculture and Food Production." *Ecologist 25* (2/3): 120–125.

Willers, Bill, Ed. (1999). *Unmanaged Landscapes: Voices for Untamed Nature*. Washington, DC: Island Press.

Williams, Nancy M. (1986). *The Yolngu and their Land: A System of Land Tenure and the Fight for its Recognition*. Canberra: Australian Institute of Aboriginal Studies.

Williams, Patricia J. (1991). "The Death of the Profane (A Commentary on the Genre of Legal Writing)." *The Alchemy of Race and Rights*. Cambridge, MA, and London: Harvard University Press: 44–51.

Wilson, Edward O. (2001). *The Diversity of Life*. London: Penguin Books.

Wilson, Kimberly A. (2001). "Exclusive Rights, Enclosure and the Patenting of Life." Tokar, Brian, Ed. *Redesigning Life: The Worldwide Challenge to Genetic Engineering*. Melbourne: Scribe Publications; London and New York: Zed Books; Montreal: McGill-Queen's University Press; Johannesburg: Witwatersrand University Press: 290–296.

Wilson, Ronald, Sir. (1997). *Bringing Them Home: Report of the National Inquiry into the Separation of Aboriginal and Torres Strait Islander Children from their Families*. Sydney: Sterling Press.

Wiseman, John. (1997). "Breaking the Spell? Alternative Responses to Globalisation." Wiseman, John, Ed. *Alternatives to Globalisation: An Asia-Pacific Perspective*. Melbourne: Community Aid Abroad: 71–112.

—— (1998). *Global Nation? Australia and the Politics of Globalisation*. Melbourne: Cambridge University Press.

Wittig, Monique. (1992). *The Straight Mind and Other Essays*. Boston: Beacon Press.

Wittig, Monique and Sande Zeig. (1979). *Lesbian Peoples: Material for a Dictionary*. New York: Avon.

Wo-Lap Lam, Willy. (1999). "Zhu Points to Global Market." Shanghai: *South China Morning Post*. 14 July: 17.

Wolfwood, Theresa. 2001. "Resistance is Creative: False Options and Real Hope". Diverse Women for Diversity List. 28 October.

Wolke, Howie. (1999). "Bureaucracy and Wilderness (The Grand Design)." Willers, Bill, Ed. *Unmanaged Landscapes: Voices for Untamed Nature*. Washington, DC: Island Press: 83–102.

Wollstonecraft, Mary. (1792/1970). "A Vindication of the Rights of Woman." Frankau, Pamela, Ed. *The Rights of Woman/On the Subjection of Women.* London: J. M. Dent: 1–215.

Wolpe, Bruce C. (2001). "Scoreboard: Globalisation 1, Terrorism 0." Melbourne: *Age.* 9 October: 19.

Woo, Jisuk. (2000). *Copyright Law and Computer Programs: The Role of Communication in Legal Structure.* New York and London: Garland Publishing Inc.

Woodfin, Max. (1997). "Bugging Out: How Monsanto's Biotech Miracle Undermines Organic Farming." *Sierra 82* (1): 27.

Woolf, Virginia. (1929/1974). *A Room of One's Own.* London: Penguin Books.

World Bank. (1993). *Pacific Island Economies: Toward Efficient and Sustainable Growth, Vol. 1, Overview.* 8 March.

"World's 100 Largest Economic Entities." (2001). Sydney: *Sydney Morning Herald.* 31 March: 32.

Wright, Judith. (1996). "Eroded Hills." *A Human Pattern: Selected Poems.* Sydney: ETT Imprint: 49.

—— (1991). "Australian Wilderness and Wasteland." *Born of the Conquerors: Selected Essays by Judith Wright.* Canberra: Aboriginal Studies Press.

Yapa, Lakshman. (1993). "What are Improved Seeds? An Epistemology of the Green Revolution." *Economic Geography 69* (3): 254–273.

Yibarbuk, Dean. (1998). "Notes on Traditional Use of Fire on Upper Cadell River." Langton, Marcia, *Burning Questions: Emerging Environmental Issues for Indigenous Peoples in Northern Australia.* Darwin: Centre for Indigenous and Cultural Resource Management, Northern Territory University: 1–6.

Young, Carole. (1991). "LESY-Adelaide: An Example of a Lesbian Economy." *Lesbian Ethics 4* (2): 62–66.

Young, Iris Marion. (1997). *Intersecting Voices: Dilemmas of Gender, Political Philosophy and Policy.* Princeton, NJ: Princeton University Press.

INDEX

If you would like to know more about Spinifex Press,
write for a free catalogue or visit our Web site.

SPINIFEX PRESS
PO Box 212, North Melbourne
Victoria 3051, Australia
<http://www.spinifexpress.com.au>